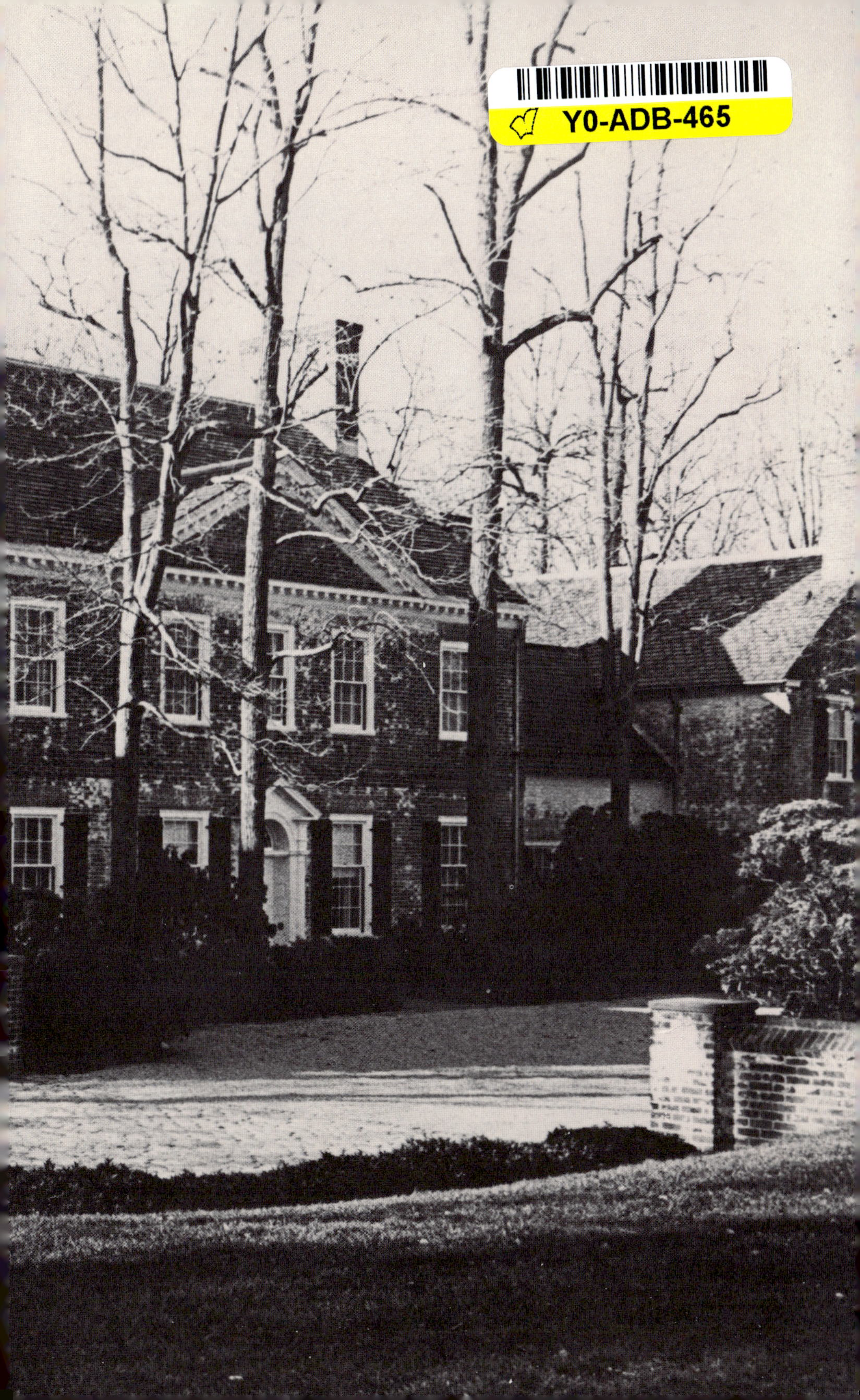

Genetics and Biology of Alcoholism

A Banbury Center Meeting

Banbury Report Series

Banbury Report 1: Assessing Chemical Mutagens
Banbury Report 2: Mammalian Cell Mutagenesis
Banbury Report 3: A Safe Cigarette?
Banbury Report 4: Cancer Incidence in Defined Populations
Banbury Report 5: Ethylene Dichloride: A Potential Health Risk?
Banbury Report 6: Product Labeling and Health Risks
Banbury Report 7: Gastrointestinal Cancer: Endogenous Factors
Banbury Report 8: Hormones and Breast Cancer
Banbury Report 9: Quantification of Occupational Cancer
Banbury Report 10: Patenting of Life Forms
Banbury Report 11: Environmental Factors in Human Growth and Development
Banbury Report 12: Nitrosamines and Human Cancer
Banbury Report 13: Indicators of Genotoxic Exposure
Banbury Report 14: Recombinant DNA Applications to Human Disease
Banbury Report 15: Biological Aspects of Alzheimer's Disease
Banbury Report 16: Genetic Variability in Responses to Chemical Exposure
Banbury Report 17: Coffee and Health
Banbury Report 18: Biological Mechanisms of Dioxin Action
Banbury Report 19: Risk Quantitation and Regulatory Policy
Banbury Report 20: Genetic Manipulation of the Early Mammalian Embryo
Banbury Report 21: Viral Etiology of Cervical Cancer
Banbury Report 22: Genetically Altered Viruses and the Environment
Banbury Report 23: Mechanisms in Tobacco Carcinogenesis
Banbury Report 24: Antibiotic Resistance Genes: Ecology, Transfer, and Expression
Banbury Report 25: Nongenotoxic Mechanisms in Carcinogenesis
Banbury Report 26: Developmental Toxicology: Mechanisms and Risk
Banbury Report 27: Molecular Neuropathology of Aging
Banbury Report 28: Mammalian Cell Mutagenesis
Banbury Report 29: Therapeutic Peptides and Proteins: Assessing the New Technologies
Banbury Report 30: Eukaryotic Transposable Elements as Mutagenic Agents
Banbury Report 31: Carcinogen Risk Assessment: New Directions in the Qualitative and Quantitative Aspects
Banbury Report 32: DNA Technology and Forensic Science
Banbury Report 33: Genetics and Biology of Alcoholism

Genetics and Biology of Alcoholism

Edited by

C. ROBERT CLONINGER
Washington University School of Medicine

HENRI BEGLEITER
State University of New York
Health Science Center, Brooklyn

33

Banbury Report

COLD SPRING HARBOR LABORATORY PRESS
1990

Banbury Report 33: Genetics and Biology of Alcoholism

© 1990 by Cold Spring Harbor Laboratory Press
All rights reserved
Printed in the United States of America
Cover and book design by Emily Harste

Library of Congress Cataloging-in-Publication Data

Genetics and biology of alcoholism / edited by C. Robert Cloninger,
   Henri Begleiter.
      p. cm.—(Banbury report, ISSN 0198-0068; 33)
   Includes bibliographical references.
   ISBN 0-87969-233-2
   1. Alcoholism—Physiological aspects. 2. Alcoholism—Genetic
aspects. I. Cloninger, C. Robert. II. Begleiter, Henri.
III. Series.
RC564.7.G46 1990   89-70879
616.86'1042—dc20   CIP

The articles published in this book have not been peer-reviewed. They express their authors' views, which are not necessarily endorsed by the Banbury Center or Cold Spring Harbor Laboratory.

Authorization to photocopy items for internal or personal use, or the internal or personal use of specific clients, is granted by Cold Spring Harbor Laboratory Press for libraries and other users registered with the Copyright Clearance Center (CCC) Transactional Reporting Service, provided that the base fee of $1.00 per article is paid directly to CCC, 27 Congress St., Salem, MA 01970. [0-87969-233-2/90 $1.00 + .00]. This consent does not extend to other kinds of copying, such as copying for general distribution, for advertising or promotional purposes, for creating new collective works, or for resale.

All Cold Spring Harbor Laboratory Press publications may be ordered directly from Cold Spring Harbor Laboratory Press, 10 Skyline Drive, Plainview, New York 11803. Phone: 1-800-843-4388. In New York (516) 367-8423. FAX: (516) 367-8432.

The meeting at the Banbury Center on which this book is based was generously supported by a financial contribution from the CHRISTOPHER D. SMITHERS FOUNDATION, New York.

Publication of the book was assisted by an anonymous donation.

Corporate Sponsors

Alafi Capital Company
American Cyanamid Company
Amersham International plc
AMGen Inc.
Applied Biosystems, Inc.
Becton Dickinson and Company
Beecham Pharmaceuticals
Boehringer Mannheim Corporation
Ciba-Geigy Corporation/Ciba-Geigy Limited
Diagnostic Products Corporation
E.I. du Pont de Nemours & Company
Eastman Kodak Company
Genentech, Inc.
Genetics Institute
Glaxo Research Laboratories
Hoffmann-La Roche Inc.
Johnson & Johnson
Life Technologies, Inc.
Eli Lilly and Company
Millipore Corporation
Monsanto Company
Oncogene Science, Inc.
Pall Corporation
Perkin-Elmer Cetus Instruments
Pfizer Inc.
Pharmacia Inc.
Schering-Plough Corporation
Tambrands Inc.
The Upjohn Company
The Wellcome Reseach Laboratories, Burroughs Wellcome Co.
Wyeth-Ayerst Research

Participants

Dharam P. Agarwal, Institute of Human Genetics, University of Hamburg, Federal Republic of Germany

Henri Begleiter, Neurodynamics Laboratory, State University of New York Health Science Center, Brooklyn

Paul R. Billings, Department of Medicine, Harvard Medical School, Boston, Massachusetts

Remi J. Cadoret, Department of Psychiatry, University of Iowa College of Medicine, Iowa City

Aravinda Chakravarti, Department of Human Genetics, University of Pittsburgh, Pennsylvania

C. Robert Cloninger, Department of Psychiatry, Washington University School of Medicine, St. Louis, Missouri

P. Michael Conneally, Department of Medical Genetics, Indiana University Medical Center, Indiana

Christopher C.H. Cook, Academic Department of Psychiatry, Middlesex Hospital School of Medicine, London, England

Conrad Gilliam, New York State Psychiatric Institute, Columbia University, New York

Daniel Flavin, National Council on Alcoholism, New York, New York

David Goldman, Laboratory on Clinical Studies, National Institute on Alcohol Abuse and Alcoholism, National Institutes of Health, Bethesda, Maryland

Enoch Gordis, National Institute on Alcohol Abuse and Alcoholism, National Institutes of Health, Rockville, Maryland

Andrew C. Heath, Department of Psychiatry, Washington University School of Medicine, St. Louis, Missouri

Victor Hesselbrock, Department of Psychiatry, University of Connecticut School of Medicine, Farmington

Eric S. Lander, Whitehead Institute for Biomedical Research, Cambridge, Massachusetts

Ting-Kai Li, Indiana University School of Medicine, Indianapolis

N.G. Martin, Queensland Institute of Medical Research, Brisbane, Australia

Ernest P. Noble, Alcohol Research Center, University of California Neuropsychiatric Institute, Los Angeles

Jurg Ott, Department of Psychiatry, Columbia University College of Physicians & Surgeons, New York, New York

Tim J. Peters, Department of Clinical Biochemistry, King's College School of Medicine and Dentistry, London, England

John Polich, Department of Neuropharmacology, Scripps Clinic, La Jolla, California

Peter Propping, Institute of Human Genetics, University of Bonn, Federal Republic of Germany

Theodore Reich, Department of Psychiatry, Jewish Hospital of St. Louis, Missouri

Neil J. Risch, Department of Epidemiology, Yale University School of Medicine, New Haven, Connecticut

Joseph Sambrook, Department of Biochemistry, University of Texas Medical Center, Dallas

Marc A. Schuckit, University of California and Veterans Administration Alcohol Research Center, San Diego

John S. Searles, University of Pennsylvania School of Medicine and Veterans Administration Medical Center, Philadelphia

Robert S. Sparkes, Department of Medicine, University of California Health Science Center, Los Angeles

Boris Tabakoff, National Institute of Alcohol Abuse and Alcoholism, National Institutes of Health, Bethesda, Maryland

Ralph E. Tarter, Department of Psychiatry, University of Pittsburgh Medical School, Pennsylvania

James D. Watson, Director, Cold Spring Harbor Laboratory, New York

Ellen M. Wijsman, Division of Medical Genetics, University of Washington School of Medicine, Seattle

Jan A. Witkowski, Director of Banbury Center, Cold Spring Harbor Laboratory, New York

Preface

Recent research indicates the need to examine seriously the feasibility and utility of current plans to detect and map specific genes that influence susceptibility to alcoholism. On the one hand, the opportunity to map genetic loci for susceptibility to alcoholism has been facilitated by the convergence of several research advances. First, twin and adoption studies have demonstrated the substantial role of genetic factors in the development of alcoholism. Adoption studies have also helped to characterize clinical subtypes of alcoholics who differ in their patterns of inheritance. Second, studies of the children of alcoholics have identified heritable neurobiological markers that predict later risk of alcoholism in adulthood. Third, genetic selection experiments have developed strains of animals that differ in their preference for alcohol and susceptibility to tolerance and dependence on alcohol. Such findings have led to a consensus that specific alcoholism susceptibility genes must be detected and mapped in order to understand the neurobiological processes that underlie susceptibility to alcoholism. Together with improved knowledge of the human genome and improved techniques for linkage mapping, both the need and the opportunity exist to begin the search for specific genes influencing the risk of alcoholism.

Even though some pedigree analysis has suggested the presence of a major gene effect in one alcoholism subtype, the mode of inheritance of alcoholism remains uncertain. Pedigree and twin studies indicate that the alcoholism susceptibility genes are incompletely penetrant, particularly in women, and also show highly variable clinical expression. Consequently, there is extensive clinical heterogeneity among alcoholics, who manifest a wide variety of comorbid personality traits, psychiatric disorders, and medical complications. The design and analysis of linkage trials for Mendelian disorders have been well characterized, but the power and robustness of methods for the study of common disorders with complex modes of inheritance remain controversial, as evidenced by unreplicable recent reports for other psychiatric disorders, including schizophrenia and manic-depressive disorder.

Accordingly, several important questions must be answered before we embark on the search for specific alcoholism susceptibility genes: Are the current descriptive methods for diagnosing and classifying alcoholics adequate for genetic linkage trials? Are there heritable neurobiological markers that would be useful in characterizing subtypes or components of susceptibility to alcoholism? Are there plausible candidate genes or favored loci that can narrow the search to specific regions of the human genome? Are available quantitative analytic methods for genetic linkage analysis able to handle the problems of incomplete penetrance, variable expressivity, and unknown mode of inheritance? If so, how should pedigree studies be designed to maximize the power to detect linkage and assure reproducibility of the findings?

These questions became all the more urgent in the fall of 1989 because the National Institute on Alcohol Abuse and Alcoholism was about to initiate a large multisite study on the genetics of alcoholism. Accordingly, Dr. Jan Witkowski, the Director of the Banbury Center, contacted the editors of this book for the purpose of organizing a meeting to evaluate critically the current state of knowledge about the genetics and biology of alcoholism and, particularly, the feasibility and design of genetic linkage studies for alcoholism. This meeting brought together a distinguished group of clinicians, neurobiologists, and geneticists to summarize and critique the obstacles, opportunities, and possible consequences of the search for specific genes for susceptibility to alcoholism. Leading advocates and critics of the application of new genetic methods to complex phenotypes were brought together to spark spirited discussion of the problems that may hinder progress and replication in this difficult but unarguably important field.

The proceedings cover four main areas: genetic and environmental risk factors, neurobiological markers of risk, animal models and candidate genes for alcoholism, and quantitative genetic methods for analysis of linkage for complex phenotypes. The chapters and associated discussions focus primarily on the feasibility and design of genetic linkage trials of alcoholism. However, the lively exchange of ideas among the outspoken and articulate participants will be of interest to everyone concerned with the inheritance or neurobiology of any complex human disease.

The proceedings of this Banbury conference capture the field of psychiatric genetics at a crucial juncture in its development. Evidence for genetic factors in alcoholism and other psychiatric disorders is strong, but the pathway from the genotype to the phenotype appears to involve many steps that may be difficult to characterize. However, many of the tools needed to identify specific genes influencing specific behaviors are now available. Although their application may be difficult, certainly the search for major genes underlying motivated behaviors like alcohol abuse has begun in earnest.

We thank the participants of the meeting for their lucid presentations and stimulating discussion. The staff of the Banbury Center of Cold Spring Harbor Laboratory provided an ambience that facilitated the ready exchange of ideas among the participants. In particular, we thank Dr. Jan Witkowski and Bea Toliver for their help with the organization of the meeting and the Christopher D. Smithers Foundation for its generous support. We are grateful to Katya Davey, hostess of Robertson House, for her hospitality, and to Sharon Hammer for transcription of the discussions. Finally, special thanks are extended to Nancy Ford, Managing Director of Publications; Patricia Barker, Nadine Dumser, and Inez Sialiano, who worked diligently with the editors to ensure the timely publication of the proceedings.

C.R. Cloninger
H. Begleiter

Contents

Participants, vii

Preface, xi

SECTION 1: GENETIC AND ENVIRONMENTAL CONTRIBUTIONS TO RISK OF ALCOHOLISM

Inheritance of Alcohol Consumption Patterns in the Australian Twin Survey, 1981 / Andrew C. Heath, Joanne M. Meyer, and Nicholas G. Martin — 3

Twin Studies of Alcohol Consumption, Metabolism, and Sensitivity / Nicholas G. Martin — 15

Use of the Adoption Paradigm to Elucidate the Role of Genes and Environment and Their Interaction in the Genesis of Alcoholism / Remi J. Cadoret and Robert B. Wesner — 31

Vulnerability to Alcoholism: From Individual Differences to Different Individuals / Ralph E. Tarter — 43

Time-dependent Model of the Familial Transmission of Alcoholism / Theodore Reich and C. Robert Cloninger — 55

Behavioral/Social Factors That May Enhance or Attenuate Genetic Effects / Victor Hesselbrock and Michie Hesselbrock — 75

Methodological Limitations of Research on the Genetics of Alcoholism / John S. Searles — 89

Genetic Epidemiology of Alcoholism: Observations Critical in the Design and Analysis of Linkage Studies / C. Robert Cloninger — 105

SECTION 2: NEUROBIOLOGICAL MARKERS OF RISK FOR ALCOHOLISM

Individuals at Risk for Alcoholism: Neurophysiologic Processes / Bernice Porjesz and Henri Begleiter   137

Alcoholic Fathers and Their Sons: Neuropsychological, Electrophysiological, Personality, and Family Correlates / Ernest P. Noble   159

Alcohol Effect on the Electroencephalogram: Are There Possibilities for Application of Molecular Genetics? / Peter Propping   175

A Prospective Study of Children of Alcoholics / Marc Alan Schuckit   183

Two Biological Markers of Alcoholism / Boris Tabakoff, James P. Whelan, and Paula L. Hoffman   195

Open Discussion   205

Comments: The NIAAA Consortium on the Genetics of Alcoholism / Enoch Gordis   213

SECTION 3: ANIMAL MODELS AND CANDIDATE GENES FOR ALCOHOLISM

Genetic Animal Models for the Study of Alcoholism / Ting-Kai Li   217

Candidate Genes and Favored Loci for Alcoholism / Christopher Charles Holland Cook and Hugh Malcolm Douglas Gurling   227

Genetic Variation in Serotonin and ALDH Underlying Alcoholism / David Goldman and Roberta Haber   237

Human Aldehyde Dehydrogenases: Genetic Implications in Alcohol Sensitivity, Alcohol-drinking Habits, and Alcoholism / Dharam P. Agarwal and H. Werner Goedde   253

Acquired and Genetic Deficiencies of Cytosolic Acetaldehyde Dehydrogenase / Timothy J. Peters, Andrew J.S. Macpherson, Roberta J. Ward, and Akira Yoshida   265

Open Discussion   277

SECTION 4: GENETIC LINKAGE ANALYSIS IN ALCOHOLISM—OBSTACLES, OPPORTUNITIES, AND CONSEQUENCES

Genetic Approaches to the Dissection of Complex Diseases / Aravinda Chakravarti and Eric S. Lander   307

Linkage Analysis of Alcoholism: Problems and Solutions / Ellen M. Wijsman   317

Genetic Linkage Analysis under Uncertain Disease Definition / Jurg Ott   327

Brewing Genes and Behavior: The Potential Consequences of Genetic Screening for Alcoholism / Paul R. Billings   333

Open Discussion   351

Author Index   375

Subject Index   377

Genetic and Environmental Contributions to Risk of Alcoholism

Inheritance of Alcohol Consumption Patterns in the Australian Twin Survey, 1981

ANDREW C. HEATH,* JOANNE M. MEYER,† AND NICHOLAS G. MARTIN‡
*Department of Psychiatry
Washington University School of Medicine
St. Louis, Missouri 63110
†Department of Human Genetics
Medical College of Virginia
Richmond, Virginia 23298-0033
‡Queensland Institute of Medical Research
Brisbane, Queensland, Australia

OVERVIEW

We review published data from the 1981 survey of alcohol consumption patterns in the Australian Twin Register and present results from new analyses. Both genetic and shared environmental effects have a substantial influence on whether or not teenage drinking occurs (as indicated by the results of parametric model fitting); however, the timing of the onset of drinking is under purely environmental control in males though also subject to genetic influence in females. Results from both multidimensional scaling (MDS) and model-fitting analyses indicate that adult alcohol consumption patterns are determined by separate abstinence, quantity, and frequency dimensions. Twin correlations for abstinence are uniformly high across all twin groups and are consistent with nongenetic determination of this dimension. For both quantity and frequency dimensions, there are substantial genetic effects in females and, at least, moderate genetic (and, possibly, also shared environmental) influences in males. The implications of this evidence for genetic effects on alcohol exposure are considered.

INTRODUCTION

Studies of adoptees (Goodwin et al. 1974; Cadoret et al. 1980; Cloninger et al. 1981), half-siblings (Schuckit et al. 1972), and twins (Kaij 1960; Hrubec and Omenn 1981; McGue et al. 1989) indicate a significant genetic influence on alcoholism in males (although evidence for genetic influence on female alcoholism is more equivocal [Goodwin et al. 1977; Bohman et al. 1981; McGue et al. 1989]). Despite criticism of the shortcomings of individual studies (Searles 1988), the broad consistency of findings from different studies, using different sampling strategies, makes theories of alcoholism that ignore heredity untenable. Apparent negative findings (e.g., Gurling et al. 1981; Murray et al. 1983) are easily explained when one considers the low resolving power of the twin study in the presence of assortative mating (Martin et al. 1978; Heath et al. 1985), which is observed to a high degree for alcoholism (Reich et al. 1988).

Most research on the genetics of alcoholism has treated the evidence for a strong genetic influence on alcohol consumption patterns as irrelevant (Partanen et al. 1966; Cederlof et al. 1977; Clifford et al. 1981; Kaprio et al. 1981, 1987; Jardine and Martin 1984). However, exposure to alcohol is a necessary prerequisite for the development of alcoholism; and insofar as exposure is partly under genetic influence, it should be taken into account in any genetic analysis of alcoholism. Application of both nonmetric MDS (Heath et al. 1990a) and parametric model-fitting methods (Heath and Martin 1988; Heath et al. 1989, 1990b) to twin data has provided some new insights into the genetic and environmental determination of alcohol exposure.

RESULTS

Onset of Teenage Drinking

Questionnaires were mailed to 5967 adult twin pairs, aged 18–88, enrolled on the Australian National Health and Medical Research Council volunteer twin panel, between November 1980 and March 1982. Completed questionnaires were returned by 3810 pairs, including 1233 female monozygotic (MZ), 567 male MZ, 751 female dizygotic (DZ), 352 male DZ, and 907 unlike-sex DZ pairs. The questionnaire requested information both about current alcohol use and age of first use (Jardine and Martin 1984). Because assessment of onset of drinking necessarily relied on the retrospective recall of the respondents, data about onset must be interpreted with some caution. For this reason, we have published genetic analyses of age of onset of drinking only for the young cohort, aged 18–30 years at the time of the Australian survey (Heath and Martin 1988), whose memories might be expected to be less fallible.

We have computed two-way contingency tables for age of onset of alcohol use (or abstinence from alcohol use as a teenager) for the entire sample, broken down into the five sex/zygosity groups, and used these as the basis for nonmetric MDS. We have discussed the application of MDS to twin data elsewhere (Heath et al. 1990a; J. Meyer et al., unpubl.). In brief, MDS is used to determine relative locations of variables in multidimensional space and the dimensionality of that space from a matrix of distances between such variables. Thus, in one textbook example (Kruskal and Wish 1978), a matrix of distances between major airports is used to generate a two-dimensional map of the United States. In applications to twin data, we cannot use the raw contingency cell frequencies as a distance metric, because differences in marginal frequency between response categories will yield spurious results. Instead, we divide the raw cell frequencies by the product of the corresponding row and column marginal frequencies to yield a proximity measure that would be the reciprocal of the conventional distance metric. No exact statistical test is available to compare the goodness of fit of MDS solutions of different dimensionality; however, Kruskal (1964) has proposed a stress measure, which is given by

$$S = (\Sigma[d_{i,j} - d'_{i,j}]^2 [\Sigma d^2_{i,j}]^{-1})^{0.5}$$

where $d_{i,j}$ is the estimated distance between variables i and j, and $d'_{i,j}$ is a monotonic transformation of the observed distance between variables. Stress values >0.20, by convention, are interpreted as showing a poor fit.

When applied to twin data, MDS uses differences within pairs to scale response categories. In MZ twin pairs, such differences will reflect only within-family environmental effects. In DZ twin pairs, such differences will also be the result of genetic segregation within families. Separate MDS analyses were therefore performed for each twin group. Unlike-sex twin pairs were excluded from these analyses, as it was not considered appropriate to assume the equivalence of onsets at the same age in the two sexes.

Table 1 gives the stress values obtained for each twin group, for solutions of differing dimensionality. In all cases, the one-dimensional solution, which posits that teenage abstainers lie on the same dimension as drinkers with differing ages of onset, gives a very poor fit. In the two MZ groups, the two-dimensional solution gives an adequate fit and identifies a teenage age-of-onset dimension, discriminating between onset at different ages, and a late onset or abstinence dimension, discriminating between teenage drinkers and those who remained abstinent or only began drinking at age 19 or 20. In the DZ like-sex groups, however, the two-dimensional solution still gives a

Table 1
MDS Solutions for Age of Onset of Teenage Drinking: Stress Values

Twin group	one dimensional	two dimensional	three dimensional
MZ male pairs	0.23	0.12	0.10
DZ male pairs	0.48	0.27	0.19
MZ female pairs	0.31	0.14	0.10
DZ female pairs	0.37	0.24	0.17

relatively poor fit, and a third dimension must be added to give an adequate fit to the data. In each case, this third dimension was found to discriminate very early onset drinkers (≤12 years) from other drinkers or abstainers. Because this dimension was observed in the DZ, but not the MZ, groups, this raises the possibility that this is a genetically determined dimension, with no corresponding environmental dimension.

Table 2 gives item weights derived from the MDS analyses for the MZ female pairs (two-dimensional solution) and the DZ female pairs (three-dimensional solution). Results for male like-sex pairs were comparable and are not shown here. Even with the very large sample sizes obtained by pooling older and younger cohorts, these solutions are far from perfect. Nonetheless, the interpretation of the first factor as an age-of-onset dimension and the second factor as a teenage drinking versus late onset or abstinence dimension is broadly consistent across the two groups.

The results of fitting genetic and environmental models to the twin age-of-onset data have been published elsewhere (Heath and Martin 1988). These analyses, which used only data from the younger cohort, give support to the notion that the determinants of teenage abstinence are quite different from the determinants of timing of onset of drinking in those who become teenage drinkers. Specifically, when onset of teenage drinking was treated as a dichotomous variable and analyzed under the assumption of an underlying normal liability distribution (Olsson 1979), additive genetic effects and shared environmental effects accounted for 35% and 32% of the variance in liability in females and 47% and 48% of the variance in liability in males. Environmental effects shared by members of like-sex pairs were largely uncorrelated over unlike-sex pairs, suggesting that peer influences or other sex-specific environmental influences were important. The age of first alcohol use, however, was purely determined by shared and nonshared environmental effects in males but was also influenced by genetic effects, and influenced only weakly by shared environmental effects, in females.

In subsequent analyses motivated by the MDS results, we have attempted to explore genetic influence on very early onset of drinking, treating onset of drinking by age 12 as a dichotomous variable. However, the number of twins reporting this early onset was very low in this general community sample, and the power of our test for genetic effects was correspondingly slight. In male twin pairs, tetrachoric correlations were consistent with a simple genetic model, but the standard errors of these correlations were so large as to make it impossible to exclude a nongenetic model (MZ males, $r = 0.77 + 0.10$; DZ males, $r = 0.39 + 0.26$). In female like-sex pairs, data were consistent with a nongenetic model (MZ females, $r = 0.71 + 0.10$; DZ females, $r = 0.79 + 0.11$). Only when data are available on larger samples will it be possible to resolve this issue.

Table 2
Category Weights for Female Like-sex Pairs Derived from MDS

	\u2264 12	13–14	15	16	17	18	19–20	abstinent
				Age-of-onset category				
				Monozygotic female pairs				
Dimension 1	−0.43	−0.49	−0.22	−0.05	0.41	0.61	0.23	−0.07
Dimension 2	−0.08	−0.28	−0.41	−0.39	−0.32	0.10	0.61	0.77
				Dizygotic female pairs				
Dimension 1	−0.12	0.14	0.54	0.33	0.31	0.65	0.41	0.06
Dimension 2	0.10	0.74	0.08	0.21	−0.52	−0.08	0.53	0.76
Dimension 3	0.76	−0.00	−0.12	0.36	−0.05	0.09	0.35	0.32

Adult Consumption Patterns

The first publication on the inheritance of alcohol consumption patterns in the Australian Twin Survey was that of Jardine and Martin (1984). This focused on total weekly alcohol consumption, both as derived from a 7-day retrospective diary (Redman et al. 1987) and as assessed using standard quantity and frequency questions (Straus and Bacon 1953). That study reported a significant and substantial genetic influence on level of alcohol consumption in female twins and young male twins but no genetic effect in the cohort of male twins aged 31 years and older. However, the data analysis included abstainers and twins who were infrequent users of alcohol, as well as those who were more regular drinkers, and thus may have confounded the inheritance of two different characters, abstinence and level of consumption by drinkers.

When we applied nonmetric MDS to an alcohol consumption scale derived from the items about abstinence, quantity, and frequency of consumption (Heath et al. 1990a), separate abstinence, frequency, and quantity dimensions emerged. Subsequent model-fitting analyses of the quantity/abstinence and frequency/abstinence data confirmed that there were separate dimensions controlling abstinence from alcohol use and level of alcohol consumption (Heath et al. 1990b). Neither a single liability dimension (SLD) model (Eaves et al. 1978) nor a conventional two-dimensional model that postulated independent abstinence and quantity (or frequency) dimensions—the latter influencing level of consumption in those who were not abstainers on the first dimension (Eaves and Eysenck 1980)—gave an adequate fit to the data. It was necessary to fit a combined model (CM), which recognized that those who were not abstainers on the first abstinence dimension could nonetheless be abstainers by virtue of their position on the second dimension, i.e., that some people were so low in liability on the consumption dimension that they were effectively abstainers (Heath et al. 1990b).

Model fitting revealed substantial twin correlations for all twin groups for the abstinence dimension and no evidence for genetic effects on this dimension, but strong genetic effects on the second, frequency (or quantity) dimension. In females, genetic effects accounted for 57–66% of the variance in consumption level on the second dimension. In males, a purely genetic model for twin resemblance and a model allowing for both genetic and shared environmental effects gave equally good fits to the data. Under the former model, genetic effects explained as much as 61–75% of the variance, comparable to the heritability observed in females; however, under the latter model heritability was no higher than 24–42% with shared environmental effects explaining an additional 32–35% of the variance on the second frequency (or quantity) dimension. No significant evidence for an interaction of genetic and environmental effects with cohort was found in either sex ($x^2_{10} = 5.95$, $P =$

Table 3
Comparison of Polychoric Correlations Under SLD, ILD, and CM Models for Quantity of Alcohol Consumed When Drinking

	SLD	ILD abstinence	ILD quantity	CM abstinence	CM quantity
Young cohort					
MZ female pairs	0.57	0.71	0.56	0.86	0.65
MZ male pairs	0.61	0.72	0.69	0.84	0.75
DZ female pairs	0.43	0.51	0.21	0.76	0.29
DZ male pairs	0.51	0.63	0.47	0.72	0.56
Unlike-sex DZ pairs	0.24	0.40	0.22	0.66	0.29
Older cohort					
MZ female pairs	0.59	0.63	0.46	0.61	0.70
MZ male pairs	0.60	0.73	0.46	0.87	0.71
DZ female pairs	0.34	0.41	0.05	0.84	0.34
DZ male pairs	0.52	0.68	0.23	0.97	0.45
Unlike-sex DZ pairs	0.33	0.47	0.14	0.97	0.21

0.82 for the frequency/abstinence data; $x^2_{10} = 5.98$ for the quantity/abstinence data). However, because the standard errors of parameter estimates under the two-dimensional CM were somewhat large, this may reflect a lack of statistical power for detecting heterogeneity of twin correlations across cohorts.

Table 3 summarizes the correlations estimated under the SLD, independent liability dimension (ILD), and CM models for the young and the older Australian cohorts, for the quantity/abstinence data (correlations for the frequency/abstinence data were comparable). Comparison of the estimates of correlations under the general model and the two submodels that were rejected by goodness-of-fit or likelihood-ratio Chi-square test gives some indication of the biases that can arise when incorrect assumptions about the dimensionality of the determinants of alcohol consumption patterns are made.

The SLD correlations suggest a relatively weak genetic influence on male consumption and consumption by younger female twins. A much more pronounced genetic effect is apparent for the quantity dimension under the CM. This suggests that it is the confounding of abstinence and quantity traits, having very different modes of inheritance, that explains the SLD results and supports our interpretation that such confounding was also the cause of the failure of Jardine and Martin (1984) to find significant heritability for total consumption in the older male cohort. The ILD quantity correlations underestimate those obtained under the CM, particularly in the older cohort. We would expect this because the ILD model truncates the second dimension by not allowing for any individuals who are abstainers because of their position on this second dimension.

DISCUSSION

Onset of drinking emerges from our analyses as at least a two-stage process. Both genetic and shared environmental effects influence whether or not an individual is at risk of becoming a teenage drinker. The timing of onset of drinking in those at risk, in males at least, appears to be environmentally determined, although there appears to be some genetic influence in females. From the analyses of quantity/abstinence and frequency/abstinence data, it also appears that there are two types of abstainers: those who abstain for familial environmental reasons, probably related to religious and similar beliefs; and those who abstain because of factors relating to personality or intolerance of alcohol, which are, in part, under genetic control.

Model-fitting analyses have indicated substantial genetic influence on frequency and quantity dimensions of alcohol consumption in females and, at least, moderate genetic influence in males. Because alcoholism cannot develop without exposure to alcohol, total abstainers have no risk of alcoholism. It has yet to be determined whether there are levels of alcohol use that are the equivalent of total abstinence, i.e., that involve no increased risk of alcoholism even for the first-degree relatives of alcoholics, and what such levels might be. The methods of model fitting and MDS that have been reviewed in this paper and elsewhere (Heath et al. 1990a,b), when applied to twin or other family data on both alcoholism and alcohol consumption patterns, can be used to address this question with considerable power.

If there are "safe" levels of alcohol consumption, even for those at high genetic risk of alcoholism, then the fact that alcohol exposure, itself, is partly under genetic control has important implications for genetic studies of alcoholism. It will be necessary to analyze jointly the inheritance of alcoholism and the inheritance of alcohol consumption patterns. Only in this fashion will it be possible to separate out the contributions to alcoholism of genes that influence level of exposure and genes that determine differences in risk of developing symptoms of alcohol abuse or dependence in response to a given degree of exposure.

ACKNOWLEDGMENTS

This work was supported by Alcohol, Drug Abuse and Mental Health Administration grants (AA07728, AA07535, MH40828, and DA05588) and by a grant from the Australian National Health and Medical Research Council. We are grateful to Theodore Reich and Lindon Eaves for their provocative and stimulating comments.

REFERENCES

Bohman, M., S. Sigvardsson, and C.R. Cloninger. 1981. Maternal inheritance of alcohol abuse: Cross-fostering analysis of adopted women. *Arch. Gen. Psychiatry* **38**: 965.

Cadoret, R.J., C.A. Cain, and W.M. Grove. 1980. Development of alcoholism in adoptees raised apart from alcoholic biologic relatives. *Arch. Gen. Psychiatry* **37**: 561.

Cederlof, R., L. Friberg, and T. Lundman. 1977. The interactions of smoking, environment and heredity and their implications for disease aetiology: A report of epidemiological studies on the Swedish twin registries. *Acta Med. Scand. Suppl.* 612.

Clifford, C.A., D.W. Fulker, H.M.D. Gurling, and R.M. Murray. 1981. Preliminary findings from a twin study of alcohol use. In *Progress in clinical and biological research* (ed. L. Gedda et al.), vol. 69, part C, p. 47. Alan R. Liss, New York.

Cloninger, C.R., M. Bohman, and S. Sigvardsson. 1981. Inheritance of alcohol abuse: Cross-fostering analysis of adopted men. *Arch. Gen. Psychiatry* **38**: 861.

Eaves, L.J. and H.J. Eysenck. 1980. The genetics of smoking. In *The causes and effects of smoking* (ed. H.J. Eysenck), p. 140. Maurice Temple Smith, London.

Eaves, L.J., K.A. Last, P.A. Young, and N.G. Martin. 1978. Model-fitting approaches to the analysis of human behavior. *Heredity* **41**: 249.

Goodwin, D.W., F. Schulsinger, J. Knop, S. Mednick, and S. Guze. 1977. Psychopathology in adopted and nonadopted daughters of alcoholics. *Arch. Gen. Psychiatry* **34**: 1005.

Goodwin, D.W., F. Schulsinger, N. Moller, L. Hermansen, G. Winokur, and S.B. Guze. 1974. Drinking problems in adopted and nonadopted sons of alcoholics. *Arch. Gen. Psychiatry* **31**: 164.

Gurling, H.M.D., C.A. Clifford, and R.M. Murray. 1981. Genetic contributions to alcohol dependence and its effect on brain function. In *Twin research* (ed. L. Gedda et al.), vol. 3, p. 77. Alan R. Liss, New York.

Heath, A.C. and N.G. Martin. 1988. Teenage alcohol use in the Australian twin register: Genetic and social determinants of starting to drink. *Alcohol Clin. Exp. Res.* **12**: 735.

Heath, A.C., R. Jardine, and N.G. Martin. 1989. Interactive effects of genotype and social environment on alcohol consumption in female twins. *J. Stud. Alcohol* **50**: 38.

Heath, A.C., K.S. Kendler, L.J. Eaves, and D. Markell. 1985. The resolution of cultural and biological inheritance: Informativeness of different relationships. *Behav. Genet.* **15**: 439.

Heath, A.C., J. Meyer, L.J. Eaves, and N.G. Martin. 1990a. The inheritance of alcohol consumption patterns in a general population twin sample: I. Multidimensional scaling of quantity/frequency data. *J. Stud. Alcohol* (in press).

Heath, A.C., J. Meyer, R. Jardine, and N.G. Martin. 1990b. The inheritance of alcohol consumption patterns in a general population twin sample: II. Determinants of consumption frequency and quantity consumed. *J. Stud. Alcohol* (in press).

Hrubec, Z. and G.S. Omenn. 1981. Evidence of genetic predisposition to alcoholic cirrhosis and psychosis: Twin concordance for alcoholism and its biological endpoints by zygosity among male veterans. *Alcohol Clin. Exp. Res.* **5**: 207.

Jardine, R. and N.G. Martin. 1984. Causes of variation in drinking habits in a large twin sample. *Acta Genet. Med. Gemellol.* **33**: 435.

Kaij, L. 1960. *Alcoholism in twins: Studies on the etiology and sequels of abuse of alcohol.* Almqvist and Wiksell, Stockholm.

Kaprio, J., M. Koskenvuo, and S. Sarna. 1981. Cigarette smoking, use of alcohol, and leisure-time physical activity among same-sexed adult twins. In *Progress in clinical and biological research* (ed. L. Gedda et al.) vol. 69, part C, p. 37. Alan R. Liss, New York.

Kaprio, J., M.D. Koskenvuo, H. Langinvainio, K. Romanov, S. Sarna, and R.J. Rose. 1987. Genetic influences on use and abuse of alcohol: A study of 5638 adult Finnish brothers. *Alcohol Clin. Exp. Res.* **11**: 349.

Kruskal, J.B. 1964. Multidimensional scaling by optimizing goodness of fit to a nonmetric hypothesis. *Psychometrika* **29**: 1.

Kruskal, J.B. and M. Wish. 1978. Multidimensional scaling. In *Sage University Paper Series on Quantitative Applications in the Social Sciences,* no. 07-011. Sage Publications, Beverly Hills, California.

Martin, N.G., L.J. Eaves, M.J. Kearsey, and P. Davies. 1978. The power of the classical twin study. *Heredity* **40**: 97.

McGue, M., R.W. Pickens, and D.S. Svikis. 1989. Sex differences in the inheritance of alcoholism. *Behav. Genet.* **19**: 768.

Murray, R.M., C.A. Clifford, and H.M.D. Gurling. 1983. Twin and adoption studies: How good is the evidence for a genetic role? In *Recent developments in alcoholism* (ed. M. Galanter), vol. 1, p. 25. Plenum Press, New York.

Olsson, H. 1979. Maximum likelihood estimation of the polychoric correlation coefficient. *Psychometrika* **44**: 443.

Partanen, J., K. Bruun, and T. Markkanen. 1966. *Inheritance of drinking behavior: A study on intelligence, personality, and use of alcohol of adult twins.* The Finnish Foundation for Alcohol Studies, Helsinki (distributed by Rutgers Center of Alcohol Studies, New Brunswick, New Jersey).

Redman, S., R.W. Sanson-Fisher, C. Wilkinson, P.P. Fahey, and R.W. Gibberd. 1987. Agreement between two measures of alcohol consumption. *J. Stud. Alcohol* **48**: 104.

Reich, T., C.R. Cloninger, P. VanEerdewegh, J.P. Rice, and J. Mullaney. 1988. Secular trends in the familial transmission of alcoholism. *Alcohol Clin. Exp. Res.* **12**: 458.

Schuckit, M.A., D.W. Goodwin, and G. Winokur. 1972. A study of alcoholism in half siblings. *Am. J. Psychiatry* **128**: 1132.

Searles, J.S. 1988. The role of genetics in the pathogenesis of alcoholism. *J. Abnorm. Psychol.* **97**: 153.

Straus, R. and S.D. Bacon. 1953. *Drinking in college.* Yale University Press, New Haven, Connecticut.

Twin Studies of Alcohol Consumption, Metabolism, and Sensitivity

NICHOLAS G. MARTIN
Queensland Institute of Medical Research
Brisbane, Australia

OVERVIEW

It is a common observation that individuals differ greatly in their consumption of alcohol and in their sensitivity to it. Some people appear greatly affected by even small doses; others consume large amounts of alcohol with little apparent effect on their behavior or performance. The causes of this normal variation, both in consumption and sensitivity, are of considerable interest, partly because they may provide clues to the etiology of the abnormal condition, alcoholism.

Comparison of identical (MZ) and nonidentical (DZ) twins is perhaps the best available design for estimating the relative contributions of environmental and genetic factors to individual differences. We have conducted a laboratory study of alcohol metabolism and psychomotor sensitivity in >200 twin pairs. Serum enzymes and hematological variables used to diagnose alcohol-related liver damage were also measured in these twins. Independently, we have studied drinking habits in nearly 4000 twin pairs who responded to a mailed questionnaire. Detailed reports of these studies have appeared elsewhere; in this paper, I highlight some of the insights we have gained into causes of normal individual differences in drinking habits, ethanol metabolism, and sensitivity to alcohol and the relationships between these variables.

Alcohol Consumption

A questionnaire, which included items on drinking patterns, was mailed to all 5967 pairs of adult (>18) twins enrolled on the Australian Twin Register. Completed replies were obtained from 3810 pairs, a 64% pairwise response rate, including 1233 MZ female, 567 MZ male, 751 DZ female, 352 DZ male, and 907 unlike sex pairs. The distribution of alcohol consumption reported by our volunteer twin sample was similar to that found in a random sample of the population surveyed by the Australian Bureau of Statistics. Because the distribution is highly skewed, genetic analysis was carried out on log-transformed scores.

Alternative hypotheses concerning the causes of individual differences in alcohol consumption were fitted to the mean squares for MZ and DZ twins.

One cause considered was additive genetic variance, which produces differences between MZ pairs but not within them and is divided equally between and within DZ pairs. Two sources of environmental variance are distinguished: exogenous influences that make siblings differ from each other (individual or specific environment—E1) and those that affect both cotwins but differ between twin pairs (shared or family environment—E2). The distinction is important; E1 estimates the influence of environmental factors unique to the individual and also includes measurement error, whereas E2 includes the influence of social and familial environments that are of primary interest to sociologists, for example. Models comprising various sensible combinations of these parameters were fitted to the data by the method of iterative weighted least squares, and criteria including goodness of fit and parsimony were used to decide upon a preferred hypothesis for the cause of individual differences (see Eaves et al. 1978).

The median age of the sample was ~30 years, so separate analyses were performed for twins aged 30 and under and for pairs over 30. Percentages of variance in alcohol consumption due to the three sources of variance considered are shown in Table 1 (Jardine and Martin 1984).

These percentages are calculated from the preferred models, and because the sample is subdivided four ways, the power to detect all three sources of variance in a subgroup is low if any one source is small (Martin et al. 1978). Thus, it is unlikely that there is no influence of shared environment on females nor of genetic factors on older males.

Our results confirm the importance of genetic factors in determining individual differences in alcohol consumption and echo the results of other twin studies (see, e.g., Kaprio et al. 1981). However, the differences in etiology between age and sex groups are highly significant, and our analysis makes the point that the relative importance of genetic and environmental factors depends crucially on the group under consideration. In males, genetic differences are important in youth but are increasingly overshadowed by environmental influences shared by brothers as they age. Genetic factors are of major importance in determining the alcohol consumption of females, al-

Table 1

Sources of Variance (%) for Alcohol Consumption According to Sex and Age of Twins

	Females		Males	
	≤30	>30	≤30	>30
Individual environment	42	45	34	49
Shared environment	—	—	21	51
Genetic	58	55	45	—

though both genetic and individual environmental variances for this measure increase considerably with age. In further analyses, we have shown that the causes of variation in female alcohol consumption depend critically on marital state. In unmarried females, genetic factors account for as much as 76% of the variance, whereas in married females, it is as low as 31% (Heath et al. 1989 and this volume). These patterns echo the causes of variation in age of onset of drinking; primarily social factors seem to determine when males start drinking, whereas genetic factors play a larger role in determining when females reach this landmark (Heath and Martin 1988; Heath et al., this volume).

We are currently following up this large twin sample 8 years after the initial contact to investigate the stability and sequelae of different drinking patterns and the extent to which genetic and environmental factors modify persistence and change in these behaviors over time. This study will be augmented with a new cohort of 18- to 26-year-old twins to resolve cohort versus developmental effects as the cause of the age differences we have observed in genetic architecture, and with the parents, spouses, and siblings of both new and already registered twin cohorts to address more subtle questions about genetic and environmental causes of family similarities and differences in drinking habits.

Alcohol Metabolism

In a laboratory study, we measured psychomotor performance in 206 pairs of 18- to 34-year-old twins before consuming alcohol and three times at hourly intervals after a standard dose of ethanol (0.75 g/kg body weight) was ingested. Blood alcohol concentration (BAC) was measured at frequent intervals after ingestion. There were 43 MZ female, 42 MZ male, 44 DZ female, 38 DZ male, and 39 DZ pairs of opposite sex. Repeat measurements were obtained for 41 of these pairs approximately 4 months after their first trial (Martin et al. 1985a,b).

At least six assays for blood ethanol were made from finger-prick samples on each subject. To correct for slight inequalities in sampling times, a curve was fitted to the BACs for each subject, from which the peak BAC, time to peak, and the rate of elimination were calculated. Repeatabilities (test/retest reliabilities) between occasions (averaging 4.5 months apart) were surprisingly low. For the individual readings, the average repeatability across different sampling times was only 0.64, 0.66 for peak BAC, 0.39 for rate of elimination, and a barely significant 0.27 for time of peak. Because the correlation between duplicate assays of the same sample was 0.97, little of this nonrepeatable variation can be attributed to errors in aliquot measurements or to machine fluctuations.

Genetic analysis found heritabilities of 0.62 ± 0.06 for peak BAC and 0.49 ± 0.07 for rate of elimination, but no significant genetic variance could be detected for time to peak. Heritabilities do not differ significantly from the respective repeatabilities of the BAC parameters, suggesting that all repeatable variation between people in the way they metabolize alcohol is determined genetically. Our results are at variance with those of Vesell (1972), who estimated a heritability of 0.98 for alcohol elimination rate in 14 pairs of twins, but are close to those of Kopun and Propping (1977), who used a larger sample of 40 pairs and found a heritability of 0.41. Our much larger sample of twins confirms the extensive role of environmental influences on rates of alcohol metabolism and suggests that these are ephemeral in nature and cannot be detected systematically over a period of months.

Our subjects were instructed to have a light, nonfatty breakfast before the trial and not to drink after midnight the previous evening. But in an effort to identify the ephemeral influences that account for so much of the variance in ethanol metabolism, we examined the relationship between BACs and the size of breakfast eaten on the day of the trial, and also whether the subject had consumed any alcohol on the previous evening. Neither factor accounted for more than several percent of the variance in BACs. Larger correlations were obtained with normal weekly alcohol consumption and also with the number of years that the subject had been drinking regularly. However, these variables still only accounted for 5–10% of the variance in BACs; in any case, we have shown that they are fairly stably reported and quite heritable, particularly in women (see above). Similarly, significant correlations were found between BACs and physical variables, including weight, adiposity, and lung function, although the relationships were a complex function of age, sex, and time of sampling. Once again, however, these physical variables are fairly stable over a period of several months, are moderately to highly heritable (Clark et al. 1980; Gibson et al. 1983), and will therefore not explain much of the ephemeral environmental variation detected.

Our study (Martin et al. 1985a) could only provide the broadest description of major influences on alcohol metabolism, namely, genetic factors and ephemeral environmental factors. We have failed to identify the nature of these environmental influences, although we have established that they are not merely due to measurement error. Further pharmacological experiments of the most traditional kind—investigations of the influence of A on B—are needed to identify and quantify these influences, which may well reside in quite subtle aspects of life-style, small-scale life events, and associated moods.

Polygenic factors that affect drinking habits and adiposity also appear to influence ethanol metabolism but are unlikely to account for more than a small proportion of variance in the latter. There is not yet sufficient evidence of polymorphism at alcohol or aldehyde dehydrogenase loci in Europeans to account for the observed genetic variance in BACs (Goedde et al. 1979), although this may change with the availability of DNA probes for these enzymes. Clearly, we have barely begun to explain individual differences in alcohol metabolism.

Psychomotor Sensitivity to Alcohol

Twins taking part in the above experiment were trained to plateau on a variety of psychomotor tasks, measured once before and three times after alcohol ingestion at hourly intervals. From previous work, the tasks had all been found to exhibit a monotonic relationship between alcohol dose and psychomotor response (Franks et al. 1976). We were therefore in a position to ask whether genetic factors that affected individual differences in psychomotor response to alcohol could be identified (Martin et al. 1985b). On the basis of work by Martin and Eaves (1977), an analysis was designed that would distinguish genes affecting all four measurements of psychomotor performance on a given task (general genetic factor) from independent genes that only influenced performance on the three postalcohol trials, but not the prealcohol trial (alcohol genetic factor).

Our psychomotor battery measured four essentially independent aspects of performance, which we term coordination, steadiness, cognitive time, and reaction time. We detected alcohol-specific genetic variation for all four factors. That is, there are genetic differences between individuals that help determine how one will perform at a given task under the influence of alcohol, and these genes are quite independent of those that determine one's general level of performance with or without alcohol. Yet another viewpoint is that an environmental factor, alcohol, unmasks genetic variation between people, which is hidden when they are sober.

The most striking example of this phenomenon in our study was the body sway task. Individuals were asked to stand with their eyes closed on a platform beneath which was a transducer that measured the amount of sway in the forward/backward dimension. Not surprisingly, sway was a function of center of gravity, so raw scores were corrected for height and weight before analysis. Table 2 shows the proportions of variance due to genetic and environmental factors for males at each trial.

Genetic differences are either general in influence or are only expressed after alcohol ingestion. Environmental variance is partitioned between those influences affecting performance on all four occasions (general factor), which might include sporting prowess and general state of well-being on the day, and specific environment, which influences a particular trial and that trial only. It is significant that estimates of the specific environmental variance are

Table 2
Body Sway in Male Twins: Variance (%) in Performance Before and After Alcohol Ingestion

	Environment		Genetic	
	general	specific	general	alcohol
Before alcohol	4	26	70	—
1 hr after	7	26	23	44
2 hr after	21	26	13	40
3 hr after	55	13	22	10

very close to independent estimates of the unreliability of the measurements from the test/retest data.

Genetic variance, as discussed above, is partitioned between that due to the general factor affecting performance, both before and after ingestion, and the alcohol genetic factor that reflects genetic differences exposed only in the presence of alcohol. The trends in Table 2 are striking. Before alcohol ingestion, a set of genes that affects body sway accounts for 70% of variance in the sober state. One hour after ingestion, these genes account for only 23% of the variance, and a new set of genes, whose effects are only "switched on" in the presence of alcohol, account for 44% of variance. As the influence of alcohol diminishes, these genes account for less and less of the variance— 40% at 2 hours and only 10% at 3 hours after ingestion (Boomsma et al. 1989).

Similar, though smaller, alcohol-specific genetic effects were found for the other dimensions of psychomotor performance and also for physiological variables, including heart rate, blood pressure, and skin temperature. There were also large genetic effects on subjective impressions of drunkenness (Neale and Martin 1989) and on willingness to drive a car after alcohol ingestion (Martin and Boomsma 1989). Clearly, there are genetic polymorphisms that have great influence on sensitivity to alcohol. To what extent are these polymorphisms the same as those reflected in genetic variation for drinking habits and ethanol metabolism?

A first approach to this question is to examine the correlates of change scores in psychomotor performance. We calculated the difference between performance before alcohol ingestion and 1 hour after (the time of maximum effect for most measures) and carried out stepwise multiple regression on a number of independent variables, including measures of drinking habits, BAC at 1 hour postingestion, and personality measures, incuding extraversion and psychoticism. For body sway in males, normal weekly alcohol consumption accounted for 11% of the change score, reflecting the fact that heavier drinkers were less steady than average before alcohol but more steady after alcohol. Only a further 2% of variance was accounted for by BAC, and another 3% by the number of years of regular drinking by the subject. For body sway in females, regular alcohol consumption and BAC each accounted for <2% of variance in the change score. For some other psychomotor tasks, notably hand/eye coordination, BAC did account for somewhat more of the variance in change score.

The striking finding remains, however, that psychomotor change scores are predicted very poorly by BAC, at least within the range of BACs obtained in our experiment (at 1 hr, mean 89 mg/100 ml EtOH, s.d. 18 for males; 95 ± 19 for females). Our results suggest that very little of the genetic variation in psychomotor sensitivity to alcohol can be accounted for either by variation in drinking habits or by BACs. This suggests that clues to the biochemical basis of variation in alcohol sensitivity in Europeans will not be found in the early parts of the metabolic pathway. To this end, we are now recontacting the twins who took part in this experiment, on whom valuable sensitivity data have been obtained, to obtain blood samples with a view to establishing Epstein-Barr virus lines. As probes for genes implicated in ethanol sensitivity become available (neurotransmitters?), we will look for associations between genetic variants and our earlier phenotypic measurements of alcohol sensitivity.

How Well Does Psychomotor Performance Discriminate between Groups with Different Blood Alcohol Levels?

As already noted, we observed low correlations between psychomotor performance and BAC after alcohol ingestion. We may ask how well these psychomotor measures discriminate between persons with BACs above or below a certain level, e.g., 80 mg/100 ml.

One hour after alcohol ingestion, 59 males had BACs < 80 mg/100 ml, and 139 had BACs greater than this level. The best discriminant function of performance variables measured at this time only classified 60% of these cases correctly. At other times, in both males and females, the best discrimination achieved between groups was only 71%. Thus, at any given time, the fact that individuals had a BAC greater than or less than 80 was a very poor guide to their performance on our battery of tests.

This result may arise from a restriction of range in both performance measures and BACs at a given time. Consequently, we recalculated the discriminant function by regarding each BAC reading and its associated performance measures at a given time as a separate case. The sets of observations are thus not independent, because each individual is now regarded as four "cases," but the analysis should afford the maximum opportunity for performance measures to discriminate between the two classes of BACs over a wide range of values, including the prealcohol values at which BAC was zero. Because the aim was to discriminate between BACs greater than or less than 80, regardless of sex, all 412 individuals were included in the analysis, generating 1648 cases.

At least one variable from each of the four groups of psychomotor measures contributed to the discriminant function and two measures each from the body sway and pursuit rotor tests, which appear to be the most discriminating tasks. Although the function made a highly significant discrimination between groups on either side of the BAC of 80 mg/100 ml, there is a great deal of overlap between the two groups. About 29% of cases with actual BACs <80 performed poorly enough to fall into the group predicted to be >80, whereas 34% with actual BACs >80 performed well enough that they were predicted to fall into the low BAC group. Only 69% of cases were correctly classified. A further discriminant analysis attempted to classify BACs into three groups: 0, 1–80, and >80 mg/100 ml; the classification results are shown in Table 3. Of those who were actually completely sober, 9.5% of cases performed so badly that they were predicted to have BACs >80, whereas of those who actually did have BACs >80, 19.3% were predicted to fall into the sober group. Overall, only 54% of cases were correctly classified.

We conclude that our battery of tests provides only very crude predictive power about the BACs of individuals. Conversely and more importantly, BACs in the considerable range that we have observed are a poor predictor of psychomotor performance on our battery of tests. This range was 0 mg/100 ml to 162 mg/100 ml, including 412 zero readings; the mean of nonzero readings is 83 and s.d. 17. This range of BACs is the main focus of legislative and police attention in attempts to lower the road toll.

Two possible interpretations of our results are (1) the psychomotor tests we have used have little to do with driving competence, and our results are

Table 3
Classification Results for Discriminant Analysis between BACs on the Basis of Psychomotor Performance Scores

	Predicted group (%)			
	0	1–80	>80[a]	n
Actual group				
0[a]	72.5	18.0	9.5	411
1–80	33.1	32.1	34.8	202
>80	19.3	19.8	60.9	653

54% of cases correctly classified.
[a]Concentrations are milligram per milliliter.

therefore irrelevant for practical purposes; or (2) preventive action would be better aimed at testing driving competence than measuring concentrations of alcohol or other drugs in the blood. It is ironic that the traditional test for drunkenness in many countries, in which the suspect was asked to walk a white line (a task closely related to our body sway test) was superseded by blood alcohol testing. Perhaps those interested in road safety should be pressing for roadside psychomotor testing rather than for lower legal BACs. If the psychomotor tasks we used in our study have any correlation with driving safety, such legislation penalizes many drivers who are competent and leaves unpenalized many drivers who are not competent.

In conclusion, our studies have shown the important role played by genetic differences in determining how much people drink and how they are affected by alcohol. In an ideal world, each individual would determine his own level of responsible drinking, but this would ignore individual differences in responsibility and judgment.

ACKNOWLEDGMENTS

This work was supported by grants from the Australian Associated Brewers and the National Health and Medical Research Council of Australia. This paper is based on work done in collaboration with my colleagues Drs. J. Gibson, R. Jardine, J. Oakeshott, G. Starmer, and J. Whitfield, although none of them is responsible for the remarks made herein.

REFERENCES

Boomsma, D.I., N.G. Martin, and P.C.M. Molenaar. 1989. Factor and simplex models for repeated measures: Application to two psychomotor measures of alcohol sensitivity in twins. *Behav. Genet.* **19:** 79.

Clark, P., R. Jardine, N.G. Martin, A.E. Stark, and R.J. Walsh. 1980. Sex differences in the inheritance of some anthropometric characters in twins. *Acta Genet. Med. Gemellol.* **29:** 171.

Eaves, L.J., K.A. Last, P.A. Young, and N.G. Martin. 1978. Model-fitting approaches to the analysis of human behaviour. *Heredity* **41:** 249.

Franks, H.M., V.R. Hensley, W.J. Hensley, G.A. Starmer, and R.K.C. Teo. 1976. The relationship between alcohol dosage and performance decrement in humans. *J. Stud. Alcohol* **37:** 284.

Gibson, J.B., N.G. Martin, J.G. Oakeshott, D.M. Rowell, and P. Clark. 1983. Lung function in an Australian population: Contributions of polygenic factors and the Pi locus to individual differences in lung function in a sample of twins. *Ann. Hum. Biol.* **10:** 547.

Goedde, H.W., D.P. Agarwal, and S. Harada. 1979. Alcohol metabolising enzymes: Studies of isozymes in human biopsies and cultured fibroblasts. *Clin. Genet.* **16:** 29.

Heath, A.C. and N.C. Martin. 1988. Teenage alcohol use in the Australian Twin Register: Genetic and social determinants of starting to drink. *Alcohol Clin. Exp. Res.* **12:** 735.

Heath, A.C., R. Jardine, and N.C. Martin. 1989. Interactive effects of genotype and social environment on alcohol consumption in female twins. *J. Stud. Alcohol* **50:** 38.

Jardine, R. and N.C. Martin. 1984. Causes of variation in drinking habits in a large twin sample. *Acta Genet. Med. Gemellol.* **33:** 435.

Kaprio, J., M. Koskenvuo, and S. Sarna. 1981. Cigarette smoking, use of alcohol and leisure-time physical activity among same sexed adult male twins. In *Twin research 3: Part C* (ed. L. Gedda et al.), p.37. Alan R. Liss, New York.

Kopun, M. and P. Propping. 1977. The kinetics of ethanol absorption and elimination in twins supplemented by repetitive experiments in single subjects. *Eur. J. Clin. Pharmacol.* **11:** 337.

Martin, N.G. and D.I. Boomsma. 1989. Willingness to drive when drunk and personality: A twin study. *Behav. Genet.* **19:** 97.

Martin, N.G. and L.J. Eaves. 1977. The genetical analysis of covariance structure. *Heredity* **38:** 79.

Martin, N.G, L.J. Eaves, M.J. Kearsey, and P. Davies. 1978. The power of the classical twin study. *Heredity* **40:** 97.

Martin, N.G., J. Perl, J.G. Oakeshott, J.B. Gibson, G.A. Starmer, and A.V. Wilks. 1985a. A twin study of ethanol metabolism. *Behav. Genetics* **15:** 93.

Martin, N.G., J.G. Oakeshott, J.B. Gibson, G.A. Starmer, J. Perl, and A.V. Wilks. 1985b. A twin study of psychomotor and physiological responses to an acute dose of alcohol. *Behav. Genetics* **15:** 305.

Neale, M.C. and N.C. Martin. 1989. The effects of age, sex and genotype on self-report drunkenness following a challenge dose of alcohol. *Behav. Genet.* **19:** 63.

Vesell, E.S. 1972. Ethanol metabolism: Regulation in normal volunteers under a controlled environment and the effect of chronic ethanol administration. *Ann. N.Y. Acad. Sci.* **197:** 79.

COMMENTS

Schuckit: Did you determine the reproducibility of the body sway data?

Martin: Yes, it was about 0.8.

Chakravarti: The data that Andrew presented, concerning frequency and quantity of drinking, you said this was self-reported data?

Heath: Yes.

Chakravarti: Are you making an attempt to verify it?

Martin: We have test-retest data. In that particular study, we had the same questions answered three months later by 100 individuals. It's not a very large sample. Test-retest correlations were about 0.8 for the quantity and frequency questions. Of course, that doesn't answer the question about validity.

Heath: We are trying in the follow-up to actually get information from informants about it.

Chakravarti: Given all the social taboos now about drinking, I'm just wondering whether there are changes in your classification.

Heath: In the Virginia study, we asked people to report about themselves, their twins, their parents, and so on. We get correlations on the order of about 0.7–0.75 between what an individual says and what other members of the family say about that individual. It's not an ideal measure. Obviously, we would rather have someone from the outside, as it were.

Reich: Is your repeatability different in different parts of the distribution, since the alcohol consumption curve is really skewed?

Martin: The repeatability of alcohol consumption?

Reich: Consumption frequency and frequency. If they're real alcoholics, they may not be able to know exactly.

Heath: We don't have enough data points. We only had a retest for about 120.

Begleiter: I'm always a little surprised about the lack of BAL reliability over time. Maybe this is because for the most part people only take one parameter out of the wealth of data included in the whole BAL curve. For instance, you have rise time, decay time, onset time, and frequency. Typically, people only look at one thing, which is peak, and, of course, most people don't find it to be highly reliable.

Martin: I showed you the reliability and heritability at each time point and in the four measured statistics, the four computer statistics, as well. I looked at the raw time point data there, and the best reliability was around 0.68 for a single time point. The problem is that when you then start combining those into computer statistics or working out the first differential, which is the maximum, you just combine the zeroes and they've actually even got worse characteristics.

Li: For the test-retest reliability, was what you stated for both without alcohol and with alcohol?

Martin: The test-retest reliability was higher after alcohol than before alcohol—about 0.8 for females, and a bit lower for males.

Begleiter: This is in direct contradiction to the Nagoshi and Wilson data.

Martin: That's test-retest data. I can't remember how large their test-retest sample was. We had about 80 subjects in our test-retest sample.

Begleiter: They had a larger sample than that.

Schuckit: We find a high level of similarity testing the same man on three different occasions.

Martin: For psychomotor?

Schuckit: For body sway. We test men at two different doses of alcohol and we find a high correlation between the amount of increase in sway after low dose and the amount of increase after high dose. It's very, very similar. I don't have data on the same man at the same dose twice, but my data would be more similar to yours than it would be to Nagoshi-Wilson's.

Martin: We need to look at that Nagoshi and Wilson data. I think there was something problematic about the way they did their analysis.

Reich: Since the biology of the ascending and descending forces on the curve was different, wouldn't you expect the heritability and the performance characteristics to be different also?

Martin: It's so difficult to get anything on the ascending path because it's so quick. Certainly, getting breath alcohol measurements during that time is useless anyway because there is so much residual breath alcohol. Unless you are taking samples every five minutes, you just miss it for most people.

Risch: When you did modeling with two genetic components, you said upon alcohol consumption there was a new heritability elicited. Is this reflecting the fact that the heritability goes up, basically, after alcohol consumption?

Martin: Yes, but the fascinating thing is, if you do it on the raw measurements, you can actually see the variance go up dramatically after alcohol, and you can actually show that all that new variance is genetic, and environmental variance is actually more or less remaining as a constant. Of course, the problem is when you then start studying the proportion, you see that the environmental variance goes down as a proportion, but actually, in absolute terms, it's constant.

Heath: It's not just the case that you can estimate a single common factor with increase in loading?

Martin: No. You have to put a second factor in there to account for it, which is a very clumsy way to do it. We have redone it as a time series problem with the inputs at each time point, which is the correct way to do it, and you can actually show a large chunk of new genetic variance coming at time 1, and that just gets carried forward, but diminishes at the subsequent time points. That's the only innovation you need to put in.

Risch: Did you do any regression on the other covariates, like weight and blood alcohol concentration? I would think those things are heritable also.

Martin: I didn't in the genetic model because from just the correlation tables that I showed you the correlations were so slight that you're only going to mark up 4% or 5% variance at most due to any of the covariates. If that is a phenotypic correlation, that is going to split between genetic and environmental effects anyway, so you're going to be looking at effects down around 2% or 3% of the variance. Even if I can estimate that, who cares?

Chakravarti: But those are all individual, because you have cases where you found an effect not at time zero or you found an effect in females even after correcting the measurement for body weight. So there may be other interactions.

Martin: Yes. That shows that our attempts to dose for weight are not good enough. There are all sorts of inner body fat deposits which even taking some subscapular readings and subcutaneous readings are not going to fix up. My guess is that, while we are trying to do that very carefully, there is still such a huge range of variation left in BAC that other factors are operating which are quite independent of those physical kinds of things.

Risch: High-weight people got a higher dose, right?

Martin: Yes.

Risch: They also showed up with a higher blood alcohol content; is that right?

Martin: Yes.

Risch: Maybe you overcompensated, because they got a higher dosage of alcohol.

Martin: Yes, but we're talking about a correlation of 0.2–0.25, which was the maximum correlation with weight or with adiposity.

Risch: I didn't know what happened when you put them all together. You probably did that.

Martin: As I say, that would account for that 2%, or 3%, or 4% variance, but there is a massive chunk of variance out there that is not accounted for in that.

Li: There is a new observation which I think is probably important in understanding some of these differences, and that has to do with first pass metabolism, that is now known in humans and is really quite significant when the dose of alcohol is low. But with the dose you're giving and which we normally give—which is really about half a bottle, not quite a whole bottle of wine...

Schuckit: What he gave is close to six drinks.

Li: Yes, five to six drinks. Then, first pass metabolism can be quite significant because of alcohol dehydrogenase in the stomach. It is almost absent in women and it's quite prominent in men.

Martin: I don't know what you mean by first pass metabolism.

Li: When you drink, the alcohol is metabolized and never reaches the blood stream, so you are measuring breath (and we are too) and blood alcohol, and you don't see the amount because it has been metabolized already.

Martin: Before it even gets there?

Li: Yes. It has been shown quite recently that it is due to the metabolism by the stomach and not first pass through the liver.

Martin: And you're saying that could account for that sex difference?

Li: Sex difference, as well as maybe differences in pernicity of drinking, because that changes with drinking, and also, individuals differ in the amount of the forms present. It's a different form. We're calling it σ ADH.

Reich: The more you drink the less you have?

Li: Yes. Chronic alcoholics have less of a first pass.

Heath: What are the typical drinking histories of the people who agreed to participate in that study?

Martin: There was a range. The age range was 18–34, with the preponderance toward the younger people. There were quite a number of naive drinkers in the study. We tried to get young people who hadn't shot their livers, but, nevertheless, there were some people who drank heavily; for example, one guy showed up whose pre-alcohol breathalyzer was 0.12.

Tabakoff: One important thing I didn't see in the data is some attention to the recent history of alcohol abuse. You have average weekly consumption, you have consumption over the past year or so. How well did you know what they were doing the day before or the night before?

Martin: I think I went too quickly over that. We actually asked them when they had their last drink and how much they drank. I made that into a single variable we regressed out which I just called "last drink." There was no correlation, either, in the time points. It ranged from 0.1 to negligible across the whole sample. That's not to say that for certain individuals it may not have been important, but across the whole sample it was negligible.

Use of the Adoption Paradigm to Elucidate the Role of Genes and Environment and Their Interaction in the Genesis of Alcoholism

REMI J. CADORET AND ROBERT B. WESNER
Department of Psychiatry
University of Iowa College of Medicine
Iowa City, Iowa 52242

OVERVIEW

Separation or adoption designs are uniquely able to assess genetic, environmental, and genetic-environmental effects. At the present state of linkage studies in alcoholism, information from adoption designs could be used profitably to determine the possibility of affected individuals being phenocopies. This information could be included in current mathematical models used to detect genetic linkage.

Adoption studies are one type of separation paradigm that includes experiments such as Harlow's removal of infant monkeys from their mothers and placement with various maternal surrogates. In the investigation of human behaviors, separation studies most commonly involve adoptees separated at birth and placed with nonrelatives who become the adoptive parents. The study of adoptees thus reared in different environments was first proposed in 1912 by Richardson as a method to determine the importance of nature versus nurture (or heredity vs. environment) in determining human intelligence (Richardson 1912–13). The relevant issue is the contribution such an old technique can make to molecular genetics.

In the recent past, adoption studies have become more common in psychiatry and have been used to demonstrate that a number of important psychiatric conditions have a genetic factor in their etiology. Such conditions are alcoholism (Goodwin et al. 1973, 1974; Cadoret and Gath 1978; Cadoret et al. 1980, 1985a; Bohman et al. 1981; Cloninger et al. 1981), drug abuse (Cadoret et al. 1986), schizophrenia (Heston 1966; Rosenthal and Kety 1968; Kety et al. 1971, 1978; Rosenthal et al. 1971; Wender et al. 1974), bipolar affective disorder (Mendelwicz and Rainer 1977), various schizophrenia-related conditions, etc. (Kendler et al. 1981a,b, 1982). Thus, the most recent contribution of adoption studies to the question of psychiatric etiology has been the evidence for a genetic factor. However, the separation design can also be used to investigate other factors of etiologic importance such as environmental effects—gene-environment interaction (Cadoret 1986). A variety of environmental effects can be studied, such as the environmental factors that are shared by all family members, unique environmental factors that occur only with certain individuals in a family and may determine individual differences, and gene-environment correlations or the tendency for some individuals to seek out certain environments due to their genotypes. Recently, adoption studies have implicated environmental effects in alcoholism (Bohman et al. 1981; Cloninger et al. 1981; Cadoret et al. 1985a), criminality (Bohman et al. 1982; Cloninger et al. 1982; Sigvardsson et al. 1982), schizophrenia (Wender et al. 1974), and major depression (von Knorring et al. 1983; Cadoret et al. 1985b). As discussed below, this ability of the separation study to assess the effect of the environment can be very important in determining the expression of the genotype, as well as the production of phenocopies. However, we shall review the general separation paradigm first to see how environmental and genetic effects can be assessed.

The purpose of the separation paradigm is to isolate, measure, and control for factors that would ordinarily be confounded. The unconfounding is accomplished usually by the physical separation and its timing. By removing a child from its biologic parents and environment at birth and placing the child in an adoptive home with nonrelatives, genetic effects can be assessed separately from the environment. Figure 1 shows one subdivision of the genetic and environmental factors that impinge on the adoptee and on each other. The vertical line separating biologic family factors from adoptive family factors depicts the result of the separation in unconfounding biologic parental factors from adoptive family factors. With the separation at birth, relationship 1 can be considered a measure of genetic endowment and can be assessed if other factors are controlled, especially prenatal, perinatal, and postnatal environments. Relationship 2 can be considered as a measure of adoptive parental behavior effect or as a reaction of parental behavior to adoptee behavior (e.g., temperament). Relationship 3 reflects similarities between adoptive and biologic parents, such as socioeconomic status, drinking behavior, and IQ. Its importance lies in the fact that adoption practices might result in significant correlations between adoptive and biologic parents, leading to potential overestimating of the genetic effect, relationship 1. This effect, known as selective placement, can be minimized by design and controlled, in part, by statistical methods. Thus, the separation element allows relationship 7, postnatal environmental factors, to be assessed, as well as the genetic factor (relationship 1). Other relationships, 4, 5, and 8, can be assessed and controlled either by design or by statistical methods. Thus, by measuring the factors shown in Figure 1, it is possible to use each as a variable to control the remainder and thus to determine which conditions are affecting adoptee behavior. Modern statistical techniques such as logistic regression

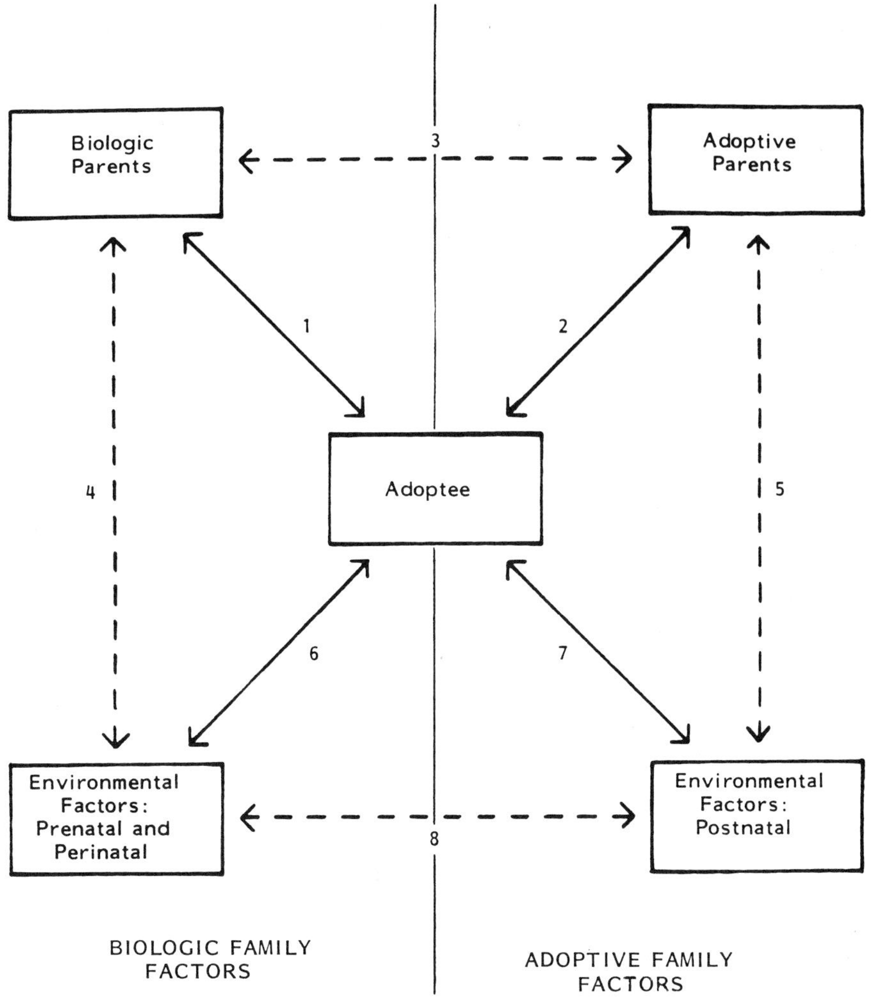

Figure 1
The adoption paradigm showing relationship between hereditary and environmental factors.

and log-linear modeling can be used to identify genetic and environmental factors and their interaction, and to control for possible confounding factors.

From the historical perspective, adoption studies have contributed to the study of alcoholism by providing evidence for a genetic factor (for review, see Cadoret 1989). What further contribution can be expected of the adoption paradigm? As shown above, etiologic environmental factors can be identified as effectively as genetic factors, and current adoption studies have indicated a role for environmental factors in the etiology of alcoholism (Bohman et al. 1981; Cloninger et al. 1981; Cadoret et al. 1985a). The ability of the environment to produce in an individual a picture of alcoholism that may be independent of a genetic factor is important information. Such phenocopies confuse analyses currently in vogue to detect genetic linkage. However, if environmental factors could be identified for alcoholism, appropriate weightings could be included in the mathematical paradigm used to measure genetic linkage. To be so used, a factor would have to be identifiable. Adoption studies would provide an ideal way to identify such factors.

Another role for adoption studies is the determination of genetic-environmental interactions. Environmental factors that markedly increase the chance of the expression of the alcohol genetic factors or, conversely, environments that markedly inhibit the genetic expression could confuse linkage studies. For example, potential phenylketonurics in an environment devoid of or low in phenylalanine are much less likely to manifest mental retardation. If mental retardation were the clinical end point used to define the phenotype, linkage analyses would be difficult to carry out. Again, as with independent environmental factors, the adoption design can detect such genetic-environmental interactions. Once specific environmental conditions are identified, appropriate weightings are entered into the equations to measure genetic linkage.

There is an additional contribution that adoption studies can make to untangle the genetic etiology of alcoholism. Alcoholism is known to occur more frequently in conjunction with a number of other psychiatric illnesses: antisocial personality (ASP), major depression, drug abuse, various anxiety and panic disorder states, to name the most frequent comorbid conditions (Hesselbrock et al. 1985; Helzer and Pryzbeck 1988). Clinical heterogeneity suggests that there may be more than one genetic pathway to alcoholism, e.g., antisocial traits that lead to excessive drinking behavior. Some of these conditions comorbid with alcoholism may have genetic factors in their etiology that are independent of factors leading to alcoholism. ASP is such a case; both family and adoption studies show separate and independent inheritance of factors involved with ASP and factors leading to alcoholism (Lewis et al. 1983; Vaillant 1983; Cadoret et al. 1987). However, ASP appears to play a predisposing role in alcoholism in view of ASP's manifestation in childhood and early adolescence and its high correlation with early substance use and adult alcoholism. ASP alcoholics probably are included in Cloninger's type II alcoholism (Cloninger et al. 1981). Adoption designs can clarify the role of these other genetic pathways to alcoholism such as the ASP route. Identification of alternate pathways to alcoholism would result in selection of subtypes of families with alcoholism to detect linkage using current model-fitting procedures.

The remainder of this paper presents results from adoption studies done over the last decade in Iowa. These results will demonstrate each of the points made above. The experimental paradigm for these studies is shown in Figure 2. Our practice has been to use adoption agency records to identify adoptees, 18–40 years of age, who have some type of psychopathology in a biologic parent. Psychopathology is defined in Cadoret and Gath (1980), Cadoret et al. (1980), Cadoret and Cain (1981), and Cadoret et al. (1985a) and includes conditions such as alcohol problems, criminal or delinquent behavior, and mental retardation. A control group of adoptees matched for age, sex, and age of biologic mother is selected from the same agency. The controls have no record of psychopathology in the biologic parents. These adoptees are separated at birth from their biologic parents and placed with nonrelatives. To measure environmental factors and adoptee early development, adoptive parents are given an extensive structured interview. The adoptees are given a structured psychiatric interview to diagnose psychiatric conditions such as alcohol abuse, depression, and antisocial personality. Interviews are conducted by research assistants who are blinded to the biologic parent background. The validity of the paradigm in measuring genetic effects depends, in part, on random placement in environments (see Fig. 2). Although randomness with regard to every selection factor probably does not hold, we have never found evidence in these data to suggest that biologic parent psychopathology has influenced the type of home placement. The design shown in Figure 2 allows us to estimate a genetic effect by comparing adoptee out-

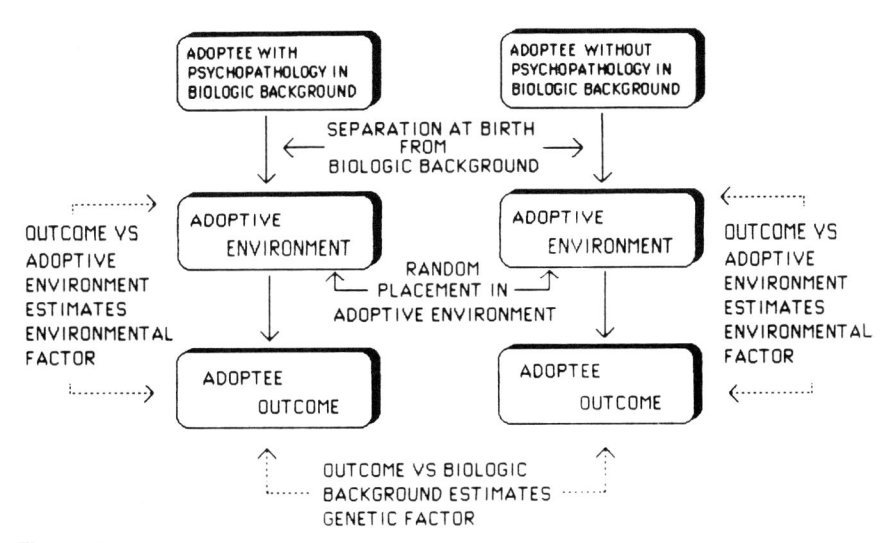

Figure 2
The adoption paradigm for estimating genetic and environmental effects on psychopathology.

comes between groups with and without parental psychopathology and to estimate environmental effects by correlations (within psychopathology and control groups) between environmental factors and adoptee outcome. Statistically different correlations between control and psychopathologic groups would estimate a genetic environmental interaction effect.

Results are presented for 286 male adoptees collected from two adoption agencies: Lutheran Social Services of Iowa and Iowa Family and Children's Services. The analysis is by log-linear modeling, which relates relevant adoptee outcomes such as ASP and alcohol abuse to genetic and environmental factors. Figure 3 shows the results of such an analysis (analysis and methodology described in Cadoret et al. 1989). The thin arrows depict correlations "forced" into the model to control for selective placement. None of these correlations was significant, except for the relationship between biologic parent with antisocial behavior and with alcohol problems. This correlation is a measure of (1) nonrandom mating and (2) the tendency for antisocial behavior and alcohol problems to occur in the same individual. The heavier arrows indicate statistically significant correlations found in the analysis. Beside each arrow is the odds ratio describing the magnitude of the correlation found. Each correlation is corrected for the effect of all other variables in the model. Arrows with one head suggest a directionality of cause and effect; those with two heads indicate that direction of effect is not clear.

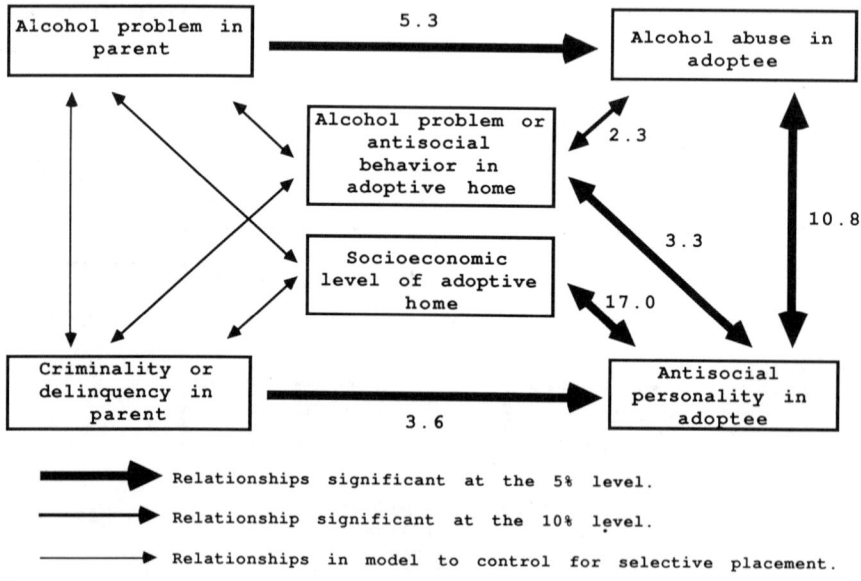

Figure 3
Genetic and environmental precursors of alcohol abuse.

The results show a clear-cut genetic factor operating from biologic parent to adoptee and increasing the chance of alcohol abuse in the adoptee. There is evidence for an environmental factor: An alcohol or antisocial problem in the adoptive home increases the chance of both alcohol abuse and ASP in the adoptee. This environmental factor acts independently of the genetic background of alcohol problem, criminality, or delinquency (in the biologic parent) and suggests that the environmental factor is able to produce phenocopies, since we are unable to find clinical differences between alcohol abuse stemming from these different factors in adoptees.

ASP is very strongly correlated with alcohol abuse. ASP, itself, is related to biologic parent criminality/delinquency, and as the diagram suggests, inheritance of ASP appears to be independent of the alcohol diathesis. This finding, which is compatible with family studies of alcoholics, suggests that ASP must be considered in linkage analyses as a separate genetic factor influencing alcohol abuse, as shown in the diagram.

The model in Figure 3 also demonstrates the importance of gene-environment interaction. The very significant odds ratio shown between socioeconomic status (SES) of the adoptive home and ASP holds only for adoptees from a criminal/delinquent background who are placed in a lower SES adoptive home. This interaction is shown in Table 1, where it can be seen that adoptive home SES has little influence on ASP if the adoptee is from a noncriminal/nondelinquent biologic parent but that ASP increases dramatically in lower SES adoptive homes, given a criminal/delinquent background. In view of the implication of ASP in the etiology of alcoholism, this interaction could be of considerable importance in controlling for ASP in linkage models. The interaction factor could be controlled by including in the model a weighting factor based on SES; alternatively, it could be controlled by selecting families for study from the same SES, a process that could minimize variability in the effect of SES but that would limit generalizability.

Table 1
Interaction between SES and Biological Parent Background

Biologic parent	Adoptee outcome	SES of adoptive home		
		high	medium	low
Criminal/	antisocial (%)	6	43	67
delinquent	no.	17	21	12
Not				
criminal/	antisocial (%)	11	10	13
deliquent	no.	82	94	60

DISCUSSION

How can adoption studies improve moleclular genetic linkage studies in psychiatry? On the surface, it may appear that adoption studies are of little use to molecular genetic linkage studies. Detecting genetic markers for psychiatric disorders requires families (preferably large) with a mixture of affected and unaffected individuals. Additionally, informative families should have a unilateral source of illness and should suggest some mode of transmission, such as X-linked or autosomal dominant, when subjected to segregation analysis. Adoption studies usually involve broken families, and the methodology of these types of studies does not allow easy answers to hypotheses about the mode of transmission. Furthermore, biologic relatives are usually unavailable for investigation and drawing of blood for cell lines, etc.

The thesis of this paper is that adoption studies can add to our understanding of certain problems associated with genetic linkage studies. Phenocopies, gene penetrance, and gene environment interaction are three major issues in genetics that presently remain unsolved but to which adoption studies may help provide some answers. As mentioned earlier, phenocopies are cases that are clinically identical to the illness under study but have an entirely different etiology. Nongenetic factors, such as an adverse environment, trauma, or infection, may be the causal factor for phenocopies. Adoption studies may be able to identify nongenetic factors that are likely to result in illness. When properly identified, such cases can be dealt with properly in a linkage analysis, for example, by weighting the affected individual on the basis of the probability that the affectation is due to environmental factors, including genetic-environmental interaction. Failure to identify phenocopies seriously impairs linkage analysis, because such cases appear to be obligate recombinants and greatly reduce LOD scores (Gottesman and Bertelsen 1989). Before we are successful in finding any genetic marker for a psychiatric illness, the problem of phenocopies must be solved.

Once valid genetic markers are found for mental disorders, adoption studies will continue to help us understand how the gene, or genes, for these disorders are expressed. It is unlikely that any gene for a mental disorder is completely penetrant, i.e., some individuals will probably carry the specific genotype for a mental disorder but will never express it during their lives (Gottesman and Bertelsen 1989). The factors necessary for a gene to express itself are unknown at this time (Morton and Kidd 1980). Because of this, there is now no way to calculate the exact penetrance of any disease gene for any psychiatric disorder (Kennedy et al. 1989). This leaves molecular geneticists in a quandary when performing linkage analysis, because a penetrance value must be set to calculate LOD scores. Adoption studies may help us to calculate accurate penetrance values for mental disorders more accurately.

For example, a sample of adoptees who all carry a specific genetic marker for the disorder could be studied. The proportion of adoptees who manifest the illness while controlling for specific environmental factors may provide a reasonably accurate estimate of gene penetrance. It would certainly be an improvement over current methods of penetrance estimation, which are often based on general population figures that do not control for environmental effects or phenocopies.

It was mentioned previously that adoption studies examine the issue of nature versus nurture, with regard to the expression of behavior and illness. Combining adoption studies with molecular genetic linkage studies will allow the molecular geneticist to go beyond the nature versus nurture issue and ask, What is the effect of environmental factors on a given genetic diathesis? Because it is reasonably clear that phenocopies exist and that gene penetrance is probably never 100%, the environment most likely plays a significant role in the expression of these illnesses. Uncovering these factors will undoubtedly help in the search for valid genetic markers and may lead to the characterization of the gene, or genes, for mental disorders.

REFERENCES

Bohman, M., S. Sigvardsson, and R. Cloninger. 1981. Maternal inheritance of alcohol abuse: Cross-fostering analysis of adopted women. *Arch. Gen. Psychiatry* **38**: 965.

Bohman, M., C.R. Cloninger, S. Sigvardsson, and A.L. von Knorring. 1982. Predisposition to petty criminality in Swedish adoptees: I. Genetic and environmental heterogeneity. *Arch. Gen. Psychiatry* **39**: 1233.

Cadoret, R.J. 1986b. Adoption studies: Historical and methodological critique. *Psychiatr. Dev.* **1**: 45.

―――. 1989. Genetics of alcoholism. In *Alcohol and the family* (ed. R.L. Collins et al.). Guilford Press, Inc. New York. (In press.)

Cadoret, R.J. and C. Cain. 1981. Environmental and genetic factors in predicting adolescent antisocial behavior in adoptees. *Psychiatr. J. Univ. Ottawa* **6(4)**: 220.

Cadoret, R.J. and A. Gath. 1978. Inheritance of alcoholism in adoptees. *Br. J. Psychiatry* **132**: 252.

―――. 1980. Biologic correlates of hyperactivity: Evidence for a genetic factor. In *Human functioning in longitudinal perspective* (ed. S.B. Sells et al.), p. 103. Williams and Wilkins, Baltimore.

Cadoret, R.J., C.A. Cain, and W.M. Grove. 1980. Development of alcoholism in adoptees raised apart from alcoholic biologic relatives. *Arch. Gen. Psychiatry* **37**: 561.

Cadoret, R.J., E. Troughton, and T.W. O'Gorman. 1987. Genetic and environmental factors in alcohol abuse and antisocial personality. *J. Stud. Alcohol* **48**: 1.

Cadoret, R.J., T.W. O'Gorman, E. Heywood, and E. Troughton. 1985a. Genetic and environmental factors in major depression. *J. Affective Disord.* **9**: 155.

Cadoret, R.J., T. O'Gorman, E. Troughton, and E. Haywood. 1985b. Alcoholism and antisocial personality: Interrelationships, genetic and environmental factors. *Arch. Gen. Psychiatry* **42**: 161.

Cadoret, R.J., E. Troughton, J. Bagford, and G. Woodworth. 1989. Genetic and environmental factors in etiology of antisocial personality. *Eur. Arch. Psychiatry Neurol. Sci.* (in press).

Cadoret, R.J., E. Troughton, T.W. O'Gorman, and E. Heywood. 1986. An adoption study of genetic and environmental factors in drug abuse. *Arch. Gen. Psychiatry* **43**: 1131.

Cloninger, C.K., M. Bohman, and S. Sigvardsson. 1981. Inheritance of alcohol abuse: Cross-fostering analysis of adopted men. *Arch. Gen. Psychiatry* **38**: 861.

Cloninger, C.R., S. Sigvardsson, M. Bohman, and A.L. von Knorring. 1982. Predisposition to petty criminality in Swedish adoptees: II. Cross-fostering analysis of gene-environment interaction. *Arch. Gen. Psychiatry* **39(11)**: 1242.

Goodwin, D.W., F. Schulsinger, and L. Hermansen. 1973. Alcohol problems in adoptees raised apart from alcoholic biologic parents. *Arch. Gen. Psychiatry* **28**: 238.

Goodwin, D.W., F. Schulsinger, and N. Moller. 1974. Drinking problems in adopted and nonadopted sons of alcoholics. *Arch. Gen. Psychiatry* **31**: 164.

Gottesman, I.I. and A. Bertelsen. 1989. Confirming unexpressed genotypes for schizophrenia. *Arch. Gen. Psychiatry* **46**: 867.

Helzer, J. and T. Pryzbeck. 1988. The cooccurrence of alcoholism with other psychiatric disorders in the general population and its treatment. *J. Stud. Alcohol* **49**: 219.

Hesselbrock, V.M., M.N. Hesselbrock, and J.R. Stabenau. 1985. Alcoholism in men patients subtyped by family history and antisocial personality. *J. Stud. Alcohol* **46**: 59.

Heston, L.L. 1966. Psychiatric disorders in foster home reared children of schizophrenic mothers. *Br. J. Psychiatry* **112**: 819.

Kendler, K.S., A.M. Gruenberg, and J.S. Strauss. 1981a. An independent analysis of the Copenhagen sample of the Danish adoption study of schizophrenia: II. The relationship between schizotypal personality disorder and schizophrenia. *Arch. Gen. Psychiatry* **38**: 982.

———. 1981b. An independent analysis of the Copenhagen sample of the Danish adoption study of schizophrenia: III. The relationship between paranoid psychons (delusional disorder) and schizophrenia. *Arch. Gen. Psychiatry* **38**: 985.

———. 1982. An independent analysis of the Copenhagen sample of the Danish adoption study of schizophrenia: V. The relationship between childhood social withdrawal and adult schizophrenia. *Arch. Gen. Psychiatry* **39(11)**: 1257.

Kennedy, J.L., L.A. Giuffra, H.W. Moises, L.L. Cavalli-Sforza, A.J. Pakstis, J.R. Kidd, C.M. Castiglione, B. Ssjogren, L. Wetterberg, and K.K. Kidd. 1989. Evidence against linkage of schizophrenia to markers on chromosome 5 in a northern Swedish pedigree. *Nature* **336**: 167.

Kety, S.S., D. Rosenthal, P. Wender, and F. Schulsinger. 1971. Mental illness in the biological and adoptive families of adopted schizophrenics. *Am. J. Psychiatry* **128(3)**: 82.

Kety, S.S., D. Rosenthal, P. Wender, F. Schulsinger, and B. Jacobsen. 1978. The biologic and adoptive families of adopted individuals who became schizophrenic: Prevalence of mental illness and other characteristics. In *The nature of schizophrenia* (ed. L.C. Wynne et al.), ch. 2. Wiley, New York.

Lewis, C., J. Rice, and J. Helzer. 1983. Diagnostic interactions: Alcoholism and antisocial personality. *J. Nerv. Ment. Dis.* **171:** 105.

Mendlewicz, J. and J. Rainer. 1977. Adoption study supporting genetic transmission in manic-depressive illness. *Nature* **268:** 327.

Morton, L.A. and K.K. Kidd. 1980. The effects of variable age of onset and diagnostic criteria on the estimates of linkage: An example using manic-depressive illness and color blindness. *Soc. Biol.* **27:** 1.

Richardson, L.F. 1912–13. The measurement of mental "nature" and the study of adopted children. *Eugen. Rev.* **4:** 391.

Rosenthal, D. and S.S. Kety. 1968. *Transmission of schizophrenia.* Pergamon Press, Oxford, England.

Rosenthal, D., P.H. Wender, and S.S. Kety. 1971. The adopted-away offspring of schizophrenics. *Am. J. Psychiatry* **128:** 307.

Sigvardsson, S., A.L. von Knorring, M. Bohman, and C.R. Cloninger. 1982. Predisposition to petty criminality in Swedish adoptees: III. Sex differences and validation of the male typology. *Arch. Gen. Psychiatry* **39(1):** 1248.

Vaillant, G. 1983. *The natural history of alcoholism.* Harvard University Press, Cambridge, Massachusetts.

von Knorring, A.L., C.R. Cloninger, M. Bohman, and S. Sigvardsson. 1983. An adoption study of depressive disorders and substance abuse. *Arch. Gen. Psychiatry* **40(9):** 943.

Wender, P.H., D. Rosenthal, S.S. Kety, F. Schulsinger, and J. Welner. 1974. Crossfostering: A research strategy for clarifying the role of genetic and experimental factors in the etiology of schizophrenia. *Arch. Gen. Psychiatry* **30:** 121.

COMMENTS

Searles: I was struck by the fact that you found an increased effect with the alcohol problems in the adoptive family. I think this morning you said that you didn't find the effect, or there was a decreased trend. Do you think that's probably just cultural or sample dependent?

Cadoret: I really don't know. It would be very interesting to see in our current study whether we can find this same effect again.

Searles: Do the double-headed arrows mean that you can't tell the direction of the effect?

Cadoret: Usually, yes. All you can do is get a correlation and at least correct for the other correlations in the model.

Cloninger: I wonder if we could get Remi to say a little bit more about the adoptive family effect. In my Swedish study, I was only looking at adoptive parents. In contrast, in Iowa you referred to looking at adoptive parents and other relatives in the family?

Cadoret: Yes.

Cloninger: If you did it the way that I did, how much agreement would we have?

Cadoret: It was also significant for the adoptive parent only. I don't have the isolated two-by-two tables here so I can't tell you what the difference was. For the parents, the odds ratios were all about the same, around 3. It was significant for the parents because there were more parents.

Cloninger: How many alcoholic adoptive parents are we talking about all together, roughly?

Cadoret: It wouldn't be very many.

Reich: Remi, how did you diagnose the adoptive families?

Cadoret: You mean as to whether there is an alcohol problem?

Reich: Alcohol or antisocial, whatever.

Cadoret: It was based on the kinds of reported behaviors, if the parent said that they had a problem with alcohol or if they were treated for alcohol problems.

Reich: Was that at the time they adopted the child or after?

Cadoret: In most cases it was after, because the adoption agency would probably veto the adoption otherwise.

Reich: You couldn't adopt a child if you said you had been to prison and you were drinking heavily.

Cadoret: That's right, one would hope.

Vulnerability to Alcoholism: From Individual Differences to Different Individuals

RALPH E. TARTER
Department of Psychiatry
University of Pittsburgh Medical School
Pittsburgh, Pennsylvania 15213

OVERVIEW

Evidence accrued from investigations of children of alcoholics, chronic alcoholics, and behavior-disordered adolescents indicates that high behavioral activity level may be a risk factor for alcoholism. Activity level, as a temperament trait, is hypothesized to be normally distributed in the population. The developmental pathway to an alcoholism outcome in a subset of the alcoholic population is contingent on a genetic predisposition, namely, high activity level, interacting with both micro- and macroenvironmental influences.

INTRODUCTION

Several lines of evidence converge to implicate high childhood behavioral activity level as a risk factor for alcoholism. Although the biological mechanisms underlying this behavioral disposition are unknown, studies of both animals and humans leave little doubt that this is a heritable trait.

Hyperactive boys, compared to normal youngsters, are more likely to have alcoholic biological fathers (Cantwell 1972). This overrepresentation of paternal alcoholism is present even if the child is reared by adoptive nonalcoholic parents (Morrison and Stewart 1973). Paralleling these findings, investigations of alcoholic men have revealed that their male offspring are more likely to exhibit high general activity level than children of normal parents (Tarter et al. 1985). Symptoms of childhood hyperactivity are also more likely to be present in adopted sons of alcoholics, and among these individuals, there is a higher prevalence of alcoholism when they attain adulthood (Goodwin et al. 1975).

Investigations of alcoholics, albeit relying primarily on retrospective recall, generally support the findings that hyperactivity predisposes to alcoholism. Preliminary studies of alcoholics in treatment suggest that 30–40% of them qualify for a diagnosis of attention deficit disorder, residual type; this DSMIII-R diagnosis typically is conjoint to a behavioral disorder featured by high and dysregulated behavioral activity (Wood et al. 1976; Horton 1985).

In addition, adolescents diagnosed as hyperactive are more likely to become problematically involved with alcohol than their peers (Mendelson et al. 1971; Blowin et al. 1978). Furthermore, high behavioral activity level (McCord et al. 1960; Jones 1968) or a rapid behavioral tempo (Vaillant 1983) has been reported in prospective studies of children who subsequently developed alcoholism in adulthood.

The available findings, although not consistent across all studies, suggest that a disorder of behavioral regulation, manifest as high activity level, may comprise an important risk factor for alcoholism. Moreover, the demonstration that children of alcoholics exhibit circumscribed cognitive deficits of the type commonly found in individuals with anterior cerebral lesions (Tarter et al. 1989) has prompted the intriguing hypothesis that alcoholism vulnerability may be characterized by a dysfunction of frontal neural systems. It is significant to note that the anterior cerebral region subserves the executive cognitive functions, specifically, the linguistic mediation of goal-motivated behavior (Luria 1966). Injury in this cortical region commonly results in disturbances in planning ability, behavioral inhibition, self-monitoring, and goal persistence. In support of this hypothesis, alcoholics and boys who subsequently develop alcoholism have been commonly reported to be deficient in these capacities (Tarter et al. 1985). Furthermore, because the cognitive and behavioral processes subserved by the frontal cortical regions do not mature functionally until mid-adolescence, it is plausible to hypothesize that the psychological basis of alcoholism vulnerability may comprise a disturbance of neurobehavioral maturation. The research described below, utilizing neuropsychologic and behavioral assessment procedures to evaluate alcoholics and nonalcoholic high risk individuals, has been aimed at comprehensively characterizing the neurobehavioral manifestations of alcoholism vulnerability.

RESULTS

Investigations of Alcoholics

In our first study, alcoholics were dichotomously classified as being either the primary or secondary type. Primary alcoholics met criteria indicating that alcohol use onset was unrelated to psychiatric illness or life stress. Their drinking began at an early age and without a known triggering event. In contrast, secondary alcoholics commenced drinking following either an identifiable stressor or concomitant with a psychiatric disturbance. As Table 1 illustrates, the primary alcoholics endorsed four times as many characteristics of childhood hyperactivity and minimal brain dysfunction as either the secondary alcoholics or normal controls; the latter two groups were almost

Table 1
Association between Childhood Hyperactivity and Alcoholism

	X̄	Standardization
Primary alcoholics ($n = 34$)	15.1	7.1
Secondary alcoholics ($n = 28$)	4.2	3.7
Normal controls ($n = 27$)	3.4	2.7

Alcoholic	Primary alcoholics (%)	Secondary alcoholics (%)	Controls (%)
Father	42.1	21.4	25.9
Mother	10.5	7.1	3.7
Other relative	52.6	28.5	22.2

identical with respect to the number of hyperactivity features that they retrospectively ascribed to themselves. In addition, the primary alcoholics had a higher prevalence of paternal alcoholism than the secondary alcoholics. They also first met criteria for alcoholism approximately 20 years earlier (mean age, 25) than the secondary alcoholics did (mean age, 44).

In a subsequent study employing the more traditional essential-reactive method for dichotomizing alcoholism, it was found that the former subjects, broadly characterized as psychosocially immature, described themselves as more hyperactive as children than reactive alcoholics, who have a normal premorbid adjustment but drink in reaction to a life stressor. The same childhood behavior checklist as employed in the first study discriminated the two groups on 40 of the 50 items. In addition, the score on the essential-reactive scale combined with the score on the childhood hyperactivity checklist explained almost 50% of the variance on the overall alcoholism severity scale on the alcohol use inventory.

Investigations of High Risk Subjects

Investigations of alcoholics are limited with respect to the confidence that can be attached to retrospective reporting. Although, at least with respect to reporting of childhood behavior, alcoholics agree with reporting by a parent (DeObaldia and Parsons 1984), it is preferable for obvious reasons to ascertain the presence of anomalies or disturbances prior to the onset of the disorder in question—in this case, alcoholism. Several studies have been conducted in our laboratory on sons of alcoholics; these boys have a four- to sixfold risk of becoming alcoholic as adults and, hence, are at high risk. The features that discriminate alcoholics' offspring from nonalcoholics' offspring may therefore reflect the characteristics, possibly having a heritable basis, that are concomitant with alcoholism vulnerability.

Table 2
Cognitive Test Results in Delinquent Sons of Alcoholics and Nonalcoholics

	Sons of alcoholics $\bar{X}$ (n = 16)	Sons of nonalcoholics $\bar{X}$ (n = 25)
WISC-R[a]		
VIQ	90	94
PIQ	95	98
FSIQ	92	90
PIAT (grade level)[b]		
mathematics	7.9	8.7
reading recognition	7.4	8.8
reading comprehension[c]	7.2	9.5
spelling	5.9	7.8
general information[c]	7.4	9.3
total score	6.9	8.7
DTLA[d]		
auditory attention—words[c]	41.3	47.5
visual attention—objects[c]	47.0	51.1
auditory attention—syllables	70.2	74.8
visual attention—letters	60.3	63.0
disarranged pictures	19.4	29.5
Peabody picture vocabulary[c]	89	99
Weschler memory scale		
digit span (total)	10.5	10.8
mental control	7.3	7.1
logical memory—immediate[c]	12.8	17.1
—delay[c]	7.1	12.7
figural memory—immediate	10.5	11.6
—delay	9.8	11.6
paired associate—immediate	24.8	25.2
—delay	8.5	9.2
Reitan aphasia score[c]	2.38	0.92
Perceptual-motor		
finger tapping	93.8	90.5
Purdue pegboard	38.7	37.7
star tracing	47.3	43.3
symbol digit	45.6	48.5
block design	27.1	21.0
trail making[c]	114.0	92.2
Boston aphasia exam		
fluency	21.3	21.1
phrase repetition	14.6	15.3
confrontation naming	101.9	102.9
responsive naming	29.6	29.7

[a] WISC-R = Weschler Intelligence Scale for Children (Revised).
[b] PIAT = Peabody Individual Achievement Test.
[c] $p < 0.05$.
[d] DTLA = Detroit Tests of Learning Aptitude.

In our first study of high risk youth, delinquent adolescents were divided into two groups: Group 1 consisted of boys whose fathers had either a current or lifetime history of alcoholism, and group 2 consisted of delinquent boys who did not have a biological father who was alcoholic. Delinquent youths were selected for initial study because this behavioral disposition is known to be associated with subsequent alcohol abuse, and it was of interest to determine whether there was a specific effect of paternal alcoholism independent of antisocial behavior. The results, summarized in Table 2, indicate that the sons of alcoholic fathers were somewhat more impaired than the sons of nonalcoholics on certain cognitive tests measuring primarily linguistic abilities. Both groups of delinquents reported a large number of hyperactivity characteristics and were not different in this respect.

Our second series of studies focused on community-dwelling alcoholics. To accrue a sample as representative of the population as possible, alcoholic men

Table 3
Cognitive Test Performance in Sons of Community-dwelling Alcoholics

	Sons of alcoholics $\bar{X}$ (n = 33)	Sons of nonalcoholics $\bar{X}$ (n = 30)
Porteus mazes[a]	14.0	15.2
Matching familiar figures—errors[a]	9.9	7.9
Arithmetic speed		
part 1	44.9	40.6
part 2[a]	59.4	52.7
Stroop		
words[a]	12.2	12.0
colors	19.3	16.4
interference[a]	34.8	28.1
Tail making		
part A	36.7	30.7
part B	78.7	74.2
Tactual performance		
dominant hand	193.6	231.8
nondominant hand	139.9	118.9
both hands	65.5	67.1
Symbol digit[a]	41.1	47.3
Grooved pegboard		
dominant hand	69.2	68.9
nondominant hand	77.6	73.1

[a] $p < 0.05$.

were recruited who had sons between the ages of 9 and 17 living at home with them and the biological mothers and who had never been diagnosed or clinically treated for alcoholism. Table 3 presents the results of the cognitive assessment. Although robust or generalized impairments were not observed in the sons of alcoholics, it is noteworthy that the deficits in the sons of alcoholic group, where manifest, were circumscribed to neuropsychologic tests requiring attentional and planning skills.

Because of the importance of learning and memory capacities for optimal school and psychosocial adjustment, a complement of such tests was administered to sons of alcoholics and nonalcoholics. No between-group differences were found on verbal paired associate learning or on a test of short-term memory for digits; however, as can be seen in Figure 1, the sons of alcoholics are inferior to the sons of normal social drinking men on a test measuring the capacity to hold verbal information in storage where there is no opportunity for mental rehearsal.

Paralleling these results, the mother's report of the child's behavior on the dimensions of temperament scale (DOTS) indicates that male offspring of alcoholic men are characterized by high activity level. In Table 4 the factorial structure of the DOTS is described. Only the waking and sleeping scales, loading on the same construct, discriminated the two groups. Moreover, as

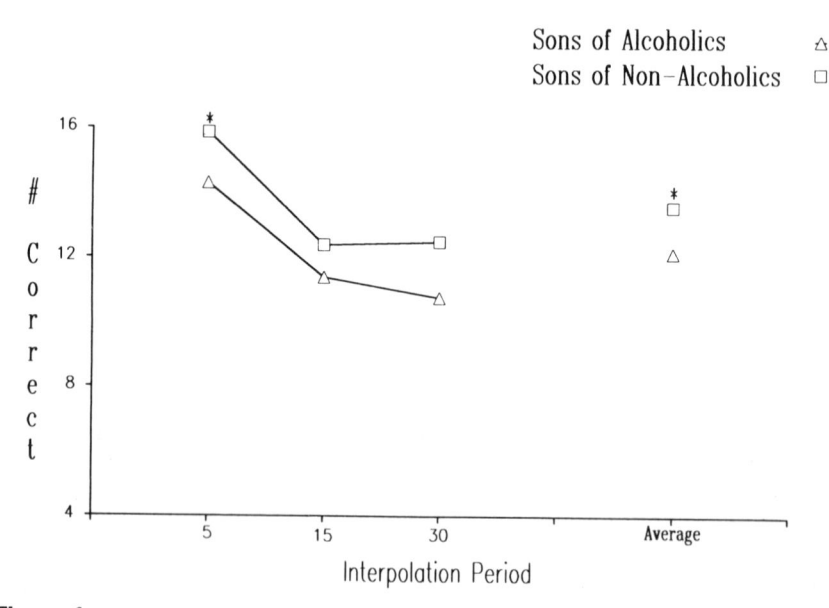

Figure 1

Retention as a function of interpolation interval in sons of alcoholics and nonalcoholics.

Table 4
Varimax Rotated Matrix for the DOTS

	Factor 1	Factor 2	Factor 3
Eating rhythm	0.8674		
Daily rhythm	0.7829		
Sleep rhythm	0.7064		
Mood		0.8016	
Flexibility/rigidity		0.7322	
Approach/withdrawal		0.6508	
Task orientation		0.5181	
Sleep activity			0.8608
General activity			0.7008

revealed in Table 5, the temperament scores were unrelated to family atmosphere, as measured by the family environment scale. Finally, it is important to observe that motor impairment involving gross movement or eye/hand coordination was not found in the sons of alcoholics. They did, however, exhibit greater upper body sway, as determined by a quantified Romberg test. As confirmed in Table 6, the sons of alcoholics swayed significantly more while tested in a stationary position, either with eyes open or closed.

Table 5
Correlations between the Family Environment Scale Scores and the DOTS Factors in the Sons of Alcoholic Group

		DOTS	
FES	factor 1	factor 2	factor 3
Cohesion	−0.28	0.06	−0.16
Expressiveness	0.03	0.15	−0.24
Conflict	−0.01	−0.04	0.08
Independence	0.17	−0.17	0.23
Achievement orientation	−0.23	−0.05	−0.03
Intellectual/cultural orientation	0.09	0.05	−0.23
Active-recreational orientation	0.05	0.24	−0.33[a]
Moral-religious emphasis	−0.08	−0.15	−0.17
Organization	0.14	0.37[a]	−0.20
Control	0.02	−0.11	0.13

[a] $p < 0.05$.

Table 6
Static Ataxia in Sons of Alcoholics and Nonalcoholics

	Sons of alcoholics ($\bar{X}$)	Sons of nonalcoholics ($\bar{X}$)
Eyes open[a]	29.5	19.4
Eyes closed[a]	41.0	28.8

[a] $p < 0.05$.

DISCUSSION

The question of central concern pertains to how individual differences in cognitive and behavioral processes in childhood culminate in categorically different individuals, namely, alcoholic or nonalcoholic. Figure 2 depicts the major factors occurring during development that affect the vulnerable child to either augment or attenuate the risk of an alcoholism (or other drug abuse)

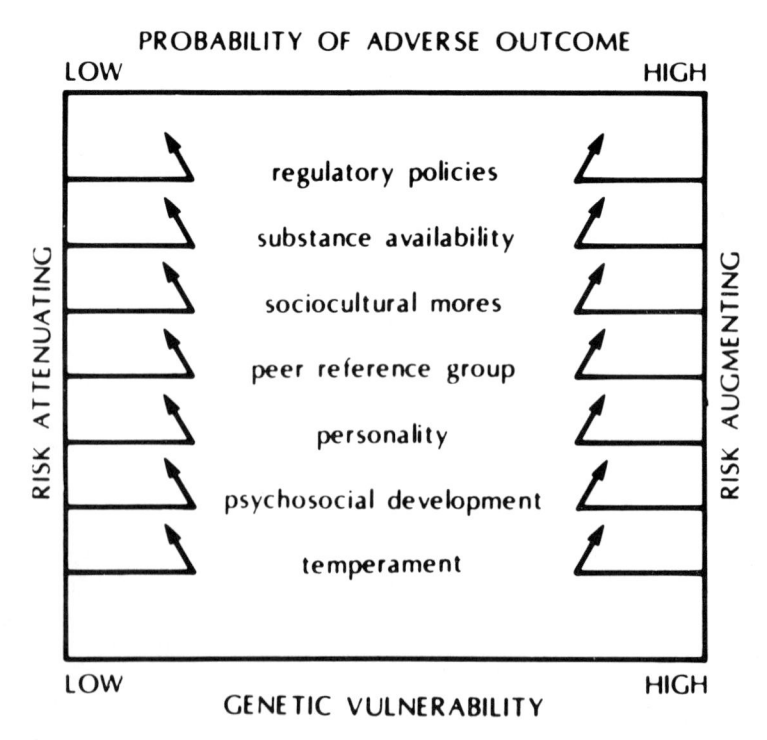

Figure 2
Factors affecting risk for an alcoholism outcome.

outcome. It is important to emphasize that this model does not specify either a necessary or sufficient cause of alcoholism but, rather, conceptualizes vulnerability as existing within a normal distribution in the population and risk status, changing over time as a function of events occurring during the child's development. For example, how the parent responds to the infant who is highly active and restless influences the subsequent developmental course of the child. It is noteworthy that mothers of highly active children use more punishing disciplinary techniques than mothers of children who are characterized by more normative activity levels (Webster-Stratton and Eyberg 1982). On the basis of the early experience of physical punishment, the child learns to legitimize physical aggression in the context of socialization. By priming the child to an adjustment pattern featured by dispositionally externalizing behavior that, clinically defined, is a conduct disorder, the stage is set for the child to select a non-normative peer group, to fail in school, and because of deficiencies in age-normative social skills, be further predisposed to alcohol or other drug use. The point to be made is that high activity level, evidenced as a dimensional trait in infancy, potentially can culminate in a non-normative disinhibited behavior style that ultimately is characterized by alcohol abuse.

In addition to eliciting certain types of behavior from their parents that predispose to conduct problems, hyperactive children may affect their parents' behavior such that alcohol use becomes role-modeled behavior. It has been shown, e.g., that professionally trained child actors, skilled in simulating the behavior patterns of hyperactive children, induce alcohol consumption in normal men in laboratory settings (Lang et al. 1989). Generalizing to naturalistic settings, it would appear that child and parents reciprocally affect each other's behavior, and in this case, alcohol consumption is observed and modeled by the child.

This discussion has focused on one temperament trait, namely, activity level. Other traits have been identified that have a strong heritable basis and, where deviant from the norm, may additionally augment the vulnerability to alcoholism. Tarter et al. (1985), integrating the behavior-genetic research findings by Buss and Plomin (1975) and developmental studies by Thomas and Chess (1984), have argued that deviations in temperament traits such as sociability, emotionality, attention span, and soothability may also be contributing vulnerability features, particularly where the alcoholism outcome has an early age onset and conjointly presents with psychosocial immaturity and social deviancy. Whether the various temperament traits aggregate to comprise one or more temperament types that predispose to alcoholism subtypes remains to be determined. However, from the findings described herein and the etiologic model described in Figure 2, it is apparent that myriad pathways to an alcoholism outcome may derive from the few predisposing temperament traits.

No claim is advanced implicating high behavioral activity level as predisposing specifically to alcoholism. On the basis of psychological research, the risk may be nonspecific. Considering the close similarity between alcoholism and other disorders of excess, the vulnerability may predispose to a variety of topologically distinct outcomes, the particular one being shaped by culture and idiosyncratic and unique experiences occurring during the child's development. The specific outcome, be it alcoholism, other types of drug abuse, gambling, bulimia, or other dysregulated and excessive behavior, may reflect more the impact of the micro- and macroenvironmental influences, especially cultural and social regulatory mechanisms, than a unique and specific vulnerability. Not coincidentally, these latter behaviors of excess commonly coexist in the same individual and aggregate in families.

In summary, it is hypothesized that the extreme manifestation of certain temperament traits predisposes to a variety of adverse outcomes. These outcomes, although arbitrarily classified into distinctive taxonomic categories in contemporary psychiatric practice, share the common cardinal feature of excessive and dysregulated behavior. Whether alcohol abuse or dependence is, in fact, a unique and distinctive biologically determined syndrome is questioned. This taxonomic category, like others in the DSMIII-R classification system, may comprise little more than a convenient labeling of individuals according to the salience of one behavior—alcohol consumption. The extent to which individuals assigned to this category are similar with respect to etiology or natural history is questionable, especially because over 400 variations of clinical presentations are possible to qualify the person for a diagnosis of alcohol abuse or dependence according to DSMIII-R criteria (Tarter et al. 1987).

ACKNOWLEDGMENT

This work was supported by National Institute on Drug Abuse grant DA-05605.

REFERENCES

Blowin, A., R. Bornstein, and R. Trites. 1978. Teenage alcohol use among hyperactive children. A five-year follow-up study. *J. Pediatr. Psychol.* **3**: 188.

Buss, A. and R. Plomin. 1975. *A temperament theory of personality development.* John Wiley, New York.

Cantwell, D. 1972. Psychiatric illness in the families of hyperactive children. *Arch. Gen. Psychiatry* **27**: 414.

DeObaldia, R. and O. Parsons. 1984. Reliability studies on the primary secondary alcoholism classification questionnaire and the NK/MBD childhood symptoms checklist. *J. Clin. Psychol.* **40:** 1257.

Goodwin, D., F. Schulsinger, L. Hermansen, S. Guze, and G. Winokur. 1975. Alcoholism and the hyperactive child syndrome. *J. Nerv. Ment. Dis.* **160:** 349.

Horton, A. 1985. Prevalence of attention deficit disorder, residual type in alcoholics: A cross validation. *Int. J. Clin. Neuropsychol.* **8:** 52.

Jones, M. 1968. Personality correlates and antecedents of drinking pattern in adult males. *J. Consult. Clin. Psychol.* **32:** 2.

Lang, A., W. Pelham, C. Johnston, and S. Gelernter. 1989. Levels of adult alcohol consumption induced by interaction with child confederate exhibiting normal versus externalizing behaviors. *J. Abnorm. Psychol.* **98(3):** 294.

Luria, A. 1966. *Higher cortical functions in man.* Basic Books, New York.

McCord, W., J. McCord, and J. Gudeman. 1960. *Origins of alcoholism.* Stanford University Press, Stanford, California.

Mendelson, W., N. Johnson, and M. Stewart. 1971. Hyperactive children as teenagers: A followup study. *J. Nerv. Ment. Dis.* **153:** 273.

Morrison, J. and M. Stewart. 1973. The psychiatric status of the legal families of adopted hyperactive children. *Arch. Gen. Psychiatry* **28:** 888.

Tarter, R., A. Alterman, and K. Edwards. 1985. Vulnerability to alcoholism in men: A behavior-genetic perspective. *J. Stud. Alcohol.* **46:** 329.

———. 1989. Neurobehavioral theory of alcoholism etiology. In *Theories of alcoholism* (ed. C. Chaudron and D. Wilkinson), p. 73. Addiction Research Foundation, Toronto.

Tarter, R., A. Hegedus, and J. Gavaler. 1985. Hyperactivity in sons of alcoholics. *J. Stud. Alcohol.* **46:** 259.

Tarter, R., A. Arria, H. Moss, N. Edwards, and D. Van Thiel. 1987. DSMIII criteria for alcohol abuse: Association with alcohol consumption behaivor. *Alcohol. Clin. Exp. Res.* **11:** 541.

Thomas, A. and S. Chess. 1984. Genesis and evolution of behavioral disorders. From infancy to early adult life. *Am. J. Psychiatry* **140:** 1.

Vaillant, G. 1983. *The natural history of alcoholism.* Harvard University Press, Cambridge, Massachusetts.

Webster-Stratton, C. and S. Eyberg. 1982. Child temperament: Relationship with child behavior problems and parent-child interactions. *J. Clin. Child Psychol.* **11:** 123.

Wood, D., F. Reimherr, P. Wender, and G. Johnson. 1976. Diagnosis and treatment of minimal brain dysfunction in adults. *Arch. Gen. Psychiatry* **33:** 1453.

COMMENTS

Searles: I want to ask about the comparison between the sons of high-risk and low-risk. I know you have shown in your data that the sons of alcoholics have a much greater probability of having closed head trauma and have lost consciousness sometime in their life. Is there any connection between the neurocognitive deficits and that?

Tarter: In these latter studies we controlled for that. I think one can't ignore the fact that children of alcoholics experience more physical and sexual abuse and have more experiences of loss of consciousness from parental abuse as well as from other accidents. The other accidents are particularly important with respect to high activity level and poor behavioral regulation. In these kinds of studies, those are critical variables. We have looked at it in the community sample. In the first study of delinquents we didn't control for those variables.

Time-dependent Model of the Familial Transmission of Alcoholism

THEODORE REICH AND C. ROBERT CLONINGER
Washington University School of Medicine and Department of Psychiatry, Jewish Hospital of St. Louis, St. Louis, Missouri 63110

OVERVIEW

The design of studies to search for genes that influence susceptibility to alcoholism requires at the outset a description of the familial transmission of the disorder. Because there has been a sustained increase in per capita consumption of alcohol in the United States over the past four decades, time-dependent methods were used. To explore secular trends in the familial transmission of alcoholism, new models of familial transmission were developed and applied to a large sample of alcoholic probands and their first-degree relatives. The methods of survival analysis established the presence of strong secular trends in the age of onset and lifetime prevalence of alcoholism in both the families of alcoholic probands and the general population, so the multifactorial model of disease transmission was modified to include these trends.

Our analyses confirmed that more recently born cohorts of individuals had increased expected lifetime prevalences of alcoholism and earlier ages of onset when compared with older cohorts. Although the disorder is much more common in men, differences between males and females appear to be narrowing in younger cohorts. Despite strong shifts in the base rate, the intergenerational transmissibility of the disorder has increased over time, suggesting that the excess risk occurring in more recently born cohorts occurs disproportionately in the children of alcoholics.

The magnitude of the effects described in this article is large and demonstrates clearly that the search for specific genetic abnormalities using techniques such as linkage analysis should be modified to allow for complex, time-dependent phenotypic variation.

INTRODUCTION

Characterizing the population and familial distribution of alcoholism is an important first step in the design and interpretation of molecular and genetic studies. Since alcoholism is probably the result of complex social factors and equally complex susceptibility factors, new models of familial transmission have been required.

Between 1950 and 1981, the apparent United States per capita consumption of pure alcohol rose from approximately 2 gallons to 2.76 gallons for all individuals age 14 and older (Fig. 1) (Heckler 1983). To the extent that alcohol consumption is related to the onset of alcohol abuse and dependence, secular changes in the frequency of these disorders can be expected. During the last four decades, the drinking practices of Americans have changed markedly in terms of legal age of drinking, attitudes of women toward consumption, and public awareness of adverse consequences; it is against this background that familial models of alcoholism must be constructed.

Robins et al. (1984), reporting data from a large-scale epidemiological survey, found that the lifetime prevalence of alcohol abuse and dependence (DSM-III) was greatest in males and females under the age of 44 years. Further subdivision of their data into subjects 25 years and younger, and comparing these with subjects ages 26–44, two of the three epidemiologic sites reported rates in the younger group that were higher than or almost as high as the older group. Age adjustment of the results in the younger group suggests that the lifetime prevalence of alcohol abuse and dependence in younger individuals is higher than in individuals born in older cohorts. One interpretation of these data is that more recently born individuals are at higher risk for the onset of alcoholism at an earlier age than older individuals.

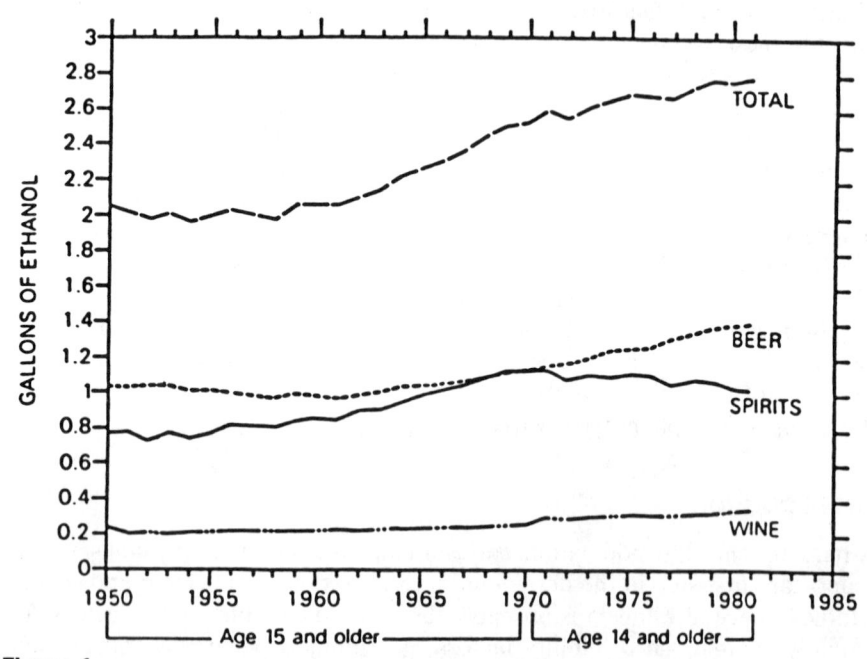

Figure 1

Apparent U.S. consumption of alcoholic beverages in gallons of ethanol per capita 1950–1981.

Since the epidemiologic survey referred to above was conducted in 1980–81, the period of highest per capita consumption of alcohol in the United States, secular trends in alcohol abuse and dependence might well be the consequence of changes in consumption.

Using data collected approximately 10 years ago, strong secular trends were also reported for major depressive disorder (Klerman et al. 1985), completed suicides (Wetzel et al. 1987), and drug abuse and dependence (Dinwiddie and Reich 1990). As with alcoholism, it appeared that more recently born cohorts of individuals were at greater risk than older individuals.

The implications of secular trends in the epidemiological and family data referred to above are important for both clinicians and the design of genetic studies. Before proceeding, however, it is necessary to consider whether artifacts inherent in the retrospective assessment of lifetime diagnosis are responsible for all or most of the changes in risk.

Although there are many potential sources of artifact in measuring secular trends, four important possibilities suggested by Lavori et al. (1987) are (1) decreased recall of a mild syndrome that occurred early in life by persons who are interviewed later in life; (2) the possibility that younger individuals are less likely to "deny" the presence of alcohol abuse and dependence because the disorder has become more socially acceptable; (3) the rapid increase in treatment programs that might lead younger individuals into treatment more often, resulting in their alcohol abuse becoming more memorable; and (4) that differential mortality may have reduced the frequency of alcohol abuse and dependence in older cohorts of living individuals. A definitive answer to the nature of secular trends in alcoholism and related disorders awaits a large-scale prospective study, but, even if artifactual, these effects must be taken into account when multigenerational family resemblance is characterized (Lavori et al. 1987).

In this paper, a modified form of the multifactorial model of disease transmission is used to quantify familial transmission of alcoholism in the presence of secular trends. Age-of-onset distributions are included, which may be different in males and females and may also differ as a function of the cohort of birth of individuals. The goal of the analyses presented here is to characterize the transmissibility of alcoholism taking into account secular trends in expected lifetime prevalence, age of onset, sex effect, environmental effects common to siblings, and assortative mating (Reich et al. 1988).

A Family Study of Alcoholism

Data in this paper are taken from a family study of alcoholism conducted in St. Louis between 1978 and 1983. Probands were a random sample of white inpatients at four St. Louis area psychiatric hospitals, which included a specialized private hospital for alcoholics. A random sample of convicted felons was also ascertained from the local probation and parole office.

Subjects were included if they met the Feighner criteria (Feighner et al. 1972) for definite alcoholism, if they were born within 100 miles of the St. Louis metropolitan area, and if they agreed to participate. All families had at least one first-degree relative who was personally interviewed. These data are part of an ongoing family and genetic study of alcoholism being conducted by C.R. Cloninger and T. Reich (Cloninger et al. 1986).

All first-degree relatives and spouses age 17 and over were personally interviewed, using a comprehensive self-coding diagnostic interview developed for this project. The interview was administered by trained nonphysicians following a reliability study which indicated that there was satisfactory agreement between physicians and nonphysician interviewers (Coryell et al. 1978). In addition to the interview, hospital records and family history data were collected, and a conference was held to collate all available information and to make the final diagnosis. Feighner criteria were used throughout. The study was conducted in a blind fashion so that interviewers were not aware of the proband's diagnosis, and family diagnostic information was not included during the professional diagnostic conference. The relatives of a control group of nonalcoholic, nonfelon probands were interspersed with the relatives of the alcoholic probands in order to maintain blindness.

An estimate of the lifetime population prevalence of alcoholism in St. Louisans was provided by analyzing data collected as part of the epidemiologic catchment study (Reiger et al. 1984; L. Robins, pers. comm.). Diagnoses were made using the Feighner criteria. Lifetime rates were stratified by cohort of birth so that the relationship of secular trends in population prevalence could be compared with rates in the families of alcoholic probands.

Familial Transmission of Time-dependent Data

Kaplan-Meier (Kalbfleisch and Prentice 1980) estimates of the time to onset of alcoholism and the asymptotic proportion of those who are affected by a specified age were used to test for the presence of secular trends in the male and female relatives subdivided by their age at interview. Similar estimates were made for the general population. These analyses were undertaken to guide the formulation of a quantitative transmission model that was used to characterize the familial transmission of alcoholism.

The multifactorial model disease transmission was used to compute cohort- and sex-specific correlations between parents and offspring, siblings and spouses. This model assumes that familial and nonfamilial factors that influence the development of a disorder can be summed into a single underlying variable termed the "liability" and that individuals whose liability exceeds a threshold develop the disorder sometime during their lives. The distribution of liability in a family is assumed to be a multivariate normal, and the position of the thresholds truncates a portion of the liability distribution equal in area to the sex- and cohort-specific lifetime population prevalence (Reich et al. 1979).

The analysis proceeds one family at a time by estimating the probability of each family, conditional on the proband's being affected, and taking into account the age and cohort of birth of each member. In this way, correction for ascertainment is included, and relevant population prevalences can be computed. The probability of each family is also modified by correcting for variable age of onset. In this approach, the liability of the family of size "n" is assumed to be an n variate normal distribution. Accordingly, a new method for integrating a multivariate normal distribution was developed to estimate more accurately the probability of a family. Hypothesis testing is done using a likelihood ratio criterion. In the analyses that follow, the entire family data are used including parents, siblings, offspring, and spouses. Each family, including all of its members, is used as a single data point. Single ascertainment is assumed, since each family was ascertained only once when the data was collected.

The familial correlations were quantified using the "TAU path analytic model" developed by Rice et al. (1980). In this model, the liability of each individual is partitioned into transmissible and nontransmissible components for each sex. The proportion of the variance in liability accounted for by transmissible factors is termed the "transmissibility" (t^2). Transmission between parents and offspring is described by a standardized path coefficient (TAU=τ) which measures the sex-specific contribution of the transmissible factors of the parent to the transmissible factors of that offspring. Correlations between the liability of mates (R_m) and between the nontransmissible elements of siblings (c) are also included. The path parameters are used to compute correlations in liability between relatives. These in turn are used, after correcting for variable age of onset and ascertainment, to compute the probability of observing a particular family. This model combines path analytic methods and the tectrachoric correlations between liabilities within families. The TAU model does not assume that the causes of resemblance between parents and offspring are entirely genetic. Cultural as well as genetic factors might be present and are assumed to be additive. If familial transmission were entirely due to polygenic factors, then the value of the parameter TAU would be 0.5. Deviations from this value suggest that nongenetic mechanisms of familial transmission are present.

Sex-specific secular trends in lifetime population prevalence, age of onset, and the transmissibility of the liability were included in a reformulation of the multifactorial model. This was accomplished using a logistic function to relate cohort of birth to each variable (Province and Rao 1985). Secular trends were thus introduced into the model by assuming that individual nonfamilial environmental factors are a function of cohort of birth. In this application, the parameters of the logistic distribution were estimated along with other cohort-specific parameters when the model was fit to the data. In fitting the model, it was assumed that there was no secular variation for individuals born prior to 1928. This assumption was made to minimize the effect of differential mortality in older alcoholics. In addition, it was assumed that there was no secular variation for individuals born since 1963. This was done because of the small number of very young individuals in the sample.

Variable age of onset was modeled by means of a quadratic regression of the mean and variance of the natural log of age of onset on the natural log of cohort of birth. Censoring of age of onset was taken into account. A log normal and normal distribution of age of onset were compared and the log normal distribution was chosen because it better fit these data. This novel approach to age adjustment was used because preliminary analyses indicated that cohort-specific ages of onset fit the data better than customary methods. During the analyses, it was established that secular trends in age-of-onset distributions from males and females were different, and so, sex-specific functions were used. It was assumed that there were no correlations between the ages of onset of relatives and between age of onset and underlying liability distributions.

Using the computerized search program GEMNI (Gemini 1979), the method of maximum likelihood was used to fit a generalized transmission model, including secular trends, to the family and epidemiological data. Then the likelihood ratio chi-square test was used to test subhypotheses of the general model and hence produce an increasingly parsimonious description of familial transmission. A more detailed description of this approach is found in Reich et al. (1988).

RESULTS

The frequency of alcoholism in interviewed spouses and first-degree relatives of 60 female and 240 male alcoholics is displayed in Table 1 along with their average age at interview. Comparable population prevalence data collected in St. Louis are displayed in Table 2.

In keeping with the results of other epidemiological and family studies, the frequency of alcoholism in females is much less than that in males. The rates in siblings are nearly as high or higher than those in the same-sex parent, even though they are, on the average, considerably younger. Likewise, the frequency of alcoholism in the sons and daughters of male and female probands

Table 1
Frequency of Alcoholism in Interviewed Spouses and First-degree Relatives of 300 Alcoholic Probands (Feighner Criteria)

	Male probands			Female probands		
	n	% affected	mean age	n	% affected	mean age
Fathers	80	37.5	54.1	13	38.5	61.2
Mothers	125	20.8	51.2	27	3.7	59.3
Brothers	192	56.8	29.3	36	52.8	36.7
Sisters	196	14.8	31.1	49	20.4	35.3
Sons	28	32.1	23.8	20	50.0	26.3
Daughters	47	19.1	23.1	18	16.7	24.9
Spouses	100	13.0	35.9	25	56.0	41.0

is higher than that in the fathers and mothers, even though the parents are approximately 30 years older. Age-adjusting these frequencies leads to the prediction that the illness would be most common in offspring when compared with siblings and parents.

The frequency of alcoholism in the first-degree relatives of males and females is very similar, indicating that the sex of the proband has little influence on the familial distribution of the disorder (Reich et al. 1980). One interpretation of these results is that nonfamilial environmental factors may be sufficient to explain differences in population prevalence of alcoholism in males and females. Alternately, these data might reflect the existence of a "male-limited" form of the disorder, along with another form which occurs in both sexes (Cloninger et al. 1981).

The lifetime prevalences of alcoholism, based on the epidemiological catchment area study conducted in St. Louis and displayed in Table 2, are subdivided by the age of the respondent to illustrate that the frequency of alcoholism in younger males and females is much higher than in older subjects.

Table 2
Population Prevalence of Alcoholism in White Males and Females Based on the ECA (Feighner Criteria)

Age	Males		Females	
	n	% affected	n	% affected
18–24	45	11.1	45	4.4
25–44	289	21.8	331	5.1
45–64	141	19.9	169	0.6
65+	272	9.9	418	1.4

Comparing the frequency of alcoholism in the first-degree relatives and spouses (Table 1) with the data in Table 2 shows that in every group the disorder is strongly familial, irrespective of sex and generation. Although the population prevalences of alcoholism appear to be increasing, the familial aggregation of the disorder has been maintained. No evidence of a "generation gap" is observed. In Tables 1 and 2 it can also be seen that the spouses of alcoholic probands are at high risk for a similar diagnosis when compared with age-specific members of the general population. This is true for both husbands and wives of alcoholic probands. Assortative mating for this disorder has the effect of amplifying familial transmission, since it increases the proportion of the population that are the offspring of two alcoholics beyond that which would ordinarily be expected.

Kaplan-Meier survival distributions stratified by age groups are displayed in Figures 2 and 3. The survival distribution function is the proportion of subjects who remain well at each age corrected for the varying number of relatives within each age group. If there were no secular trends, the three survival curves displayed in these figures would fall on the same line; this possibility can be statistically rejected at the 0.001 level for both males and females.

survival estimates females

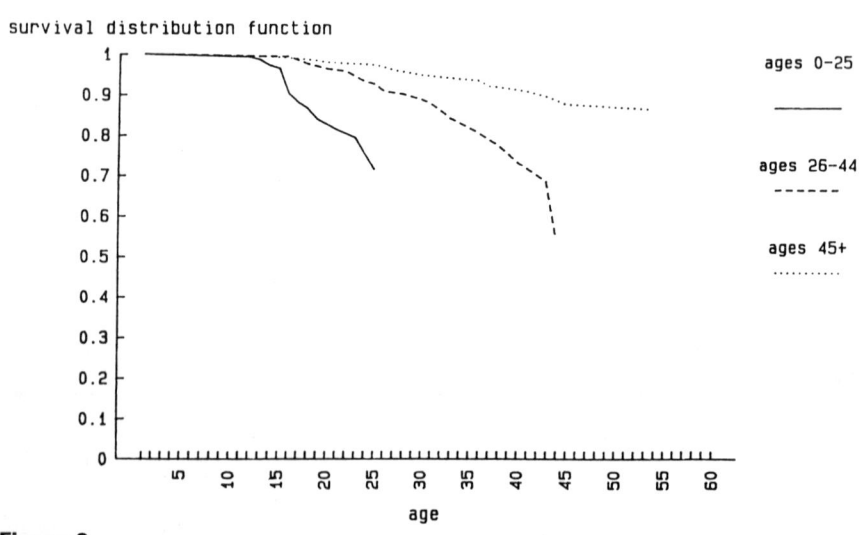

Figure 2
Age-specific distribution of alcoholism in the female first-degree relatives of alcoholic probands, subdivided by current age.

survival estimates
males

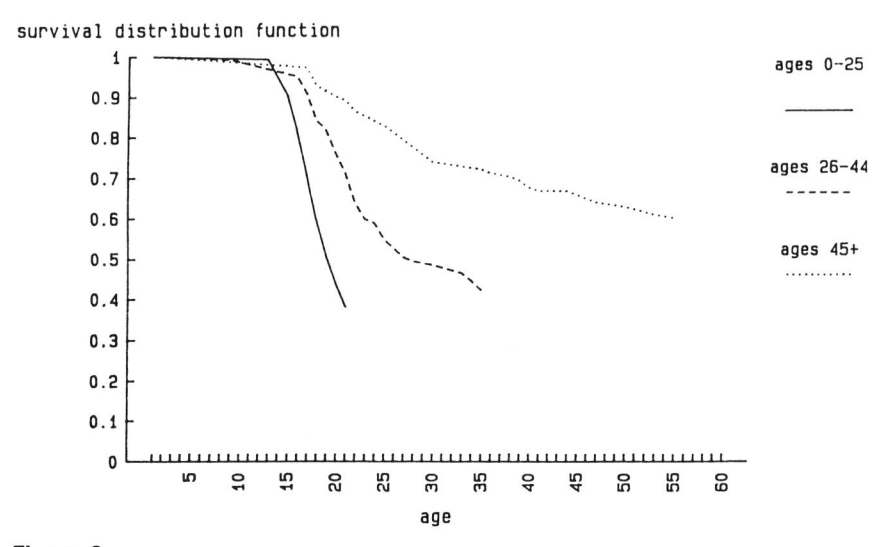

Figure 3
Age-specific distribution of alcoholism in the male first-degree relatives of alcoholic probands, subdivided by current age.

The magnitude of the secular trends can be appreciated by noting that in the youngest group of male relatives, the rate of alcoholism is approximately 52% by age 20. In contrast, the rate by age 20 in male relatives age 26–44 is only 22%, and for male relatives over the age of 45, it was less than 10%. The secular trends in the female group are also very striking, since the rate of the youngest group of females is approximately 18% by age 20, but in older cohorts, it is less than 5% by this age.

By comparing the slopes of the various survival distribution functions in different age groups, it appears that the slopes of the time-to-onset curves for younger male and female cohorts are much steeper than for older relatives. This suggests that the age of onset of alcoholism has been decreasing and that the rate of onset is different in males and females. Secular trends in the age of onset were studied, first, to determine whether or not cohort-specific age-of-onset distributions were required, and second, to estimate the parameters of these distributions.

The age-of-onset distributions in Figures 4 and 5 were computed by means of a quadratic regression of the mean and variance of the natural log of age of onset on the natural log of the birth cohort in each sex. These analyses showed that separate age-of-onset distributions were necessary for males and

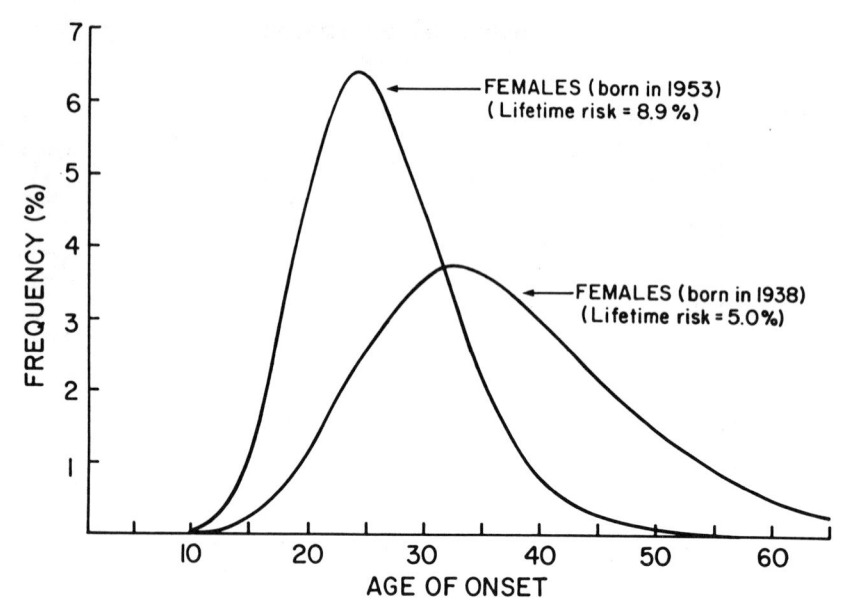

Figure 4
Age of onset and lifetime population prevalence of alcoholism in females.

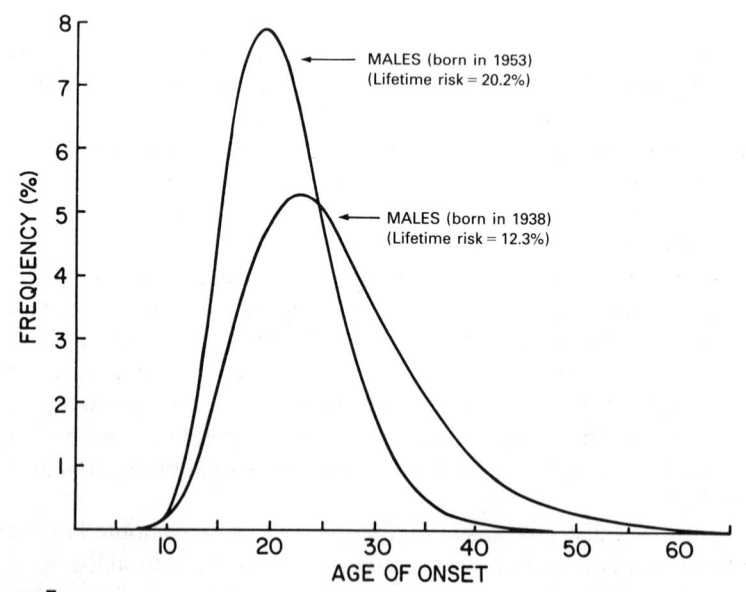

Figure 5
Age of onset and lifetime population prevalence of alcoholism in males.

females and that the probands' and relatives' birth cohorts contributed significantly to the onset distribution. The quadratic terms themselves were not significant and were dropped during the analysis.

In Figures 4 and 5, the age-specific frequency of onset is displayed for each year for males and females born in 1953 and in 1938. The area under each curve represents the distribution of ages of onset for individuals who will become affected sometime during their lifetime. From these curves, we may note that the modal age of onset of males has decreased by about 4 years when older and younger individuals are compared. For females the effect is much more dramatic, since the modal age of onset has decreased from approximately 32 years to approximately 24 years.

It is also important to note that the variance age of onset of both males and females is also decreased, which further amplifies the rapid increase in the frequency of alcoholism in younger cohorts. The decrease in modal age of onset and the decrease in variance are highly statistically significant. The decreased variance in age of onset suggests that alcoholism currently has an earlier age of onset and offset when compared with older cohorts.

It is important to note that not all the relatives in our sample were through the ages of risk. Accordingly, the right-hand tail of the age-of-onset distributions are produced by extrapolation based on current observations. The precision of this prediction is lower for more recently born cohorts who are earlier in the period of risk. However, the consistency in these findings throughout the age range of the sample strengthens these conclusions.

In fitting the family data using the multifactorial analysis, an estimate of the expected lifetime population prevalences for alcoholism was computed for individuals living to age 80. Separate distributions were fitted for males and females, and the logistic function was used to relate the expected lifetime prevalence in younger and older cohorts.

At the point of best fit of the model to the data, lifetime prevalence of alcoholism in males born since 1955 is approximately 22% and in females approximately 10%. In contrast, the prevalence for males and females born before 1940 is approximately 12.3% and 4%, respectively. The possibility that the lifetime prevalences were equal in all birth cohorts was tested and statistically rejected ($p < 0.001$). Similarly, the possibility that the lifetime prevalences of males and females were equal was statistically rejected.

Data collected over the past 5 years suggests a decrease in per capita consumption of alcohol in the United States (although not in Missouri). Accordingly, we may expect a decrease in the frequency of onset of alcoholism in these families when they are followed. Many of the relatives are being followed up as part of a genetic linkage study, but an analysis of these data is not available. Future inferences about younger cohorts may be modified by taking into account current trends in alcohol consumption.

The findings of the multifactorial analysis of the family and population data parameterized using the TAU model are displayed in Table 3. The primary object of these investigations is the study of the transmissibility of alcoholism, taking into account secular trends in age of onset and expected population prevalence. At issue is the possibility that the "excess risk" we have observed in younger cohorts might have occurred in individuals who do not necessarily come from the families of alcoholic probands. If this were true, the disorder in more recently born cohorts would be less familial, and the increased frequency of alcoholism in younger subjects would be independent of the disorder in prior generations. This phenomenon might have occurred if

Table 3
Parameters of the TAU Path Analytic Model of Disease Transmission for Alcoholism Comparing the Presence and Absence of a Secular Trend in Transmissibility

	No secular trend in transmissibility	Secular trend in transmissibility
R_m	0.63	0.64
t^2 male		
born before 1929	0.85	0.65
born 1929–1962	0.85	0.65–0.97
born after 1962	0.85	0.98
t^2 female		
born before 1929	0.35	0.27
born 1929–1962	0.35	0.27–0.58
born after 1962	0.35	0.59
Lifetime pop. prev. of males		
born before 1929	0.11	0.12
born 1929–1962	0.12–0.24	0.12–0.22
born after 1962	0.24	0.22
Lifetime pop. prev. of females		
born before 1929	0.03	0.04
born 1929–1962	0.04–0.11	0.04–0.10
born after 1962	0.11	0.10
c	0.37	0.22
τ	0.58	0.63
Loglikelihood	−2617.26	−2614.00

$\chi^2_2 = 6.51$

nonfamilial environmental factors were the most important cause of this secular trend.

A decrease in familial transmission would also be observed if an early-onset form of alcoholism were due to independent familial factors that had greatly increased in frequency, i.e., a juvenile form of the disorder. In this case, a "generation gap" would be observed in transmission from parent to offspring. In Table 3 it can be seen that there is a statistically significant secular trend in transmissibility and that the disorder is more transmissible in younger cohorts. Furthermore, the transmissibilities are significantly less for females. These data support the unity of alcoholism across generations and also support the hypothesis that the excess risk in more recently born cohorts occurs differentially in the children of alcoholics. The transmissibility (t^2) for males varied between 0.65 and 0.98 and for females between 0.27 and 0.59.

Many different versions of the TAU model were fitted to these data; however, the parameters we found were quite stable. Throughout our analysis, the expected lifetime rates were higher in more recently born cohorts, and the transmissibility was greater for younger individuals. An important characteristic of our data is that the secular trends in population prevalence, age of onset, and transmissibility have resulted in decreasing differences between males and females. This effect is most striking for age of onset but also occurred for other variables.

In keeping with other analyses, the correlations between nontransmissible factors of siblings were estimated to test the hypothesis that these factors contribute to family resemblance for alcoholism. The correlations between nonfamilial environmental factors common to sibs varied between 0.22 and 0.41 and was significantly different from 0. Similarly, a high degree of assortative mating was observed, and these are included in the analyses.

The presence of a maternal effect for alcoholism was studied by comparing the value of τ from mother to offspring with τ from father to offspring, but they did not differ significantly. Sex-specific transmission (i.e., a deficiency of cross-sex transmission) was also modeled but could not be demonstrated in these data at a statistically significant level.

The parameter τ was studied to determine if its value deviated significantly from 0.5—its value under the assumption that familial transmission is entirely due to polygenic factors. The analyses reported here consistently found this parameter to be significantly greater than 0.5, indicating that nongenetic transmissible mechanisms are operating in addition to polygenic transmission. A similar result was found during the analysis of an earlier data set. Another interpretation of this finding is that the data are heterogeneous and that a more and a less transmissible form are present. A more detailed review of these results is given in Reich et al. (1988).

DISCUSSION

The observation that more recently born relatives of alcoholic probands have a higher risk for alcoholism than older relatives is strongly supported by the presence of a similar observation in epidemiological data. Additional support is offered by a striking increase in the rate of suicide among teenagers since the 1950s and similar secular trends in the affective disorders. Determining the extent to which these findings are artifactual requires prospective longitudinal follow-up studies of sufficient duration to directly test hypotheses about "forgetting" or shifts in recall of age of onset. Preliminary data from a prospective longitudinal follow-up study of the relatives of probands with major forms of affective disorder suggest that the secular trends we have observed are not entirely artifactual and that retrospective estimates of age of onset are very stable, when estimated at a 6-year interval. The 6-year prospective follow-up study referred to above is large scale ($n \sim 2500$) but is not directly comparable, since the Schedule for Affective Disorder and Schizophrenia (SADS) interview schedule was used and the research diagnostic criteria were implemented (J. Rice, pers. comm.).

Since alcoholics die at an earlier age than nonalcoholics, differential mortality might in part explain these results. The secular trends, however, are observed throughout the age range of our subjects, suggesting that this explanation would only explain the effect in the older part of the data set.

To the extent that the secular trends are real, we must look for causative mechanisms that influence both the families of alcoholic subjects and the general population. This might include changes in drinking age, increases in alcohol consumption, and changes in the drinking behavior of women. It seems clear that with respect to both alcohol consumption and alcohol abuse, women are increasingly like men in terms of age of onset and lifetime population prevalence.

The finding that the transmissibility of alcoholism has increased when younger cohorts are compared with their older counterparts suggests that children of alcoholics have disproportionately more of the excess risk. The magnitude of the effect is large and strongly recommends prevention programs targeted at the most susceptible groups. Because more recently born relatives of alcoholic probands are increasingly exposed to both drugs and alcohol, the rates of definite drug dependence (Feighner criteria) among the alcoholic relatives was also estimated. These are displayed in Table 4. These data show an increasing risk for drug dependence among the younger alcoholics when compared with their older counterparts. Thus, the excess risk for alcoholism is accompanied by an increasing risk for drug dependence as well.

The method of analysis we have developed models the secular trend as a

Table 4
Rates of Definite Drug Dependence among Alcoholics

	Definite drug dependence		
	age 17–30	age 31–40	age 41+
Men	$n = 52$ 26(50.0)	$n = 30$ 5(16.7)	$n = 57$ 0(0.0)
Women	$n = 19$ 7(36.8)	$n = 14$ 4(28.6)	$n = 23$ 2(8.7)

"cohort effect." Each successive cohort was assumed to be at higher risk when compared with preceding ones. An alternative formulation is that a "period effect" has occurred, that is, the change in the base rate has resulted from an environmental factor that affects all cohorts of susceptible individuals. If the secular trend were modeled as a period effect, then the age-of-onset distribution would be different; however, it is likely that conclusions about the transmissibility of the disorder would be unchanged. Unfortunately, age, period, and cohort effects are confounded so that a direct partitioning of the secular trend into these components is not possible. This is an active area of research, and as new approaches are developed, they will be applied to these data (J. Rice et al., in prep.).

The characteristics of familial transmission that have been described in this paper have strong implications for the design and analysis of linkage studies in alcoholism. Age- and sex-specific age-of-onset distributions will be required, and penetrance vectors should be modified to reflect secular variation. The secular trend has occurred too rapidly to be accompanied by changes in gene frequency, and it is likely that similar genetic risk factors are present in more recently born and older cohorts.

Genetic linkage studies have traditionally been conducted either when a candidate gene is found or when unambiguous statistical evidence for a major locus is available. Unfortunately, statistical methods for detecting major loci in the presence of complex intergenerational phenotypic variation such as that demonstrated here are not available. A number of groups, including our own, are extending current approaches to genetic linkage so that increasingly complex phenotypes can be studied. Complexities being modeled include diagnostic instability, secular trends, bilineality and genetic heterogeneity.

Accelerated efforts are under way to provide a fine-grained map of the human genome, including many highly polymorphic markers. Thus, we will be able to search for abnormal genes that influence susceptibility to develop disorders such as alcoholism, where Mendelian transmission does not occur and where environmental factors play a large role. Simulation studies are being conducted to extend linkage analysis to the study of complex genetic mechanisms. Of particular interest in the field of alcoholism are preliminary reports which indicate that additive genetic effects that result from variation at four to six loci can be resolved with reasonable sample sizes (B. Suarez, pers. comm.).

ACKNOWLEDGEMENTS

This research was supported in part by U.S. Public Health Service grants AA-08401, AA-08403, AA-03539, MH-31302, and AA-08028.

REFERENCES

Cloninger, C.R., M. Bohman, and S. Sigvaardson. 1981. Inheritance of alcohol abuse: Cross-fostering analysis of adopted men. *Arch. Gen. Psychiatry* **38:** 861.

Cloninger, C.R., T. Reich, S. Sigvardsson, A.-L. von Knorring, and M. Bohman. 1986. Effects of changes in alcohol use between generations on inheritance of alcohol abuse. In *Alcoholism: Origins and outcome*, Proceedings of the 76th Annual Meeting of the APPA, New York, March 1986 (ed. R.M. Rose and J.E. Barrett), p. 49. Raven Press, New York.

Coryell, W., C.R. Cloninger, and T. Reich. 1978. Clinical assessment: Use of nonphysician interviews. *J. Nerv. Ment. Dis.* **166:** 599.

Dinwiddie, S.H. and T. Reich. 1990. Epidemiological perspectives on children of alcoholism. *Recent Adv. Alcohol.* **23:** (in press).

Feighner, J., E. Robins, S.B. Guze, R.A. Woodruff, G. Winokur, and R. Munoz. 1972. Diagnostic criteria for use in psychiatric research. *Arch. Gen. Psychiatry* **26:** 57.

Gemini: Technical Report Number 14. 1979. Department of Biophysics and Medical Computing, University of Utah, Salt Lake City.

Heckler, M.M. 1983. *Fifth special report to the U.S. Congress on Alcohol and Health*. U.S. Department of Health and Human Services (NIAAA), U.S. Government Printing Office, Washington, D.C.

Kalbfleisch, J.D. and R.L. Prentice. 1980. *The statistical analysis of failure time data*. Wiley, New York.

Klerman, G.L., P.W. Lavori, J. Rice, T. Reich, J. Endicott, N.C. Andreasen, M.B. Keller, and R.M. Hirschfeld. 1985. Birth cohort trends in rates of major depressive disorder among relatives of patients with affective disorder. *Arch. Gen. Psychiatry* **42:** 689.

Lavori, P.W., G.L. Klerman, M.D. Keller, T. Reich, J. Rice, and J. Endicott. 1987. Age-period-cohort analyses of secular trends in onset of major depression: Findings in siblings of patients with major affective disorder. *J. Psychiatr. Res.* **21:** 23.

Province, M.A. and D.C. Rao. 1985. Path analysis of family resemblance with temporal trends. *Am. J. Hum. Genet.* **37:** 178.

Regier, D.A., J.K. Myers, W.W. Clinton, and D.Z. Locke. 1984. The NIMH epidemiologic catchment area program. *Arch. Gen. Psychiatry* **41:** 934.

Reich, T., J.P. Rice, C.R. Cloninger, and C. Lewis. 1980. The contribution of affected parents to the pool of affected individuals: Path analysis of the segregation distribution for alcoholism. In *The social consequences of psychiatric illness* (ed. L.N. Robins et al.), p. 91. Brunner/Mazel, New York.

Reich, T., C.R. Cloninger, P. Van Eerdewegh, J.P. Rice, and J. Mullaney. 1988. Secular trends in the familial transmission of alcoholism. *Alcoholism* **12:** 458.

Reich, T., J.P. Rice, C.R. Cloninger, R. Wette, and J. James. 1979. The use of multiple thresholds in segregation analysis in analyzing the phenotypic heterogeneity of multifactorial traits. *Annu. Num. Genet.* **42:** 371.

Rice, J.P., C.R. Cloninger, and T. Reich. 1980. General causal models for sex differences in the familial transmission of multifactorial traits: An application to human spatial visualizing ability. *Soc. Biol.* **26:** 36.

Robins, L.N., J. Helzer, M.N. Weismann, H. Orvaschel, E. Gruenberg, J.D. Burke, and D.A. Regier. 1984. Lifetime prevalence of specific psychiatric disorders in three sites. *Arch. Gen. Psychiatry* **41:** 949.

Wetzel, R.D., T. Reich, G.E. Murphy, M. Province, and J.P. Miller. 1987. The changing relationship between age and suicide rates. *Psychiatr. Dev.* **3:** 179.

COMMENTS

Billings: Was the number of assessed people similar?

Reich: No. I don't have those numbers in my head. The entire group was about 1200 subjects.

Billings: Did you have more cases in the older age group than in the younger age group?

Reich: Yes. The biggest group would be in the middle years.

Noble: I want to make a point that there is a comorbidity in this. In your own studies, you show that there is a clear entity with alcoholism. For a long time this disorder has not been seen as caused in part by anxiety, in part by depression, etc.

Reich: There is comorbidity.

Noble: There is a comorbidity, but I think you have managed to separate that. That is important at the policy level, because we have been hearing Fred Goodwin going around the country and stating that this all belongs to the same thing, that it all comes under one umbrella. It is an important point for policy.

Reich: I think at the biological level we will see that, in terms of the transmissibility of these disorders, alcoholism and depression are independent. We understand some aspects of transmission. They include sociocultural phenomena, and biological and genetic phenomena. There will probably be more than one factor in each group.

Billings: I'm a little unclear about your explanation about the secular trend in depression or alcoholism.

Reich: I think they're different.

Billings: Your data show secular trends in both. Are you arguing that a different genetic mechanism was applying to the older than to the younger people, or that there is a different allele that is now more frequent?

Reich: From what we know about genetics, if the environment changes radically—and a secular trend of this magnitude is a radical change—the genetic mechanisms could easily be changed.

Billings: So it's a different locus?

Reich: A radical change in environmental exposure might lead in turn to a new set of genetic mechanisms which result in a disease phenotype. For example, early in this century a large proportion of cases of coronary artery disease were probably due to Mendelian genetic abnormalities in cholesterol metabolism. After decades of sedentary living, obesity, and very high fat and cholesterol diets, the types of coronary artery cases we observe and their relative frequencies are probably very different.

Chakravarti: I think you are confusing two issues. You raise two points: one, that controlled exposure to anything could change the frequencies of genes, and two, change of course could make the frequencies zero or high.

Reich: I don't think any of these changes are gene frequency changes.

Chakravarti: Were you talking of the sort of usual situation where there is some underlying genetic variable that all populations have and that new environmental components act on that variable to create what looks like the same phenotype?

Reich: No, it doesn't look like the same phenotype in fact.

Chakravarti: You keep saying that the genetics has changed. I don't understand.

Reich: No, I keep saying that in a new environment different kinds of genes can be turned on and off.

Chakravarti: What do you mean different kinds of genes can be turned on or off?

Reich: When an organism is exposed to a new environmental challenge or when there is a large shift in the usual environment, then new disease phenotypes or susceptibilities may be found. Perhaps the development of pesticide resistance in insects might be an example.

Chakravarti: I don't think there is any example in genetics where we think that that's the case. Usually all the work done in other plants and animals suggests that at the same locus you have alleles, some that give rise to resistance and others to susceptibility. So I don't understand, when you're talking of new genes that would not have had any alcoholism related.

Conneally: DDT resistance in some insects was simply an enormous change in gene frequency by selection; it was nothing else.

Gordis: The insect model would correspond to a long evolutionary change in man. The point you are making, I think, is that if a 40-year-old was seeing alcohol for the first time and a 20-year-old was seeing alcohol for the first time, the same phenotype might result in the action of different genes. Isn't that what you're really saying?

Reich: Yes.

Sambrook: I would feel happier about that argument if there were populations in the world (there may well be, for all I know) in which the instance of alcoholism is decreasing, but all these examples are increasing.

Reich: In the United States we have had a decrease in alcohol consumption in the last 4 or 5 years. I think probably the onset of alcoholism will be decreasing as a consequence of that. It would be very interesting to see who's stopping drinking, whether it's alcoholics who proportionately are stopping drinking, which I doubt, or whether it's the nonalcoholics who are stopping. That is research that has yet to be done.

Behavioral/Social Factors That May Enhance or Attenuate Genetic Effects

VICTOR HESSELBROCK* AND MICHIE HESSELBROCK[†]
*Department of Psychiatry
University of Connecticut Health Center
Farmington, Connecticut 06032
[†]Department of Social Work
Southern Connecticut State University
New Haven, Connecticut 06515

INTRODUCTION

Although it is clear that alcoholism is a familial disorder and that offspring of an alcoholic parent are at increased risk for alcoholism, only a small percentage of offspring actually go on to develop alcoholism. Reports from the literature indicate that only about one-third of sons of alcoholic fathers eventually develop alcohol dependence (Goodwin et al. 1973), whereas the rate is ~10% for daughters (Goodwin et al. 1977). Thus, it would seem that a variety of factors may serve either to enhance genetic effects and their expression leading to alcohol dependence or to attenuate genetic effects and their expression. In this paper, we examine the evidence regarding the role of nongenetic factors in terms of either increasing or reducing the risk of alcoholism in those individuals who have a family history of alcoholism.

Behavioral Factors That May Enhance Genetic Effects

Several childhood behavioral factors have been identified that appear to be related to increased use of alcohol, an essential ingredient for the development of alcohol dependence, in adolescence and adulthood.

Attention Deficit Disorder/Hyperactivity

The essential features of the childhood attention deficit disorder (ADD) include developmentally inappropriate degrees of inattention, impulsiveness, and hyperactivity (Committee on Nomenclature and Statistics [DSM-III-R] 1987). The condition is typically worse in settings requiring sustained attention such as school, whereas its expression may be minimal or absent when the person is receiving frequent reinforcement or is under very strict control. The frequency of the disorder is overrepresented in families with alcohol dependence (Vaillant 1983), conduct disorder (Wood et al. 1983), and antisocial personality (ASP) disorder (Stouthamer-Loeber and Loeber 1988). Many of the studies cited above are not based on samples at high genetic risk for alcoholism. This suggests that behavioral factors are not necessarily part of the genetic expression of the risk for alcoholism, but are more likely to be present even in general population samples. Furthermore, inattention has been found to distinguish high-risk from low-risk samples in several studies of neuropsychological vulnerability to alcoholism (Tarter et al. 1985; Schaeffer et al. 1986).

The importance of ADD as a potentiating factor can also be found in its relationship to an individual's drinking history. In two separate studies of young adult nonalcoholic subjects, we have found that an increased frequency of such behavior in childhood was predictive of an earlier age at which the first drink of beverage ethanol was consumed and also when regular drinking began (Hesselbrock et al. 1985; Workman-Daniels and Hesselbrock 1987). The findings were not specific to offspring at high risk for alcoholism. Other studies have reported similar findings (e.g., Tarter et al. 1985).

Several key features of ADD have been examined in relation to the risk for developing alcoholism, particularly as indicators of central nervous system functioning. Impulsiveness, for example, was first identified as a distinguishing characteristic of positive family hypercholesterolemia (FH^+) subjects compared with FH^- subjects in the Danish cohort study (Knop et al. 1985). More recently, impulsiveness has been hypothetically related to the amine system and personality characteristics as having etiological significance for the development of alcoholism (Cloninger 1987). One hypothesis contends that an increased level of impulsiveness may serve as a mediator of vulnerability. The difficulty in inhibiting responses leads impulsive individuals to seek immediate gratification without regard for the potential for punishment at a later time. Thus, if drinking becomes problematic, highly impulsive individuals are less likely to develop effective inhibitory control. Instead, they may choose to continue to enjoy the effects of intoxication with little regard for the possible social and biological consequences of repeated intoxication.

Impulsivity may also lead to impaired coping (K. Sher, unpubl.). Because successful coping is thought to require a relatively high degree of reflection and consideration of available behavioral options, the impulsive person may not be able to formulate appropriate strategies to resist high-risk drinking situations.

ADD appears to persist into adulthood in a rather high percentage of individuals, rather than dissipate in early adolescence as thought previously (Wender et al. 1981; Wood et al. 1983). Thus, ADD may have etiological significance in several ways. It may enhance genetic effects related to the development of alcoholism in that persons at risk for alcoholism may begin to drink to self-medicate as a way of attempting to control the disorder. It could also be suggested that the impulsiveness associated with ADD may lead high-risk individuals to drink when restraint should be excercised. In both situations, behavior problems lead to increased ethanol exposure, providing an opportunity for the genes associated with alcoholism to be expressed.

Conduct Problems

Conduct problems have a very early onset and are easy to identify. Increased aggressiveness, risk-taking, antisocial activity, and rebelliousness are typical of children with conduct problems. Conduct problems in general, however—not just conduct disorder or antisocial personality—have consistently been related to the development of alcohol abuse/dependence in late adolescence and early adulthood (Robins 1966; Vaillant 1983; Hesselbrock et al. 1984; Drake and Vaillant 1988). These findings are consistent across youthful clinical samples (Robins 1966) and studies of children sampled from the general population (cf. the Oakland Growth Study; Jones 1968). Furthermore, several of these studies have indicated that minor, and not major, deviance is most predictive of later problems with alcohol and other substances.

It should be noted that only about one-third of boys with conduct disorder in childhood go on to develop ASP disorder in adulthood; however, persons with ASP frequently begin early use and abuse of alcohol and other drugs. ASP individuals are also likely to continue abusing a variety of substances as they progress through adolescence and young adulthood; thus, conduct problems may have etiological significance by providing a mechanism for early chronic exposure to ethanol in persons vulnerable to its effects.

Poor School Achievement

A number of studies have identified poor school achievement as a marker for later problems in several areas, including alcoholism (cf. Robins 1966; Ensminger et al. 1983; Johnson and Rolf 1988). This is particularly true if the pattern of early school failure continues into later life (Zucker and Lisansky-Gomberg 1986). The continued pattern of failure from primary schooling into the vocational arena may indicate incompetence in several areas necessary for effective functioning. The ineffective coping may then provide a context for abusive drinking that eventually leads to chronic abuse.

Several vulnerability factors may underlie the marker variable of poor school achievement. Difficulties in school may result from cognitive deficits present in the "at risk" child (cf. Hegedus et al. 1984; Knop et al. 1985). Deficits in learning, memory, and concept formation, for example, may impair the child's learning process. ADD or conduct disorder, if present, may also affect school performance. These behavioral problems may affect school achievement by reducing the child's ability to concentrate or impairing the development of social skills necessary for effective school performance.

A caution should be noted, however. Poor school performance may also have an organic basis. Studies indicating that poor school achievement distinguishes children of alcoholics from children of nonalcoholics have not always examined the drinking history of the mother carefully. Because there is a substantial degree of assortative mating among alcoholics, as well as an increase in heavy drinking among nonalcoholic spouses (Hall et al. 1983), the mothers of high-risk children may have been regular consumers of ethanol during gestation. The poor school performance reportedly found among children of nonalcoholics therefore may be due to fetal alcohol effects (Streissguth et al. 1986) rather than a direct or indirect expression of genetic effects.

Social Factors That May Enhance Genetic Effects

Social factors may be important for the expression of genetic effects in a number of ways. Such factors probably have their impact by providing a nurturant context in which the genetic effects become manifest. Social factors frequently enhance genetic effects by providing an environment in which the person becomes initiated into early drinking (i.e., exposure) that leads to alcohol dependence—not just heavy drinking.

Socioenconomic Status

A variety of studies of persons at risk for the development of psychopathology—not just alcoholism—have found that low socioeconomic status of the family of origin contributes to the genetic risk provided by the proband parent. Although low socioeconomic status per se is not predictive of future alcoholism, Drake and Vaillant (1988) and Cloninger (1987) found that low socioeconomic status in childhood was predictive of later alcohol dependence in persons with a family history of alcoholism. It is not clear which aspects of low socioeconomic status contribute to this prediction, but poorer general health, the environment (e.g., increased availability of ethanol at a younger age), or the nature of peer relationships where early heavy drinking is condoned and encouraged might be factors.

Parenting

Because it is well-established that alcoholism is a familial disorder, a number of different factors have been posited to account for this relationship. One factor that has received considerable attention over the years is parenting. More specifically, how do parent-child interactions affect the offspring's vulnerability to alcoholism? Robins (1966) found that a lack of discipline and structure in the relationships of parents with their children, particularly sons, was predictive of later alcohol problems. A lack of maternal control (McCord

1983) and a poor relationship with both parents (Wechsler and Thum 1973; Prendergast and Schaefer 1974) have also been cited as factors that contribute to the risk for developing alcoholism.

Another aspect of parenting that has been related to increased risk for alcoholism is the attitudes of parents toward alcohol consumption. It has been suggested that parental approval of early drinking (Barnes and Welte 1985; McCord 1988) is associated with increased exposure to alcohol. On the other hand, a disparity between parental attitudes (negative) and those of the adolescent's peer group (positive) also seems predictive of increased exposure to alcohol that could potentially lead to abusive drinking (Jessor and Jessor 1975).

Poor parenting may enhance genetic effects in several ways. First, poor parental control and discipline fail to put limits on impulsive behavior in early childhood. As the child reaches adolescence, the impulsive behavior may lead to drinking at an early age and an inability of the maturing adolescent to put appropriate limits on ethanol consumption. Second, parental behavior may serve as a model for later alcohol use by the child. Parental approval of early consumption and heavy alcohol consumption by parent(s) provides little guidance as the offspring begins his/her drinking career. The failure of the parent to provide a model indicating the limits of drinking behavior may also lead to increased consumption by offspring at risk for alcoholism. Finally, lack of parental control over the offspring's behavior and a disparity between peers and parental attitudes toward drinking may lead to increased peer pressure to drink. Peer pressure has been identified as an important source of influence leading to early initiation into drinking and possibly to abusive drinking (see below).

Family Environment

Another social factor that has been suggested as contributing to the familial nature of alcoholism is the environment in which the offspring are reared. Several attempts to characterize aspects of the home environment have been made. In their attempts to type environments of normal families and families containing a psychiatrically ill parent, Moos and Moos (1984) found that alcoholic families are less expressive and less cohesive. This is thought to lead to increased familial stress and may possibly lead to the heavy use of alcohol as a coping mechanism among family members.

Reich et al. (1988) and Earls et al. (1988) found that among children of alcoholics, the more disturbed child was distinguished by having had increased exposure to the drinking parent and an increased frequency of parent-child conflicts, as well as having experienced less parent-child interaction. The more routine aspects of family life, such as mealtime habits and the celebration of holidays and special events, have been studied by Wolin et al. (1980) as "family rituals." They have found these events to be associated with the transmission of alcoholic behavior from parent to child in some families. Families in which the daily rituals have been disrupted or subsumed by alcohol use are more likely to be "transmitter" families than those families in which usual routines are maintained. Failure to provide guidance and structure for the developing child due to the disrupted routine may have etiological relevance. Furthermore, family acceptance of excessive drinking and family initiation into drinking provide models for offspring of an alcoholic parent(s) to follow (Jacob and Leonard 1985).

Peer Influences

The role of peers and peer influences on the initiation into substance use, including alcohol, is well documented (Kandel and Logan 1984; Jessor and Jessor 1975; Margulies et al. 1977). Data from a variety of samples, ranging from general population surveys to samples of youths at high risk for developing substance abuse problems, consistently implicate peer behavior (including acceptability of use) and peer pressure as factors related to increased exposure and increased substance intake. Peer-related influences appear to be more important for adolescent females than males. Peers may also have an indirect influence on substance-taking behavior by providing inadequate socialization into acceptable adult behavior. Poor socialization could permit the expression of conduct problems, as well as fail to set appropriate limits on alcohol use. Such constraints may be necessary for the genetically vulnerable person to avoid developing alcohol problems.

Life Events

Although several early studies suggested that stressful life events may be instrumental in the etiological course of both medical and psychiatric problems, later studies have not always supported this conclusion (Dohrenwend and Dohrenwend 1978). Thus, the importance of stressful major life events as a precipitant of abusive drinking, leading to alcohol dependence, is equivocal.

However, the role of stressful life events in the development of alcoholism cannot be totally discounted. More recent studies have implicated the role of daily stress rather than major stressors as being important for a variety of psychological and medical problems (Brantley et al. 1987). Some studies have suggested that alcohol use may arise as a way to cope with the stress of living in a disruptive family (rather than the incidence of major stressful events); therefore, drinking may be provoked in an effort to dampen these chronic levels of stress (Jacob and Leonard 1985; McCord 1988). It has also been found that the stress of living in a disruptive family may have an indirect effect on the onset of drinking. Novy and Donohue (1985) found that stress levels were predictive of minor delinquency which, in turn, was predictive of initiation into drug use, alcohol use, and other delinquent acts.

Behavioral Factors That May Attenuate Genetic Effects

Studies of a variety of groups at risk for alcoholism have indicated the importance of nongenetic effects with respect to good adjustment, resiliency, or invulnerability to poor outcome, e.g., psychopathology, including alcoholism (cf. Garmezy and Streitman 1973). Two behavioral factors, particularly social competence and academic competence, have shown some promise as protective factors against poor psychiatric outcome, including alcoholism.

Social Competence

Social competence, or the ability of the individual to respond effectively in a variety of social situations, has been the focus of a number of investigations on factors that may protect individuals at high genetic risk for the future development of psychopathology. Rolf (1976) found that academic achievement, participation and competition in a variety of activities (not just athletic events), and an ability to relate well to others (high self-esteem, self-efficacy) in childhood and adolescence were predictive of good adult adjustment in the progeny of a schizophrenic parent. More recently, similar findings were reported in a study of children of alcoholics (Rae-Grant et al. 1988). Social competence is thought to provide an effective response to a variety of environmental hazards that predispose the individual to maladaptive outcomes, such as peer pressure to use alcohol and the general availability of alcohol. The studies mentioned above suggest that socially competent children—even those that carry a possible genetic predisposition—have a reduced risk for future psychopathology.

Academic Competence

Academic competence is defined as the ability to work to one's level of proficiency and to be consistently successful at that level. Good communication skills are an important aspect of academic competence. Studies by Werner (1985) and Rae-Grant et al. (1988) identified academic competence as a protective factor in children who were resilient to early substance use and abuse. In both studies, the importance of academic competence as a protective factor persisted even when the children carried a genetic predisposition for alcoholism, as indicated by a family history for alcoholism.

Social Factors That May Attenuate Genetic Effects

In a previous section, a number of social factors were identified as possible contributors to the enhancement of genetic effects leading to the development of alcoholism. In this section, their antithesis will be examined as environmental influences that may reduce a person's risk for developing alcohol-related problems.

Parenting

Just as poor parenting may enhance genetic effects by permitting certain behaviors to be expressed, effective parenting may serve to diminish the untoward influences of having a family history positive for alcoholism. Consistency of affection and discipline seemed to identify that group of boys referred to a child guidance clinic who did not develop problems in adulthood (Robins 1966). It is possible that inconsistency of discipline fails to control the impulsivity leading conduct-disordered boys without such parental discipline into criminality and substance abuse. With respect to alcohol use, parental disapproval of drinking has been associated with later abstinence among offspring (Barnes and Welte 1985), and daughters of alcoholics who are reared in a supportive home environment are more likely to have good adjustment in adolescence and young adulthood (Benson and Heller 1987).

Family Environment/Interaction

Family factors have long been considered by clinicians as having prophylactic effects against alcoholism, particularly for children of alcoholic parents. In their family study of alcoholism, Jacob and Leonard (1985) found that families displaying coping behaviors that prohibit drinking produce offspring with better outcomes. Families actively seeking to prevent drinking (e.g., finding hidden bottles and pouring out contents, etc.) produce offspring who are less likely to develop alcohol-related problems in adolescence or young adulthood. Bennett et al. (1987) examined the daily routines and most valued activities of families with an alcoholic parent for their protective value against alcoholism in offspring. Their work suggests that when these family rituals are taken over by alcohol use, poor outcomes for the children are more likely; however, if family rituals are maintained and preserved as distinct from alcohol use, the family is less likely to transmit alcoholism to the offspring. The family and the environment that it provides are seen as an important mechanism for furnishing structure and controls for the behavior (including alcohol use) of the offspring. When these controls are operative, exposure to alcohol is reduced. Reduced alcohol consumption thereby reduces the likelihood of the activation of the genes responsible for the development of alcoholism.

A more recent study of female twin pairs suggests that marital status may serve as a modifier of genetic effects on drinking habits (Heath et al. 1989). For those subjects under the age of 30 years, genetic differences accounted for 31% of the variance in alcohol consumption. For unmarried twins, genetic differences accounted for 60% of the variance in alcohol consumption. For married twins over the age of 31, genetic differences accounted for 46–59% of the variance in alcohol consumption compared to 76% in unmarried female twins. Given the rather high rate of assortative mating that occurs among persons with a family history of alcoholism (Hall et al. 1983), the influence of the spouse as a factor that may serve to limit alcohol consumption cannot be ignored.

Peer Relations

Peer relations provide a context in which alcohol and other drug use is either supported or discouraged. Just as peer pressure and acceptance of alcohol and other substance use may lead to increased exposure, the opposite also seems to hold. In a general population study of teens and substance use, Marston et al. (1988) found that the peer group is often a source of alternative activities to chronic exposure for those youths reporting minimal or no use.

The importance of the above social and behavioral factors for the development and maintenance of alcohol and other substance abuse problems is further supported in a recent study by Kandel and Raveis (1989). They found that the above factors (social role performance, social context unfavorable to alcohol/drug use, etc.), which are predictive of delayed onset of use in adolescence, are also predictive of cessation of use in young adulthood.

SUMMARY

This review indicates that a variety of social and behavioral factors are important in the etiology of alcoholism. Some social and behavioral factors may enhance the risk of developing alcoholism, particularly in persons with a family history of alcoholism. Conversely, a number of social and behavioral factors appear to protect the individual against the risk of developing alcoholism. The importance of these factors for the expression of alcoholism lies in their potential effects on either limiting or increasing an individual's exposure to ethanol. Although it is unlikely that these factors make a direct contribution to the genetic risk for alcoholism, they do seem to provide the context that leads to the expression of the genes responsible for the disorder.

ACKNOWLEDGMENTS

This work was supported by grants AA-3510 and U10-AA08403 from the National Institute of Alcohol Abuse and Alcoholism.

REFERENCES

Barnes, G. and J. Welte. 1985. Patterns and predictors of alcohol use among 7–12th grade students in New York State. *Alcohol* **14:** 53.

Bennett, L., S. Wolin, D. Reiss, and M. Teitelbaum. 1987. Couples at risk for transmission of alcoholism: Protective influences. *Fam. Process.* **26:** 111.

Benson, C. and K. Heller. 1987. Factors in the current adjustment of young adult daughters of alcoholic and problem drinking fathers. *J. Abnormal Psychol.* **96:** 305.

Brantley, P., C. Waggoner, G. Jones, and N. Rappaport. 1987. A daily stress inventory. *J. Behav. Med.* **10:** 61.

Cloninger, R. 1987. Neurogenetic adaptive mechanisms in alcoholism. *Science* **236:** 410.

Committee on Nomenclature and Statistics (DSM-III-R). 1987. *Diagnostic and statistical manual of mental disorders.* American Psychiatric Association, Washington, D.C.

Dohrenwend, B. and B. Dohrenwend. 1978. Some issues in research on stressful life events. *J. Nerv. Ment. Dis.* **106:** 7.

Drake, R. and G. Vaillant. 1988. Predicting alcoholism and personality disorder in a 30 year longitudinal study of children of alcoholics. *Br. J. Addict.* **83:** 799.

Earls, F., W. Reich, K. Jung, and R. Cloninger. 1988. Psychopathology in children of alcoholic and antisocial parents. *Alcohol. Clin. Exp. Res.* **12:** 481.

Ensminger, M., C. Brown, and S. Kellam. 1983. Social control as an explanation of sex differences in substance use among adolescents. In *Problems of drug dependence* (ed. L. Harris), vol. 49, p. 296. National Institute on Drug Abuse, Washington, D.C.

Garmezy, N. and S. Streitman. 1973. Children at risk: The search for the antecedents of schizophrenia. *Schizophr. Bull.* **8:** 14.

Goodwin, D., F. Schulsinger, L. Hermansen, S. Guze, and G. Winokur. 1973. Alcohol problems in adoptees raised apart from alcoholic biological parents. *Arch. Gen. Psychiatry* **28:** 238.

Goodwin, D., F. Schulsinger, J. Knop, S. Mednick, and S. Guze. 1977. Alcoholism and depression in adopted-out daughters of alcoholics. *Arch. Gen. Psychiatry* **34:** 751.

Hall, R., V. Hesselbrock, and J. Stabenau. 1983. Familial distribution of alcohol use: II. Assortative mating of alcoholic probands. *Behav. Genet.* **13:** 373.

Hegedus, A., A. Alterman, and R. Tarter. 1984. Learning achievement in sons of alcoholics. *Alcohol. Clin. Exp. Res.* **8:** 330.

Heath, A., R. Jardine, and N. Martin. 1989. Interactive effects of genotype and social environment on alcohol consumption in female twins. *J. Stud. Alcohol* **50:** 38.

Hesselbrock, V., J. Stabenau, and M. Hesselbrock. 1985. Minimal brain dysfunction and neuropsychological test performance in offspring of alcoholics. In *Recent developments in alcoholism* (ed. M. Galanter), p. 65. Plenum Press, New York.

Hesselbrock, M., V. Hesselbrock, T. Babor, J. Stabenau, R. Meyer, and M. Weidenman. 1984. Antisocial behavior, psychopathology, and problem drinking in the natural history of alcoholism. In *Longitudinal research in alcoholism* (ed. D. Goodwin et al.), p. 197. Kluwer-Nijhoff, Boston.

Jacob, T. and K. Leonard. 1985. Psychosocial functioning in children of alcoholic fathers, depressed fathers and control fathers. *J. Stud. Alcohol* **47:** 373.

Jessor, R. and S. Jessor. 1975. Adolescent development and the onset of drinking: A longitudinal study. *J. Stud. Alcohol* **36:** 27.

Johnson, J. and J. Rolf. 1988. Cognitive functioning in children from alcoholic and nonalcoholic families. *Br. J. Addict.* **83:** 849.

Jones, M. 1968. Personality correlates and antecedents of drinking patterns in adult males. *J. Consult. Clin. Psychol.* **32:** 2.

Kandel, D. and J. Logan. 1984. Patterns of drug use from adolescence to young adulthood: I. Periods of risk for initiation, continued use, and discontinuation. *Am. J. Public Health* **74:** 660.

Kandel, D. and V. Raveis. 1989. Cessation of illicit drug use in young adulthood. *Arch. Gen. Psychiatry* **46:** 109.

Knop, J., T. Teasdale, F. Schulsinger, and D. Goodwin. 1985. A prospective study of young men at high risk for alcoholism. *J. Stud. Alcohol* **46:** 273.

Margulies, R., R. Kessler, and D. Kandel. 1977. A longitudinal study of onset of drinking among high-school students. *J. Stud. Alcohol* **38:** 897.

Marston, A., D. Jacobs, R. Singer, K. Widaman, and T. Little. 1988. Adolescents who apparently are invulnerable to drug, alcohol, and nicotine use. *Adolescence* **23:** 593.

McCord, J. 1988. Alcoholism: Toward understanding genetic and social factors. *Psychiatry* **51:** 131.

Moos, R. and B. Moos. 1984. The process of recovery from alcoholism. *J. Stud. Alcohol* **45:** 111.

Novy, D. and S. Donohue. 1985. The relationship between adolescent life stress events and delinquent conduct including conduct indicating a need for supervision. *Adolescence* **20:** 313.

Prendergast, T. and E. Schaefer. 1974. Correlates of drinking and drunkenness among high school students. *Q.J. Stud. Alcohol* **35:** 232.

Rae-Grant, N., J. Thomas, D. Offord, and M. Boyle. 1988. Risk, protective factors, and the prevalence of behavioral and emotional disorders in children and adolescents. *J. Am. Acad. Child Adolesc. Psychiatry* **28:** 262.

Reich, W., F. Earls, and J. Powell. 1988. A comparison of the home and social environments of children of alcoholic and nonalcoholic parents. *Br. J. Addict.* **83:** 831.

Robins, L. 1966. *Deviant children grownup*. Williams and Wilkins, Baltimore.

Rolf, J. 1976. Peer status and the directionality of symptomatic behavior: Prime social competence predictors of outcome for vulnerable children. *Am. J. Orthopsychiatry* **46:** 74.

Schaeffer, K., O. Parsons, and J. Yomans. 1986. Neuropsychological differences between male familial and nonfamilial alcoholics and nonalcoholics. *Alcohol. Clin. Exp. Res.* **12**: 347.

Stouthamer-Loeber, M. and R. Loeber. 1988. The use of prediction data in understanding delinquency. *Behav. Sci. Law* **6**: 333.

Streissguth, A., H. Barr, and P. Sampson. 1986. Attention, distraction, and reaction time at 7 years and prenatal alcohol exposure. *Neurobehav. Toxicol. Teratol.* **8**: 717.

Tarter, R., A. Alterman, and K. Edwards. 1985. Vulnerability to alcoholism in men. *J. Stud. Alcohol* **46**: 329.

Vaillant, G. 1983. *The natural history of alcoholism.* Harvard University Press, Boston.

Wechsler, H. and D. Thum. 1973. Teenage drinking, drug use, and social correlates. *Q. J. Stud. Alcohol.* **34**: 1220.

Wender, P., F. Reihmherr, and D. Wood. 1981. Attention deficit disorder (minimal brain dysfunction) in adults. *Arch. Gen. Psychiatry* **33**: 449.

Werner, E. 1985. Resilient offspring of alcoholics: A longitudinal study from birth to age 18. *J. Stud. Alcohol* **47**: 34.

Wolin, S., L. Bennet, D. Noonan, and M. Teitelbaum. 1980. Disrupted family rituals, a factor in the intergenerational transmission of alcoholism. *J. Stud. Alcohol* **41**: 199.

Wood, D., P. Wender, and F. Reihmherr. 1983. The prevalence of attention deficit, residual type, or minimal brain dysfunction, in a population of male alcoholic patients. *Am. J. Psychiatry* **140**: 95.

Workman-Daniels, K. and V. Hesselbrock. 1987. Childhood problem behavior and neuropsychological functioning in persons at risk for alcoholism. *J. Stud. Alcohol* **48**: 187.

Zucker, R. and E. Lisansky-Gomberg. 1986. Etiology of alcoholism reconsidered, the case for a biopsychosocial process. *Am. Psychol.* **41**: 783.

COMMENTS

Begleiter: The two things you didn't mention, Victor, are accessibility and availability of alcohol, which are really important environmental factors.

Hesselbrock: Yes, certainly, but that depends on sampling issues. If you sample from the Amish or from Moslem groups, neither of those are factors. SES may influence availability. That might be the mechanism for low SES increasing access in some locations. In the deep South with very fundamental religion, that is not going to work. Maybe in northern areas where religion is not as important, SES might influence availability and accessibility.

Gordis: It goes beyond region. It's national and sector as well, because one of the problems in studying transmissibility of drugs compared to alcohol is that 30 years ago that generation didn't have as much access to crack and heroin. Furthermore, if there is a regulatory policy that makes pricing higher across the board, there will be secular trends in excess that will also somewhat contaminate genetic studies. So, it's not just the Amish versus the world; it's time variant also.

Hesselbrock: Yes. I think that's why Dr. Reich's data are so important, looking at secular trends. It's not only secular trends for alcohol use, but certainly secular trends in why there might be much less specificity in terms of children of alcoholics also getting involved in the other types of things.

Begleiter: Ken Sherr has repeatedly mentioned that the single most important variable associated with high risk for alcoholism is being a school dropout; that is, they almost never finish high school. Therefore, I wonder what it means to study, for example, a college population, like Marc does.

Hesselbrock: Nothing.

Cloninger: Does Ken think he knows what the direction of effects there is: Does drug use lead to school dropout or vice versa?

Hesselbrock: A single best predictor. My guess is, in talking with him about some of his data, he gets into the type 1/type 2 argument very clearly because early school dropout is one of the cardinal signs of people with antisocial personality. Also, antisocials begin early alcohol and drug abuse and frequently get into abusive patterns. It's that type of mixture. I don't know that it is a predictive factor for children of alcoholics.

Tarter: Picking up a bit on Henri's point, looking for specific risk factors is very difficult. Rolfe Loburg at our center in Pittsburgh has been conducting a longitudinal study of children from grade 2 through high school and beyond, a community-wide sampling study, going into the homes, interviewing parent and kids in homologous fashion. He has found that the best single predictor of adolescent-onset alcohol abuse is consuming their first unsupervised drink of liquor by grade 3.

Chakravarti: In view of the strong secular trends that you see, have there been any studies that try to correlate how the availability of alcohol has changed over the same period of time?

Hesselbrock: I will tell you, that has absolutely wrecked my prospective study. What has happened in the United States makes prospective studies, particularly those that began very early, absolutely impossible to deal with. I will give you my own history. We started a prospective study in Connecticut in 1978. We picked up adolescents, 14 or 15 years old. The drinking age was 21 at that time. In 1980, it went down to 20, then a year later it went down to 19, then it went to 18, then it went back up again. But, because of its going down, what happens is that as you get closer in age to that, you get availability from brothers and sisters and peers and things of that nature. So, it's not nice and clean any more. The availability has changed in the period of time that I have been studying these kids. It has happened in almost every state in the country.

Reich: Yes. Incidentally, there is an interaction between availability and age, so that the way people drink is very different at different ages. People who start to drink at a young age drink very, very differently than, for example, people who start to drink later. The relationship of that to eventual outcome is really complex and not carefully studied. Those are important variables.

Billings: Although you have constructed your presentation describing socioeconomic factors as an environmental factor that might modify genetic factors, there have been investigators who have published in reputable journals who have talked about the genes that might determine socioeconomic status. I'm thinking in particular of blood markers that are associated with socioeconomic status in England. So, you might just be talking about genetic interactions in that as well. Some people might think that.

Reich: There is an old literature with respect to psychiatric disorders comparing one's social class to that of one's father in terms of one's own psychopathology. But it's perfectly clear that different psychiatric disorders are differentially represented socially. If one looks at, for example, the excess of schizophrenics, the first demonstration was that the excess of schizophrenics among the poor was due to downward social drift. With respect to other psychiatric disorders, both antisocial personality and alcoholism, the upward migration of individuals with those disorders is much slower than for other individuals in the American populations. The socioeconomic distributions within populations of these disorders is quite complex because it's partly influenced by the presence of those disorders in the families, especially in the fathers.

Methodological Limitations of Research on the Genetics of Alcoholism

JOHN S. SEARLES
Department of Psychiatry
Addiction Research Center
University of Pennsylvania
Philadelphia, Pennsylvania 19104 and
Department of Veterans Affairs Medical Center
Philadelphia, Pennsylvania 19104

OVERVIEW

A substantial research effort has gone into establishing a genetic mechanism in the etiology of at least some forms of alcoholism. In this paper, I challenge this approach by examining the conceptual focus of putative high risk designs and reviewing significant methodological limitations of three major adoption studies of alcoholism. High risk designs confound genetic and environmental effects, which makes unambiguous interpretation of the results difficult. Results across different studies are sometimes contradictory, and adoption studies vary so widely on diagnostic criteria that comparisons across studies are problematic. Prevalence rates range from 0% to 32%, suggesting that different phenomena are being investigated. Research that focuses on etiologically significant environmental factors has been underemphasized; however, recent research implicates an important function for environmental influences in a complete etiologic model.

INTRODUCTION

Few serious scientists currently doubt the familial aggregation of at least some types of alcoholism; it is a well-documented phenomenon (Cotton 1979). However, because familial and genetic are not isomorphic, there is legitimate dispute about the source and the implications of familial alcoholism. The results of research in this area directly affect prevention and treatment efforts; therefore, it is especially important to provide an etiologic model as complete and precise as possible.

Recently, there has been a substantial effort to differentiate individuals who are at putative high risk for becoming alcoholics by virtue of their family history. This quasi-genetic approach seeks to identify factors (e.g., personality traits, physiological, neuropsychological, and biochemical processes) that distinguish those individuals who will and will not eventually exhibit behavioral or social problems with alcohol. It should be clear that except for the most basic biochemical processes, high risk studies cannot disentangle genetic from environmental effects. That is, individuals defined at high risk to develop alcoholism in terms of the diagnostic status of relatives (usually the father) share both genetic material and environmental forces that could substantially affect the later development of alcohol abuse. Therefore, at least three sources of etiologic factors (not necessarily independent) could be operating: genetic predisposition, environmental effects, or some combination of the two such as gene × environment interaction or gene-environment correlation (Scarr and McCartney 1983; Searles 1988). Often in the literature and in common parlance, there seems to be a genetic component independent of environmental influences imbedded in the high risk design. Thus, it is not uncommon to see high profile research efforts included in popular press reports about the genetics of alcoholism (e.g., CBS's *48 Hours,* July 6, 1989).

Adding to the confusion is the fact that not all high risk studies have reported similar results. Sometimes differences can be attributed to sample characteristics. For example, in previous work, I have pointed out that one of the most ephemeral of all the differences between high and low risk individuals appears in the electrophysiological domain (Searles 1988). Begleiter and colleagues (Begleiter et al. 1984; Begleiter 1988) have consistently reported significant differences in the magnitude of the P300 wave between sons of alcoholics and sons of nonalcoholics. However, a number of other studies have reported no such effect (see, e.g., Polich 1984; Neville and Schmidt 1985; Polich and Bloom 1986, 1987, 1988; Polich et al. 1988). Because both Henri Begleiter and John Polich attended this conference, the issue arose as to why such different results should obtain. Both Begleiter and Polich suggested substantial differences in sample characteristics. Begleiter et al. recruit only sons of diagnosable alcoholics who are in treatment, whereas the Polich group has typically employed a college sample who self-report their father as alcoholic. In addition, differences in the type of signal (auditory or visual) and the nature of the signal (simple or complex) can produce varying results. Whipple and Noble (1986) and Noble (this volume) reported no differences between high and low risk individuals on a simple task, but reported significant differences on a complex discrimination task. The meaning of these electrophysiological differences is not at all clear and requires further research specification (e.g., indicative of increased reinforcement value for alcohol and impairment of important cognitive functions and decision-making processes). It is especially important in these studies and others that investigate possible neuropsychological markers to control for the fact that children of alcoholic fathers, compared to controls, are at an increased risk to suffer closed head trauma and loss of consciousness, which may have important implications that are quite independent from a genetic mechanism (Tarter et al. 1984; Searles 1988). Moreover, it would be useful to test daughters of alcoholics, as well as sons, because even the simplest genetic model would not predict differential electrophysiological response patterns across gender.

Not all differences reported from various high risk studies are totally a function of sample characteristics or stimulus properties. For example, Hill et al. (1987) reported an increase in static ataxia following an ethanol challenge in offspring of alcoholics compared to controls; Nagoshi and Wilson (1987) reported no differences between high and low risk groups at baseline or after an ethanol challenge; Schuckit (1985) reported a decrease in body sway in high risk individuals compared to controls. Although there are some sample differences across these three studies, this should not account for such disparate results.

Interpretation of results from the high risk design should be made with caution, especially when postulating a genetic mechanism to account for obtained differences between high and low risk groups. For example, there appear to be no differences between high and low risk groups on metabolic processes involving alcohol such as clearance rates, time to peak blood alcohol concentration (BAC), or maximum BAC (Schuckit 1981; Nagoshi and Wilson 1987). In addition, no single biological marker appears to reliably differentiate high and low risk individuals. Although this does not vitiate a genetic hypothesis of alcoholism, it does require a more complex genetic scheme that could account for no differences in obvious mechanisms (e.g., biological) but differential effects in more subtle processes (e.g., electrophysiological).

The most powerful evidence adduced thus far demonstrating a genetic basis for alcoholism comes from the adoption studies carried out in Denmark, Sweden, and the United States. I have been somewhat critical of the methodology and interpretation of the results of these studies (Searles 1988, 1989a,b). Therefore, I will highlight in this chapter what I consider to be the most serious problems with each of the three major adoption studies: the Danish Adoption study by Goodwin and colleagues (Goodwin et al. 1973); the Stockholm Adoption Project reported by Cloninger et al. (1981); and the Iowa Studies directed by Remi Cadoret (Cadoret et al. 1985, 1987). For a more exhaustive critique, see Searles (1988).

Danish Adoption Study

There are two principal difficulties with the Danish Adoption Study (Fig. 1). First, as was also pointed out by Murray et al. (1983), the entire genetic effect depends on a rather artificial distinction between what Goodwin et al. (1973) term problem drinking and alcoholism. There is actually a higher percentage

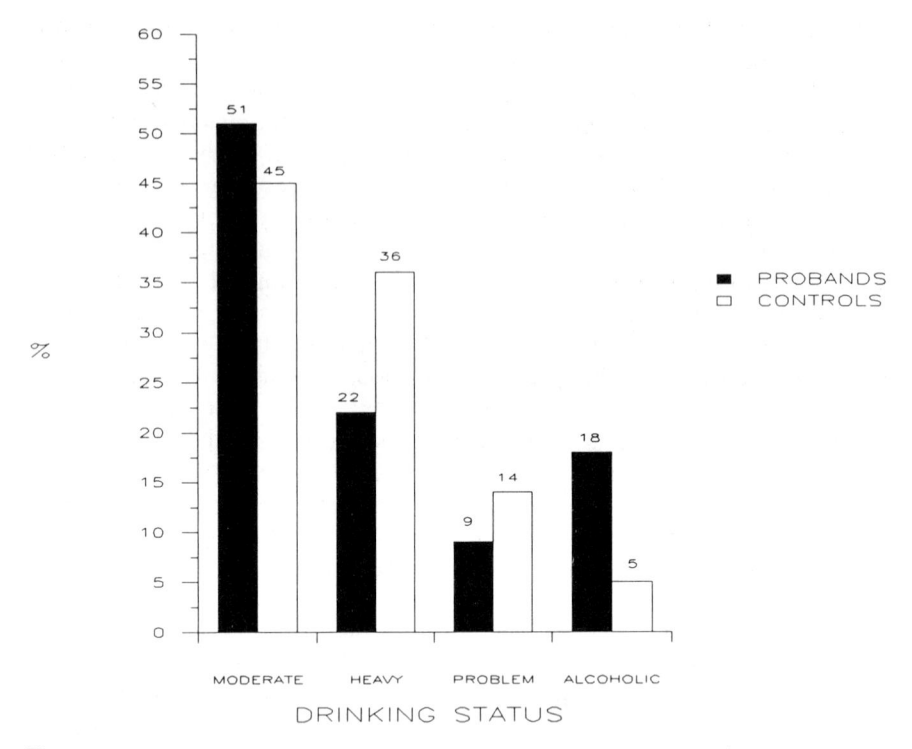

Figure 1
Percent in each drinking category. (Data from Goodwin et al. 1973.)

of heavy and problem drinkers in the control group (those adoptees without alcoholism in a biological relative). When the problem drinkers and alcoholics are combined, there is no statistical difference in rates of alcoholism between the probands and controls.

The second significant problem with the Danish study is primarily one of omission. That is, over 60% of both probands and controls were under 30 years of age at the time of the study, which may be too young to be considered through the lifetime risk for alcoholism. Thus, a re-evaluation of these individuals seems warranted. So far, no such follow-up has been published.

Stockholm Adoption Study

One of the main incentives for this conference is the work of Cloninger et al. (1981) on alcoholism of Swedish adoptees with and without a biological family history of alcohol problems. Their findings implicated both a genetic effect *and* a gene × environment interaction effect and described two different varieties of alcoholism. Cloninger (1986) has also developed an elegant and comprehensive neurobiologically rooted theory of personality functioning, partially on the basis of the Stockholm data. It is difficult to overestimate the impact this work has had on the field of alcoholism. At the Research Society on Alcoholism annual meeting two years ago at which Dr. Cloninger gave the plenary address (Cloninger 1988), almost every talk that covered psychosocial and biological issues in the etiology or treatment of alcoholism was followed by questions pertaining to the applicability of the type 1 and type 2 scheme to the topic at hand. To my knowledge, no one has yet applied the typology to animal models of alcoholism, but it may only be a matter of time before we are hearing about type 1 and type 2 alcoholic rats.

Despite the wave of enthusiasm for this work subsequent to publication in 1981, several critical papers surfaced that pointed out several problems with the design and interpretation of the genetics of alcoholism in general and the Swedish study in particular (Murray et al. 1983; Lester 1988; Littrel 1988; Searles 1988). Although I have delineated a number of difficulties previously (Searles 1988), in this paper I will focus on two of the most significant ones. The most problematic issue concerns adoptees being classified as mild, moderate, or severe alcohol abusers.

The temperance boards, one for each county, record instances of alcohol-related family violence and traffic offenses, as well as behavioral and social problems associated with alcohol abuse. It is not clear who may report abuses (law enforcement persons, health professionals, family, and friends), nor are the criteria for reporting or recording made clear. The temperance boards have no American counterpart, and this makes direct diagnostic comparisons difficult.

As shown in Table 1, 7.4% of the abusers were classified as mild abusers, 4.2% were classified as moderate abusers, and 5.9% were classified as severe abusers. It is not at all clear whether any but the severe abuse criteria could be considered alcohol abuse by standard criteria in the United States (e.g., DSM-III; American Psychiatric Association 1980). It is quite possible that the majority of American college students could qualify as at least mild abusers by the Swedish criteria. These data should be reanalyzed by redefining levels of abuse within the severe category. Cloninger (this volume) has clarified the issue somewhat by stating that the temperance boards do not automatically register individuals when a complaint is filed, but they apparently evaluate the information impartially and decide rationally whether or not registration is justified. Although this is important information, it still does not provide objective criteria for requirements of temperance board registration and does not take into account the differences between the social and behavioral criteria of Sweden and those of the United States. Michael Bohman has

Table 1
Criteria for Alcohol Abuse Diagnosis in the Stockholm Adoption Project

Mild abuse (7.4%)
   one registration with the county temperance board
   never been treated for alcoholism

Moderate abuse (4.2%)
   two or three registrations with the temperance board
   never been treated for alcoholism

Severe abuse (5.9%)
   four or more temperance board registrations, compulsory treatment, or psychiatric hospitalization with a diagnosis of alcoholism

---

commented on this point: "Sweden today is a stable country with a stable population, a high living standard, and a well-developed social security system. We do not have the large differences between social classes that we find in other countries, including some states or cities in the United States, and this gives us an opportunity to study the importance of genetic factors. We cannot generalize our findings concerning criminality or alcohol abuse to the United States. The United States, as a whole, is a country with very different circumstances" (Bohman et al. 1983). Furthermore, Schuckit and Irwin (1989) report difficulty in replicating the type 1/type 2 structure in a sample of young American men with a family history of alcohol abuse.

The second major problem is also related to, and is a consequence of, the classification system. Specifically, the results of this study suggest that both mild *and* severe abuse cluster into the environmentally mediated type 1 alcoholic, whereas the type 2, highly heritable, male-limited subtype consists of the moderate abusers. Thus, the hypothesized genetic liability is greatest with the moderate abusers and less robust with *both* mild and severe abusers. This seems to be a rather implausible mechanism and will need further explanation by Cloninger et al.

A misunderstanding has also arisen from this typology. The type 2 abuser is often described as being associated with extensive alcohol treatment history and a high level of criminality. Actually, these characteristics are associated with the fathers of the identified type 2 abusers. The abusers, themselves, are classified as moderate (i.e., two to three temperance board registrations), with no history of treatment or criminality. This is a widespread misinterpretation of the Swedish data that has obvious and dramatic implications for treatment and research.

Iowa Studies

Cadoret et al. (1985, 1987) have reported on two separate cohorts of adoptees in Des Moines, Iowa. These have been, by far, the most influential American studies of the genetics of alcoholism and antisocial personality reported to date; however, there are two major problems that I would point out.

First, these studies suffer from a lack of objective information about the biological parents, particularly the biological father. That is, much of the critical information used to derive an alcoholism diagnosis in the biological father is not obtained directly and may even be based on information provided by the biological mother. The veracity and reliability of such data must be considered suspect unless confirmed by an additional source.

The second issue in the Iowa studies concerns diagnosis of alcoholism in the adoptees. Diagnoses were made by Cadoret, himself, blind to the biologic background of the adoptees. Diagnosis was based primarily on interviews with the adoptee and the adoptee's parents. Additional data were garnered from available records of treatment for psychiatric or behavioral problems. From this information, Cadoret was able to ascertain alcoholism in accordance with DSM-III criteria, which is a real strength of these studies. However, data analyses were not only conducted on the individuals who met criteria, but also on those who were "possible" alcohol abusers, defined as "when one criterion behavior was lacking to make the definite diagnosis." Given the rather restrictive nature of the DSM-III criteria, it is not clear how the possible diagnosis was made.

This problem is of some consequence, since the 1985 study reported 14 men who met definite criteria for alcohol abuse or dependence and an additional 23 men who were classified as possible alcohol abusers. However, the data are analyzed and reported on the combined sample of 37 definite *or* possible alcohol abusers. The basic diagnostic data are not reported in the more recent paper (Cadoret et al. 1987), but presumably were similar to the earlier description (Cadoret et al. 1985).

It might be said that despite some minor methodological and statistical anomalies, these three adoption studies all converge on a similar result. Given the widely varying diagnostic criteria that the studies employed, this is a difficult argument to sustain. Table 2 lists the minimum criteria for an alcohol abuse diagnosis for each of the three major adoption studies. These criteria, in turn, determine the reported rates of abuse. In the three groups of studies discussed above, diagnoses of alcohol abuse that are genetically influenced range from 7.1% to 29.7%; environmentally induced diagnoses range from 4.1% to 32.4%; and gene × environment interaction diagnoses range from 0% to 26.7%. This suggests that the samples may be too diverse to

Table 2
Minimum Criteria for Alcohol Diagnosis

Goodwin et al. (1973)

a. Drank daily for at least 1 year *and* had six or more drinks at least two or three times a month, *or* drank six or more drinks at least once a week for over a year.
b. Must have had alcohol-related problems in at least three of the following four groups:

Group 1
  social disapproval of drinking by friends, parents
  marital problems from drinking

Group 2
  job trouble from drinking
  drinking-related traffic arrests
  other police trouble from drinking

Group 3
  frequent blackouts
  tremors
  withdrawal hallucinations
  withdrawal convulsions
  delirium tremens

Group 4
  loss of control
  morning drinking

Cadoret et al. (1985)

DSM-III: [37.8% (14) definite; 62.2% (23) possible]
  pattern of pathological alcohol use, impairment in social or occupational functioning, and duration of disturbance for at least 1 month

Cloninger et al. (1981)

One temperance board registration; never been treated for alcoholism

---

draw any general conclusions or that these research groups are studying qualitatively different phenomena.

Two very important considerations have been overlooked in most of the research that investigates the genetics of alcoholism. First, most individuals with a biological family history of alcoholism do not become alcoholic themselves. In fact, a rather small proportion of these individuals go on to abuse alcohol. Second, the majority of individuals from these studies who are diagnosed as alcoholics do not have a biological family history of alcoholism. That is, unspecified environmental factors are the predominant influence in most cases of alcohol abuse, and these environmental factors are likely not to be shared by individuals in the same family—nonshared environmental effects. Recent studies of monozygotic twins reared apart suggest that for most variables studied, genetic factors account for about half of the variance, and nonshared environment accounts for the majority of environmental effects. This has been demonstrated both in the Minnesota Study of Twins Reared Apart (Tellegen et al. 1988) and the Swedish Adoption and Twin Study of Aging (SATSA; Bergeman et al. 1988; Pedersen et al. 1988, 1989; Plomin et al. 1988a,b).

Research investigating environmental influences in the transmission of alcoholism is rare, because as Schuckit has said, "It's easier to study the biology [of alcoholism]. I know I'm only studying part of the pie, but there are no good environmental measures at this point." (Bower 1988). This is true only to the extent that it is easier to identify individuals at putative high risk for alcoholism as a function of their family history of alcohol abuse. However, recent research that specifically focuses on environmental factors has shown significant effects. For example, Richardson et al. (1989) have shown that children who are not supervised more than 11 hours per week are at a significantly increased risk for substance abuse compared to children who are supervised after school; this relationship obtained across all levels of sociodemographic status, involvement in extracurricular activities, social influences, and stress. The results reported by these workers also suggest an active gene-environment correlation effect, i.e., risk-taking individuals who select friends who smoke and smoke-inducing situations increased the relationship between time spent in self-care and substance use. Holmes and Robins (1988) report that differential parental disciplinary practice recalled retrospectively discriminates siblings who do and do not become alcoholics. Preliminary data from an ongoing project at the Addiction Research Center at the University of Pennsylvania demonstrate a significant relationship between alcoholism risk status and perception of the impact of very early life history events. Specifically, young men with an alcohol-abusing father report a significantly greater negative impact score of life events for preschool, elementary school, and junior high school periods than do young men without an alcohol-abusing father (J.S. Searles and A.I. Alterman, in prep.). These and other studies should encourage research that at least takes into account environmental factors. They are likely to be important etiological factors, as well as motivational and catalytic influences.

I am not suggesting that we abandon the search for a genetic mechanism that may underlie *some*, but certainly not the majority, of alcoholism; however, I think that we should pursue environmental factors with the same enthusiasm and research vigor that has been apparent in the genetic area. Multifocal studies that consider both genetic and environmental influences, as well as gene × environment interactions and gene-environment correlations will allow for a more accurate specification of an etiological model that considers developmental processes in both biology and environment.

REFERENCES

American Psychiatric Association (DSM-III). 1980. *Diagnostic and statistical manual of mental disorders,* 3rd edition. American Psychiatric Association, Washington, D.C.

Begleiter, H. 1988. Stimulus intensity and evoked brain potentials in subjects at risk for alcoholism. Paper presented at the annual meeting of the Research Society on Alcoholism, Wild Dunes, S.C.

Begleiter, H., B. Porjesz, B. Bihari, and B. Kissin. 1984. Event-related brain potentials in boys at risk for alcoholism. *Science* **225:** 1493.

Bergeman, C.S., R. Plomin, G.E. McClearn, N.L. Pedersen, and L. Friberg. 1988. Genotype-environment interaction in personality development: Identical twins reared apart. *Psychology Aging* **3:** 399.

Bohman, M., C.R. Cloninger, S. Sigvardsson, and A.-L. von Knorring. 1983. Gene-environment interaction in the psychopathology of Swedish adoptees: Studies of the origins of alcoholism and criminality. In *Childhood psychopathology and development* (ed. S.B. Guze et al.), p. 265. Raven Press, New York.

Bower, B. 1988. Alcoholism's elusive genes. *Sci. News* **134:** 74.

Cadoret, R.J., E. Troughton, and T.W. O'Gorman. 1987. Genetic and environmental factors in alcohol abuse and antisocial personality. *J. Stud. Alcohol* **48:** 1.

Cadoret, T.J., T.W. O'Gorman, T.W. Troughton, and R. Heywood. 1985. Alcoholism and antisocial personality: Interrelationships, genetic and environmental factors. *Arch. Gen. Psychiatry* **42:** 161.

Cloninger, C.R. 1986. A unified biosocial theory of personality and its role in the development of anxiety states. *Psychiat. Dev.* **3:** 167.

Cloninger, C.R., M. Bohman, and S. Sigvardsson. 1981. Inheritance of alcohol abuse: Cross fostering analysis of adopted men. *Arch. Gen. Psychiatry* **38:** 861.

Committee on Nomenclature and Statistics (DSM-III). 1980. *Diagnostic and statistical manual of mental disorders.* American Psychiatric Association, Washington, D.C.

Cotton, N.S. 1979. The familial incidence of alcoholism. *J. Stud. Alcohol.* **40:** 89.

Goodwin, D.W., F. Schulsinger, L. Hermansen, S.B. Guze, and G. Winokur. 1973. Alcohol problems in adoptees raised apart from biological parents. *Arch. Gen. Psychiatry* **28:** 238.

Hill, S.Y., J. Armstrong, S.R. Steinhauer, T. Baughman, and J. Zubin. 1987. Static ataxia as a psychobiological marker for alcoholism. *Alcohol. Clin. Exp. Res.* **11:** 345.

Holmes, S.J. and L.N. Robins. 1988. The role of parental disciplinary practices in the development of depression and alcoholism. *Psychiatry* **51:** 24.

Lester, D. 1988. Genetic theory: An assessment of the heritability of alcoholism. In *Theories on alcoholism* (ed. C.D. Chaudron and D.A. Wilkinson), p. 1. Addiction Research Foundation, Toronto.

Littrell, J. 1988. The Swedish studies of the adopted children of alcoholics. *J. Stud. Alcohol* **49:** 491.

Murray, R.M., C.A. Clifford, and H.M.D. Gurling. 1983. Twin and adoption studies: How good is the evidence for a genetic role? In *Recent developments in alcoholism* (ed. M. Galanter), vol. 1, p. 25. Plenum Press, New York.

Nagoshi, C.T. and J.R. Wilson. 1987. Influence of family alcoholism history on alcohol metabolism, sensitivity, and tolerance. *Alcohol. Clin. Exp. Res.* **11:** 392.

Neville, H.J. and A.L. Schmidt. 1985. Event-related brain potentials in subjects at risk for alcoholism. In *Early identification of alcohol abuse* (ed. N. Chang and H. Chao), res. monog. 17, p. 228. National Institute on Alcoholism and Alcohol Abuse, Rockville, Maryland.

Pedersen, N.L., R. Plomin, G.E. McClearn, and L. Friberg. 1988. Neuroticism, extraversion, and related traits in adult twins reared apart and reared together. *J. Pers. Soc. Psychol.* **55:** 950.

Pedersen, N.L., P. Lichtensen, R. Plomin, U. DeFaire, G.E. McClearn, and K.A. Matthews. 1989. Genetic and environmental influences for type A-like measures and related traits: A study of twins reared apart and twins reared together. *Psychosom. Med.* **51:** 428.

Plomin, R., G.E. McClearn, N.L. Pedersen, J.R. Nesselroade, and C.S. Bergeman. 1988a. Genetic influence on childhood family environment perceived retrospectively from the last half of the life span. *Dev. Psychol.* **24:** 738.

Plomin, R., N.L. Pedersen, G.E. McClearn, J.R. Nesselroade, and C.S. Bergeman. 1988b. EAS temperaments during the last half of the life span: Twins reared apart and twins reared together. *Psychology Aging* **3:** 43.

Polich, J. 1984. P300 latency reflects personal drinking history. *Psychophysiology* **21:** 592.

Polich, J. and F.E. Bloom. 1986. P300 and alcohol consumption in normals and individuals at risk for alcoholism. *Prog. Neuro-psychopharmacol. Biol. Psychiatry* **10:** 201.

———. 1987. P300 from normals and children of alcoholics. *Alcohol* **4:** 301.

———. 1988. Event-related brain potentials in individuals at high and low risk for developing alcoholism: Failure to replicate. *Alcohol. Clin. Exp. Res.* **12:** 368.

Polich, J., R.J. Haier, M. Buchsbaum, and F.E. Bloom. 1988. Assessment of young men at risk for alcoholism with P300 from a visual discrimination task. *J. Stud. Alcohol* **49:** 186.

Richardson, J.L., K. Dwyer, K. McGuigan, W.B. Hansen, C. Dent, C.A. Johnson, S.Y. Sussman, B. Brannon, and B. Flay. 1989. Substance use among eighth-grade students who take care of themselves after school. *Pediatrics* **84:** 556.

Scarr, S. and K. McCartney. 1983. How people make their own environments: A theory of genotype-environment effects. *Child Dev.* **54:** 424.

Schuckit, M.A. 1981. Peak blood alcohol levels in men at high risk for the future development of alcoholism. *Alcohol. Clin. Exp. Res.* **5:** 64.

———. 1985. Ethanol-induced changes in body sway in men at high alcoholism risk. *Arch. Gen. Psychiatry* **42:** 375.

Schuckit, M.A. and M. Irwin. 1989. An analysis of the clinical relevance of type 1 and type 2 alcoholics. *Br. J. Addict.* **84:** 869.

Searles, J.S. 1988. The role of genetics in the pathogenesis of alcoholism. *J. Abnorm. Psychol.* **97**: 153.

———. 1990a. Behavior genetic research and risk for alcoholism among children of alcoholics. In *Children of alcoholics: Critical perspectives* (ed. M. Windle and J.S. Searles), p. 99. Guilford Press, New York.

———. 1990b. The contribution of genetic factors to the development of alcoholism: A critical review. In *Alcoholism and the family* (ed. R.L. Collins et al.). Guilford Press, New York. (In press).

Tarter, R.E., A.M. Hegedus, G. Goldstein, C. Shelly, and A.I. Alterman. 1984. Adoloescent sons of alcoholics: Neuropsychological and personality characteristics. *Alcohol. Clin. Exp. Res.* **8**: 216.

Tellegen, A., D.T. Lykken, T.J. Bouchard, Jr., K.J. Wilcox, N.L. Segal, and S. Rich. 1988. Personality similarity in twins reared apart and together. *J. Pers. Soc. Psychol.* **54**: 1031.

Whipple, S. and E.P. Noble. 1986. The effects of familial alcoholism on visual event-related potentials. *Psychophysiology* **23**: 470.

COMMENTS

Billings: What comprises a negative life event?

Searles: Actually, that's an interesting question, because you would think something like divorce of parents would be a prototypical negative life event, although it could be rated positively by some people, and that has actually occurred. So, it's death of a parent, death of a friend, doing something terrible in school, failing a grade, things of that nature. It's fairly easy to clarify whether they're positive or negative, although again, in many cases they can mean both positive and negative things to the individual.

Begleiter: I think in reviewing the influence of the genetics of alcoholism, you have taken a very selective view of the literature. That is to say, you have focused in your formal published review, as well as in today's presentation, on adoption studies. Indeed, there are other data that are at the very least equally interesting, if not more compelling.

Searles: I have talked about the other studies in the paper. I didn't talk about them today.

Begleiter: But you focus primarily on adoption. Your major criticisms deal with the adoption studies.

Searles: Actually, when I first submitted that paper I did not have anything in there on high-risk studies at all.

Begleiter: I wasn't just talking about high-risk studies. I mean, there are other studies.

Searles: I do talk about twin studies, too, in the paper. The reason I focus on the adoption studies, even though I did write a section on high-risk, is that they certainly provide the most compelling evidence to date that I know about, that converge in this finding.

Begleiter: In your high-risk study do you worry at all about sporadic cases, since you define high-risk as someone with an alcoholic father? Is that, in fact, the best genetic definition that you can come up with?

Searles: Yes, it is, in fact. I'm not sure how else we can do that.

Begleiter: Are you troubled by your statistical results when you do 12, 15, 20 comparisons and only one finding comes up significant? In some quarters these may be referred to as spurious findings.

Searles: I agree with you, and I'm not comfortable with that. The reason we are taking so many measures and doing so many scales is to try to do some model-building. I think it's a legitimate criticism. I didn't want to make a big deal about those differences.

Tabakoff: Then, in terms of all the scales that you have administered, there were a very limited number of significant findings and some close significance. Can you review those significant findings for low impersistence?

Searles: Low impersistence on the dots are—and low in control on the MPQ—and also, we have a rather large effect on what is called the childhood history questionnaire—it's called the leisure activities blank, which is the Zucker and Noll ASP measure. That is a fairly large effect; that's the biggest effect we have.

Tabakoff: How are persistence and control related?

Searles: They seem to be related to some sort of ASP-type non-delay of gratification or to impulsivity, which is one of the major dimensions of most measures of ASP.

Schuckit: Although I disagree with a number of the things you have said, and although I have some problems with some of your statements about what percentage of alcoholics have a close family member who is alcoholic, I want to tell you how much I appreciate the fact that you come before a group like this. Although I disagree again with some of your conclusions, the fact of the matter is every now and then somebody needs to hit us with a sledgehammer and say, "Rethink some of those things. I'm telling you I look at it differently. At least stop and rethink some of those things." So, thank you.

Goldman: I'm sure that we all second Marc's comment. I would like to focus some attention now on some sensitive data that was presented, which was on the so-called nonshared environmental effects on various personalities. I would just point out that not included in that analysis was measurement error.

Searles: Right. Well, that's part of the nonshared effect.

Goldman: That's part of the nonshared effect. How large is it? We know that for a number of traits, for instance, heritability is between 40% and 60%. For example, I noted that the three traits that interest me most—extroversion, harm avoidance, and impulsivity—were all between 40% and 50%.

Searles: Right.

Goldman: Just what that measurement error is we don't know. We do know that when one looks at personality variables as Kagan did for introversion and extroversion, it appears that the differences between individuals are set early. One really wonders just what these nonshared environmental effects are.

Searles: I quite agree with you. I think that it's an intriguing finding, nonetheless.

Li: In your study when you find lack of differences between the two groups, how much of that is a selection bias because you are looking at college students and you really left out a large proportion of people who might be, let's say, high risk and yet unable to get into college because of personality differences, high school dropout, et cetera?

Searles: That's why we're doing the other part of the study, which is the VA part. The whole purpose of that part of the study is to pick up those individuals.

Li: You can pick up young VA people?

Searles: No. We're picking up their fathers and having them refer their sons. You're right, that is an important consideration, and also, part of the findings (the non-findings, I should say) is a function of power. Again, that's a very small sample size.

Li: That's right. There's no power there.

Reich: I want to remind us that just because someone is a geneticist does not mean he is a hereditarian at all. I know people in this room, and I could tell you who are the hereditarians and who aren't, and you would be very, very surprised. In general, the people who are closest to the genes on a hereditarian scale would be the least hereditarian. Interest in the genetics of alcoholism is blind-sided, I could say, by certain Southern California wizards from time to time who assume that anybody interested in genetics is a hereditarian. It's a very important distinction that I think we should all make in our presentations and in thinking about these things.

Sambrook: Maybe we should give Dr. Searles a purple heart.

Genetic Epidemiology of Alcoholism: Observations Critical in the Design and Analysis of Linkage Studies

C. ROBERT CLONINGER
Washington University School of Medicine
St. Louis, Missouri 63110

The search for specific genes causing susceptibility to alcoholism is difficult because of the complex developmental pathway from the genotype and environment of alcoholics to their alcohol-related behavior. To justify and design appropriate experimental designs for linkage studies of alcoholism, we need to know as much as possible about its mode of inheritance. Prior pedigree studies show that the mode of inheritance of alcoholism is complex and non-Mendelian (see below). The number of relevant susceptibility genes and the distribution or the size of their effects remain uncertain, but the number is likely to be large and to include both major and minor effects on penetrance and expression.

The non-Mendelian characteristics of alcoholism include both incomplete penetrance and variable expression of relevant genotypes, but truly sporadic cases without underlying heritable predisposition appear to be infrequent. Strong evidence of the incomplete penetrance of genotypes that can cause alcoholism is based on studies of the prediction of risk in grandchildren of alcoholics and the incomplete concordance of monozygotic twins for alcoholism. Evidence of the variable expressivity of alcoholic genotypes is shown by adoption studies in which the effects of genetic and environmental factors can be separated. Furthermore, prospective studies of adoptees have also confirmed the important interaction of genetic and environmental factors in development of different clinical subgroups of alcoholics.

In view of the importance of such observations for the design and analysis of linkage studies, the key aspects of the genetic epidemiology of alcoholism are described and critically discussed from the perspective of a linkage analyst. First, studies of recurrence risk in pedigrees and segregation analysis studies are summarized to describe the non-Mendelian pattern of inheritance. Second, studies that document that the penetrance of relevant genotypes is incomplete are presented. Third, the variable expressivity of alcoholigenic genotypes is described in family members, including adoptees. Fourth, the interaction of genetic and environmental factors is considered in cross-fostering analyses of adoptees and in prospective studies of adoptees. Finally, these findings are discussed in relation to critiques by the few psychosocial scientists who have yet to recognize the importance of genetic factors in alcoholism and in relation to the difficulties investigators face in their efforts to identify specific susceptibility genes and other specific risk or protective factors in the environment.

Non-Mendelian Mode of Inheritance of Alcoholism

Susceptibility to alcoholism is strongly familial, but its mode of inheritance cannot be explained by simple Mendelian patterns of inheritance, such as the effects of a single autosomal or X-linked gene with complete penetrance. In addition, there have been large group differences in the prevalence of alcoholism because of sociocultural influences: Both consumption and complications have varied widely from one historical era to another and currently vary from country to country, between social classes, between persons of different occupation, and between men and women (Cloninger et al. 1981). To assess compatibility of the familial transmission of alcoholism with alternative patterns of inheritance, information is needed about the lifetime risk of alcoholism in multiple classes of relatives under comparable conditions and from segregation analyses of systematically ascertained pedigrees.

Fortunately, a wide range of observations have been made over the past four decades in Sweden during a time that country has been relatively stable and homogeneous socially. Sweden has maintained excellent records about the consumption and complications of alcohol. Observations about the cumulative lifetime risk of recurrent alcohol problems or alcoholism in family members of recurrent alcoholics with varying degrees of genetic relationship are summarized in Table 1. The lifetime risk of recurrent alcohol problems in men increases from 7% in the general population to 12% probandwise concordance in those who share about one-quarter of their genes (grand-

Table 1
Family Studies of Recurrent Alcohol Abuse in Swedish Men

Source	Relationship	Probandwise concordance n	%
Kaij (1960)	MZ twins	27	70
Kaij (1960)	DZ twins	60	33
Amark (1951)	singleton sib		
	one alcoholic parent	97	33
	no alcoholic parent	252	17
Bohman (1978)	adopted-away sons	50	20
Kaij and Dock (1975)	grandsons	270	12
Census of 1968	general population		7

sons), to 20-33% in those who share about one-half of their genes (sons and brothers), to 70% in those who are genetically identical (monozygotic twins). If multifactorial inheritance is assumed, the heritability of liability to alcoholism can be computed from these data to be about 67%.

Furthermore, vertical genetic inheritance from parent to child is confirmed by two observations about Swedish families. First, there is greater concordance in brothers who have at least one alcoholic parent than in those who have no alcoholic parents (33% vs. 17%; Amark 1951). Second, adopted-away sons of alcoholics are at threefold increased risk overall compared to other men in the general population (20% vs. 7%; Bohman 1978). Therefore, the familial aggregation of alcoholism cannot be attributed to stratification of social groups with variable rates of alcohol consumption and complications.

Similar findings are available in the United States and other countries, but care must be exercised to compile data that use similar clinical criteria, assessment procedures, and controls that permit estimates of the lifetime risk in the general population at the time of study stratified by sex and age. This is illustrated later for the varying estimates of concordance in monozygotic twins that have been reported. In particular, variation by sex and age is highly marked in the United States (Cloninger et al. 1988b). Use of odds ratios or relative risks to compare data in secondary analysis of pooled data, as done recently by some authors (Merikangas 1990), is not fully satisfactory because relative risk ratios are inversely related to the base rate in the general population even when the correlation in liability remains constant (Cloninger et al. 1975). Therefore, it is prudent to use data from a single source rather than pooling data using variable disease definitions in samples in which the base rate of disorder varies across region and time of observation.

Accordingly, it is fortunate that many observations about the familial transmission of alcoholism in the United States have used fairly uniform diagnostic criteria devised by Guze and incorporated in studies conducted by many investigators trained at Washington University, such as George Winokur, Don Goodwin, Marc Schuckit, Ted Reich, and myself. These polythetic criteria are summarized in Table 2 and require symptoms in at least three of four problem groups for a definite diagnosis and in at least two groups for a probable diagnosis. These criteria have the advantages of good correspondence to traditional disease concepts of alcoholism and widespread use in studies of families and the general population. They also have the disadvantage that a wide variety of different kinds of problems are treated as indices of a single discrete diagnosis, even though the risk of different medical and social problems may be influenced by different genetic and social antecedents. For example, twin studies have shown that different susceptibility genes influence the risk of alcoholic liver disease and alcoholic dementias (Hrubec and Omenn 1981). Similarly, animal selection experiments reveal

Table 2
Alcohol-related Symptoms Surveyed for Alcoholism Diagnoses

Medical problems
  withdrawal
    shakes
    hallucinations
    withdrawal seizures
  organ damage
    cirrhosis
    gastritis/bleeding
    polyneuropathy
    chronic brain syndrome
  blackouts (at least 2)
  benders
  impotence

Control problems
  trouble stopping
  admits no control
  tried to limit
  morning drinking
  nonbeverage alcohol

Social problems
  arrests
  automobile trouble
  lost job
  fighting
  lost friends

Prior identification
  family objects to level of individual's drinking
  self-admitted excessive drinking
  others thought individual drank too much
  guilt about drinking

Alcoholic diagnoses were made using Guze's criteria (Guze et al. 1988). Definite alcoholism required at least three symptoms in each of three symptom categories. Probable alcoholism required two symptoms in each of two symptoms groups.

different susceptibility genes for alcohol-seeking behavior, susceptibility to behavioral tolerance ("holding liquor well"), and susceptibility to seizures upon withdrawal of alcohol following chronic intoxication.

Lifetime risk of alcoholism in first-degree relatives of alcoholics is summarized in Table 3 from a study of a large consecutive series of white men and women hospitalized for treatment of their alcoholism (Cloninger et al.

Table 3
Alcoholism in Adult First-degree Relatives of White Hospitalized Alcoholics in St. Louis

Sex and severity in relatives	Male probands (n = 132) f/n	%	Female probands (n = 52) f/n	%
Father/son				
definite alcoholism	24/67	35.8	13/32	40.6
probable alcoholism	7/67	10.4	6/32	18.8
Brother				
definite alcoholism	52/108	48.1	16/35	45.7
probable alcoholism	23/108	21.3	6/35	17.1
Mother/daughter				
definite alcoholism	16/102	15.7	3/45	6.7
probable alcoholism	7/102	6.9	4/45	8.9
Sister				
definite alcoholism	17/113	15.0	10/46	21.7
probable alcoholism	7/113	6.2	2/46	4.3

Data from Cloninger et al. (1988b).

1988b). It is noteworthy that in studies of intact families the risk is the same in relatives regardless of the sex of the alcoholic proband, even though alcoholism is three to five times more frequent in men than women. It is also important to recognize that the risks are the same whether probands are ascertained from hospitals, as shown here, or whether probands are ascertained from other high-risk populations like criminal men (Cloninger et al. 1988b).

Age and birth cohort have a substantial effect on risk of alcoholism, however. Figure 1 shows the cumulative probability of alcoholism in male first-degree relatives of alcoholic probands in the St. Louis study as a function of the age of the individual and the year of birth of the relative. The cumulative risk of definite alcoholism by age 25 years increases with the year of birth from 26% in the 61 men born before 1924 to 34% in the 56 born 1925–1934, 52% in the 54 born 1935–1944, 63% in the 76 born 1945–1954, and 67% in the 141 born after 1954. It should be remembered that the younger birth cohorts have yet to pass through their full period of risk. For example, the risks of alcoholism at 25 and 40 years of age increase from 22% to 38% in men born before 1924, from 36% to 48% in men born 1925–1934, and from 53% to 63% in men born 1935–1944. As a consequence of such variation, it is necessary to distinguish multiple liability classes according to

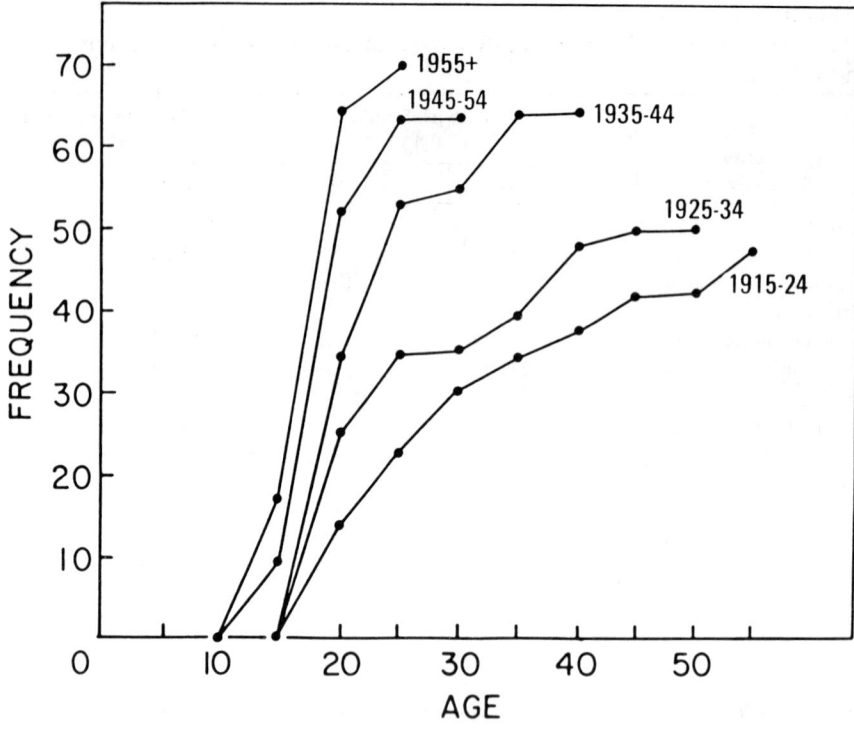

Figure 1
Cumulative risk of alcoholism in first-degree male relatives of alcoholics by the age and year of birth of the relatives.

age, sex, and birth cohort in carrying out complex segregation analyses of alcoholism.

Complex segregation analysis of alcoholism has been carried out in these families taking variation in risk according to age and sex into account (Gilligan et al. 1987). Pedigree analyses were carried out using the computer program POINTER to obtain maximum likelihood estimates of parameters defining a mixed model including effects of a putative single diallelic autosomal locus superimposed on a multifactorial background. The major locus parameters included the allele frequency (q), the displacement between the two homozygotes (t), and a dominance parameter (d) defining the relative position of the heterozygote between the homozygotes as the product dt. The multifactorial heritability in liability to alcoholism was estimated as the proportion (H) of the total variance in liability attributable to additive polygenic or sociocultural effects. The ratio (Z) of adult to child heritability in liability was also estimated.

Table 4
Complex Segregation Analysis of Definite Alcoholism in White Hospitalized Alcoholics in St Louis

Gender of proband	Number of families	d	t	q	H	Z	$-2\ln L + c$
Total sample	288	1.00	1.69	0.18	0.39	0.10	−1406.66
Male probands	209	0.00	5.44	0.07	0.74	(1)[a]	−1088.14
Female probands	79	(0)	(0)	(0)	0.83	0.31	− 319.73

Overall heterogeneity $\chi^2 = 1.21$ (1–3 df)[b]

Models were used to separate families of male probands into two groups reflecting patterns of inheritance. Data from Gilligan et al. (1987).
[a]Parameters set in parentheses were fixed at value.
[b]Degrees of freedom were between 1 and 3, because three nonboundary parameter estimates were obtained for families of male probands and only one for families of female probands.

The segregation parameter estimates obtained are summarized in Table 4 for the total sample and for families of male and female probands, as reported by Gilligan et al. (1988). Although heterogeneity among the families of male and female probands was not statistically significant overall, the patterns of transmission of liability to alcoholism appeared to be markedly dissimilar. Accordingly, we tested the hypothesis that the families of male probands were composed of two etiologically heterogeneous subtypes: type 1, which is similar to that of most women ("female-like"), and type 2, which is typical of most men ("male-like"). This hypothesis, which had been generated by the Stockholm Adoption Study described below, was supported by the finding that two subtypes explained the segregation significantly better than did the assumption of homogeneity. For example, heritability estimates were 88% for type 2 families of male probands compared to 21% for type 1 families of male probands, which significantly fits the data better than the composite heritability of 69% under the assumption of homogeneity of 69% (heterogeneity chi-square=14.22 with 1 degree of freedom, $p < 0.01$).

The segregation analyses of the type 2 families indicated significant evidence of a major gene effect, with maximum likelihood estimates of allele frequency $q=0.11$, displacement between homozygotes $t=2.30$, dominance parameter $d=1.0$, and multifactorial background $H=0.15$. Compatibility to Mendelian transmission was tested by estimating the transmission probability of the susceptibility allele from parent to child, which was found to be close to the value of 0.5 expected under Mendelian transmission. In contrast, there was no evidence for any effect of a major locus in type 1 families. The results of the segregation analyses are summarized in Figure 2.

Overall, the results of segregation analyses in St. Louis and other data about risks of alcoholism in different classes of relatives of alcoholics indicate

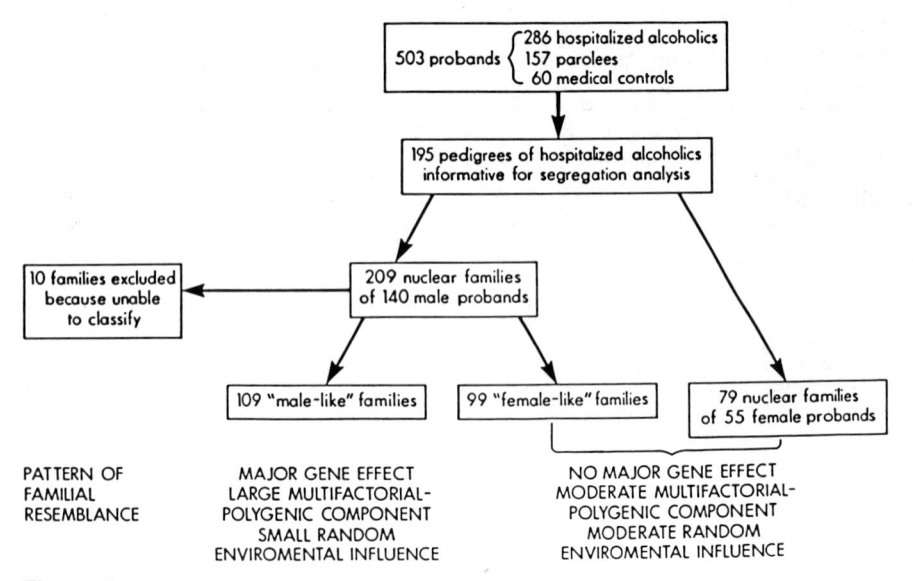

```
                    ┌─ 286 hospitalized alcoholics
        503 probands ┤  157 parolees
                    └─ 60 medical controls

        195 pedigrees of hospitalized alcoholics
             informative for segregation analysis

                    209 nuclear families
                    of 140 male probands

10 families excluded
because unable
to classify

  109 "male-like" families   99 "female-like" families    79 nuclear families
                                                          of 55 female probands
```

PATTERN OF FAMILIAL RESEMBLANCE	MAJOR GENE EFFECT LARGE MULTIFACTORIAL-POLYGENIC COMPONENT SMALL RANDOM ENVIROMENTAL INFLUENCE	NO MAJOR GENE EFFECT MODERATE MULTIFACTORIAL-POLYGENIC COMPONENT MODERATE RANDOM ENVIROMENTAL INFLUENCE

Figure 2
Summary of segregation analysis in St. Louis family study of alcoholism.

that alcoholism has a complex mode of inheritance. No single Mendelian gene with complete penetrance can explain its pattern of familial transmission. Segregation analyses are compatible with either of two possible modes of inheritance: (1) genetic heterogeneity, in which there are two distinct subtypes, including type 1 with moderate multifactorial inheritance and no major gene locus and type 2 with both a major dominant gene locus and high polygenic heritability; or (2) a mixed model comprising the effects of a major gene with a multifactorial background. In many ways, these are not practically different from one another, because under the mixed model the effects of the major gene will vary in its importance. The only practical question is whether there are clinical indices that allow investigators to distinguish families in which the effects of the major susceptibility allele are operative from those in which they are not. This will be examined in more detail after considering other more direct evidence of incomplete penetrance and variable expression.

Diagnostic Stability and Incomplete Penetrance

To assess evidence of incomplete penetrance based on concordance between relatives, it is first necessary to evaluate diagnostic stability or the concordance for diagnosis in the same individual at different times. Studies of diagnostic stability in alcoholism indicate moderate to high reliability. Even when observations are made independently over many years, more than 80% of individuals receive the same diagnosis at follow-up, as shown in Table 5. Furthermore, individuals whose alcoholism was only diagnosed at follow-up had reported more alcohol problems at index than others, but were younger and required more time for the full disorder to become evident. Other inconsistent subjects tended to have fewer and less severe features of alcoholism. Overall, consistency of diagnosis is highest in individuals with the early onset of a large number of severe symptoms, such as benders, loss of control, blackouts, and withdrawal symptoms. Definite and/or primary alcoholics are more likely to be diagnostically stable than probable and/or secondary alcoholics, particularly those with early onset of depression and later alcohol abuse (Guze et al. 1988). It is noteworthy that the diagnostically stable features of early-onset severe symptoms have also been described in alcoholics who are most likely to have a positive family history; prototypic descriptions of familial alcoholics may have been confounded with the characteristics of diagnostic certainty and severity of illness (Cloninger et al. 1979; Cloninger 1987).

If 84% diagnostic consistency is found in alcoholics assessed at two independent interviews, what is the diagnostic consistency in the monozygotic cotwin of an alcoholic? Since monozygotic (MZ) twins have the same genotype, diagnostic concordance in MZ twins provides an upper limit to the penetrance of genotypes that cause alcoholism. Lack of concordance in MZ twins is caused by incomplete penetrance and/or truly sporadic cases.

Twin studies of alcoholism are summarized in Table 6. The MZ concordance of recurrent alcohol abuse or alcoholism in men was found to be about 70% in two studies with personal examination of subjects in both Sweden and the United States. The estimate of 26% by Hrubec and Omenn (1981) is a lower limit based on military records of veterans. The estimate of 33% by

Table 5
Consistency of Diagnosis of Alcoholism in 500 Psychiatric Outpatients Reinterviewed after 6–10 Years

Lifetime alcoholism diagnosis at index interview	n	Lifetime diagnosis of alcoholism at follow-up	
		% yes	% no
Yes	70	84	16
No	430	13	87

Data from Guze et al. (1988).

Table 6
Concordance in Twin Studies of Alcoholism

| Source and zygosity | Probandwise concordance for alcoholism ||||
| | men || women ||
	n	%	n	%
Kaij (1960)				
MZ	27	70	—	
DZ	60	33	—	
Hrubec and Omenn (1981)				
MZ	271	26	—	
DZ	444	12	—	
Gurling et al. (1981)				
MZ	15	33	13	8
DZ	20	30	8	13
Pickens and Svikis (1988)				
MZ	40	70	24	29
DZ	53	53	22	36

Gurling et al. (1981) was obtained by personal examinations in a small sample of alcoholics identified in a psychiatric sample in which 55% of the alcoholics were also diagnosed as depressives. Gurling and his associates defined alcoholism according to the presence or absence of the dependence syndrome that is emphasized in Great Britain, rather than in terms of multiple problems as described by Guze et al. (1988). (Later work in adoption studies suggested that such severe dependence syndromes are too narrow a definition for genetic purposes and depend much more on environmental interactions than do other definitions, as discussed below in the section on genetic heterogeneity and gene/environment interaction.) Omitting the military record sample, the 82 MZ twins with personal examinations had an overall concordance of 63%.

Such concordance rates in individuals with the same genotype are probably lower than the expected diagnostic stability, suggesting some effects of incomplete penetrance or sporadic cases in men. In contrast, the concordance in MZ female twins is about 22% in the 47 pairs reported in two series. This suggests either that penetrance is lower in women than in men, or that sporadic cases are more frequent in women.

Kaij and Dock (1975) reported equal risk of alcoholism in the grandsons of alcoholics regardless of the sex of the grandparent or parent. They concluded quite properly that this made X-linked transmission unlikely. It also suggests that penetrance for alcoholism is more complete in men than in women, who often carry a heritable susceptibility to alcoholism without manifesting it.

Variable Expressivity and Clinical Heterogeneity

Alcoholics have a wide range of associated psychiatric disorders, and these comorbid disorders are associated with differences in the distribution of illness in their family members. The most common primary diagnoses in alcoholics are major depressive disorder and antisocial personality disorder (ASP). Table 7 shows that the psychiatric disorders in relatives are associated with the primary diagnosis of alcoholic probands. These comorbid psychiatric disorders must be taken into account in family studies of alcoholism.

To understand the familial relationship of alcoholism to other disorders like ASP, it is necessary to examine psychopathology in relatives of probands who are not necessarily alcoholics themselves. Note that all of the probands described in Table 7 were alcoholics. The only disorders other than substance abuse that are associated with the substantially increased familial risk of primary alcoholism are ASP and somatization disorder (also called Briquet's syndrome or hysteria) (Cloninger et al. 1979). Although primary alcoholics have an increased likelihood of relatives with primary depression, primary depressive probands who are not also alcoholics have only slightly increased likelihood of relatives with primary alcoholism (for a detailed analysis of this asymmetric relationship, see Cloninger et al. 1979). However, individuals with ASP and/or somatization disorder consistently have an excess of relatives with primary alcoholism; most primary alcoholics have few antisocial relatives. Table 8 summarizes data about the familial relationship of ASP and alcoholism. Together, Tables 7 and 8 show that ASP increases the risk of alcoholism both in the same individual and in relatives. These data contradict the hypothesis of Schuckit (this volume) that primary alcoholism and ASP are discrete diseases that do not share etiologic factors.

Table 7
Psychiatric Disorders in First-degree Relatives of Alcoholic Probands by Primary Diagnosis

| Diagnosis of proband | Primary diagnosis of first-degree relatives ||||||
| | alcoholism || depression || ASP ||
	f/n	%	f/n	%	f/n	%
Alcoholism	184/807	23[a]	78/535	15	19/516	4
Depression	19/130	15	24/89	27[a]	3/70	4
ASP	18/106	17	14/72	19	15/68	22[a]

Diagnoses are based on all available data about subjects over 17 and age-adjusted by Stromgren method. Prevalence of ASP is given for male relatives only; other prevalences include both sexes (Cloninger et al. 1979).
[a]Relatives with same primary diagnosis as the proband are significantly increased compared to the other (contingency χ^2, <0.05).

Table 8
Primary Alcoholism (1° Alc) and Antisocial Personality in the General Population and the First-degree Relatives of Alcoholic or Antisocial Probands (Men Only)

Diagnosis of proband	Prevalence in general population n	%	Proportion of affected first-degree relatives				
			1° Alc			ASP		
			n	%	r ± S.E.	n	%	r ± S.E.
1° Alc	751	7.6	270	35.2	0.59 ± 0.04^a	516	3.7	0.03 ± 0.06
ASP	329	3.3	120	15.0	0.18 ± 0.07^a	120	16.7	0.43 ± 0.07^a

[a]Correlation between proband and illness in relatives significant ($p < 0.05$).

The asymmetry in familial overlap of ASP and alcoholism, or depression and alcoholism, which arise in probandwise studies can be explained by the etiologic heterogeneity of these disorders. ASP, which is much less common than alcoholism, accounts for only a minority of the alcoholics in the general population. If a consecutive series of primary alcoholics are sampled, most will have no antisocial relatives; on the other hand, if a consecutive series of antisocials are sampled, most will have alcoholic relatives. This heterogeneity was suggested initially by quantitative genetic analysis of family studies (Cloninger et al. 1979). Later adoption studies have confirmed that the clinical and familial heterogeneity was caused by genetic heterogeneity.

Gene/Environment Interaction and Genetic Heterogeneity

Prior to the Stockholm Adoption Study (Bohman et al. 1981; Cloninger et al. 1981), adoption studies of alcoholism had produced inconsistent results that were difficult to reconcile. In the United States, Roe and Burks (1945) found that good foster placement was associated with no alcohol abuse in all but one of 27 children of alcoholic parents and in all but one of 22 children of normal parents. They found that none of 21 adopted-out sons of alcoholics had drinking problems as adults. In contrast, Goodwin et al. (1974) observed that chronic alcoholism was four times more common in 55 adopted-out sons of Danish alcoholics than in 78 such sons of nonalcoholics. However, the risk of alcoholism in adopted-out daughters of Danish alcoholics (nearly all were fathers) was not significantly increased compared with adopted controls (Goodwin et al. 1977). Unfortunately, these different observations were difficult to compare because of differences in the clinical characteristics of alcohol abuse in the biological parents and differences in the adoptive placement. Goodwin studied children of alcoholics who required hospitalization, but none of the parents studied by Roe was treated. In addition, the children of alcoholics studied by Roe were more often placed in rural areas where there was infrequent drinking than were the children of nonalcoholics. Neither study was large enough to subdivide alcohol abusers according to sex, severity, and other clinical characteristics, such as associated antisocial or criminal behavior.

Accordingly, the Stockholm Adoption Study provided an important opportunity to consider the effects of sex, severity of illness, and comorbid features on the pattern of inheritance of alcoholism. The study is described in detail elsewhere (Cloninger et al. 1981, 1985, 1988a). Briefly, all the adopted children born to single women in Stockholm, Sweden, from 1930 to 1949 were studied, along with their biological and adoptive parents. The average age of separation from their biological parents was 4 months, and all were placed in the adoptive home prior to 3 years of age. The biological fathers were nearly always identified because of Swedish legal practices. Clinical information about alcohol abuse was available for the lifetimes of all children and parents based on multiple sources including temperance board registrations, criminal convictions, and a truly comprehensive system of medical records maintained by the National Health Insurance Board. Unfortunately, several critiques of these studies have been in error about the method of case detection despite the explicit nature of our description of the methods in every report. Let it suffice to say here that alcohol abuse was detected if it was identified by any psychiatrist, other physician, police, or other social agencies. This multisource method has been estimated to have a sensitivity of 70% for alcoholism diagnosed by any source including personal interviews (Cloninger et al. 1988b). Furthermore, this multisource method is not biased in favor of detection of subgroups of alcoholics, such as criminal alcoholics, because it identifies subjects from a comprehensive set of sources.

The effect of the sex of the biological parent on the risk of alcohol abuse in the adopted-away children in the Stockholm Adoption Study is shown in Table 9. Alcohol abuse in either the biological father or biological mother increased the risk in adopted-away sons from 14.7% in the sons of nonalcoholics to 22–33% of the sons of alcoholic parents. In contrast, only alcohol abuse in the biological mothers increased the risk in adopted-away daughters from 3% to about 10%. That is, most alcoholic biological fathers did not have an increased risk of alcohol abuse in their adopted-out daughters. This suggested the possibility of a form of sex-limited heterogeneity in which one type of alcoholism was expressed in both men and women, and a second type of alcoholism was expressed only in men.

The hypothesis of genetic heterogeneity was further evaluated by analyzing the relationship of severity of alcohol abuse to genetic background. Following earlier studies of Swedish alcoholics by Kaij (1960), we distinguished (1) men who had single registrations by the temperance board but no treatment

Table 9
Effect of Sex on Inheritance of Susceptibility to Alcoholism in Stockholm Adoption Study

Alcohol abuse in biological parents		Alcohol abuse in adoptees			
		sons		daughters	
father	mother	n	%	n	%
No	no	571	14.7	577	2.8
Yes	no	259	22.4	285	3.5
No	yes	23	26.0	29	10.3
Yes	yes	9	33.3	22	9.1

Data from Cloninger et al. (1985).

(called mild abusers), (2) men who had two or three registrations by the temperance board but no treatment (called moderate abusers), and (3) men with more than three registrations by the temperance board, compulsory treatment for alcoholism, or psychiatric hospitalization with a diagnosis of alcoholism (called severe abusers).

Information about the biological parents of the adopted-away children was used as an index of their genetic background. Discriminant function analyses were carried out to determine what characteristics of the biological parents discriminated the four groups of subjects (i.e., sons with no, mild, moderate, or severe alcohol abuse). The men with either mild or severe abuse had identical genetic backgrounds in all variables except one. In both groups, the biological fathers and biological mothers had increased incidence of adult-onset alcohol abuse and absence of criminality, and the social status of the biological fathers of the severe abusers was lower than that of all the other groups of men. Because of this extensive similarity, the mild and severe alcohol abusers were together called "type 1" alcohol abusers. In contrast, the biological fathers of the moderate abusers were characterized by teenage onset of both alcohol abuse and criminality, and their biological mothers were seldom alcoholic. As a result of this pattern, the mild and severe alcohol abusers were together called type 1 alcohol abusers, and the moderate abusers were called "type 2" or "male-limited" alcoholics.

A comparable effort was made to identify environmental factors that predisposed to later alcoholism. Information about the adoptive parents and early life experiences of the adoptees was used as an index of postnatal environment. Low social status of the adoptive parents, but not alcohol abuse by the adoptive parents, was found to increase the risk of alcohol abuse in the children. Taken together with information about genetic background, environmental factors were particularly important in predicting the severity of

Table 10
Cross-fostering Analysis of Mild and Severe Type 1 Alcoholism

Is genetic background type 1?	Is environmental background mild or severe?	total n	% with mild abuse	% with severe abuse
No	—	448	6.5	4.2
Yes	no	237	7.2	6.3
Yes	mild	91	15.4[a]	7.7
Yes	severe	86	4.7	11.6[a]

[a] Abuse is increased only given both genetic and postnatal predisposition ($p < 0.05$).

alcohol abuse in men with a type 1 genetic background, as shown in Table 10. The major environmental discriminant of mild versus severe alcohol abuse was the occupational status of the adoptive father: Low social status was associated with an increased probability of rapid progression to severe complications. Accordingly, type 1 alcoholism was also called "milieu-limited" alcoholism.

In contrast, environmental background was less predictive of risk of type 2 (or male-limited) alcohol abuse, as shown in Table 11. However, it should be recalled that the sons were only moderate abusers and the fathers were severe criminal alcoholics, so the improved social circumstances of rearing in the adoptees, who were mostly adopted into stable middle class homes, were associated with markedly different outcomes than their biological fathers had manifest.

The observation of gene/environment interaction on severity of alcohol abuse has critical implications for pedigree studies. Often geneticists assume that the most extremely severe definition of the phenotype will define the most heritable subgroup, but this does not appear to be so in alcoholism. The traditional medical predisposition of alcohol dependence develops from un-

Table 11
Cross-fostering Analysis of Type 2 Alcohol Abuse in Men

Is genetic background type 2?	Is environmental background type 2?	total n	% with type 2 abuse
No	no	567	1.9
No	yes	196	4.1
Yes	no	71	16.9[a]
Yes	yes	28	17.9[a]

[a] Risk is significantly increased in those with type 2 genetic background compared to others ($p < 0.01$).

derlying genetic predisposition only under particular environmental conditions. Most cases with a predisposition to type 1 abuse that are reared in stable adoptive homes develop only mild abuse with no treatment. Likewise, most cases with a predisposition to type 2 abuse that are reared in stable adoptive homes develop recurrent abuse but do not receive treatment. Alcohol abuse that requires treatment is usually the consequence of nonadditive interactions between genetic and environmental factors, according to the results of the Stockholm Adoption Study.

Given the importance of the initial findings of genetic heterogeneity and gene/environment interaction in the Stockholm Adoption Study, we carried out further tests of these hypotheses. First, we tested predictions in a large sample of adopted daughters in the Stockholm Adoption Study (Cloninger et al. 1985). The genetic background of the daughters was classified using the exact discriminant functions derived from the sample of sons. We predicted that the daughters of type 1 alcoholic mothers and fathers would have an increased risk of alcohol abuse because the mothers in these families had been alcohol abusers. In contrast, we predicted that the daughters of type 2 alcoholic fathers would have no increased risk of alcoholism, but would show other psychopathology, such as somatization disorder. These predictions were confirmed, as shown in Tables 12 and 13.

Next, we tested the topology by analysis of pedigree data from the United States (Gilligan et al. 1987, 1988). In the Stockholm Adoption Study, we had found that the vast majority of alcoholic women were type 1 alcoholic, whereas alcoholic men were a mixture of type 1 and type 2. As described

Table 12

Psychopathology in the Adopted-out Daughters of Type 1 Biologic Parents and of Nonalcoholic Biologic Parents

Observed psychopathology[b]	Classification of daughters[a]		
	type 1 ($n = 110$) row %	low risk ($n = 282$) row %	significance level p
Alcohol abuse	7.3	2.5	<0.05[c]
Criminality only	0	1.4	n.s.
Somatization only	16.3	16.3	n.s.
Other disability	13.6	15.2	n.s.

n.s. indicates not significant.
[a]Classification of the biologic parents of the women was based on discriminant analysis of an independent sample of parents of adopted men.
[b]The classification system for adoptees was hierarchical, proceeding from alcohol abuse to other psychiatric disability. Thus criminality only indicates criminality and no alcohol abuse with or without somatization or other disability; somatization only indicates neither alcohol abuse nor criminality.
[c]Risk is increased compared with low-risk daughters.

Table 13
Psychopathology in the Adopted-out Daughters of Type 2 Biologic Parents and of Nonalcoholic Biologic Parents

Observed psychopathology[b]	Classification of daughters[a]		significance level p
	type 2 ($n = 105$) row %	low risk ($n = 282$) row %	
Alcohol abuse	4.8	2.5	n.s.
Criminality only	2.9	1.4	n.s.
Somatization only	26.7	16.3	<0.05[c]
Other disability	13.3	15.2	n.s.

n.s. indicates not significant.
[a] Classification of the biologic parents of the women was based on discriminant analysis of an independent sample of parents of adopted men.
[b] The classification system for adoptees was hierachical, proceeding from alcohol abuse to other psychiatric disability. Thus criminality only indicates criminality and no alcohol abuse with or without somatization or other disability; somatization only indicates neither alcohol abuse nor criminality.
[c] Risk is increased compared with low-risk daughters.

earlier, we found evidence supportive of etiologic heterogeneity in families of alcoholic men (see Fig. 2). However, our findings that type 1 men were either mild or severe, but seldom moderate, abusers implied that they differ from type 2 abusers in the rapidity with which they develop loss of control over their drinking. Therefore, we predicted that there should be differences in the characteristic alcohol-related symptoms of alcoholic men in type 1 families compared to men in type 2 families. This was tested by discriminant analyses to characterize the alcohol-related symptoms of men in the families of either male or female alcoholic probands (Table 14). This showed that type 1 alcoholism was characterized by onset of benders, guilt, and loss of control after age 25 years, whereas type 2 is associated with early onset of antisocial conduct associated with alcohol abuse, such as fighting and reckless driving. The type 1 features had often been described as characteristic of alcoholic women, but our results showed that these same features were characteristic of the men in the families of female alcoholics.

These symptom profiles also helped to explain the motivational differences between drinkers in type 1 and type 2 families. Personal interviews with type 1 alcoholics in both the United States and in Sweden revealed that type 1 alcoholics usually had passive-dependent or anxious personalities and enjoyed the antianxiety effects of alcohol. In contrast, type 2 alcoholics usually had antisocial or impulsive-aggressive personality traits and enjoyed the euphoriant or stimulatory effects of alcohol.

To test this motivational hypothesis, we carried out a critical analysis of prospectively collected longitudinal data about the childhood personality of

Table 14
Alcohol-related Symptoms Distinguishing Male Relatives of Female Probands from Those of Male Probands

Distinguishing characteristics of male relatives[a]	Discriminant coefficient	Variable means of relatives by sex of proband male proband ($n = 176$)	female proband ($n = 67$)
Type 1 features			
benders	+0.55	0.16	0.22
guilt	+0.45	0.20	0.30
onset after 25[b]	+0.40	0.18	0.30
loss of control	+0.33	0.25	0.30
cirrhosis/liver disease	+0.25	0.02	0.06
Type 2 features			
inability to abstain	−0.23	0.19	0.15
fights while drinking	−0.44	0.42	0.24
reckless driving while drinking	−0.45	0.32	0.20
treatment for alcohol abuse	−0.46	0.11	0.06
Discriminant function score	—	−0.24	+0.62
Number of alcoholic symptoms[c]			
type 1	—	1.1	2.0
type 2	—	1.0	0.6

[a]Variables were selected by stepwise discriminant function analysis (total explained variance = 12.8%, Wilk's $\lambda = 0.87$, $p = 0.0002$).
[b]Denotes the proportion of relatives with age at onset of a second alcohol-related problem after 25 years of age.
[c]After regression on the total number of Feighner alcoholic symptoms, the residual number of type 1 and type 2 symptoms were negatively correlated in male relatives ($r = 0.23$).

adoptees and their later risk of alcoholism (Cloninger et al. 1988). We studied 431 children including 233 boys born in Stockholm in 1956 or 1957 and followed prospectively to age 27. According to our prior hypotheses, we expected that most alcoholism up to age 27 would be type 2, so that boys with antisocial personality traits defined by high novelty seeking, low harm avoidance, and low reward dependence would be at highest risk for early-onset alcoholism. However, we also expected some incidence of type 1 alcoholism associated with the opposite personality profile of high harm avoidance, high reward dependence, and low novelty seeking. These personality traits were rated on a quantitative 7-point scale (+3 to 0 to −3) by Cloninger on the basis of interview ratings made with teachers when the children were in the fourth grade and without any knowledge whatsoever of later behavior. The results are summarized in Table 15. Low harm avoidance (−1 to −3) was associated with a 2.7 increased relative risk of alcohol abuse. High novelty seeking (+1 to +3) was associated with a 2.4 increased relative risk of alcohol abuse. Average reward dependence had 0.4 relative risk of alcohol abuse compared to nonaverage subjects. Deviations of harm avoidance and reward dependence from average were associated with increased risk, but novelty seeking had a predominantly unidirectional effect with high novelty seeking increasing risk. The predictions of our motivational theory will be further evaluated by following the men to age 36 in order to test whether those with onset between 27 and 36 are predominantly those with anxiety-prone personalities (Fig. 3).

The logistic function relating childhood personality to later risk of alcohol abuse is depicted in Figure 3, which shows variation from 4% risk in boys low in novelty seeking and high in harm avoidance to 75% risk in boys with the opposite profile. This emphasizes that risk of alcoholism is a function of quantitative variation, not something that is either present or absent. This has

Table 15
Quantitative Personality Deviations and Nonlinearity of Risk for Later Alcohol Abuse

Childhood personality rating	No. of boys	Percentage alcohol abuse	Risk ratio[a]
Harm avoidance			
+2 or +3	21	14	1.6
+1	49	8	0.9
0	99	9	1.0
−1	39	18	2.0
−2 or −3	25	28	3.1
Novelty seeking			
−2 or +3	65	25	2.3
+1	24	4	0.4
0	101	11	1.0
−1	27	0	0.0
−2 or −3	16	13	1.2
Reward dependence			
+2 or +3	30	20	2.5
+1	67	12	1.5
0	89	8	1.0
−1	29	17	2.2
−2 or −3	18	22	2.8

[a] Risk ratio is the ratio of the risk in the specified group to the risk of average individuals.

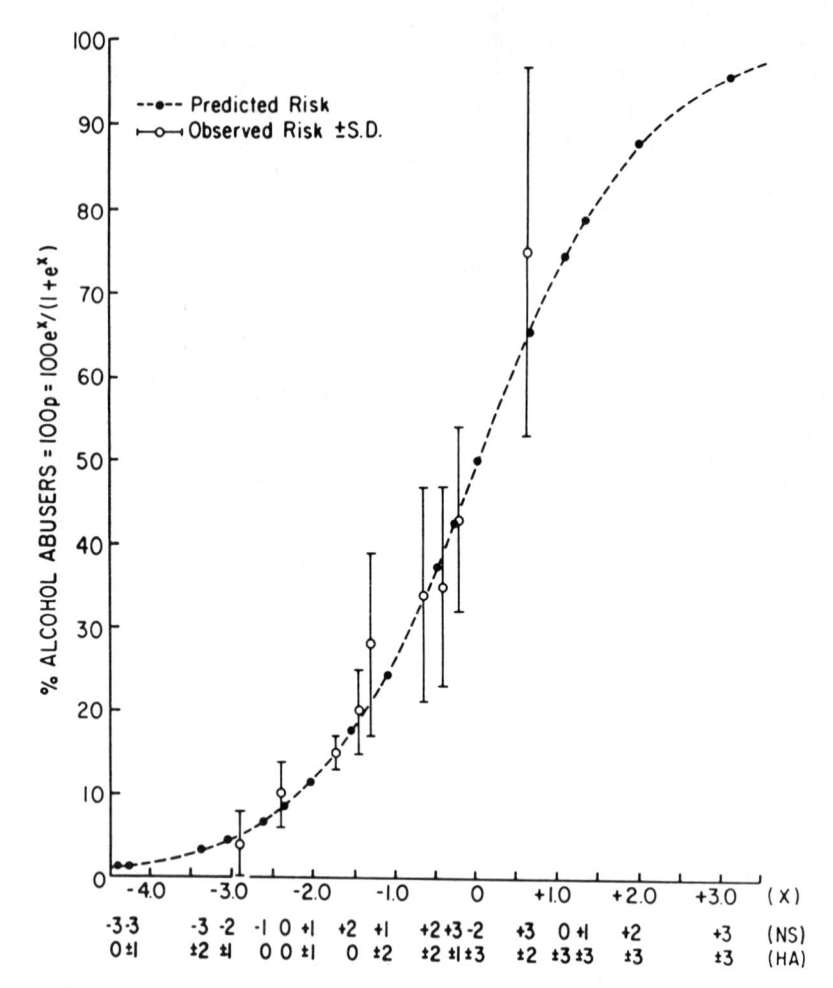

Figure 3
Logistic risk function (X) of novelty seeking (NS) and harm avoidance (HA).

strong implications for risk prediction because only a small proportion of individuals have extremely deviant personality profiles. Table 16 shows that only 10% of alcohol abusers have more than a 50% risk of alcoholism (RR=5). To detect 67% of alcohol abusers based on childhood personality, the threshold must be lowered to the point that 74% of those identified as at risk will not develop alcoholism (that is, positive predictive value is 26%).

Table 16
Reliability of Prediction of Alcohol Abuse by Level of Relative Risk

Index of reliability (%)	Level of relative risk (RR) for alcohol abuse		
	severe (RR = 5)	moderate (RR = 3)	mild (RR = 2)
Sensitivity	10	30	67
Specificity	99	93	67
Predictive value			
positive	75	43	26
negative	86	88	92
overall	86	84	67

DISCUSSION

These observations show that the inheritance of alcoholism cannot be explained by a simple Mendelian mode of transmission, such as a single autosomal or X-linked gene with complete penetrance. The mode of inheritance of alcoholism is developmentally complex and affected by incomplete penetrance, variable expressivity, and gene/environment interaction demonstrated in studies of twins, adoptees, and multigenerational pedigrees. Segregation analyses are compatible with either of two hypotheses: (1) genetic heterogeneity, in which there are two distinct subtypes, including type 1 with moderate multifactorial inheritance and no major gene locus, and type 2 with both a major dominant gene locus and high polygenic heritability; or (2) a mixed model comprising the effects of a major gene with a multifactorial background. These alternative models are not of practical difference unless the two putative subtypes can be distinguished on the basis of clinical features or biological markers.

The latest findings in the adoption studies show that childhood personality traits account for most of the predictable risk of adult alcoholism. Recalling that studies of the inheritance of personality indicate the importance of polygenic inheritance of quantitative variation, this suggests that the clinical subtypes that have been described in the Stockholm Adoption Study are prototypes of two developmental pathways. Some personality profiles predispose to development of anxiety, which positively reinforces use of alcohol for its relief and leads to rapid development of tolerance and loss of control, as in type 1 alcoholism. Such individuals are generally inhibited, and so their exposure to heavy alcohol use is highly dependent on social reinforcement. Accordingly, the heritability of liability to type 1 alcoholism is only moderate because of the important effects of milieu-limitation or gene/environment interaction.

In contrast, ASP profiles predispose to a wide variety of risk-taking behaviors, including teenage onset of substance abuse and antisocial behavior in men, and somatization in women. Such individuals seek out risks regardless of their social setting, and so their exposure to heavy alcohol use is essentially built-in; environmental interactions primarily determine severity of recurrent problems, rather than recurrence itself. Even in good social circumstances, like adoptive homes, recurrent problems are typical of type 2 alcohol abusers.

These observations also answer the questions that have sometimes been raised by critics like Searles (this volume). For example, the generalizability of our findings between Sweden and the United States has been supported by our analyses of American pedigrees that show two types of families with different patterns of inheritance and different clinical profiles similar to those in Sweden. Furthermore, the effects of sex and severity on inheritance have been carefully considered in relation to a coherent motivational theory of the development of alcoholism. Finally, in all of our studies, we have expended as much effort to identify environmental factors as we have expended to identify genetic factors. For example, the interaction of genetic and environmental factors has been carefully studied in our cross-fostering analyses. Unfortunately, both geneticists and environmentalists sometimes oversimplify available information about the genetic epidemiology of alcoholism. Accordingly, presentations and opportunities for open-minded critical discourse, such as those organized at the Banbury Center, are essential to maintaining effective communication about such developmentally complex disorders as alcoholism.

It seems unlikely that one or two genes will account for a large proportion of the variance in risk for alcoholism. It is more likely that there are several genes that make contributions to risk that are detectable with current methods for detecting and mapping genes in the human genome. Studies of polygenic systems in animals have usually revealed that such systems are composed of a few major genes and a much larger number of minor genes (Wright 1968). Such expectations about the complexity of both genetic and environmental contributions to risk have led us to design linkage studies that can be analyzed in multiple ways. First, my colleague Ted Reich and I decided to begin with systematic ascertainment of multiplex sibships (at least two alcoholic sibs) and then extend these systematically beyond the nuclear family to multigenerational pedigrees. This allows us to analyze the data using both affected sib methods (which are robust in the face of incomplete penetrance) and extended pedigree methods (which can be more informative if genetic heterogeneity and sporadics are not too common).

We recognized that it is not only difficult, but probably doubtful, to classify family members as affected or unaffected. Accordingly, we conduct exhaustive personal interviews to describe psychiatric comorbidity, associated personality traits, and social circumstances. These data are based on multiple sources, including personal interviews, and medical records. Then the clinical information is classified using explicit criteria that distinguish varying levels of severity and certainty of the diagnosis of alcoholism, as well as varying levels of severity and certainty of disorders that aggregate in the same families with primary alcoholism, such as somatization disorder and antisocial personality. This creates ambiguity about how to extend pedigrees through affected individuals because what is affected may vary according to different hypotheses about the diagnostic hierarchy. We have elected a wide definition of spectrum to avoid premature closure. However, different groups need to standardize their procedures to produce comparable results.

Finally, because of the complexities about clinical heterogeneity and uncertain mode of inheritance of the phenotype of alcoholism, we have also favored the simultaneous collection of biological markers that can help refine the phenotype and suggest candidate genes. Fortunately, alcoholism is one of the richest psychiatric disorders in terms of biological markers and candidate genes because it is unarguably a pharmacogenetic disorder caused by exposure to ethyl alcohol.

Overall, I suspect that the search for specific genes in alcoholism will be difficult but fruitful eventually. We can optimistically hope for quick success in finding at least one major gene contributing to risk, but it is more realistic to be prepared for exhaustive search of the entire genome along with exclusion mapping of candidate loci suggested by studies in animals. A multisite study like the NIAAA project has the advantages of replication across site and pooling of data to generate large enough samples for increased power to detect and map relevant loci.

Such studies are necessarily longitudinal. Alcoholism is associated with high mortality, so there will be opportunities to study the brains of subjects with alcoholism as well as those at risk for alcoholism. Furthermore, the prolonged developmental course of risk and abuse will afford opportunities for joint studies of biogenetic and sociocultural influences on risk. Such collaborative efforts are likely to be critical as a result of the gene/environment interaction on risk of alcoholism.

The meeting at the Banbury Conference Center on which this volume is based is likely to be a landmark because it documented what the status of our knowledge and methods were at the point that a challenging linkage mapping experiment began. At least as we undertake the challenge, we know nearly as much about the genetic epidemiology of the disorder as we can with available methods of clinical description and pedigree analysis.

ACKNOWLEDGMENTS

This work was supported in part by grants from the National Institute of

Alcoholism and Alcohol Abuse (AA-03539, AA-07982, AA-08028, AA-08401) and the National Institute of Mental Health (MH-31302).

REFERENCES

Amark, C. 1951. A study in alcoholism. *Acta Psychiatr. Scand. Suppl.* **70**: 1.

Bohman, M. 1978. Some genetic aspects of alcoholism and criminality: A population of adoptees. *Arch. Gen. Psychiatry* **35**: 269.

Bohman, M., S. Sigvardsson, and C.R. Cloninger. 1981. Maternal inheritance of alcohol abuse: Cross-fostering analysis of adopted women. *Arch. Gen. Psychiatry* **38**: 965.

Cloninger, C.R. 1987. Recent advances in family studies of alcoholism. In *Genetics and alcoholism* (ed. H.W. Goedde and D.P. Agarwal), p. 47. Alan R. Liss, New York.

Cloninger, C.R., M. Bohman, and S. Sigvardsson. 1981. Inheritance of alcohol abuse: Cross-fostering analysis of adopted men. *Arch. Gen. Psychiatry* **38**: 861.

Cloninger, C.R., T. Reich, and S.B. Guze. 1975. The multifactorial model of disease transmission: II. Sex differences in the familial transmission of sociopathy (antisocial personality). *Br. J. Psychiatry* **127**: 11.

Cloninger, C.R., T. Reich, and R. Wetzel. 1979. Alcoholism and affective disorders: Familial associations and genetic models. In *Alcoholism and affective disorders: Clinical, genetic, and biochemical studies* (ed. D.W. Goodwin and C.K. Erickson), p. 57. SP Medical and Scientific Books, New York.

Cloninger, C.R., M. Bohman, S. Sigvardsson, and A.-L. von Knorring. 1985. Psychopathology in adopted-out children of alcoholism: The Stockholm Adoption Study. *Recent Dev. Alcohol.* **3**: 37.

Cloninger, C.R., S. Sigvardsson, A.-L. von Knorring, and M. Bohman. 1988a. The Swedish studies of the adopted children of alcoholics: A reply to Littrell. *J. Stud. Alcohol* **49**: 516.

Cloninger, C.R., T. Reich, S. Sigvardsson, A.-L. von Knorring, and M. Bohman. 1988b. Effects of changes in alcohol use between generations on inheritance of alcohol abuse. In *Alcoholism: Origins and outcome* (ed. R.M. Rose and J.E. Barrett), p. 49. Raven Press, New York.

Gilligan, S.B., T. Reich, and C.R. Cloninger. 1987. Etiologic heterogeneity in alcoholism. *Genet. Epidemiol.* **4**: 395.

―――. 1988. Alcohol-related symptoms in heterogeneous families of hospitalized alcoholics. *Alcohol. Clin. Exp. Res.* **12**: 671.

Goodwin, D.W., F. Schlusinger, J. Knop, S. Mednick, and S.B. Guze. 1977. Psychopathology in adopted and non-adopted daughters of alcoholics. *Arch. Gen. Psychiatry* **34**: 1005.

Goodwin, D.W., F. Schlusinger, N. Moller, L. Hermansen, G. Winokur, and S.B. Guze. 1974. Drinking problems in adopted and non-adopted sons of alcoholics. *Arch. Gen. Psychiatry* **31**: 164.

Gurling, H.M.D., R.M. Murray, and C.A. Clifford. 1981. Investigations into the genetics of alcohol dependence and into its effects on brain function. In *Twin research 3: Epidemiologic clinical studies* (ed. L. Gedda et al.), p. 77. Alan R. Liss, New York.

Guze, S.B., C.R. Cloninger, R. Martin, and P.J. Clayton. 1988. Alcoholism as a medical disorder. In *Alcoholism: Origins and outcome* (ed. R.M. Rose and J.E. Barrett), p. 83. Raven Press, New York.

Hrubec, Z. and G.S. Omenn. 1981. Evidence of genetic predisposition to alcoholic cirrhosis and psychosis: Twin concordances for alcoholism and its biological end points by zygosity among male veterans. *Alcohol. Clin. Exp. Res.* **5:** 207.

Kaij, L. 1960. *Alcoholism in twins: Studies on the etiology and sequels of abuse of alcohol.* Almqvist and Wiksell, Stockholm.

Kaij, L. and J. Dock. 1975. Grandsons of alcoholics. *Arch. Gen. Psychiatry* **32:** 1379.

Merikangas, K.R. 1990. The genetic epidemiology of alcoholism. *Psychol. Med.* **20:** 11.

Pickens, R.W. and D.S. Svikis. 1988. The twin method in the study of vulnerability to drug abuse. *Natl. Inst. Drug Abuse Res. Monogr. Ser.* **89:** 41.

Roe, A. and B. Burks. 1945. Adult adjustment of foster children of alcoholic and psychotic parentage and the influence of the foster home. No 3. In *Memoirs of the Section on Alcohol Studies.* Yale University, New Haven, Connecticut.

Wright, S. 1968. *Evolution and the genetics of populations;* volume 1. *Genetic and biometric foundations.* University of Chicago Press, Chicago.

COMMENTS

Cadoret: How did you assess home environments to decide what affected the severity of alcohol abuse?

Cloninger: I wish we had a fine-grain classification of those home environments in terms that would be satisfying. We only had assessments of the social status of the fathers, plus a couple of other variables having to do with contacts with the biological mothers and home placement. Having to be hospitalized more often prior to adoption and having very low social status in the home were characteristic of several alcohol abusers.

Li: What about drinking status?

Cloninger: We didn't have direct information about alcohol consumption. We also had some adoptive parents who had become alcoholic, so we looked to see whether alcohol abuse in the adoptive parents increased the risk in their children. It did not. There was a nonsignificant trend to have less abuse if the adoptive parent was an alcoholic. It's as if people see the problems, see that it's not desirable, and try to avoid it. There is certainly no increased risk if the adoptive parents are alcohol abusers. We have to look for things short of overt alcohol abuse in the rearing parents to explain the exposure effects. We think that it is probably mediated by attitudes toward drinking, encouragement of heavy drinking, and so on, so that these people are exposed.

Sambrook: In the genetic background for type 1 it says "No." What happens if you split that into environment?

Cloninger: No difference.

Sambrook: Are you saying that a mild environmental background gives rise to a mild abuse and a severe background gives rise to severe abuse?

Cloninger: Given the genetic predisposition. You've got to have both. You've got to have the genetic vulnerability and the relative exposure pattern as you grow up.

Sambrook: So there's no progression in this disease from mild to severe?

Cloninger: That is a good question, because obviously you know that some people go through mild in order to get to severe. People make that progression rapidly if they ever will do so.

Schuckit: You are also looking at one data set and a theoretical construct that Bob has been brave enough to put forward and to test. That doesn't mean the final outcome will look like this. It just means that this data set suggests that possibility.

Cloninger: Now we are doing prospective studies from birth, through childhood personality, into adulthood, and we have followed children up to age 30.

Schuckit: If you're talking about a multifactorial disorder with probably multiple genes involved, are you bothered by a 90% heritability?

Wijsman: No.

Schuckit: That doesn't bother you?

Wijsman: No, especially since he said that the environment is constant.

Schuckit: Constant?

Wijsman: Well, not constant, but more similar.

Cloninger: Don't be overblown by the heritability estimate of liability to something, because we're still only talking about 18% of the kids.

Schuckit: How old were these kids when they were studied?

Cloninger: They ranged from 23 to 43, most over 30. I think the average age was something like 34.

Martin: Marc, it probably has a standard error of about 0.3, so I wouldn't get too excited.

Cloninger: That's right. The heritability estimate there has a standard error of 0.2-something, 0.21, 0.22.

Gordis: Could you just comment on the point that was raised before, the sort of counterintuitive thing, that the mild and the severe constitute the type 1 genetic background, whereas in the most genetically influenced type, type 2, it's the moderate rather than the severe?

Cloninger: Let me do that in relation to the fuller description of the phenotypes later.

Billings: What's the percentage of alcoholism in the Swedish population?

Cloninger: Here, for any registration, it's about 15%, and it's about one-fifth that in the women, about 2–3%. For recurrent, you can cut that in half.

Billings: That's longitudinal?

Cloninger: Yes, that's a prospective cohort of 431 children.

Billings: Did any of those children develop manic-depressive illness, for instance, during that time?

Cloninger: We have looked at depression, and we find no increased association with psychotic mood disorders leading to treatment.

Searles: You can't assess shared and nonshared environment in this kind of sample. Even though, perhaps, the adoptive homes did vary—I think he said that the adoptive parenting made a difference in the progression of the disorder—it's not statistically possible to assess that effect.

Cloninger: If you have characteristics of the rearing parents, then that's what most people have meant by "home environment." It's true that we don't have a control group of separately reared siblings, which provides one way to get a shared environment. However, another way is to look at the characteristics of the adoptive home directly, which is what we did.

Billings: Since this is a meeting about the genetics of alcoholism, let me ask a genetic question about your data. It's true in some multifactorial polygenic models that have showed sexual dimorphism that if you choose the least affected sex (for instance, females of the type 2) then, if you find index cases that are female type 2s, their offspring should be severely affected. That has been true for some polygenic multifactorial conditions. It that true in your cohort as well?

Cloninger: What we have found is that the women who have a high frequency of bodily pain complaints have an excess of biological fathers with early-onset alcoholism associated with criminality.

Billings: No, my question is: If you look at the children of a type 2 antisocial alcoholic woman, do you find a higher frequency of type 2 or any kind of alcoholism in those as compared with other type 2s?

Cloninger: In the adoption material, we have only been able to look back at the parents. However, we have done family studies of women who have somatization disorder, and there is an increased risk of both antisocial personality and alcoholism in their sons and daughters. They don't have an excess of somatization.

Billings: They should have the most. By some genetic models, they should be far less the most likely to show a genetic effect.

Cloninger: I think that the heritable factors that increase risk of alcoholism are largely the intervening personality traits. Personality traits do not show sex-dependent threshold effects.

Chakravarti: Bob, you talked earlier about the stability of the diagnosis, but now I see that the phenotype has been stretched out into obviously more severe and more mild. So, it seems that certain individuals, based on personality traits and other things, have a more stable diagnosis.

Cloninger: The problem in the linkage analysis would be, if you had a mother or a brother who was antisocial and a teetotaler, for the sake of argument, what would you do in a linkage analysis? Would you count those people as affected or not?

Chakravarti: Did you have personality trait data on all the families you looked at in St. Louis?

Cloninger: Yes, we did, in the St. Louis study.

Risch: I'm confused about the sex effect also. As I recall, you showed that there was an increased risk of the female adoptees if the biological mother was affected, but if the biological father was affected there was no increase in risk.

Cloninger: That was the original table from 1981 that was using information only on the presence or absence of any alcohol abuse in the father. Later, we went back and classified the fathers using a discriminant function that also included information about criminal behavior, age of onset, and social status. We then could pick type 1 fathers and type 2 fathers. The type 1 fathers do have an excess of alcoholism in their daughters.

Risch: The type 2s did also. There was about a doubling of risk in the offspring of the type 2 fathers. I would have thought those two groups comprised the vast majority of the alcoholic fathers. Those data suggest that there was at least a doubling of an increased risk in their daughters. I wonder why the two look so different.

Cloninger: The only thing I can say is that one is based on a discriminant function and uses more of the information, whereas the other is simply a dichotomy.

Risch: One prediction of the model in the separation of type 1 and type 2 is specificity, so that type 1 biological parents have only type 1 children, and type 2 biological parents have type 2 children; you shouldn't see the crossovers.

Cloninger: Yes, that is the prediction if the subtypes are simply discrete entities. However, it is more complex than that. My personality model actually presumes (and this is still yet to be rigidly tested) that the three dimensions I have described correspond to the genetic structure underlying personality, so those are three separate polygenic traits independently inherited, even though they may functionally interact. The inheritance is thought to be independent. So, you don't just get type 1 with type 1, and type 2 with type 2. That should be the overall effect. We do show patterns like that, but the traits that underlie the risk are separately inherited.

Neurobiological Markers
of Risk for Alcoholism

Individuals at Risk for Alcoholism: Neurophysiologic Processes

BERNICE PORJESZ AND HENRI BEGLEITER
Neurodynamics Laboratory
Department of Psychiatry
State University of New York Health Science Center at Brooklyn
Brooklyn, New York 11203

INTRODUCTION AND BACKGROUND

Over the last few decades, electrophysiological aberrations in alcoholics have been extensively investigated with the use of electroencephalograms (EEGs) and event-related-potentials (ERPs) (for reviews, see Begleiter and Platz 1972; Porjesz and Begleiter 1983, 1985). The evoked-potential (EP) or ERP techniques offer a unique approach for assessing level of brain functioning, as electrophysiological activity and cognition can be observed simultaneously. An ERP is obtained by using noninvasive scalp electrodes to record the time-locked electrical brain activity following the delivery of a discrete stimulus to any sensory modality (e.g., auditory, visual). Signal-averaging techniques make it possible both to extract these time-locked neuroelectric signals (ERPs) and to cancel out background random "noise." These time-locked signals represent afferent activity over neural pathways from the generators in the peripheral end organ, to higher integrative centers, to output areas of the brain. The quantification of salient features extracted from ERP recordings provides objective measures of neural processes involved in sensory reception, cognition, and integrative functions, allowing the assessment of the functional integrity of various neuroanatomical systems of the brain.

Recording electrical activity from the brain has proven to be a technique that is differentially sensitive to the various phases of alcohol-related functioning; namely, acute and chronic alcoholization, tolerance, withdrawal, and long-term brain dysfunction characteristic of abstinent alcoholics. Acute alcohol ingestion in humans results in delays in the brain stem auditory evoked response (BAER) (Fukui et al. 1981; Church and Williams 1982), whereas alcohol withdrawal is marked by shortened BAER latencies. In addition, decreases in amplitudes of ERP components (N1–P2) and delays in P3 latencies have been observed following ingestion of alcohol in healthy subjects (for review, see Porjesz and Begleiter 1985). Electrophysiological studies in abstinent alcoholics indicate they have low EEG alpha production and produce an excessive amount of fast frequency activity (Begleiter and Platz 1972; Naitoh 1973; Jones and Holmes 1976). BAER has been found to be delayed in alcoholics (Chu and Squires 1980; Rosenhamer and Silfverskiold 1980; Begleiter et al. 1981; Chu et al. 1982; Chu and Yang 1987). Alcoholics manifest low-amplitude P3 components of the ERP to target stimuli (Porjesz et al. 1980, 1987; Patterson et al. 1987; Pfefferbaum et al. 1987). Furthermore, alcoholics manifest delayed N2 components of the ERP. With prolonged abstinence from alcohol, some of these electrophysiological aberrations (e.g., BAER) recover, whereas others (e.g., P3 amplitude) do not (Porjesz and Begleiter 1985).

For many years, these brain aberrations were attributed to the neurotoxic effects of prolonged chronic alcohol exposure, nutritional deficits, or an interaction of alcohol and nutrition-related factors. More recently, the evidence is amassing that some of these electrophysiological aberrations may antecede the development of alcoholism and may be related to a genetic predisposition to alcoholism.

There is increasing evidence from population genetic studies that certain individuals are at risk for developing alcoholism. Specifically at higher risk seem to be sons of alcoholic fathers, who are four times more likely to develop alcoholism than sons of nonalcoholic fathers (Goodwin and Guze 1974; Goodwin 1979), even when they are separated from their biological parents soon after birth (Cloninger et al. 1981). Studies of male adoptees in Scandinavia indicate that the biological rather than the adoptive parent is predictive of later drinking problems (Goodwin et al. 1973; Goodwin and Guze 1974; Bohman 1978; Cadoret and Gath 1978; Cadoret et al. 1980). Furthermore, the concordance rate for alcohol abuse between identical twins is almost double the rate for fraternal twins (Kaij 1960), and patterns of alcohol consumption have been reported to be highly concordant among identical twins (Partanen et al. 1966; Jonsson and Nilsson 1968; Loehlin 1972). Taken together, these population genetic studies suggest that genetic factors predispose sons of alcoholic fathers to alcoholism.

The identification of genetically transmitted biological marker(s) would provide more definitive evidence that the etiology of alcoholism involves genetic factors. In addition, it could perhaps elucidate the potential nature of these genetic factors. There is a good deal of evidence that characteristics of both the EEG and ERP are genetically determined; e.g., the production of fast EEG activity has been demonstrated to be genetically transmitted (Vogel 1970; Young et al. 1972; Propping 1977). In various studies, Vogel has reported on the hereditary nature of several EEG variants (monomorphic alpha, low-voltage EEG, EEG with alpha and beta diffusely mixed, EEG with fronto-precentral beta) (Vogel 1970; Vogel et al. 1986). He maintains that the low-voltage and regular alpha EEG are inherited via an autosomal dominant mode, whereas the poor alpha or diffuse beta variants are under polygenic control (Vogel 1970). EPs recorded to flashes of different intensities have been reported to be under genetic control (Buchsbaum and Pfefferbaum 1971). Monozygotic twins manifest EP waveforms that are as concordant with each other as EPs obtained from the same individual tested twice (Dustman and Beck 1965; Surwillo 1980). The P3 component of the ERP is more similar in identical twins than in controls (Polich and Burns 1987).

It is quite likely that a genetic predisposition to alcoholism is manifested in brain function, and it is possible that electrophysiological events may serve as biological markers. Therefore, investigating these genetically determined electrophysiological measures of brain function provides an important approach to the study of possible genetic factors in alcoholism.

EEG

For the last several decades a number of investigators have observed that resting-state EEG activity recorded from awake abstinent male alcoholics manifests an overabundance of high-frequency activity (beta, fast EEG) and a deficiency in lower frequency EEG activity (e.g., alpha) (for review, see Begleiter and Platz 1972). The production of fast EEG activity has been demonstrated to be genetically transmitted (Vogel 1970; Young et al. 1972; Propping 1977).

These EEG findings in alcoholics, coupled with the population genetic studies of alcoholism, suggest that subjects at risk for alcoholism (male offspring of male alcoholics) would be more likely to manifest an excess of fast EEG activity. Gabrielli et al. (1982) tested this hypothesis in a sample of 27 Danish children of alcoholics compared with children of nonalcoholics. As hypothesized, they observed that male (but not female) offspring of alcoholics manifested fast EEG activity compared to controls.

A number of studies in subjects at risk for alcoholism have investigated EEG responses to alcohol. In one study, Pollock et al. (1983) report that high risk (HR) sons of alcoholics (19–21 years old) exhibit more changes in alpha activity after ingesting 0.5 g/kg of alcohol compared to low risk (LR) subjects. After alcohol ingestion, HR subjects manifested greater decreases in fast alpha activity (9.75–12.10 Hz) and greater increases in slow alpha activity (7.42–9.46 Hz). The decreases in fast alpha activity were observed at 120 minutes post-ethanol, and the increases in slow alpha were observed at both 90 and 120 minutes. In addition, HR subjects manifested greater decreases in alpha frequency than did LR subjects at 30, 60, and 120 minutes after alcohol administration.

Despite the earlier findings from their group (Gabrielli et al. 1982) that sons of alcoholic fathers produce excessive beta activity without ingesting alcohol, Pollock et al. (1983) did not report any EEG differences between

HR and LR groups prior to ethanol ingestion; furthermore, their analyses were limited to theta and fast and slow alpha activity, and beta activity was not discussed. In a subsequent paper, Pollock et al. (1984) did not replicate Gabrielli's findings. Although the HR subjects did not report a higher amount of alcohol consumption than LR subjects, they reported needing significantly more drinks to "feel tipsy." These results suggest that HR subjects are more sensitive to the physiological effects of alcohol and less sensitive to its subjective effects.

Another group of investigators has reported that males with family histories of alcoholism have more power in the fast frequency alpha range (9–12 Hz) than males without family histories of alcoholism, prior to alcohol ingestion (Ehlers and Schuckit 1990b). Family history positive (FHP) males responded less intensely to an ethanol challenge than family history negative (FHN) males in terms of the stability of their fast frequency of alpha. Furthermore, Ehlers and Schuckit (1990a) report that FHP men manifested more beta (12–20 Hz) activity than did FHN men, 90 minutes post-ethanol. In the FHN group, "moderate" drinkers were found to have more energy in the beta frequency range than the "low" drinkers, both at baseline and at 90 minutes post-ethanol. In contrast, no differences in beta activity between "low" and "moderate" drinkers were found in the FHP group.

Both laboratories have investigated fast frequency alpha activity in subjects at risk for alcoholism, but their EEG findings are different. Ehlers and Schuckit (1990b) report less physiological responsiveness and "sensitivity" to ethanol in the FHP compared to the FHN group, whereas Pollock et al. (1983) report more responsiveness and more sensitivity. Yet both groups agree that HR males report feeling less intoxicated after a single dose of alcohol (Schuckit 1980, 1984; Pollock et al. 1983).

In another interesting study, Pollock et al. (1988) attempt to resolve the issue of physiological and subjective sensitivity by testing two hypotheses, namely:

1. HR subjects will manifest greater physiological change and less subjective sensitivity to alcohol compared to controls (Tarter et al. 1984). Tarter et al. (1984) speculate that pre-alcoholics are particularly vulnerable to the effects of alcohol; they exhibit a great deal of physiological lability, and alcohol may regulate their physiological functioning. They have difficulty identifying their subjective states because of this physiological lability.
2. HR subjects will manifest less physiological and subjective sensitivity to alcohol (Goodwin 1981). Goodwin (1981) speculates that in order to develop alcoholism, individuals possess high initial tolerance for alcohol effects (defined as individual variation in sensitivity to alcohol, not acquired tolerance associated with development of dependence).

To test these hypotheses, Pollock et al. (1988) divided a sample of FHP males into those exhibiting the most EEG change (in terms of mean alpha frequency) following ethanol administration, and those exhibiting the least EEG change (similar to controls). They found that the two groups differed in terms of the time course of their subjective ratings. The group manifesting the most EEG change differed from controls at 55 but not 25 minutes post-ethanol, whereas the group manifesting the least EEG change differed from controls at 25 but not 55 minutes post-ethanol. The group with the least EEG change did not report higher levels of intoxication at 25 than at 55 minutes post-ethanol, whereas both the controls and subjects with the greatest EEG changes did.

The characteristics of the groups manifesting the greatest EEG change can be related to Tarter's hypothesis, and those manifesting the least change can be related to Goodwin's hypothesis. However, Tarter's hypothesis about physiological lability was not adequately addressed in this study, as neither placebo data nor measures of within-subject variability of mean alpha frequency were obtained.

Since differential responses to ethanol challenge have been reported depending on an individual's pre-ethanol resting EEG signature (Propping 1983), it is important to ascertain whether there are EEG differences between HR and LR groups prior to alcohol ingestion. Propping (1983) found that subjects manifesting poor alpha activity prior to ethanol manifested the most synchronization following alcohol, whereas those with regular pre-ethanol alpha exhibited slight change. Thus the effect of alcohol on EEG depends on pre-alcohol EEG pattern, which is under genetic control. Propping (1983) maintains that EEG with poor alpha or beta reflects a stronger ascending reticular activating system. As mentioned previously, Vogel (1970) has identified different genetic EEG patterns. He postulates that low-voltage and regular alpha are autosomal dominant, whereas poor alpha and diffuse beta are under polygenetic control. On the basis of the work of Propping (1983), it would seem that subjects with poor alpha or beta in their pre-alcohol EEG are more susceptible to ethanol effects. Therefore, it is important to know if Pollock's HR sample consisted of more subjects manifesting more beta activity and poor alpha than the LR group—perhaps explaining their greater response to alcohol.

In addition, it is important to characterize the EEG in the control groups before alcohol, since they may consist of individuals with different EEG variants as well. Possibly the lack of agreement between EEG laboratories is a function of differences in the EEG patterns in the subjects forming both their control and HR groups.

Because alcoholics have been reported to have poorly synchronized EEG, it can be postulated that their offspring would be more likely to inherit this pattern. However, Propping et al. (1981) found that female and not male alcoholics manifested this poorly synchronized EEG pattern, as did their relatives.

Taken together, the aforementioned findings indicate that alcoholism is not a homogeneous disease and suggest that subjects at risk may be characterized by different EEG patterns. Perhaps the alcoholics with desynchronous resting EEG (predominantly females) represent a group that uses alcohol to relax and synchronize their alpha activity (Cloninger's type 1) (Cloninger 1987), thus normalizing their physiological functions. These alcoholics probably correspond to Pollock's HR group that are more responsive to alcohol, and are most likely more labile, supporting Tarter's hypothesis. Alcoholics with stable synchronous EEG are probably those who are not as responsive to alcohol; this corresponds to Ehlers's FHP group as a whole, and to Pollock's HR subgroup that show less responsiveness. However, until studies are performed in which EEG patterns are characterized before and after ethanol and placebo challenges, these conclusions remain speculative.

ERP

The ERP is a very sensitive index of the functional integrity of the brain. In addition to being sensitive to sensory aspects of information processing, ERP techniques have proven to be very useful in indexing electrophysiological concomitants of complex cognitive tasks (Donchin et al. 1978; Hillyard et al. 1978; Donchin 1979). ERPs consist of characteristic, highly reproducible waveforms lasting between 250 and 500 milliseconds. The early components (less than 100 msec) of the EP reflect stimulus characteristics (e.g., intensity), whereas the later components are more influenced by psychological factors. ERPs can be recorded in conjunction with behavior, or even when no behavioral response is required; they can be recorded to attended and unattended stimuli. Because the ERP is sensitive to genetic (Polich and Burns 1987), sensory, cognitive, and motor aspects of information processing, it can be a valuable tool in studying the genetics of alcoholism.

A great deal of attention has focused on the P3 component of the ERP, a prominent positive component occurring between 300 and 500 milliseconds after the stimulus, related to stimulus significance. We have investigated P3 with numerous paradigms and have reported that it is markedly reduced or absent in abstinent alcoholics. Although other ERP component differences in alcoholics (e.g., BAER) reverse with prolonged abstinence, reduced P3 amplitudes do not (Porjesz and Begleiter 1985).

For the last decade, our laboratory has studied ERPs in subjects at risk for alcoholism. In our first study, the HR group consisted of boys between the ages of 7 and 13 who had no prior exposure to alcohol (Begleiter et al. 1984).

In each case, the father had received a diagnosis of alcoholism (DSM-III) and had been in treatment for alcoholism at some time. We excluded boys whose mothers had either ingested alcohol during pregnancy or who drank excessively after birth. Only boys with neither medical problems nor exposure to alcohol or other substances of abuse were included in this study. The LR group consisted of healthy normal boys matched for age and socioeconomic status to the HR subjects. They were included only if they had no prior exposure to alcohol or other substances of abuse, and if they had no first- or second-degree relatives with a history of alcoholism or other psychiatric disorder. With the exception of family history of alcoholism, the same exclusion criteria were used in both the LR and HR groups.

A complex visual P3 head-orientation paradigm was used. The target stimulus was a rarely occurring aerial view of the head with the nose and either the right or left ear drawn in, rotated in one of two possible positions. This yielded four possible targets, namely: nose up and right ear, nose up and left ear, nose down and right ear, nose down and left ear. These targets were interspersed randomly among non-targets (ovals). Subjects were required to press one of two microswitches to the targets, as quickly and accurately as possible, indicating whether the right or left ear was presented. In the "easy condition," the head was facing forward (nose up on screen) and the left or right ear appeared on the same side as the appropriate button; in the "difficult" condition, the head was facing back (nose down on screen) and the left or right ear appeared on the side opposite the corresponding button.

P3 amplitudes were significantly smaller in the HR compared to the LR groups to all target stimuli. This group difference was most significant at the parietal electrode (where P3 is maximum) for the difficult condition. Principal component analyses with Varimax rotation (PCAV) performed on the data indicated that only the factor representing the P3 component was significantly different between the HR and LR groups.

This study was the first in the field to indicate that P3 amplitude is significantly reduced in boys at risk for alcoholism, without exposure to alcohol. Since this original study, several laboratories, including our own, have replicated these findings; namely, O'Connor at the University of Connecticut, Whipple at UCLA, and Steinhauer at the University of Pittsburgh. O'Connor et al. (1986) replicated the findings of Begleiter et al. (1984) using the identical head-orientation paradigm; specifically, they reported reduced P3 amplitudes without the administration of alcohol in an older group of HR males.

Begleiter et al. (1987b) studied another group of sons of alcoholics to determine whether the reduced P3 amplitudes observed in HR subjects was task- or modality-specific. A modified auditory oddball task was used, in which subjects pressed a button in response to rarely occurring tones presented at a random rate; accuracy was stressed over speed. Twenty-three matched pairs of FHP and FHN males between the ages of 7 and 16 were studied; they were carefully interviewed to ascertain that they had no exposure to alcohol or illicit drugs.

The fathers of HR boys in this sample met the criteria for male-limited (type 2) alcoholism (Cloninger 1987). They manifested early-onset alcoholism and a high rate of recidivism, often accompanied by petty criminality, and they required extensive treatment. Additionally, the HR boys came from families in which alcoholism was highly heritable and was limited to males.

As in the previous visual study, the FHP boys manifested reduced P3 amplitudes. The reduced P3 voltages in HR males in this auditory paradigm suggest that these reduced P3 voltages are not task- or modality-specific; they seem to be present in auditory and visual paradigms under conditions of speed and accuracy.

Another laboratory (Whipple et al. 1988) used a continuous performance test (CPT) to examine ERPs in prepubescent boys at high risk for alcoholism. This visual paradigm consisted of a complex series of visual stimuli that changed along three dimensions: shape, color, and identity of a number. The subject silently counted each time a stimulus identically matched the one preceding it on all three dimensions. In agreement with both Begleiter et al. (1984, 1987b) and O'Connor et al. (1986, 1987), Whipple et al. (1988) report a reduction in the amplitude of the late positive complex (LPC), including a P3 component.

In our own laboratory, we have recently replicated our original findings of reduced P3 voltages without the administration of alcohol in an older sample (18–23) of sons of male alcoholics (Porjesz and Begleiter 1990). The sample consisted of 25 male offspring of carefully diagnosed (DSM-IIIR/RDC) male alcoholics and was selected from high-density alcoholic families (mean number of alcoholic family members = 4). Thus, sons of alcoholic fathers were excluded in cases where alcoholism may have been sporadic. Furthermore, individuals with mothers who abused alcohol before, during, or after pregnancy were excluded. Controls were matched to the sons of male alcoholics on the basis of age, education, and socioeconomic status. They were selected from families in which there was no history of alcohol abuse or alcoholism in any first- or second-degree relatives. FHP and FHN subjects were carefully matched on drinking history, including duration and quantity-frequency information.

We used a different visual-spatial paradigm involving easy and difficult line discriminations. Previously we had demonstrated that abstinent alcoholics manifested reduced P3 amplitudes with this design. The stimuli consisted of a non-target (vertical line) and two targets: an easy target that deviated from vertical by 90 degrees (horizontal line) and a difficult target that deviated from vertical by only 3 degrees. The subject pressed a button as quickly as possible (reaction time [RT]) to all non-vertical stimuli.

The results indicated that prior to alcohol ingestion, P3 amplitude is significantly lower in HR subjects compared to controls. This replicates our previous findings (Begleiter et al. 1984, 1987b) of lower voltage P3s in an older sample of HR males as well as the findings of O'Connor et al. (1986, 1987) and Whipple et al. (1988). The largest differences in P3 amplitude between groups occurred to the easy target, to which LR subjects manifested extremely high voltages. These results are the same as those we obtained in alcoholics with the same paradigm where the easy target elicited the greatest significant difference in P3 amplitude between groups (Porjesz et al. 1987). This P3 amplitude difference between groups was most apparent at Pz and Cz electrodes.

Most recently, in another auditory target selection task, we have observed that adolescent HR males manifest lower amplitude P3s than LR males (B. Porjesz and H. Begleiter, in prep.). In this paradigm (modified after Hillyard et al. 1978), rare or frequent tones were randomly presented rather quickly (600–800 msec) to either the right or left ear. The rare tones to a specific ear were designated as targets, and the subject pressed a button to these as quickly as possible. The same rare tones to the other ear were ignored. In the absence of other differences between groups (N1 amplitude), HR males manifested lower amplitude P3 components to targets.

The amplitude of P3 to both the rare attended (P3b) and unattended (P3a) tones were of lower voltage in HR subjects, indicating that HR subjects do not make probability matches as well as controls. In an inattention auditory oddball paradigm, we have also found that P3a is of lower amplitude in HR adolescent males. In this experimental design, subjects read a book while rare and frequent tones were randomly presented binaurally via headphones.

Taken together, the foregoing results examining P3 amplitudes indicate they are reduced in voltage in HR males both to attended and unattended stimuli, and to easy and difficult discriminations in visual and auditory modalities. Despite the general consensus that P3 amplitudes are of lower voltage in HR males, some studies have failed to replicate these findings. Polich and Bloom (1987, 1988) and Baribeau et al. (1987) have not observed significantly reduced P3 amplitudes in sons of alcoholics.

Baribeau et al. (1987) examined HR and LR subjects who were further subdivided according to the amount of alcohol they consumed (heavy vs. light drinkers). They used an auditory selective attention paradigm in which rare (500 Hz) and frequent (600 Hz) tones were randomly presented to either the right or left ear at a random rate (630–880 msec). Subjects were instructed to count the signals in one ear and ignore those in the other ear.

Although HR subjects did not exhibit reduced P3 amplitudes, the light drinkers manifested insignificantly smaller P3s in the *inattention* condition. These results suggest that when attention is mobilized, P3 deficits are not apparent in the attended channel. Perhaps the lower P3 amplitude in the unattended channel would reach significance with a larger number of subjects. As mentioned previously, we have found reduced P3 amplitudes to rare tones in the unattended channel in HR subjects with a Hillyard paradigm similar to the one described by Baribeau et al. (1987).

HR subjects manifested significantly larger N100 components than did LR subjects in the attention condition; this perhaps indicates that the HR subjects paid more attention than the LR subjects to the stimuli. Furthermore, it is possible that the HR subjects find the tone discrimination task more difficult than the LR group (500 Hz vs. 600 Hz) and hence need to pay more attention.

Finally, it seems that the subject sample represents an older group of HR individuals. There is a rather large age range (19–35) with mean ages of 27 (HR, heavy drinking), 22 (HR, light drinking), 24 (LR, heavy drinking), and 25 (LR, light drinking). It seems that these HR subjects may have passed the age of risk, and perhaps the sample is not representative of a group at high risk for alcoholism, considering that those who already manifested alcoholic problems were excluded. If by this age they have not developed alcohol-related problems or become alcoholic, the likelihood is that they will not, and this represents a skewed sample of HR subjects, perhaps endowed with protective mechanisms. Certainly, their larger N100 component suggests they are atypical. In a P3 study by Hill et al. (1988), increased cognitive efficiency in nonaffected siblings of alcoholics was reported. They observed shorter P3 latencies in these nonaffected siblings, and they suggest that this offers protection against the development of alcoholism.

In various studies at the University of California at San Diego examining ERPs in college students with positive family histories of alcoholism, conflicting ERP results have been reported. This is mostly the work of Neville (Elmasian et al. 1982; Neville and Schmidt 1985; Schmidt and Neville 1985) and Polich (Polich and Bloom 1986, 1987, 1988; Polich et al. 1988; Schuckit et al. 1988).

Following the administration of either alcohol or a placebo, differences in P3 characteristics have been found between subjects at high risk and at low risk for alcoholism. Elmasian et al. (1982) studied the P3 and slow-wave components of the ERP in HR and LR male college students (ages 20–25) under placebo, low doses, and high doses of alcohol. Unfortunately, different sets of subjects were used for each dose, and there were only five pairs of subjects per group.

After alcohol or placebo administration, Elmasian et al. (1982) reported significant P3 amplitude decreases in the HR compared to the LR subjects.

They explained their results in terms of differential expectancies for alcohol characterized by different brain events and also suggested that the results may be due to higher than normal alcohol intake in the mothers of the HR subjects.

In a subsequent study in the same laboratory (Neville and Schmidt 1985), the LPC of the ERP in HR individuals was investigated without the ingestion of any liquid. In this study, mothers of all subjects were interviewed with respect to their alcohol and drug use, and the experimental design eliminated expectancy effects. Group differences in the LPC were still observed between groups.

In another study, Schmidt and Neville (1985) investigated ERPs in HR males while they were engaged in a visual language task. They found that the N430 component (a component related to semantic processing) was significantly smaller in men at high risk for alcoholism than in men at low risk. Moreover, in the HR group, the latency of N430 was directly related to the amount of alcohol consumed per occasion. These fascinating results imply that neuronal function associated with language processes is affected by family history of alcoholism and that there is an interaction between family history and alcohol consumed per occasion and N430.

Investigating ERPs in male college students with and without family histories of alcoholism, Polich and Bloom (1987, 1988) and Schuckit et al. (1988) did not find P3 amplitude differences between groups. Schuckit et al. (1988) did not find any ERP differences between FHP and FHN subjects prior to ethanol ingestion or following a placebo dose, using an auditory oddball paradigm. Following a high dose of ethanol (1.1 ml/kg), P3 latency delays returned to baseline measures more rapidly in FHP men. This suggests that some electrophysiological differences between FHP and FHN individuals are apparent only in response to ethanol challenges, perhaps representing innate tolerance in the FHP subjects.

The initial placebo effect in FHP subjects (Elmasian et al. 1982) was not replicated in the same laboratory (Polich and Bloom 1988). These ERP results may be spurious, since they involve very small sample sizes. Elmasian et al. (1982) tested only five subjects per group, and Polich and Bloom (1988) tested only ten subjects per group.

An inverse correlation between the amount of alcohol consumption (drinks per sitting) and the amplitude of P3 was found by Polich and Bloom (1987) without the administration of alcohol. However, this relationship was only apparent for a difficult intensity discrimination task in FHP subjects. Although there was a trend in this direction in FHN subjects, it was not significant. The authors concluded that FHP subjects are more sensitive to the effects of alcohol than are FHN subjects. When a similar intensity discrimination study was performed in the visual modality, no correlation between P3 characteristics and amount of alcohol typically consumed was found (Polich et al. 1988). Furthermore, in yet another study designed to replicate Elmasian et al. (1982), Polich and Bloom (1988) not only did not replicate their previous findings of a placebo effect in the FHP group, but also now reported that in both FHP and FHN subjects there was a correlation between P3 *latency* and amount of alcohol consumption.

These findings relating alcohol consumption to P3 characteristics therefore do not appear to be robust. In the same laboratory, using samples drawn from the same basic population of students, their findings are not readily replicable. Previous alcohol consumption has been found to correlate with P3 amplitude only, particularly in FHP subjects (Polich and Bloom 1987), to correlate with P3 latency only (Polich and Bloom 1988), and to be uncorrelated with any previous drinking variables (Polich et al. 1988). The relationship between P3 characteristics and drinking history is as yet an unresolved issue in other laboratories as well. O'Connor et al. (1986) report no relationship between any P3 characteristic and drinking history, whereas Steinhauer et al. (1987) report a correlation between drinking history and P3 latency. In addition to correlations between P3 characteristics and drinking history, N430 latency has been reported to correlate with number of drinks per occasion in HR subjects (Schmidt and Neville 1985).

One possible explanation for the lack of results in the San Diego group is the mode of assessment of alcoholism in the fathers, and the clinical assessment of their families in general. A questionnaire is filled out by the son about his father's alcohol and psychiatric history and that of his first- and second-degree relatives. Unconventional criteria regarding the father's alcoholism are employed (a single positive symptom), and no verification of family history by other family members is used. Thus, it is possible that in a large percentage of subjects, the offspring are not offspring of alcoholics but of heavy or moderate drinkers. This weakens the possibility of obtaining ERP differences between FHP and FHN groups. Therefore, it is conceivable that there is more agreement in the literature dealing with subjects at risk for alcoholism than had been heretofore suspected.

Although it has been hypothesized that discrepancies in results between laboratories may be due to task difficulty, recent evidence fails to support this contention. O'Connor et al. (1987), using two tasks at different levels of task difficulty, obtained identical results with both paradigms. Begleiter et al. replicated their finding of a lower P3 amplitude in HR subjects without the ingestion of alcohol in four different paradigms thus far; namely: a complex visual response-compatibility/incompatibility design (Begleiter et al. 1984), an auditory modified oddball paradigm (Begleiter et al. 1987b), a visual discrimination paradigm (Porjesz and Begleiter 1990), and an auditory Hillyard paradigm (B. Porjesz and H. Begleiter, in prep.).

More recently, we investigated the effects of alcohol on cognitive ERPs in HR and LR subjects (Porjesz and Begleiter 1990). Twenty-four pairs of male HR and LR subjects (aged 19–24) received either a placebo or one of two ethanol doses (0.5 ml/kg and 0.8 ml/kg) mixed with three parts ginger ale on three separate occasions. A visual ERP paradigm involving easy and difficult line orientation discriminations was utilized. ERPs and measures of levels of intoxication were obtained pre-ethanol and at 20, 60, 90, and 130 minutes following ethanol ingestion. Blood alcohol levels (BALs) were monitored at 10-minute intervals throughout the test session.

No differences were obtained between groups in terms of BALs or intoxication ratings. The latency of P3 occurred significantly later to the difficult discrimination target than to the easy target in both groups of subjects. The high dose of alcohol significantly increased the latency of P3 to the difficult target in both groups of subjects. This effect was maximal between 60 and 90 minutes post-ethanol and was significant at all but occipital electrodes. There was a tendency for these alcohol-induced prolonged P3 latencies to recover to pre-alcohol ranges in the HR group. However, they remained delayed in the LR group throughout the study (130 min post-alcohol). In another study, Schuckit et al. (1988) report that FHP males recover more quickly from P3 latency delays induced by alcohol.

The N1 amplitude was significantly decreased by alcohol ingestion, particularly for the non-target stimulus at occipital leads. This result was more pronounced in the FHN than the FHP group. Although N1 amplitude to non-targets remained depressed in the FHN group throughout the test session, it recovered in amplitude by 90 minutes post-ethanol in the FHP group. These results suggest that the HR subjects exhibited more innate tolerance to alcohol than did the LR group. The N1 amplitude did not decrease to the difficult target and was somewhat decreased to the easy target by alcohol. These results support the finding by Roth et al. (1977) that attentional factors can counteract the N1 decreases caused by alcohol and the finding by Campbell and Lowick (1987) that the largest alcohol effects are obtained when attention is mobilized least (to non-targets). It was concluded that ERPs provide sensitive indices of state and trait variables involved in alcohol consumption and that different ERP characteristics are sensitive to different aspects of this multifaceted problem.

SUMMARY AND CONCLUSIONS

The foregoing review of the electrophysiological research in individuals at risk for alcoholism indicates that their ERPs can be characterized by low-voltage P3 amplitudes. This robust finding has been replicated in many different laboratories with different experimental paradigms. The low P3 amplitude is apparent in HR subjects without exposure to alcohol. Reduced P3 voltages have been reported in abstinent alcoholics and have not been found to recover with prolonged abstinence. In contrast, BAERs have been found to recover with prolonged abstinence in alcoholics, and do not differ between HR and LR subjects (Begleiter et al. 1987a). Taken together, this suggests that P3 deficits observed in alcoholics and HR subjects antecede alcoholism, whereas BAER abnormalities in alcoholics are the consequence of alcoholism.

There is substantial evidence indicating that electrophysiological characteristics (both EEG and ERP) are under genetic control. The P3 component has been reported to be more similar among monozygotic twin pairs than controls. In addition, ERPs have been reported to be similar in abstinent alcoholic fathers and their sons (Whipple et al. 1988). Thus, the reduced P3 voltage in HR subjects perhaps provides a phenotypic marker for alcoholism. However, it remains to be determined with longitudinal studies whether those HR individuals manifesting low P3 voltages are in fact those who go on to develop the disease of alcoholism.

HR and LR individuals have also been reported to differ in terms of other electrophysiological measures, namely, N2-P3a, MMN, and EEG. These findings, however, have not been replicated across different laboratories and may not be as robust as the P3 findings. Although it has been reported that HR subjects are characterized by excessive high-frequency EEG without the administration of alcohol, this has only been reported in one laboratory and has not been replicated even within the same laboratory.

In addition to electrophysiological measures that differentiate HR from LR individuals without exposure to alcohol, other electrophysiological measures have been reported to differentiate individuals at risk with the use of alcohol challenges (e.g., changes in alpha, recovery from N1 amplitude reductions, and P3 latency delays of the ERP). Although these electrophysiological measures could represent vulnerability markers for alcoholism, there has not been sufficient replication, and a substantial amount of disagreement remains in the literature.

The lack of consensus of results among laboratories can at least in part be attributed to differences in subject populations. The only definition of risk for alcoholism that these studies share is that at least the father must have been an alcoholic. Therefore, the density of alcoholism within the family fluctuates across studies. If only the individual's father and no other first- or second-degree relatives are alcoholic, this may not increase the genetic risk for alcoholism but may indicate a phenocopy or sporadic case. Furthermore, the clinical criteria for diagnosis of alcoholism in the father and the manner in which his alcoholism is assessed contribute to differences in the samples studied. Some studies require only one symptom of alcoholism in the father to qualify for inclusion into the FHP group. Therefore the HR subjects in some studies may include offspring of heavy drinkers or problem drinkers. This dilutes the form of familial alcoholism, making it less likely to obtain significant results between groups. Problems such as comorbidity for other psychiatric problems are also treated differently in different studies; individuals manifesting comorbid psychiatric diagnoses (e.g., antisocial personality or affective disorder) may be excluded from some studies and included in others. Because alcoholism is a heterogeneous disease, HR groups in different studies may be composed of different numbers of offspring of different types of alcoholism (e.g., type 1 and type 2). Often the HR subjects studied are beyond the age of risk, or the stringent screening criteria rule out potential pre-alcoholics. Furthermore, environmental influences must be taken into account; variables such as socioeconomic status, education, and age may affect the results obtained. Additionally, differences in selection criteria for the control group may also determine whether differences between HR and LR groups will be found.

Various types of pre-alcoholics may manifest different electrophysiological patterns before and after alcohol administration. That alcoholism is a clinically heterogeneous disease with possible genetic heterogeneity is underscored by the fact that different studies often yield inconsistent results. Therefore, subject selection remains a major problem in HR research. Ideally, the HR sample should consist of young children without prior exposure to alcohol who are offspring of alcoholic fathers from families in which alcoholism is prevalent; these alcoholic fathers should be diagnosed directly, and other psychiatric disorders should be eliminated.

Electrophysiological measures have an advantage in that they can provide indices of both trait and state characteristics. These trait indices perhaps provide phenotypic markers (e.g., P3 amplitude, high-frequency beta) distinguishing subjects at risk for alcoholism without the administration of alcohol. The electrophysiological measures of state characteristics, namely, how an individual's EEG and ERP respond to alcohol (changes in alpha and N1 amplitude), also distinguish HR from LR groups, perhaps representing vulnerability markers for alcoholism. Furthermore, these electrophysiological measures may be useful in distinguishing different subgroups at risk for alcoholism. Future studies focusing on individual differences in electrophysiological measures before and after alcohol administration will help identify individuals at risk for specific types of alcoholism.

To determine whether these electrophysiological measures provide phenotypic markers of alcoholism, longitudinal studies will be needed to assess individuals as they pass through the age of risk. At present, there is no compelling evidence demonstrating that those individuals manifesting a low P3 amplitude are in fact destined to become alcoholics. Longitudinal family studies are under way examining alcoholic and nonalcoholic families to determine which family members become alcoholic as they pass through the age of risk. It is hoped that this approach will elucidate the link between measures of risk and the development of alcoholism.

The foregoing review suggests that electrophysiological measures may serve as phenotypic markers for alcoholism. It is not suggested that these phenotypic markers are necessarily specific for alcoholism, nor is it suggested that all individuals manifesting these "markers" will necessarily go on to abuse alcohol. However, there is evidence that individuals at risk for alcoholism (sons of alcoholic fathers) can be distinguished from those not at risk for alcoholism with electrophysiological measures, both without the ingestion of alcohol and in response to alcohol challenges. Since these electrophysiological measures are genetically determined, the data imply that a predisposition or vulnerability to alcoholism is inherited. The role of environment and the gene-environment interaction are not to be minimized in determining whether an individual manifesting this predisposition goes on to abuse alcohol.

ACKNOWLEDGMENT

This work was supported by National Institute on Alcohol Abuse and Alcoholism grants AA-02686 and AA-05524.

REFERENCES

Baribeau, J.C., M. Ethier, and C.M.J. Braun. 1987. Neurophysiological assessment of selective attention in males at risk for alcoholism. In *Current trends in event-related potential research* (ed. R. Johnson, Jr. et al.), suppl. 40, p. 651. Elsevier Science Publishers B.V., The Netherlands.

Begleiter, H. and A. Platz. 1972. The effects of alcohol on the central nervous system. In *The biology of alcoholism* (ed. B. Kissin and H. Begleiter), vol. 2, p. 293. Plenum Press, New York.

Begleiter, H., B. Porjesz, and B. Bihari. 1987a. Auditory brainstem potentials in sons of alcoholic fathers. *Alcohol. Clin. Exp. Res.* 11: 477.

Begleiter, H., B. Porjesz, and C.L. Chou. 1981. Auditory brainstem potentials in chronic alcoholics. *Science* 211: 1064.

Begleiter, H., B. Porjesz, B. Bihari, and B. Kissin. 1984. Event-related brain potentials in boys at risk for alcoholism. *Science* 225: 1493.

Begleiter, H., B. Porjesz, R. Rawlings, and M. Eckardt. 1987b. Auditory recovery function and P3 in boys at high risk for alcoholism. *Alcohol* 4: 314.

Bohman, M. 1978. Some genetic aspects of alcoholism and criminality: A population of adoptees. *Arch. Gen. Psychiatry* 35: 269.

Buchsbaum, M. and A. Pfefferbaum. 1971. Individual differences in stimulus intensity response. *Psychophysiology* 8: 600.

Cadoret, R.I. and A. Gath. 1978. Inheritance of alcoholism in adoptees. *Br. J. Psychiatry* **132:** 252.

Cadoret, R.I., C. Cain, and W.M. Grove. 1980. Development of alcoholism in adoptees raised apart from alcoholic biologic relatives. *Arch. Gen. Psychiatry* **37:** 561.

Campbell, K.B. and B.M. Lowick. 1987. Ethanol and event-related potentials: The influence of distractor stimuli. *Alcohol* **4:** 257.

Chu, N.S. and K.C. Squires. 1980. Auditory brainstem response study in alcoholic patients. *Pharmacol. Biochem. Behav.* **13:** 241.

Chu, N.S. and S.S. Yang. 1987. Somatosensory and brainstem auditory evoked potentials in alcoholic liver disease with and without encephalopathy. *Alcohol* **4:** 225.

Chu, N.S., K.C. Squires, and A. Starr. 1982. Auditory brainstem responses in chronic alcoholic patients. *Electroencephalogr. Clin. Neurophysiol.* **54:** 418.

Church, M.W. and H.L. Williams. 1982. Dose- and time-dependent effects of ethanol on brain stem auditory evoked responses in young adult males. *Electroencephalogr. Clin. Neurophysiol.* **54:** 161.

Cloninger, C.R. 1987. Neurogenetic adaptive mechanisms in alcoholism. *Science* **236:** 410.

Cloninger, C., M. Bohman, and S. Sigvardisson. 1981. Inheritance of alcohol abuse: Cross-fostering analysis of adopted men. *Arch. Gen. Psychiatry* **38:** 861.

Donchin. E. 1979. Event-related brain potentials: A tool in the study of human information processing. In *Evoked brain potentials and behavior* (ed. H. Begleiter), vol. 2, p. 13. Plenum Press, New York.

Donchin, E., W. Ritter, and W.C. McCallum. 1978. Cognitive psychophysiology: The endogenous components of the ERP. In *Event-related brain potentials in man* (ed. E. Callaway et al.), p. 349. Academic Press, New York.

Dustman, R.E. and E.C. Beck. 1965. The visually evoked potentials in twins. *Electroencephalogr. Clin. Neurophysiol.* **19:** 541.

Ehlers, C.L. and M.A. Schuckit. 1990a. EEG fast frequency activity in sons of alcoholics. *Biol. Psychiatry* **27:** 631.

———. 1990b. Evaluation of EEG alpha activity in sons of alcoholics. *Am. J. Psychiatry* (in press).

Elmasian, R., H. Neville, D. Woods, M. Schuckit, and F. Bloom. 1982. Event-related brain potentials are different in individuals at high and low risk for developing alcoholism. *Proc. Natl. Acad. Sci.* **79:** 7900.

Fukui, Y., M. Mori, M. Kohga, T. Tadai, K. Tanaka, and N. Katoh. 1981. Reassessment of CNS effects of acute ethanol administration with auditory evoked response: A comparative study of brain stem auditory evoked response, middle latency response and slow vertex response. *Jpn. J. Alcohol Stud. Drug Depend.* **16:** 9.

Gabrielli, W.F., S.A. Mednick, J. Volavka, V.E. Pollack, F. Schulsinger, and T.M. Tiltil. 1982. Electroencephalograms in children of alcoholic fathers. *Psychophysiology* **19:** 404.

Goodwin, D.W. 1979. Alcoholism and heredity: A review and hypothesis. *Arch. Gen. Psychiatry* **36:** 57.

———. 1981. *Alcoholism: The Facts.* Oxford University Press, New York.

Goodwin, D.W. and S.B. Guze. 1974. Heredity and alcoholism. In *Biology of alcoholism* (ed. B. Kissin and H. Begleiter), vol. 3, p. 37. Plenum Press, New York.

Goodwin, D.W., F. Schulsinger, N. Moller, L. Hermansen, G. Winokur, and S.B. Guze. 1973. Alcohol problems in adoptees raised apart from alcoholic biological parents. *Arch. Gen. Psychiatry* **28:** 238.

Hill, S.Y., S.R. Steinhauer, J. Zubin, and T. Baughman. 1988. Event-related potentials as markers for alcoholism risk in high density families. *Alcohol. Clin. Exp. Res.* **12:** 545.

Hillyard, S.A., T.W. Picton, and D. Regan. 1978. Sensation, perception and attention: Analysis using ERPs. In *Event related brain potentials in man* (ed. E. Callaway et al.), p. 223. Academic Press, New York.

Jones, F.W. and D.S. Holmes. 1976. Alcoholism, alpha production and biofeedback. *J. Consult. Clin. Psychol.* **44:** 224.

Jonsson, E. and T. Nilsson. 1968. Alkohol konsumtion hos monorygota och dizygota tuillingpar. *Nord. Hyg. Tidskr.* **49:** 21.

Kaij, L. 1960. *Alcoholism in twins: Studies on the etiology and sequels of abuse of alcohol.* Almquist and Wiksell, Stockholm, Sweden.

Loehlin, J.C. 1972. Analysis of alcohol-related questionnaire items from the National Merit Twin Study. *Ann. N.Y. Acad. Sci.* **197:** 117.

Naitoh, P. 1973. The value of electroencephalography in alcoholism. *Am. N.Y. Acad. Sci.* **215:** 303.

Neville, H.J. and A.L. Schmidt. 1985. Event-related brain potentials in subjects at risk for alcoholism. National Institute on Alcohol Abuse and Alcoholism Research Monograph No. 15/16.

O'Connor, S., V. Hesselbrock, and A. Tasman. 1986. Correlates of increased risk for alcoholism in young men. *Prog. Neuropsychopharmacol. Biol. Psychiatry* **10:** 211.

O'Connor, S., V. Hesselbrock, A. Tasman, and N. De Palma. 1987. P3 amplitudes in two distinct tasks are decreased in young men with a history of paternal alcoholism. *Alcohol* **4:** 323.

Partanen, J., K. Brun, and T. Markkamen. 1966. *Inheritance of drinking behavior: A study on intelligence, personality, and use of alcohol of adult twins.* Finnish Foundation for Alcohol Studies, Helsinki.

Patterson, B.W., H.L. Williams, G.A. McLean, L.T. Smith, and K.W. Schaeffer. 1987. Alcoholism and family history of alcoholism: Effects on visual and auditory event-related potentials. *Alcohol* **4:** 265.

Pfefferbaum, A., M. Rosenbloom, and J.M. Ford. 1987. Late event-related potential changes in alcoholics. *Alcohol* **4:** 275.

Polich, J. and F.E. Bloom. 1986. P300 and alcohol consumption in normals and individuals at risk for alcoholism. *Prog. Neuropsychopharmacol. Biol. Psychiatry* **10:** 201.

―――. 1987. P300 from normals and children of alcoholics. *Alcohol* **4:** 301.

―――. 1988. Event-related potentials in individuals at high and low risk for developing alcoholism: Failure to replicate. *Alcohol. Clin. Exp. Res.* **12:** 368.

Polich, J. and T. Burns. 1987. P300 from identical twins. *Neuropsychologia* **25:** 299.

Polich, J., R.J. Haier, M. Buchsbaum, and F.E. Bloom. 1988. Assessment of young

men at risk for alcoholism with P300 from a visual discrimination task. *J. Stud. Alcohol* **49**: 186.
Pollock, V.E., W.F. Gabrielli, S.A. Mednick, and D.W. Goodwin. 1988. EEG identification of subgroups of men at risk for alcoholism. *Psychiatry Res.* **26(1)**: 101.
Pollock, V.E., J. Volavka, S.A. Mednick, D.W. Goodwin, J. Knop, and F. Schulsinger. 1984. A prospective study of alcoholism: Electroencephalographic findings. In *Longitudinal research in alcoholism* (ed. D.W. Goodwin et al.), p. 125. Kluwer-Nijloff, Boston.
Pollock, V.E., J. Volavka, D.W. Goodwin, S.A. Mednick, W.F. Gabrielli, J. Knop, and F. Schulsinger. 1983. The EEG after alcohol administration in men at risk for alcoholism. *Arch. Gen. Psychiatry* **40**: 857.
Porjesz, B. and H. Begleiter. 1983. Brain dysfunction and alcohol. In *The pathogenesis of alcoholism: Biological factors* (ed. B. Kissin and H. Begleiter), p. 415. Plenum Press, New York.
———. 1985. Human brain electrophysiology and alcoholism. In *Alcohol and the brain* (ed. R.D. Tarter and D. Van Thiel), p. 139. Plenum Press, New York.
———. 1990. Event-related potentials in individuals at risk for alcoholism. *Alcohol* (in press).
Porjesz, B., H. Begleiter, and R. Garozzo. 1980. Visual evoked potential correlates of information processing deficits in chronic alcoholics. In *Biological effects of alcohol* (ed. H. Begleiter), p. 603. Plenum Press, New York.
Porjesz, B., H. Begleiter, B. Bihari, and B. Kissin. 1987. The N2 component of the event-related brain potential in abstinent alcoholics. *Electroencephalogr. Clin. Neurophysiol.* **66**: 121.
Propping, P. 1977. Genetic control of ethanol action in the central nervous system: An EEG study in twins. *Hum. Genet.* **35**: 309.
———. 1983. Pharmacogenetics of alcohol's CNS effect: Implications for etiology of alcoholism. *Pharmacol. Biochem. Behav.* (suppl.1) **18**: 549.
Propping, P., J. Kruger, and N. Mark. 1981. Genetic disposition to alcoholism: An EEG study in alcoholics and their relatives. *Hum. Genet.* **59**: 51.
Rosenhamer, H.J. and B.I. Silfversköld. 1980. Slow tremor and delayed brainstem auditory evoked responses in alcoholics. *Arch. Neurol.* **37**: 293.
Roth, W.T., J.R. Tinklenberg, and B.S. Kopell. 1977. Ethanol and marijuana effects on event-related potentials in a memory retrieval paradigm. *Electroencephalogr. Clin. Neurophysiol.* **42**: 381.
Schmidt, A.L. and H.J. Neville. 1985. Language processing in men at risk for alcoholism: An event-related potential study. *Alcohol* **2**: 529.
Schuckit, M.A. 1980. Self-rating of alcohol intoxication by young men with and without family histories of alcoholism. *J. Stud. Alcohol* **41**: 242.
———. 1984. Subjective responses to alcohol in sons of alcoholics and control subjects. *Arch. Gen. Psychiatry* **41**: 879.
Schuckit, M.A., E.O. Gold, K. Croot, P. Finn, and J. Polich. 1988. P300 latency after ethanol ingestion in sons of alcoholics and controls. *Biol. Psychiatry* **24**: 310.
Steinhauer, S.R., S.Y. Hill, and J. Zubin. 1987. Event-related potentials in alcoholics and their first-degree relatives. *Alcohol* **4**: 307.

Surwillo, W.W. 1980. Cortical evoked potentials in monozygotic twins and unrelated subjects: Comparisons of exogenous and endogenous components. *Behav. Genet.* **10:** 201.

Tarter, R.E., A.I. Alterman, and K.L. Edwards. 1984. Alcoholic denial: A biopsychological interpretation. *J. Stud. Alcohol* **45:** 214.

Vogel, F. 1970. The genetic basis of the normal human electroencephalogram (EEG). *Humangenetik* **10:** 91.

Vogel, F., J. Kruger, H.P. Hopp, R. Schnobel, and E. Schalt. 1986. Visually and auditory evoked EEG potentials in carriers of four hereditary EEG variants. *Hum. Neurobiol.* **5:** 49.

Whipple, S.C., E.S. Parker, and E.P. Nobel. 1988. An atypical neurocognitive profile in alcoholic fathers and their sons. *J. Stud. Alcohol.* **49:** 240.

Young, J.P., M.H. Lader, and G.W. Fenton. 1972. A twin study on the genetic influences on the electroencephalogram. *J. Med. Genet.* **9:** 13.

COMMENTS

Searles: I want to ask Henri about the differences between your findings and John Polich's findings.

Begleiter: The findings from our lab have been replicated in a few places, including our own lab, except in Polich's lab. I think the primary difference—and I'll let John disagree if he wishes—the primary, probably the sole, difference is on two levels. One is our subject selection; we are dealing with totally different subject groups. The subjects in John's lab are recruited in a similar manner to what Marc Schuckit does. That is, a questionnaire is sent out on the UCSD campus; they recruit a different kind of individual than we would. Selection criteria, ascertainment are really totally different. I believe that's the most important difference. The second difference, and probably less important, are tasks used, our paradigms. Our tests are all visual, with the exception of one. They are fairly demanding tasks, typically more demanding than what Polich has used. I would attribute the difference in our findings to these two factors.

Polich: I agree totally. Because of equipment limitations, I wasn't able to implement a lot of visual-type tasks at the time I did those studies. Then, as the field emerged, I became very sensitized to the difference, as Henri said, in terms of the differences in his population and mine, and also this task difference, which I really think plays a big part.

Reich: Henri, you've got the six dipoles at this point.

Begleiter: We have up to six dipoles.

Reich: Yes, and, assuming each dipole is a nucleus or a generator of some import, if you think of the brain as a collection of organs, there are probably a lot more. Is there any theoretical limit to the number of dipoles?

Begleiter: At this point, it's computer bound. However, remember, we are looking to fit data to a specific physiological event. We can be sure there aren't 10 million dipoles going on where that is generated. That's a well-known fact. How many there are, I can't be sure. Indeed, when you try to see the number of dipoles, you rarely have to exceed 6. You can optimize, again using a numerical procedure, using a simplex procedure, you can account for most of your data using 2 or 3 dipoles per derived component.

Reich: That may be the consequence of a small amount of information.

Lander: One question; what about girls? You're studying boys. Any naive model I have I should expect to see in girls or I'd like to know a good reason why it's not there.

Begleiter: We have never studied girls and probably are not going to, at least in the next couple of months, but there are people who have. The group at McLean Hospital has studied some females. Does anyone know what they find? I don't.

Schuckit: Dr. Lex replicates our kind of stuff, but she hasn't looked at the electrophysiology yet. They'll get to it, I'm sure.

Alcoholic Fathers and Their Sons: Neuropsychological, Electrophysiological, Personality, and Family Correlates

ERNEST P. NOBLE
Alcohol Research Center
The Neuropsychiatric Institute and The Brain Research Institute
University of California
Los Angeles, California 90024

OVERVIEW

Twin, sibling, and adoption studies suggest that there is a clear genetic component to alcoholism. In this study, alcoholic fathers and their prepubescent sons are compared to nonalcoholic fathers and their sons across three dimensions of CNS functioning: neuropsychological, electrophysiological, and personality traits. Moreover, the family environments of these subjects are compared, and the emerging alcohol and other drug use behaviors of the sons are ascertained. The results show that (1) children of alcoholics with a positive family history of alcoholism (A^+) and their fathers are different from children of nonalcoholics without a family history of alcoholism (NA^-) in tests measuring neuropsychological and electrophysiological functioning and in personality traits; (2) significant correlations exist between personality composites and neurocognitive variables (P300 amplitude, memory, and Embedded Figures Test [EFT]); (3) A^+ families show little or no dysfunction in the family environment compared to NA^- families; (4) A^+ sons compared to NA^- sons reveal increased use of alcohol, cigarettes, and marijuana. This study suggests that children of alcoholics and their fathers possess an atypical CNS profile. Prospective studies will determine whether or not this profile is a predictor of future problems associated with alcohol and other drug use.

INTRODUCTION

In an attempt to separate genetic from environmental factors, various investigators, both in the United States and abroad, have employed twin, sibling, and adoption studies (Goodwin et al. 1974; Cloninger et al. 1981; Schuckit 1981, 1985). The data converge to suggest that genetic factors play an important role in predisposition to alcoholism. Specifically, sons of alcoholics are about four times more likely to be alcoholic than are sons of nonalcoholics (Goodwin et al. 1973). Although there is also some evidence for genetic factors in daughters of alcoholics, the data at this time are not as complete for females as for males.

If we assume that heritable factors are involved in alcoholism, it may be asked, What is transmitted to the children of alcoholics? Are they endowed with unique neuropsychological capacities, electrophysiological responses, and personality traits? Is the home environment of children of alcoholics different from that of children of nonalcoholics? Do children of alcoholics manifest altered behaviors regarding alcohol and other drugs as they enter the critical period of adolescence?

To get a better understanding of these questions, over the past 5 years, we have embarked on a multidiscipline prospective study on the assessment of CNS functioning in prepubescent sons of alcoholics and nonalcoholics and their fathers. For this study, 60 father/son pairs were screened rigorously to select three distinct groups. The 20 A^+ boys had a strong family history of alcoholism; not only were their fathers recovering alcoholics, but the fathers also had at least one first- or second-degree alcoholic relative. The 20 NA^+ boys had nonalcoholic fathers, but these fathers had at least one first- or second-degree alcoholic relative. The 20 NA^- boys had nonalcoholic fathers, and their fathers had no alcoholic relatives.

Fathers' alcoholism was diagnosed according to DSMIII-R criteria by interview and information obtained from independent, confidential collateral verification from at least three other sources. Social drinking by nonalcoholic fathers was also confirmed by collateral verification. Alcoholic fathers had to be abstinent for at least 2 years. None of the mothers was alcoholic, and their average reported alcohol consumption during pregnancy with the subject boys did not exceed two drinks per week. None of the boys at the start of the study was reported to have begun drinking or using other drugs.

The boys in each group were matched for age, years of education, and fathers' incomes. Each of the three groups of boys averaged 10 years of age and had 5 years of education. The fathers' average ages, in each of the three groups, was in the lower 40s, and they earned approximately $40,000 per annum. Not surprisingly, the A^+ fathers had consumed significantly more alcohol than either NA^+ or NA^- fathers (225 gallons of pure ethanol vs. 14 and 32 gallons, respectively). There were no significant differences on any other demographic variable. Written informed consent was obtained from both fathers and sons before their participation in the study.

RESULTS

Neuropsychological Studies

Table 1 shows the mean scores for sons and fathers on the neuropsychological battery (Whipple et al. 1988). The MANOVA indicated significant between-group differences on neuropsychological performance for the boys (Roy's maximum root=0.53, p <0.05). The t-tests showed that high-risk (A^+) boys had significantly poorer performance than low-risk (NA^-) controls on block design, picture completion, and object assembly subtests of the Wechsler Intelligence Scales for Children-Revised (WISC-R) and on the EFT. The reduced performance IQ score of the A^+ boys is primarily reflective of their poorer performance on the above three visuoperceptual subtests of the WISC-R. Moreover, A^+ boys also showed significantly poorer memory scores than NA^- boys. The NA^+ boys did not differ significantly from the NA^- boys on any of the assessed neuropsychological measures.

The MANOVA for the neuropsychological test battery for the fathers also indicated significant between-group differences (Roy's maximum root=0.49, p <0.05). t-tests showed that alcoholic fathers, compared to NA^- fathers, had significantly reduced visuoperceptual performance and poorer memory on the same set of tests (except the digit span) that differentiated their sons. The NA^+ fathers also had certain areas of reduced performance on the neuropsychological battery; compared to the NA^- fathers, they had significant reductions in the IQ scales, block design, object assembly, and digit span. Both A^+ and NA^+ fathers had significantly lower full-scale IQ scores compared to NA^- fathers, reflecting, in part, their reduced performance on the visuoperceptual and memory subtests of the Wechsler Adult Intelligence Scales (WAIS). It is of interest to note that Schaeffer et al. (1984) also found reduced neuropsychological performance in nonalcoholic men with a positive family history for alcoholism.

Electrophysiological Studies

A resting electroencephalogram (EEG) was obtained with the subjects' eyes opened for 1 minute and with eyes closed for 1 minute. The EEG was recorded from an array of 13 scalp electrodes. The electro-oculogram was recorded as well, to edit the data for eye movement artifacts. The raw EEG was fast Fourier-transformed, and the power spectral density was obtained. The average amplitude in the θ, α, and β frequency bands was subsequently analyzed. The data revealed no significant differences in these frequency bands observed among the three groups of sons or fathers.

The second type of electrical activity that we studied is the event-related potentials (ERPs). These potentials reflect the brain's response to a stimulus. By presenting stimuli that vary on one or more dimensions and requiring the subjects to make a behavioral response to stimuli, concurrent measures of behavior and CNS activity are obtained. Inferences can then be drawn concerning the relationship between the two.

Because there has been conflict in the literature as to whether ERP differences exist between the children of alcoholics and those of nonalcoholics

Table 1
Mean Scores (±S.E.M.) for Sons and Fathers on the Neuropsychological Test Battery

Measure	A⁺ (n = 15)	NA⁺ (15)	NA⁻ (15)	Contrasts[a] A⁺ vs. NA⁻	NA⁺ vs. NA⁻
		Sons			
WISC-R					
verbal IQ	115 ± 3	119 ± 3	117 ± 3		
performance IQ	105 ± 3	116 ± 2	115 ± 3	**	
full-scale IQ	111 ± 3	119 ± 3	118 ± 3		
Visuoperception					
EFT[b]: total correct	9.3 ± 0.9	12.5 ± 1.3	14.4 ± 1.5	**	
block design	11.5 ± 0.5	12.8 ± 0.6	13.3 ± 0.7	*	
picture completion	10.9 ± 0.8	12.3 ± 0.5	13.2 ± 0.6	**	
object assembly	9.9 ± 0.6	13.4 ± 0.4	12.8 ± 0.7	***	
Memory					
digit span	9.4 ± 0.8	10.5 ± 0.6	11.2 ± 0.7	*	
AVLT[c]: first recall	5.5 ± 0.4	6.7 ± 0.5	7.5 ± 0.5	***	
AVLT[c]: total recall	74.4 ± 3.2	84.2 ± 3.0	81.9 ± 2.3	*	

			Fathers		
WAIS					
verbal IQ	118 ± 3	119 ± 3		126 ± 2	*
performance IQ	110 ± 2	117 ± 3	***	129 ± 3	**
full-scale IQ	115 ± 3	119 ± 2	***	129 ± 2	**
Visuoperception					
EFT[b]: total correct	15.2 ± 1.5	18.5 ± 1.1	*	19.5 ± 1.4	
block design	12.2 ± 0.8	13.0 ± 0.6	**	14.7 ± 0.6	*
picture completion	11.1 ± 0.6	12.4 ± 0.6	**	13.1 ± 0.5	
object assembly	11.8 ± 0.9	11.5 ± 1.2	**	14.7 ± 0.8	*
Memory					
digit span	12.2 ± 0.8	11.1 ± 1.0		13.9 ± 0.9	
AVLT[c]: first recall	6.8 ± 0.4	7.7 ± 0.5	*	7.9 ± 0.5	*
AVLT[c]: total recall	78.5 ± 3.9	85.7 ± 3.4	*	89.7 ± 3.4	

Reprinted, with permission, from Whipple et al. (1988).
[a](*) $P < 0.05$; (**) $P < 0.01$; (***) $P < 0.001$.
[b]Embedded Figures Test.
[c]Rey Auditory Verbal Learning Test.

(Begleiter et al. 1984; O'Conner et al. 1987; Polich and Bloom 1987, 1988), we attempted to resolve this issue by utilizing two ERP paradigms. The first, a simple one, consisted of an easy color discrimination task. The second was a more demanding test and consisted of a continuous performance task (CPT).

In the easy color discrimination task, the subject sat at a distance of 120 cm from a video monitor, which displayed a sequence of colored triangles, one at a time. The subject was instructed to monitor the sequence of triangles and keep a mental count of triangles of one color. The two colors used were blue and orange. The color of the triangles to be counted, which occurred less frequently than that of the other triangle, was counterbalanced among the four runs of this ERP task (orange, blue, blue, orange). This paradigm results in an ERP wave form to the infrequently occurring (target) stimulus, which is characterized by a large positive deflection, the P300 component, at approximately 300–500 ms poststimulus. The results of this task revealed no significant latency or amplitude differences among the three groups of sons or fathers.

In the more demanding CPT, subjects monitored a sequence of complex visual stimuli and kept a mental count whenever two successive stimuli matched on three stimulus dimensions: shape, color, and the identity of a numeral appearing at the center of the shape. This task required not only sustained vigilance, but also short-term memory processes. A similar task has been used to gather normative ERP data on adolescents (Friedman et al. 1981).

A total of four CPT runs, each comprising 200 stimulus presentations, were given to each subject, separated by 5-minute rest periods. Separate ERPs were obtained for the matching stimuli and the nonmatching stimuli. Average ERPs were computed for each subject across the four runs. The average voltage over three latency windows—300–400, 400–500, and 500–600 ms—was computed for activity recorded at each electrode site. The means and standard errors for these measures for each group of sons and fathers are presented in Figure 1 (Whipple et al. 1988).

The data on the sons are shown in Figure 1 (top). The MANOVA revealed that significant differences existed in late positive complex (LPC) amplitude among the three groups of boys (Roy's maximum root=0.46, $p < 0.05$). The planned comparisons disclosed a significantly reduced LPC amplitude in high-risk A^+ boys compared to NA^- controls; this occurred at all three electrode locations (Fz, Cz, and Pz) for the mean amplitude over the 300- to 400-ms and 400- to 500-ms latency windows. No significant differences were found between NA^+ and NA^- sons in any of the three latency windows.

The planned comparisons for the fathers, shown in Figure 1 (bottom), revealed the amplitude of the LPCs to be significantly reduced in the A^+ group compared to the NA^- group at all electrode sites for the 400- to 500-ms

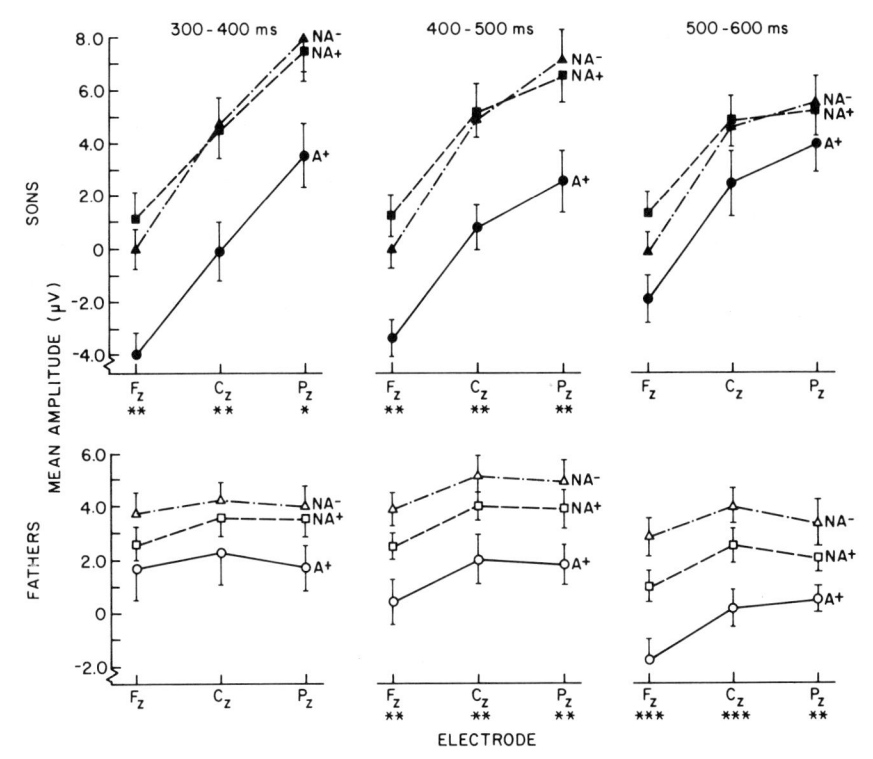

Figure 1
Mean amplitude (±s.e.m.) measures in three latency windows, 300–400, 400–500, and 500–600 ms, at three electrode locations, frontal (Fz), central (Cz), and parietal (Pz). (Filled symbols) Sons; (open symbols) fathers. (Solid lines) A⁺ sons and fathers; (dashed lines) NA⁺ sons and fathers; (dot/dash lines) NA⁻ sons and fathers. (*)$p < 0.05$; (**) $p < 0.01$; (***)$p < 0.001$; A⁺ vs. NA⁻. (Reprinted, with permission, from Whipple et al. 1988.)

and 500- to 600-ms latency windows. The NA⁺ fathers exhibited LPC amplitude values that were intermediate to the A⁺ and NA⁻ fathers who, unlike their sons, had LPC amplitudes similar to the NA⁻ controls.

The next question raised was, Is there any relationship between the neuropsychological decrements found in the sons of alcoholics and their reduced LPC amplitudes? We found that in our boys, the amplitude of the LPC at the 400- to 500-ms latency window, at Cz, was significantly ($p < 0.05$) and positively correlated with performance on the object assembly, a test for visual perception. However, measures of LPC amplitudes were not correlated with memory tasks, lending further support to a specific relationship between LPC elicited with the visual CPT and visuoperceptive processing. A similar pattern was observed in the fathers. Significant correlations were obtained between LPC amplitude in the 500- to 600-ms range at Cz and performance on the picture completion subtest ($p < 0.01$) and performance IQ ($p < 0.02$), but not between LPC amplitude and memory.

To test the viability of visuoperceptual dysfunction as a putative CNS marker for alcoholism, a discriminant function analysis (Dixon and Brown 1983) was conducted using the EFT, object assembly, and parietal and central measures of the LPC as variables at the 400- to 500-ms range. Of the boys in the two extreme groups (A^+ and NA^-), 80% were correctly classified using a jackknife test of the discriminant function. It is possible that the atypical neurocognitive profile found in the A^+ boys represents a marker for alcoholism.

Personality Traits

If children of alcoholics can be distinguished from children of nonalcoholics on the basis of neuropsychological and electrophysiological measures, can they also be distinguished on another aspect of CNS functioning, namely, personality traits?

To shed light on this question, we administered four different personality tests to both fathers and sons: (1) the Minnesota Multiphasic Personality Inventory (MMPI) (fathers) and the Personality Inventory for Children (PIC) (sons); (2) the Eysenck Personality Inventory (fathers) and the Junior Eysenck Personality Inventory (sons); (3) the 16 Personality Factor (16PF) questionnaire for adults (fathers) and the equivalent High School Personality Questionnaire (HSPQ) for children (sons); and (4) the Tridimensional Personality Questionnaire (TPQ) (Cloninger 1987) (sons and fathers).

The personality data summarized showed that A^+ fathers and sons had many similarities that distinguished them from their respective NA^+ and NA^- groups. The A^+ fathers and their sons were more tense about uncertainty or physical danger, more easily fatigued, more harm avoidant, and less adventuresome than NA^+ and NA^- fathers and sons. A^+ fathers, moreover, were more neurotic, more apprehensive/insecure, more tense/frustrated, more anxious, more pessimistic, and more shy with strangers than NA^+ and NA^- fathers. Similarly, A^+ boys were more introverted, more sensitive, more thoughtless/impulsive, and less independent/aggressive than NA^+ and NA^- sons.

To ascertain whether or not a certain constellation of variables characterized A^+ fathers and their sons, separate MANOVAs were conducted for the primary and factor scales. Following a significant MANOVA, a linear discriminant function (LDF) was computed to optimize between group differences. It was then necessary to determine which of the variables made the greatest relative contribution to the significant group difference. For this, stepwise discriminant analyses were conducted, beginning with all of the variables from the MANOVA in the stepwise analysis and then obtained the F-to-remove statistics from the last step. (Deleting a variable with a large F-to-remove is interpreted as substantially affecting group variable effect; i.e., it will significantly decrease group separation.) As a final step, a single personality index, or composite, was computed that again optimized group separation. A second LDF was obtained, using those scales from the preceding MANOVAs that were judged to contribute most to the significant group effects as variables. The LDF was then used to calculate canonical scores for each subject, which were, in turn, used to examine father/son personality correlations with the previously obtained neurocognitive variables. The results showed that the personality composite score for sons and fathers was significantly correlated with the P300 amplitude, memory, and EFT. This suggests that the underlying personality traits of the A^+ fathers and sons share a common substrate with the deficits in the visuoperceptual and CPT performance noted in these subjects and form an atypical CNS profile that may be related to the development of alcoholism.

Family Environment

Although CNS characteristics may be an important variable, how does the environment contribute to the development of alcohol problems? Could a chaotic home environment contribute to alcohol and other drug abuse? Some investigators believe that families with a recovering alcoholic member will remain dysfunctional due to the family's chronic maladaptive interactional patterns; because of these maladaptive patterns, children growing up in such families are placed at high risk for developing alcoholism.

To study whether or not our alcoholic families had dysfunctional patterns, we administered the Family Environment Scale (FES) (Moos and Moos 1986) to each father, mother, and son in the three family groups (A^+, NA^+, and NA^-). Essentially, the FES identifies and scores the subscales of the family environment, which include (1) cohesion, (2) expressiveness, (3) conflict, (4) independence, (5) achievement or orientation, (6) intellectual-cultural orientation, (7) active-recreational orientation, (8) moral-religious emphasis, (9) organization, and (10) control.

When the data were analyzed, no significant differences were found among the three groups of fathers or mothers in the ten subscales of the FES. Comparison of subscale scores among sons showed only active-recreational orientation to be significantly ($p < 0.05$) lower in the A^+ group compared to the NA^- group. Similarly, when the subscale scores were obtained for the entire family, active-recreational orientation was significantly lower ($p <$

0.05) in the A^+ group compared to the NA^- group. Overall, the present data suggest that our recovering alcoholic families, compared to nonalcoholic families, show little or no dysfunction in the family environment.

Alcohol and Other Drug-use Behaviors

At least two questions may be raised. If the family environment does not distinguish children of alcoholics from nonalcoholics, what does the atypical CNS profile represent? Does it have an etiological basis, and does it represent a trait marker for the development of alcohol problems? Or is this atypical profile, found in certain families, unrelated to the development of future alcohol problems? Clearly, to answer these questions, it is necessary to follow these children through time and assess their real-world behaviors regarding the use and abuse of alcohol and other drugs.

In an attempt to reach the above objective, we have used self-report measures developed at the University of Colorado (Jessor and Jessor 1977) to assess sensitive alcohol and other drug problem behaviors. We modified this instrument slightly in collaboration with Dr. Donovan of that university and administered a 157-item behavioral questionnaire to our boys.

Recall that the boys were 10 years old, on the average, at entry and had not yet begun to consume alcohol, tobacco, or other drugs. The behavioral questionnaire was administered 3 years later. It should be noted that our attrition rate was low at this point; of the 60 in the original sample, 58 boys were available to register their responses. The boys now averaged 13 years of age, and their numbers were subdivided into the following groups: 19 A^+, 19 NA^+, and 20 NA^-. Of the A^+ boys, 53% had already begun to use alcohol, compared to 26% of the NA^+ and 15% of the NA^- group. The difference in alcohol use between A^+ and NA^- boys was significant at the 0.015 level (Fisher's Exact Test, one-tail). When the percentage of illicit drinkers was identified, i.e., those who drank without parental permission (the type of drinking that is most prone to lead to problem drinking behaviors in the future), the following results were obtained. Of A^+ boys, 32%, compared to 11% of NA^+ and 0% of the NA^- boys, were illicit drinkers. The difference between A^+ and NA^- boys was significant at the 0.008 level.

The percentage of cigarette users was then determined. Of A^+ boys, 40% had smoked cigarettes, compared to 26% of NA^+ and 10% of NA^- boys, with the difference between A^+ and NA^- groups being significant at the 0.026 level. When the boys were asked whether they ever smoked marijuana, 21% of the A^+ boys responded in the affirmative, compared to 5% of the NA^+ and 0% of the NA^- boys. The difference between A^+ and NA^- boys was significant at the 0.047 level.

DISCUSSION

Previous clinical research in alcoholism has compared CNS functioning in alcoholic and nonalcoholic subjects. Individual studies have generally assessed a single CNS parameter: behavioral, neuropsychological, electrophysiological, neuroendocrine, or brain physical measures. Overall, differences in these assessments have been observed between alcoholic and nonalcoholic individuals. However, it has been difficult to ascertain whether the observed findings are a consequence of the chronic effects of alcohol on the CNS or whether the brains of alcoholics are innately different from those of nonalcoholic persons.

A few very recent studies have considered CNS functioning of nonalcoholic children of alcoholics. These studies, like those described above, have also used limited CNS parameters, but they too have generally found differences between children of alcoholics and those of nonalcoholics. Since these children have not experienced problems with alcohol and, in several investigations, have not even begun to drink, the evidence suggests that hereditary factors are playing a role in the differing brain function that the two groups of children demonstrate. However, environmental factors could clearly still contribute to the observed differences.

The present preliminary investigation attempts to integrate and expand on previous studies. It utilizes *both* fathers (alcoholic and nonalcoholic) and their sons in the same set and setting. It employs three parameters of CNS functioning (behavioral, neuropsychological, and electrophysiological), and it uses similar tests to compare fathers and sons. Moreover, it assesses the family environment of these subjects and prospectively follows up alcohol and other drug-use behaviors of the sons.

The evidence provided herein suggests that a transgenerational communality exists in alcoholic fathers and their sons, in that they both demonstrate a similar and an atypical CNS profile that differentiates them from nonalcoholic fathers and their sons. This profile does not appear to be dependent on the family environment. Moreover, the study shows that children of alcoholics engage in enhanced alcohol and other drug-use behaviors. Thus, the data, in toto, point to hereditary CNS factors in alcoholism. However, the conclusion that the observed atypical CNS profile represents a trait marker for alcoholism must await prospective studies that associate this profile with the future development of alcohol problems in these children.

Further studies are needed to confirm and generalize the present observations, using a large sample of subjects containing additional individuals with diverse racial/ethnic and socioeconomic backgrounds and daughters of alcoholics. Moreover, more detailed studies are necessary to consider the role that developmental and other environmental factors play in the observed CNS differentiation between children of alcoholics and those of nonalcoholics.

Given the findings of this study and the growing evidence from other human, as well as animal, investigations of the involvement of hereditary factors in alcohol-seeking behavior, there is a firm rationale to proceed for the search of gene(s) associated with alcoholism. Indeed, the recent discovery of molecular biology techniques and their application, with DNA probes that reveal restriction fragment length polymorphism (RFLP) combined with linkage analysis, has resulted in chromosomal localization of several neurological and psychiatric disorders. We are now collecting blood samples from select large families from the present study with a high aggregation of alcoholics for RFLP studies and linkage analysis. Clearly, the task will be arduous and complex; however, we feel optimistic that with hard work and good luck, the molecular genetic basis for alcoholism will be found in the not too distant future.

ACKNOWLEDGMENTS

I am grateful for the participation of Drs. Stephen Whipple and Elizabeth Parker and Ms. Laurie Meyers in various phases of this study. I also thank the families who volunteered for this study for their enduring patience and interest. This work was generously supported by The Seaver Institute and the National Institute on Alcohol Abuse and Alcoholism (AA-08020).

REFERENCES

Begleiter, H., B. Porjesz, B. Bihari, and B. Kissin. 1984. Event-related brain potentials in boys at risk for alcoholism. *Science* **225:** 1493.

Cloninger, C.R. 1987. A systematic method for clinical description and classification of personality variants. *Arch. Gen. Psychiatry* **44:** 573.

Cloninger, C.R., M. Bohman, and S. Sigvardsson. 1981. Inheritance of alcohol abuse: Cross-fostering analysis of adopted men. *Arch. Gen. Psychiatry* **38:** 861.

Dixon, W.J. and M.B. Brown. 1983. *BMDP statistical software 1983 manual.* University of California Press, Berkeley.

Friedman, E., H.G. Vaughan, and L. Erlenmeyer-Kimling. 1981. Multiple late positive potentials in two visual discrimination tasks. *Psychophysiology* **18:** 635.

Goodwin, D.W., F. Schulsinger, L. Hermansen, S.B. Guze, and G. Winokur. 1973. Alcohol problems in adoptees raised apart from biological parents. *Arch. Gen. Psychiatry* **28:** 238.

Goodwin, D.W., F. Schulsinger, H. Moller, L. Hermansen, G. Winokur, and S.B. Guze. 1974. Drinking problems in adopted and non-adopted sons of alcoholics. *Arch. Gen. Psychiatry* **31:** 164.

Jessor, R. and S.L. Jessor. 1977. *Problem behavior and psychosocial development: A longitudinal study.* Academic Press, New York.

Moos, R.H. and B.S. Moos. 1986. *Family environment scale manual,* 2nd edition. Consulting Psychologists Press, Palo Alto, California.

O'Conner, S., V. Hesselbrock, A. Tasman, and N. DePalma. 1987. P3 amplitudes in two distinct tasks are decreased in young men with a history of paternal alcoholism. *Alcohol* **4:** 323.

Polich, J. and F.E. Bloom. 1987. P300 from normals and adult children of alcoholics. *Alcohol* **4:** 301.

———. 1988. Event-related brain potentials in individuals at high risk for developing alcoholism: Failure to replicate. *Alcoholism* **12:** 368.

Schaeffer, K.W., O.A. Parsons, and T.R. Yohman. 1984. Neuropsychological differences between male familial and nonfamilial alcoholics and nonalcoholics. *Alcoholism* **8:** 347.

Schuckit, M.A. 1981. Twin studies on substance abuse: An overview. In *Twin research 3. Epidemiological and clinical studies* (ed. L. Gedda et al.), p.61. Alan R. Liss, New York.

———. 1985. Studies of populations at high risk for alcoholism. *Psychiatr. Dev.* **3:** 31.

Whipple, S.C., E.S. Parker, and E.P. Noble. 1988. An atypical neurocognitive profile in alcoholic fathers and their sons. *J. Stud. Alcohol* **49:** 240.

COMMENTS

Risch: You presented some data. There were different variables—LPC amplitude was one and personality characteristics were another—where you demonstrated a stronger group difference in the sons than in the fathers. To me, this would be counterintuitive, because you expect a regression toward the mean. You expect that, for any trait marker, the father is going to be more different than the sons are.

Noble: They are.

Risch: In the LPC amplitudes that you showed, there was a much larger difference in the sons than there was in the fathers. The fathers were much closer together. They're age effects.

Noble: Yes.

Heath: Was that just a scaling effect? Was there a difference in variability between generations?

Risch: Well, this also showed up with personality characteristics.

Heath: There was scaling effect in personality traits.

Risch: I would still expect a significant shrinking of the difference between them. That would be the case particularly if you don't have high father-son correlations. In that case, you would expect much less of a difference between those two groups.

Noble: The fathers and sons are not the same. The A^+ fathers are alcoholics, so they have gone through all the experiences that an alcoholic goes through. Moreover, the sons are adolescents; these are young children going through the developmental phases. It's basically apples and oranges, although the apple might have come from the orange. You're still comparing in that sense. The similarities we expect are there, but we would also expect to see a big difference.

Reich: How much of your results could be explained by drinking and drugging in the kids? Obviously, some of your kids have begun to consume and smoke and all that stuff.

Noble: All the data that you saw, the antecedent data, are before they start to use.

Reich: At the end you had found increased marijuana.

Noble: Yes. That was three years later.

Reich: How old were the kids in the beginning?

Noble: Ten.

Reich: They were just beginning, right?

Noble: That's right.

Reich: There could still be some differences due to experimentation and other things?

Noble: No, no. When they started at age 10, none of them were using any drugs. That's when we got the psychological measures and the electrophysiological measures. Then we followed them prospectively. Every year we give them that.

Reich: Did you try to predict from the first measures the consumption?

Noble: No. It's very hard to do that.

Reich: Well, you have the data.

Noble: In terms of alcohol consumption?

Reich: You have the variation among the kids, so you should be able to predict, by ranking or regressions, which of the kids would be expected to drink or drug.

Noble: There's just too much noise in the system. These are very young kids. They're just starting to use this stuff. We've got to wait a few more years until they start getting into problems with alcohol before we can make any definite statements. These are just consumption data, in other words.

Martin: There are a lot of correlations now between reaction time, various aspects of the evoked potential, and IQ. I can't remember what your group differences were on IQ at the beginning, but I had a feeling that the A^+s were low in IQ.

Noble: The sons were lower on the performance IQ. Overall IQ was slightly lower, but not significantly lower, in that group. On the other hand, the A^+ fathers were lower than either of the other two groups in all three IQ measures.

Martin: Yes, but could not these associations with IQ account for some of the effects that you are attributing to alcohol?

Noble: Certainly. That's exactly the point. You see the visual spatial performance: Three of those subtests come out of the performance IQ. That is the point we are making; overall IQ may be decreased, but the decrease is due to a significant decrease of the performance IQ. The visual perception aspects, which were our interest, clearly decreased in the A^+ sons, and certainly in the fathers.

Begleiter: Your very high-risk kids are higher on harm avoidance.

Noble: Correct.

Begleiter: That is counterintuitive.

Noble: Well, it depends. It could be counterintuitive, but it may be that the fathers are alcoholics of different kinds. One must always keep in mind where the subjects came from. Ours came from the newspapers. They didn't come from hospitals. There is an important difference there. You may be getting some special type there. Ours are recovered alcoholics. We require a minimum of two years. It actually turned out that five years was the average recovery time. So, we went to a variety of other criteria, too. I think these things, Henri, might account for the fact that we observed high harm avoidance.

Cloninger: I think Dr. Noble is right to point out that the alcoholics who can abstain for long periods are more likely to be high in harm avoidance. Could I follow up on that just a little? When you say there was a negative correlation between the compounded personality measure and

P3, does that mean that high harm avoidance went with low P3 amplitude?

Noble: When you look at the composite score, of course, harm avoidance is only part of that. There may be a bigger contribution made by the other factors, so I am not sure what the correlation is between P3 and harm avoidance.

Alcohol Effect on the Electroencephalogram: Are There Possibilities for Application of Molecular Genetics?

PETER PROPPING
Institute of Human Genetics
University of Bonn
D-5300 Bonn, Federal Republic of Germany

OVERVIEW

The pattern of the human electroencephalogram (EEG) examined under resting conditions is under strong genetic control. Whereas the average EEG has a multifactorial genetic basis, certain variants follow a simple mode of inheritance, thus pointing to specific genetic factors. Acute alcohol loading tests performed in healthy monozygotic (MZ) and dizygotic (DZ) twins showed that the EEG response is also under genetic control. The most pronounced alcohol effect is produced in the EEG with poor alpha activity, as evidenced by a study in carriers of extreme types of the normal EEG.

An EEG study in alcoholics exhibited a preponderance of higher frequency classes in female, but not in male, patients compared to matched controls. Because the first-degree relatives who had not abused alcohol at any time showed the same tendency, a desynchronized EEG pattern might reflect a certain predisposition to alcohol abuse in females. However, there are unexplained inconsistencies in the data that mainly apply to EEG peculiarities in alcoholics of the two sexes. Mapping and uncovering the genes responsible for variation of the normal resting EEG will certainly be a major step toward a better understanding of the genotype-phenotype relationship in human neurophysiology.

INTRODUCTION

It is an astonishing fact that the human EEG, as examined under resting conditions, is under strong genetic control. After birth, the EEG develops during childhood and youth; at the age of 18, at the latest, it has reached a stable pattern that is characteristic for a given individual. The following features of the EEG of healthy adult individuals are of importance for the geneticist (Vogel 1970; Stassen et al. 1988):

1. The EEG possesses a remarkable variation between individuals.

2. The EEG is characterized by a high intraindividual stability over time.
3. Identical twins, in contrast to fraternal twins, have identical EEG patterns, even in old age or when reared apart.
4. There is a remarkable intrafamiliar similarity of the EEG.
5. Certain variants of the EEG (extreme patterns of the electrical phenomena) follow a simple mode of inheritance, thus indicating a specific genetic peculiarity.

Thus, the phenotype of the EEG possesses all the qualities of a genetic trait. Within physiological dimensions, the EEG pattern is also influenced by sex and age (both females and older adults exhibit more beta waves on the average). Identical twins reared apart proved to differ slightly from MZ twins reared together (Stassen et al. 1988). It could not be excluded, however, that this small deviance is due solely to technical factors, because the EEG tracings of the separated twins contained more artifacts than those of the twins who grew up together.

The human EEG also possesses state characteristics, as evidenced by the typical effects of psychotropic drugs. Centrally acting agents produce typical changes of the EEG according to their pharmacological classes (Herrmann et al. 1979). When given as a single dose, ethanol increases the number of alpha and theta waves, as well as the amplitudes of all frequency classes, a phenomenon called synchronization of the EEG waves.

RESULTS

Genetic Influence on the Effect of Alcohol on the EEG

A twin study that comprised 26 MZ and 26 DZ twin pairs clearly showed that the EEG response to acute alcohol loading is under genetic control (Propping 1977). MZ twins exhibited an EEG response that is as similar as that in the same individuals in repeated experiments. On the other hand, DZ twins reacted differentially to alcohol; their EEGs became even more dissimilar. This phenomenon must have a pharmacodynamic basis, as it was not related to the metabolism of ethanol.

Because the twin study showed a considerable variation between individuals in the EEG response to alcohol, in a second step, carriers of extreme types (Fig. 1) of the normal EEG were subjected to the same alcohol loading experiments. The most pronounced synchronizing effect of alcohol was produced in the EEG with poor alpha wave activity in the pretest state (Propping et al. 1980).

Because no reliable information exists about the neurophysiological basis of interindividual EEG variation, the differential EEG response to alcohol

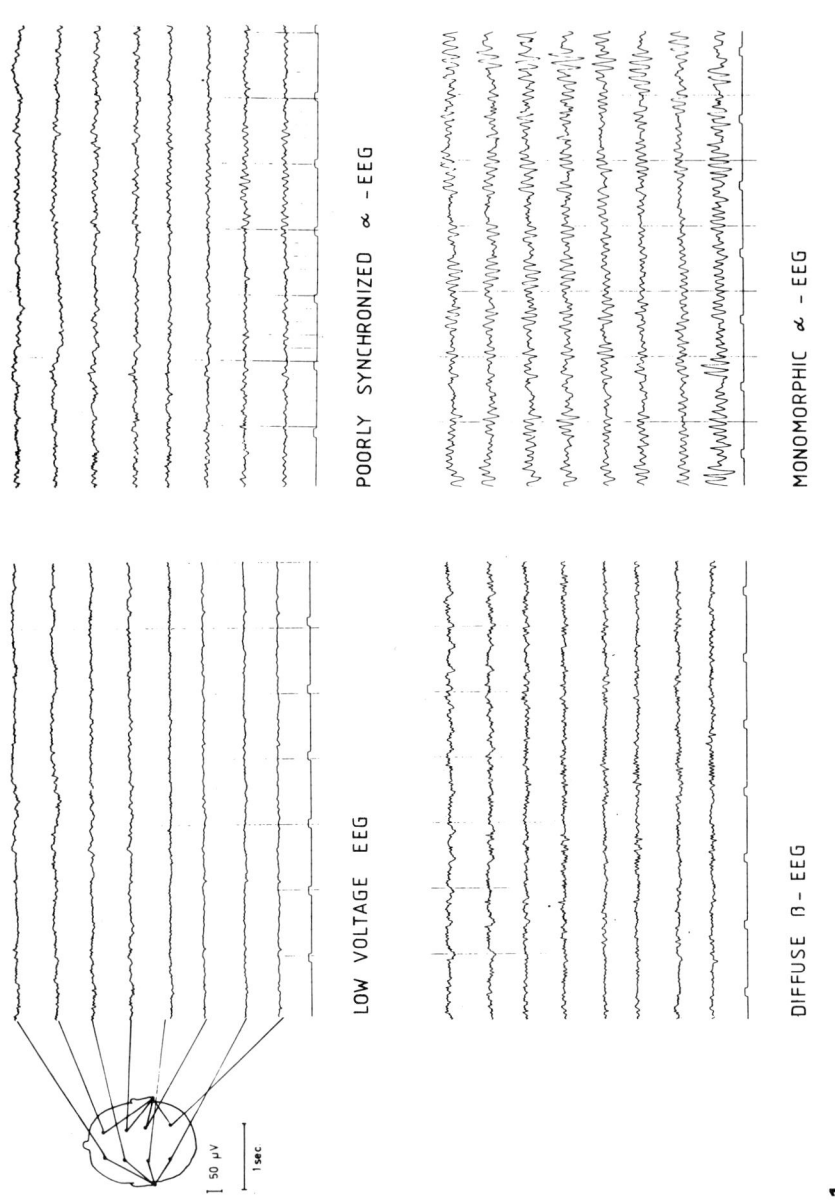

Figure 1
Examples of extreme types of the normal human resting EEG.

may serve as a clue for a certain understanding. The EEG originates in the cortex which, in turn, is under the control of deeper brain regions (Creutzfeldt and Houchin 1974). There are two main functional levels that influence cortical discharges, arising from the thalamus and the ascending reticular activating system (ARAS). The former acts as a kind of pacemaker of the alpha rhythm (synchronizing influence), and the latter is responsible for the arousal effect (desynchronizing influence) on the EEG. Alcohol is known to suppress activity of the ARAS (Caspers 1957, 1958). Individuals with an EEG characterized by poor alpha activity or a mixture of alpha and beta activity may therefore be under a stronger influence of their ARAS. This interpretation is of interest in light of a combined neurophysiological and genetic theory of alcohol abuse.

EEG Findings in Alcoholics and Their Relatives

It had been reported frequently that alcoholics, on the average, have an EEG that is synchronized more poorly than healthy controls. Two possibilities, not mutually totally exclusive, must be considered to explain this difference: Poor EEG synchronization may be the result of alcoholic brain damage or it may precede alcoholism and thus reflect a predisposition for the disease. This latter theory was demonstrated by Begleiter and Platz (1972) and Naitoh (1973).

In a study comprising 115 drug-free alcoholics (78 males; 37 females) and matched healthy controls, we obtained evidence for the predisposition hypothesis (Propping et al. 1981): Whereas the male alcoholics did not differ from their controls, the female patients were found to show a preponderance of the higher frequency classes in their EEGs. The first-degree relatives of the patients who had not abused alcohol at any time showed a comparable difference.

DISCUSSION

Neurophysiological Aspects

In the context of the described data, two other findings must be mentioned. Gabrielli et al. (1982) examined the EEGs of male children of alcoholic fathers and found them to possess less alpha activity in their resting EEG than that in control individuals. Pollock et al. (1983) performed alcoholic loading experiments in males at risk for alcoholism and found them to have a greater increase in EEG synchronization than that in controls. Thus, it seems that individuals at an increased risk for alcoholism, on the average, possess a peculiarity in brain function, as evidenced by their EEG. Carriers of a poorly synchronized resting EEG might be under the influence of a high arousal from their ARAS. Alcohol intake could therefore have a utilitarian value for them, as they might use alcohol as a medicine.

One certainly should not assume that a poorly synchronized EEG pattern is specific for a certain psychiatric disease. Instead, it presumably reflects basic, genetically controlled mechanisms that increase the risk not only for alcoholism, but for other diseases as well, such as schizophrenia. However, problems and inconsistencies remain: We found an EEG difference only in females and not in males, whereas Pollock et al. (1983), as well as Gabrielli et al. (1982), obtained their findings in males. Pollock et al., on the other hand, could not reproduce the finding of Gabrielli et al. but found an EEG difference only after alcohol application. A prospective study is needed in carriers with defined EEG patterns with respect to psychiatric outcome. Such a study can be carried out, if subjects are young adults who underwent a routine EEG examination as children or teenagers.

Possibilities for Application of Molecular Genetics

It appears that a poorly synchronized resting EEG reflects a neurophysiological state that presumably increases the risk for various psychiatric disorders, including alcohol abuse. Nothing is known about the genes involved in the brain wave pattern and its interindividual variation. Animal experiments do not offer a clue for a better understanding. Therefore, a linkage approach that applies genetic restriction fragment length polymorphisms (RFLP) might lead to the mapping of a chromosomal region, where the genetic information for a monogenic EEG variant is localized, to uncover the responsible gene and its product.

The low-voltage EEG and the EEG with monomorphic alpha waves follow an autosomal-dominant mode of inheritance (Vogel 1970), as evidenced by family studies. Both EEG variants are appreciably common in the general population (4–5%) so that suitable families should be available.

The average human EEG, as well as the poorly synchronized alpha EEG, has a polygenic basis. The genes responsible for these EEG patterns are therefore not easy to identify. However, once the genetic locus of a monogenic variant has been mapped, this information can be used for the analysis of the average EEG pattern, including the poorly synchronized alpha EEG. Model independent genetic approaches, such as haplotype sharing in affected sibling pairs or in more distant family members, may be applied.

Once the genes responsible for the pattern of the human resting EEG have been uncovered, what are the advantages and prospects of this knowledge? According to our present knowledge, certain EEG patterns such as the poorly synchronized alpha or beta EEG reflect an increased cortical arousal that, in turn, increases the risk for various psychiatric disorders. Thus, one cannot expect a direct correlation between an EEG phenotype and a certain psychological outcome.

A major problem in correlating a specific EEG pattern to a certain psychological or psychiatric phenotype is that the EEG not only possesses trait, but also state characteristics. The EEG of a disturbed and anxious patient who is also treated by psychotropic drugs mainly reflects these secondary influences rather than the "original" phenotype. The availability of DNA probes that define genetic loci responsible for the pattern of the human resting EEG would make the search for an association with the psychological and psychiatric consequences much easier. A whole new field of research—based on a genetic approach—can then be established that gives an insight into the action of genes involved in certain neurophysiological systems that relate to brain function.

REFERENCES

Begleiter, H. and A. Platz. 1972. The effects of alcohol on the central nervous system in humans. In *The biology of alcoholism* (ed. B. Kissin and H. Begleiter), vol. 2, p. 293. Plenum Press, New York.

Caspers, H. 1957. Die Beeinflussung der corticalen Krampferregbarkeit durch das aufsteigende Reticulärsystem des Hirnstammes: I. Reizwirkungen. *Z. Gesamte Exp. Med.* **129**: 128.

———. 1958. Die Beeinflussung der corticalen Krampferregbarkeit durch das aufsteigende Retikulärsystem des Hirnstammes: II. Narkosewirkungen. *Z. Gesamte Exp. Med.* **129**: 582.

Creutzfeldt, O. and J. Houchin. 1974. Neuronal basis of EEG waves. In *Handbook of electroencephalography and clinical neurophysiology* (ed. A. Rémond), vol, 2, part C, p. 5. Elsevier, Amsterdam.

Gabrielli, W.F., S.A. Mednick, J. Volavka, V.E. Pollock, F. Schulsinger, and T.M. Itil. 1982. Electroencephalograms in children of alcoholic fathers. *Psychophysiology* **19**: 404.

Herrmann, W.M., K. Fichte, T.M. Itil, and S. Kubicki. 1979. Development of a classification rule for four clinical therapeutic psychotropic drug classes with EEG power-spectrum variables of human volunteers. *Pharmacopsychiatria* **12**: 20.

Naitoh, P. 1973. The value of electroencephalography in alcoholism. *Ann. N.Y. Acad. Sci.* **215**: 303.

Pollock, V.E., J. Volavka, D.W. Goodwin, S.A. Mednick, W.F. Gabrielli, J. Knop, and F. Schulsinger. 1983. The EEG after alcohol administration in men at risk for alcoholism. *Arch. Gen. Psychiatry* **40**: 857.

Propping, P. 1977. Genetic control of ethanol action on the central nervous system: An EEG study in twins. *Hum. Genet.* **35**: 309.

Propping, P., J. Krüger, and A. Janah. 1980. Effect of alcohol on genetically determined variants of the normal EEG. *Psychiatry Res.* **2**: 85.

Propping, P., J. Krüger, and N. Mark. 1981. Genetic disposition to alcoholism: An EEG study in alcoholics and their relatives. *Hum. Genet.* **59**: 51.

Stassen, H.H., D.T. Lykken, P. Propping, and G. Bomben. 1988. Genetic determination of the human EEG. *Hum. Genet.* **80**: 165.

Vogel, F. 1970. The genetic basis of the normal human electroencephalogram (EEG). *Hum. Genet.* **10**: 91.

COMMENTS

Billings: Do you have any hypothesis about where the site of action of the gene might be for the monogenic low-voltage pattern?

Propping: Nothing is known.

Billings: And the frequency of that particular phenotype?

Propping: About 4% in the healthy adult population.

Martin: Is anyone trying to map it? That would be a lovely trait to map, wouldn't it?

Propping: Nobody has tried it so far. Vogel in Heidelberg has just begun to map it. The problem is that the families in which he studied the trait (he did it in the 1950s) are more or less no longer available.

Tabakoff: In the young adults in whom you did the analysis of alcohol effects, did you have information on their fathers and families in terms of alcohol use?

Propping: They were students at the university. We asked them, of course, if there were known alcoholics in their families. There were no alcoholics. The majority of them were social drinkers.

Schuckit: If you thought there were some leads here as to EEG patterns that might have related to familial alcoholism in the students, you could go back and get a family history now.

Propping: Yes. It will be possible.

Schuckit: It's not all that expensive.

Propping: I always thought about the possibility to do a prospective study because they are all available.

Tabakoff: Do any of the EEG patterns return to normal faster? You gave alcohol to a number of your subjects and you gave patterns of changes in EEG over time. Was there a group of those subjects who showed a fast return to normal after the administration of alcohol?

Propping: On the EEG level?

Tabakoff: Yes.

Propping: No.

Sparkes: In a sense, trying to correlate the acute effect of the alcohol with the EEG level.

Propping: All the subjects described in a very similar manner their subjective feelings, but the EEG effect has nothing to do with their subjective feelings.

Peters: Have you done any EEGs on people who flush or people on disulfiram with alcohol?

Propping: No. Among our probands who had repetitive testing, we had only one from Vietnam. He was an intensive flusher, but in this case I couldn't perform the EEG because he felt so sick.

Begleiter: Do you still have the data?

Propping: They are on tape, yes.

Begleiter: It may be worthwhile to go back and actually look at the data with fast Fourier transform procedures, which is a more efficient way of extracting information from the data. Specifically what I have in mind, Peter, is that one of the most remarkable phenomena about giving alcohol on EEG is the change that alcohol creates is totally dependent on the initial EEG, the initial baseline. That has to be studied in a very specific way. That is to say, if you look at typical α waves between 8 and 12 or 7 and 13, you are not going to see any changes. However, if you begin to break up the α into its separate bands, that is to say, into a slow α and a fast α, it has totally different topographical distribution. There are people who are fast α producers and those who are slow α producers. Again, they have different topography. One is more anterior and the other is more posterior. The people who show the greatest change subsequent to alcohol are the fast α producers. The slow α producers show practically no change. Therefore, I am now wondering whether in your females you don't have a group of essentially fast α producers. On a different level—and this is conjecture now—one might hypothesize that the females would be type 1 alcoholics, and so it would make more sense for them to show less slow α or more fast α. Therefore, you will see the greatest difference in resting EEG between the females and not the males, where the males may have more type 2 and that wouldn't show up. That could be tested.

A Prospective Study of Children of Alcoholics

MARC ALAN SCHUCKIT
Department of Psychiatry
University of California, San Diego, School of Medicine and
San Diego Veterans Affairs Medical Center
San Diego, California 92161

OVERVIEW

This paper discusses results of a 20-year series of studies scheduled to be completed by the mid-1990s. We review the reasoning upon which this research is based and present the results from baseline and postdrug challenges with sons of alcoholic fathers (family-history-positive, or FHP, group) and family-history-negative (FHN) controls. The paper concludes with the highly preliminary results from our recently initiated 8- to 12-year follow-up aimed at establishing the relationship between the initial test findings and the future development of severe alcohol-related problems.

INTRODUCTION

Background

The series of studies described below was based on the assumption that genetic factors have an impact on the alcoholism risk. Although not all studies agree, by the mid-1970s enough data had accrued from family, twin, and adoption investigations to justify a search for biological factors that might interact with environment to produce the final alcoholism risk (Goodwin 1985). Multiple avenues were available for attempting to isolate those factors responsible for increasing the risk (Schuckit 1987), but pragmatic issues based on the tools available, as well as the probable polygenic and multifactorial properties of this disorder, highlighted the assets inherent in studies of populations at high future risk for alcoholism. This paradigm takes advantage of the fourfold higher risk for severe and persistent alcohol problems among children of alcoholics, with little evidence of further enhancement of risk when the children are raised by an alcoholic biological or adoptive parent. It is probable that if biological factors exist, they might be observed by studying a large number of children of alcoholics coming from a wide array of families, and it is unlikely that these biological factors would be significantly changed through the presence of an alcoholic rearing parent (Goodwin 1985; Schuckit 1987).

A series of pilot projects were instituted in the mid-1970s that were used to develop a self-administered questionnaire as a first screening tool to identify drinking, nonalcoholic children of alcoholics, who could be evaluated further through both telephone and personal interviews. Procedures were also established for gathering a series of blood test results to help maximize the validity of the data, alcohol- and drug-challenge paradigms were piloted, and potential mechanisms to maximize future follow-ups of subjects and controls were established. The overall goal was to gather a relatively large sample of sons of alcoholic fathers who would undergo several days of intensive evaluation, with results compared to appropriate FHN controls.

Testing Procedures

As a result of the pilot investigations, each year our laboratory has mailed a structured questionnaire to approximately 1000 men, aged 18 to 25, who were either students or nonacademic staff at the University of California, San Diego and affiliated institutions. After excluding ~10% of the population who had a history of severe medical, psychiatric, drug, or alcohol-related impairment or who were total abstainers from alcohol, FHP subjects were chosen on the basis of a father's apparent diagnosis of alcohol abuse or dependence (Committee on Nomenclature and Statistics 1980). For each individual, an FHN control was selected to be similar in race, age, educational level, smoking history, and drug use history, as well as recent quantity and frequency of alcohol intake (Schuckit and Gold 1988). After corroborating the personal and family history through a telephone interview, subjects were then invited individually to the laboratory for further evaluation and testing. There, recent drinking history was corroborated through an interview, as well as via evaluation of blood tests likely to change in the presence of repeated heavy drinking (e.g., γ-glutamyl transferase; Schuckit and Irwin 1988).

Depending on the research protocol, subjects were tested on either three or four occasions, but each paradigm included separate days for challenges with a placebo (a small amount of ethanol presented with a mixer) and 0.75 ml/kg of ethanol. The latter was a 20% solution in a carbonated sugar and caffeine-free beverage and was consumed over a 7- to 10-minute period. During the three-session paradigm, carried out from the late 1970s through 1985, the remaining challenge consisted of 1.1 ml/kg ethanol (oral), whereas during the four-session paradigm, beginning in 1986, the two additional testing days utilized intravenous (IV) infusions of 0.12 and 0.20 mg/kg of diazepam administered over a period of ten minutes (M.A. Schuckit et al., in prep.).

The data from these test sessions fall into two general categories. First, in both three- and four-session paradigms, on the first test day, baseline or prechallenge evaluations were carried out. These evaluations included a variety of cognitive tests, psychomotor performance evaluations, electroencephalographic (EEG) recordings, event-related potentials, and personality tests. Following these evaluations, the drug and alcohol challenges were presented in a random order, and the intensity of reaction to the challenges was recorded in multiple test spheres. These included subjective feelings, as measured on the modified Subjective High Assessment Scale (SHAS), alterations in standing steadiness evaluated by the apparatus originally developed by Moskowitz et al., and changes in electrophysiological measures, as well as alterations in blood hormones known to change with the drug challenges being used. The specific methodologies used in these evaluations, as well as the statistical approaches invoked, are presented in greater detail in other manuscripts (Schuckit 1987; Ehlers and Schuckit 1988; Schuckit and Gold 1988; Schuckit et al. 1988a,b).

Procedures for Follow-up

The major focus of the work carried out to date has been to establish any cross-sectional differences between FHPs and FHNs. However, results from these studies would be most important if those differences at the time of initial testing predicted those men who would go on to develop severe alcohol-related life problems. As a result of these considerations, at the time subjects entered the study, they agreed to a future follow-up evaluation and supplied us with the names and addresses of individuals likely to know their whereabouts 10–20 years hence.

To maximize future follow-up results, efforts have been made to maintain contact with subjects through periodic birthday and New Year cards that contain enclosures asking for an update on any address changes. Through these methods, at the inception of the follow-up phase, beginning in March of 1989, information was known on the whereabouts of 80% of our subjects. Beginning with those men tested in 1978 and 1979, through the use of a series of procedures (contacting relatives, working through the alumnus office, driver's license records, working with social security offices, etc.), 56 of the 57 individuals eligible for follow-up from that early year have been positively identified and contacted.

RESULTS

Some generalizations can be made about the original cross-sectional evaluations of the 474 men who have been tested since the late 1970s. First, no data set has demonstrated any significant differences between the FHPs and FHNs on their expectations of the effects of alcohol using the SHAS (Schuckit and Gold 1988). Also, following active-dose challenges, the two family history groups have never shown significant differences on the time-to-peak blood alcohol concentration (BAC), the magnitude of that peak, or the rate of disappearance of ethanol following the challenge (Schuckit and Gold 1988). The latter is an indirect indicator of the accuracy of matching the family history groups on quantity and frequency of drinking, as well as on height-to-weight ratio. Similarly, our evaluation of the 62 pairs (124 men) on whom diazepam data are available demonstrates no significant family history group differences on either diazepam or desmethyldiazepam blood levels (M.A. Schuckit et al., in prep.).

The major findings from this series of protocols can be summarized as potential differences at prechallenge baseline, possible differences following ethanol, and an evaluation of potential group differences after challenge with diazepam.

Baseline Evaluations

Few consistent baseline differences have been demonstrated in these 237 pairs (474 men). However, some of the lack of group differential may reflect heterogeneity inherent in either the FHP or FHN groups, including possible mislabeling of individuals. On the other hand, these same factors make any significant differences that are observed between the groups even more impressive. In interpreting the negative results, it is also important to recognize that the population reported on here are from blue-collar and white-collar families, and although many fathers have had severe and relatively early-onset alcoholism (Schuckit et al. 1989), results might be different in relatively impoverished inner-city samples or in those gathered through alternate methods, such as through police records or actual interviews of children of hospitalized alcoholics at the time of hospitalization (Tarter et al. 1989).

A consistent finding in our laboratory over the years has been the lack of group difference on a wide variety of cognitive and motor tests (Schuckit et al. 1987a). This finding includes a lack of family group differential on the Category Test, no differences between the family groups on the Trails B or the Digit Symbol Substitution Test, a lack of differential on a divided attention test, and no evidence of family history group baseline differences in standing steadiness (Schuckit et al. 1987a).

The two family history groups were also remarkably alike on most personality measures (Schuckit 1987), including the Speilberger State Trait Anxiety Scale, the Eysenck Personality Inventory, a locus of control measure, and the Rod and Frame Test. An evaluation of potential subtests of the Minnesota Multiphasic Personality Inventory (MMPI) revealed many similarities with all test patterns within the normal range for both FHPs and

FHNs, although within this framework the FHPs did score slightly but significantly higher on the MacAndrew Subtest (Saunders and Schuckit 1981). Finally, in a very recent study, the Tridimensional Personality Questionnaire failed to differentiate between the family history groups and did not characterize the heavier drinkers within either subpopulation (Schuckit et al. 1989).

Electrophysiological measures were also used to evaluate the two groups. Relatively promising results came from evaluation of background cortical EEGs, including baseline evidence of an increased power in the fast α range for FHPs (Ehlers and Schuckit 1989). However, despite an early trend, our own work and that of Polich and Bloom (1988) were unable to establish significantly lower amplitudes of the P3 wave of the event-related potential. This latter finding might reflect the test paradigm invoked, as well as the relatively high level of functioning of our group.

Results following Ethanol Challenges

Despite similar expectations of the effects of alcohol as measured on the SHAS and identical BACs following the ethanol challenge, the two family history groups did show significant differences on their intensity of reaction to alcohol. This has been demonstrated consistently by our group after ethanol, utilizing the SHAS (Schuckit and Gold 1988), with at least trends and frequently significant differences in the same direction reported in other evaluations of young men in other parts of the United States and in Denmark (O'Malley and Maisto 1985; Pollock et al. 1986; Savoie et al. 1988).

Consistent with the diminished intensity of changes in subjective feelings was the less intense postethanol increase for FHPs on body sway (Schuckit and Gold 1988), a finding that has been replicated in women (Lex et al. 1988) with similar trends recorded in some, but not all, other laboratories (O'Malley and Maisto 1985). There are data indicating that the intensity of postethanol change in this measure may have a heritability as high as 0.8 (Martin et al. 1985; Boomsma et al. 1989).

This decreased intensity of reaction to an alcohol challenge for FHPs is also characterized by more biological measures. In our laboratory, in two separate samples of subjects, the sons of alcoholics have shown less intense or less persistent changes in prolactin and cortisol after alcohol challenges, with similar findings observed for adrenocorticotropin hormone (ACTH) (Schuckit et al. 1987b,c, 1988a). Neurophysiological differences following ethanol for the two groups included less persistent changes in P3 latency and less persistent change in EEG stability (Schuckit et al. 1988b; Ehlers and Schuckit 1989; Porjesz and Begleiter, this volume).

Family History Differences following Diazepam Challenges

The results of the ethanol sessions raised the question of whether the decreased reaction to alcohol might be part of a diminished response to all types of challenges. Thus, comparisons of FHPs and FHNs after administration of a second drug has a number of potential benefits. Documentation of these responses might demonstrate that it is not just social set or psychological beliefs that contributed to the family history group differential after ethanol. In addition, careful selection of a comparison drug might help narrow down the number of neurochemical mechanisms contributing to the family history group differential. For example, if the decreased response did not generalize to the comparison agent, it would increase the probability that the most logical avenues for further research might be the effects of ethanol that are distinct from the actions of the second drug.

As a consequence of these considerations, a second research paradigm was carried out where subjects were challenged with placebo, 0.75 ml/kg of ethanol (as an internal control), 0.12 mg/kg of diazepam (an amount shown by pilot studies to produce a level of intoxication similar to the lower dose ethanol challenge), and 0.20 mg/kg of diazepam. For this protocol, subjects were selected through the same series of questionnaires and telephone and personal interviews as had been utilized for the ethanol experiments. Here diazepam infusions occurred over a period of 10 minutes through an IV route, and subjects were tested repeatedly for subjective feelings of intoxication, motor performance, and biological measures approximately every 30 minutes during the 3-hour session.

The results of diazepam challenges were somewhat surprising. Although these same 62 pairs (124 men) still demonstrated a decreased reaction to ethanol following the 0.75 ml/kg of alcohol challenge, there was no evidence of a dampened response to diazepam. Thus, the two groups were remarkably similar on postdrug scores for all 13 SHAS items, as well as the resulting total score, on the proportion of change in body sway after the active drug challenges and on hormonal changes in response to the benzodiazepine, including prolactin, cortisol, and growth hormone (M.A. Schuckit et al., in prep.).

Follow-up

The demonstration that FHPs have a decreased reaction to ethanol but no evidence of a dampened response to benzodiazepines raised the possibility that the ethanol response might be a characteristic of FHPs that contributes to their enhanced risk for severe alcohol-related life problems. However, the more direct proof of the hypothesis rests with a future follow-up of tested subjects to determine the relationship between the initial intensity of response to ethanol and the future development of alcohol-related life problems.

In March, 1989, our research group began a follow-up of the 474 individuals tested in our laboratory over the years. During the follow-up evaluation, a structured interview is carried out separately with the subject and a resource person (usually the spouse) likely to know about the problem pattern over the 8 to 12 years. Results on drug and alcohol use patterns and related problems, social functioning, and mental health difficulties are also corroborated by a review of public records. Substance use patterns are re-evaluated through blood tests, by examining state markers of heavy drinking (Schuckit and Irwin 1988), and by urine samples obtained for a drug toxicology screen.

At the present time, approximately 45 successful follow-up interviews with subjects and resource persons, as well as blood tests, have been collected for the earliest of sample. Data from 29 of these individuals have been entered into the computer, and preliminary analyses have been carried out to ensure that data are being handled properly and that the 1978/1979 data set can be melded appropriately with the information gathered in 1989. Preliminary data analyses demonstrate that at an average age of 31 years, the follow-up sample consumed alcoholic beverages on an average of 12.4 days per month, with a maximum frequency of intake of 20.0 days per month during the 10 years of follow-up. Average drinks per drinking occasion were 2.5, with a maximum intake of 8.3 drinks per drinking day. For these purposes, a drink was defined as 4 ounces of wine, 1.5 ounces of 80-proof beverage, or a 12-ounce beer. During the follow-up, ~25% of the men have had some alcohol-related life impairment, although most were not severe enough to justify a diagnosis of alcoholism.

Three of the 29 (10%) fulfilled criteria for alcohol dependence. Focusing on the SHAS "high" item, the three men who went on to develop alcoholism originally demonstrated a score of 6.8 ± 0.28, compared to those who did not develop severe life problems with alcohol, who had a mean of 13.0 ± 4.14 on the subjective high item. Although these findings were significant at the level $p < 0.01$, the very small number of subjects involved at this highly preliminary stage of the present level of investigation underscores the very tentative characteristics of these findings.

DISCUSSION

This paper has outlined one approach used in attempting to learn more about the biological factors that might interact with environment to increase the alcoholism risk. Data from our own laboratory, as well as the majority (but not all) of additional groups focusing on alcohol challenges in children of alcoholics, support the possible importance of a decreased intensity of reaction to ethanol as a biologically related factor in the alcoholism risk. These findings are not surprising in light of what is known about pharmacogenetic influences on the responses to a variety of other drugs. Thus, some individuals are more likely to demonstrate higher levels of sensitivity to anticholinergic drugs or to antihistamines, whereas others demonstrate less response; many such factors appear to run in families and perhaps have genetic underpinnings (Weber and Nebert 1990). Therefore, one might predict that some individuals will require higher doses of ethanol to demonstrate relatively intense levels of intoxication, whereas others appear to be less responsive to lower doses of this drug. The fact that ~40% of children of alcoholics might demonstrate this dampened intensity of response (Schuckit and Gold 1988) could indicate that these individuals are not receiving enough cognitive and physiological feedback at lower alcohol levels for them to train themselves easily to use internal feelings of intoxication to avoid severe intoxication. It is equally plausible that the lack of response to lower alcohol doses, in a heavy drinking society, might increase the risk of an individual seeking out higher doses of alcohol repeatedly with resulting development of even more intense tolerance, as well as an associated risk for psychological, social, and physiological consequences inherent in heavy repeated intake of alcohol.

The phenotype described here might not require any genes unique to alcoholism. Thus, it is possible that all men and women might be part of a continuum of response to ethanol, and it is primarily those whose sensitivities place them below a hypothetical threshold level who carry the maximal risk. It is hoped that aspects of the recently initiated cooperative study on the genetics of alcoholism will help gather additional information on this possibility.

Regardless of the mechanisms involved, the initial comparisons of FHPs and FHNs, as well as the highly preliminary results from the follow-up of the first 29 subjects from our laboratory, indicate the potential validity of the diminished response to alcohol as a risk factor. At the present stage, the data might be of use to educators attempting to change the public stereotype of alcoholism as a moral weakness and might be valuable ammunition for clinicians interested in convincing children of alcoholics that they are indeed at high risk for this severe disorder. This information could also prove useful in attempts to characterize pedigrees as being positive or negative for the diminished response in relatives of alcoholics, which could help further in more focused genetic analyses of potential markers of risk. In addition, neurochemical studies might develop animal models in an attempt to isolate the neurochemical responses contributing to the diminished risk. These responses might focus on the characteristic effects of ethanol that are not shared with benzodiazepines, such as the fluidizing actions on neuronal membranes or the more direct effects of ethanol on prostaglandins.

ACKNOWLEDGMENTS

This work was supported by the San Diego Veterans Affairs Clinical Research Center on Alcoholism and the National Institute on Alcohol Abuse and Alcoholism (grant 05526).

REFERENCES

Boomsma, D.I., N.G. Martin, and P.C.M. Molenaar. 1989. Factor and simplex models for repeated measures: Application to two psychomotor measures of alcohol sensitivity in twins. *Behav. Genet.* **19:** 79.

Committee on Nomenclature and Statistics. 1980. *Diagnostic and Statistical Manual of Mental Disorders,* 3rd edition. American Psychiatric Association, Washington, D.C.

Ehlers, C.L. and M.A. Schuckit. 1988. EEG response to ethanol in sons of alcoholics. *Psychopharmacol. Bull.* **24:** 434.

———. 1990. EEG fast frequency activity in the sons of alcoholics. *Biol. Psychiatry* (in press).

Goodwin, D.W. 1985. Alcoholism and genetics. *Arch. Gen. Psychiatry* **42:** 171.

Lex, B.W., S.E. Lukas, N.E. Greenwald, and J.H. Mendelson. 1988. Alcohol-induced changes in body sway in women at risk for alcoholism: A pilot study. *J. Stud. Alcohol* **49:** 346.

Martin, N.G., J.G. Oakeshott, J.B. Gibson, G.A. Starmer, J. Perl, and A.V. Wilks. 1985. A twin study of psychomotor and physiological responses to an acute dose of alcohol. *Behav. Genet.* **15:** 305.

O'Malley, S.S. and S.A. Maisto. 1985. The effects of family drinking history on response to alcohol: Expectancies and reactions to intoxication. *J. Stud. Alcohol* **46:** 289.

Polich, J. and F.E. Bloom. 1988. Event-related brain potentials in individuals at high and low risk for developing alcoholism: Failure to replicate. *Alcohol. Clin. Exp. Res.* **12:** 368.

Pollock, V.E., T.W. Teasdale, W.F. Gabrielli, and J. Knop. 1986. Subjective and objective measures of response to alcohol among men at risk for alcoholism. *J. Stud. Alcohol* **47:** 297.

Saunders, G.R. and M.A. Schuckit. 1981. MMPI scores in young men with alcoholic relatives. *J. Clin. Psychiatry* **43:** 237.

Savoie, T.M., E.K. Emory, and S. Moody-Thomas. 1988. Acute alcohol intoxication in socially drinking female and male offspring of alcoholic fathers. *J. Stud. Alcohol* **49:** 430.

Schuckit, M.A. 1987. Biological vulnerability to alcoholism. *J. Consult. Clin. Psychol.* **55:** 301.

Schuckit, M.A. and E. Gold. 1988. A simultaneous evaluation of multiple markers of ethanol/placebo challenges in sons of alcoholics and controls. *Arch. Gen. Psychiatry* **45:** 211.

Schuckit, M.A. and M. Irwin. 1988. Diagnosis of alcoholism. *Med. Clin. North Am.* **72:** 1133.

Schuckit, M.A., N. Butters, and L. Lyn. 1987a. Neuropsychologic deficits and the risk for alcoholism. *Neuropsychopharmacology* **1**: 45.

Schuckit, M.A., E. Gold, and S.C. Risch. 1987b. Serum prolactin levels in sons of alcoholics and control subjects. *Am. J. Psychiatry* **144**: 854.

———. 1987c. Plasma cortisol levels following ethanol in sons of alcoholics and controls. *Arch. Gen. Psychiatry* **44**: 942.

Schuckit, M.A., M. Irwin, and H.I.M. Mahler. 1990. The tridimensional personality questionnaire scores for sons of alcoholics and controls. *Am. J. Psychiatry* (in press).

Schuckit, M.A., S.C. Risch, and E. Gold. 1988a. Alcohol consumption, ACTH level, and family history of alcoholism. *Am. J. Psychiatry* **145**: 1391.

Schuckit, M.A., E.O. Gold, K. Croot, P. Finn, and J. Polich. 1988b. P300 latency after ethanol ingestion in sons of alcoholics and in controls. *Biol. Psychiatry* **24**: 310.

Tarter, R.E., T. Jacob, and D.A. Bremer. 1989. Cognitive status of sons of alcoholic men. *Alcohol. Clin. Exp. Res.* **13**: 232.

Weber, W. and D. Nebert. 1990. Pharmacogenetics. In *Principles of drug activity*, 3rd edition (ed. W.B. Pratt et al.). Churchill-Livingston, New York. (In press.)

COMMENTS

Tabakoff: Marc, I'm wondering about condition factors in these studies. Many of the things you have described can be ascribed to conditioning. Have you ever tried placebo response in these individuals (family history positives)—not a placebo of nothing, but a placebo that would make them think they are getting alcohol, to see what happens?

Schuckit: For every result I gave you—body sway, subjective high, all of the other hormones—there was a placebo challenge using Jack Mendelson's drinking apparatus. The average guy thought he was getting between 1 and 1.5 drinks during that placebo challenge. The average guy's level of anxiety went up during that placebo challenge. Although there were changes, there were no differences in the two groups. Placebo responses were identical in the two groups.

Goldman: If you take all these responses that appear to distinguish the at-risks from controls, including the P3, are there any that appear to cluster together in the same individuals, or are these independent?

Schuckit: In our March 1988 paper, Schuckit and Gold, where we looked at the discriminant function analysis that I showed you, we also did a principal-components analysis to try to look at clustering. It is also something that we are going to try to do later in our new samples as well and part of the data from the additional material that we are now looking at. In that principal-components analysis, SHAS stood by itself;

the hormones and body sway tended to cluster together. The clustering was slightly different at high-dose alcohol challenge versus low-dose alcohol challenge. Personally, with no data, I think that these are all likely to be very similar phenomena. I think some people may show more sensitivity to change in one kind of system and others more sensitivity to change in another kind of system, so that you need the panoply, you need several measures of response.

Cloninger: I hope you're following up both low-risk and high-risk subjects.

Schuckit: Yes, we are. The 474 are low-risk and high-risk combined. It's 237 pairs.

Billings: The previous speaker suggested that the frequency of P3 abnormalities in the general population was about 3%. For your most discriminant function, do you have any idea what the frequency is?

Schuckit: Less than 10% of the family history negatives showed that blunted response.

Billings: I want an unselected population for that.

Schuckit: These are kind of unselected. The family history negatives were only chosen because their quantity and frequency of drinking matched the cases that we were studying.

Billings: But the normal population must have a family history positive fraction that is quite significant.

Schuckit: Indeed it does. So the answer is somewhere between 40% and less than 10%. It's going to be less than 10%. You're right. Also in our follow-up of family history negatives, some had fathers who later developed severe alcohol problems. This work is hard to do! I have never tried to do alcohol challenge studies in a random sample of the general population.

Noble: The diazepam data are somewhat puzzling, knowing that there is cross-tolerance between alcohol and diazepam. Did you do the alcohol challenge on all the subjects you did with diazepam?

Schuckit: Yes.

Noble: And there you found no difference?

Schuckit: We find alcohol difference. In these same subjects we find the alcohol difference, and we find no diazepam difference.

Noble: How do you explain that?

Schuckit: I don't think alcohol and diazepam are identical at all in what they do. Their effects on membranes are not at all identical. Their effects on the chloride channel complex are similar, they cross over in many ways, but they're not at all identical. There are things that alcohol does that benzodiazepines don't do as well or don't do as much. Those are excellent leads for potential neurochemical systems that are worth more investigation. I would have predicted that there would have been a cross-over.

Risch: My question is about the specificity to alcohol. Aren't alcoholics at increased risk for dependency on a whole range of substances?

Schuckit: That's a more complex question than it would appear. I am going to say (there will be disagreement in this room) if you pick people who are alcoholics who don't have any other preexisting major psychiatric disorder, who may have used other drugs—after all, 80% of people on the streets in San Diego have used other drugs—but haven't met criteria for abuse or dependence on drugs other than alcohol, I don't think their families are loaded with people who abuse other drugs. We are going to find out in follow-ups. I don't think these subjects, the family history positives, are at high risk for abuse of other things.

Risch: That's not really my question. Aren't the alcoholics themselves at increased risk for substance abuse for other drugs?

Schuckit: Not the primary alcoholics I study. They're not if they do not have antisocial personality disorder. It's a whole other question about whether you look at antisocial personality as a separate illness from alcoholism. All of those antisocial people are drug abusers. There are also people who got primarily into drug abuse, but they abuse alcohol. Among our alcoholics, it is a very small percentage (less than 25%) who also fulfill criteria for abuse or dependence on drugs other than alcohol.

Two Biological Markers of Alcoholism

BORIS TABAKOFF, JAMES P. WHELAN, AND PAULA L. HOFFMAN
Division of Intramural Clinical and Biological Research
National Institute on Alcohol Abuse and Alcoholism
Bethesda, Maryland 20892

OVERVIEW

Biochemical markers of a disease, in the broadest definition, range from factors that are mechanistically involved in the etiology of the disease to factors that can be correlated with the development or presence of the disease but have little to do with determining etiology or progression of the pathology. When considering biochemical markers for alcoholism, as well as other diseases, one needs to differentiate clearly between characteristics of subjects that are a result of the pathology (state markers) versus those markers that are predictive of a predisposition to disease (trait markers). Given the data for the presence of heritable components that predispose alcoholism, as described elsewhere in this volume, the identification of a biochemical trait marker of alcoholism could provide candidate genetic loci for use in linkage studies. In addition, such a marker could provide means for generating a differential diagnosis of subtypes of alcoholism, which could further aid in determining the genetic factors that predispose these subtypes.

INTRODUCTION

In trying to decide on biochemical systems that would be good candidates for a marker in studies of a behavioral disorder such as alcoholism, our attention was focused on systems important in neurotransmission that could be assayed easily in human subjects. The human platelet has provided an often-used model of the serotonergic system in brain, and given the current speculation on the importance of serotonergic transmission in the etiology of alcoholism (Cloninger 1987), we decided to examine two neurotransmitter-related enzyme systems of the platelets of alcoholic and control subjects. Examination of individuals displaying the disease are of value in the initial screen for markers, as long as both state and trait markers are evidenced in such subjects and distinctions between these types of markers are made in the future.

Our animal studies and those of other investigators have established that receptors coupled to adenylate cyclase (AC) may be important in generation or maintenance of alcohol tolerance (Szabó et al. 1988). We have also reviewed evidence and presented a hypothesis that rapid development of alcohol tolerance may be a risk factor in alcoholism (Tabakoff and Hoffman

1988). Our recent studies on β-adrenergic receptor coupling to AC in brains of alcoholics (Valverius et al. 1989) generated evidence that this coupling is compromised, compared to controls, but also provided evidence that these systems may normalize with abstinence. Because adenylate cyclase is important for generating the intracellular "second messenger," cyclic 3′,5′-adenosine monophosphate (cAMP), and is assayable in platelet as well as neuronal membranes, we focused our attention on this system as a possible biochemical trait marker in alcoholism. Another platelet enzyme, monoamine oxidase (MAO), has been the subject of numerous studies concerned with markers of schizophrenia (Rose et al. 1986), affective disorder (Belmaker et al. 1980), and personality traits (von Knorring et al. 1984), as well as alcoholism (Wiberg et al. 1977; Belmaker et al. 1980; Giller and Hall 1983; Faraj et al. 1987; Pandey et al. 1988). The most consistent findings of these studies indicate that low platelet MAO activity may be associated with sensation-seeking behavior and other personality traits that reflect a related temperament. Low platelet MAO activity has also been associated with alcoholism in a majority of studies that examined this relationship. We therefore monitored platelet MAO activity, as well as AC activity, in our population of subjects for comparative purposes.

RESULTS AND DISCUSSION

The examination of AC activity in platelets of alcoholic subjects and controls recruited in Chicago, Illinois, demonstrated that although the groups did not differ significantly in basal activity, the stimulation of AC activity by fluoride, guanine nucleotides, or prostaglandin E was lower in platelets of alcoholics than in controls (Tabakoff et al. 1988). This spectrum of effects was interpreted to reflect quantitative or qualitative differences in the stimulatory guanine nucleotide-binding coupling protein, G_s, between alcoholics and controls. Using an antibody directed at the carboxy-terminal sequence of $G_{s\alpha}$ (Spiegel et al. 1987), we performed a Western blot analysis of the quantity of $G_{s\alpha}$ in relation to fluoride-stimulated AC activity in platelet membranes of alcoholics and controls. Our data (Fig. 1) demonstrated no significant correlation between the quantity of $G_{s\alpha}$ in platelet membranes and the measure of stimulated AC activity. One may thus consider that *qualitative* differences in $G_{s\alpha}$ between alcoholics and controls may contribute to the differences witnessed in AC activity. Statistical analysis of our earlier derived data (Tabakoff et al. 1988) demonstrated that the observed differences in AC activity were not associated with race, smoking, illicit drug use, age of the subject, or duration of problems with alcohol.

In subsequent work with another group of alcoholics and controls recruited in Stockholm, Sweden, we again found that fluoride and Gpp(NH)p-stimu-

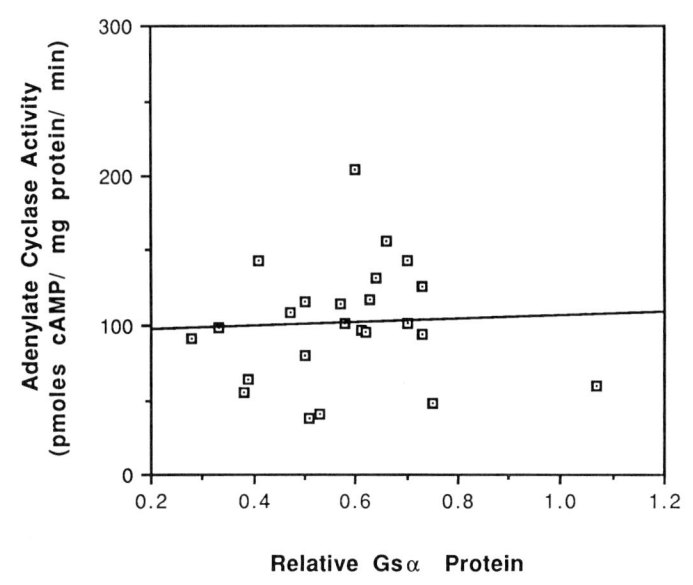

Figure 1
Correlation of quantity of $G_{s\alpha}$ and AC activity in membranes of platelets. Platelets are from control and alcoholic individuals. $G_{s\alpha}$ was quantitated by Western blot analysis, using a specific antiserum (Spiegel et al. 1987). Fluoride-stimulated AC activity was measured as described previously (Tabakoff et al. 1988). There was no significant correlation between the amount of $G_{s\alpha}$ and AC activity ($r^2=0.002$).

lated AC activities could correctly identify over 70% of alcoholics and control subjects, as was found in our earlier work (Hoffman et al. 1989). When the Swedish data were subjected to a further statistical analysis, a significant *negative* correlation was found between fluoride-stimulated AC activity and time since the last alcoholic drink in alcoholic subjects ($r^2 = -0.62$, $p < 0.003$). A similar but less robust correlation was noted in the earlier study of subjects from Chicago ($r^2 = -0.29$, $p < 0.005$). These data demonstrate that rather than regressing to normal (control) values during abstinence, the AC activity in platelets of alcoholic subjects reaches even lower values as the duration of abstinence increases. In fact, some of the lowest values of fluoride-stimulated AC activity were found in a group of long-term abstinent alcoholics (Chicago) who had not consumed alcohol for periods of 1–4 years (Tabakoff et al. 1988). These data suggest that if the differences in platelet AC activity were a result of alcohol ingestion, they reversed very slowly or not at all. Another characteristic of the Swedish alcoholics that was available for our analysis was their record of violent or criminal acts while intoxicated. No relation was noted between propensity for violence or criminality and AC activity in alcoholic subjects. The question of whether differences in platelet AC activity represent inherent characteristics of individuals predisposed to developing alcoholism is far from being answered. However, in the population of Swedish controls and alcoholics, multivariate analysis of variance did indicate that a factor significantly influencing platelet AC activity was the number of first-degree relatives in the individual's family who were alcoholic. Schuckit (1987) has summarized well the use of subjects with positive and negative family history of alcoholism as a means of distinguishing a genetic marker from a change induced by alcohol consumption.

Our examination of platelet MAO activity demonstrated no significant difference in activity between alcoholic and control subjects when the enzyme was assayed using a K_m or saturating concentration of the substrate β-phenylethylamine (Tabakoff et al. 1988). This result was contrary to a number of prior studies (Wiberg et al. 1977; Faraj et al. 1987; Pandey et al. 1988), but another recent report by von Knorring et al. (1985) also found no difference in platelet MAO activity between alcoholics and controls if the subject groups were considered as homogeneous entities. On the other hand, when von Knorring et al. (1985) subclassified their alcoholic subjects into type I and type II alcoholics, on the basis of age of onset of problems with alcohol, aggression during alcohol consumption, and social problems (e.g., job loss and drunk driving) related to alcohol, they found that low platelet MAO activity was evidenced in only the type II alcoholics (early onset of alcohol problems, aggressiveness, etc.). When we subdivided our alcoholic subjects into those whose problems with alcohol were evident prior to 21 years of age versus those whose problems with alcohol did not begin until after they were 30 years old, we also found that subjects with the earlier onset of alcohol-related problems had lower platelet MAO activity, and these activities were substantially lower than control values when measured using the K_m concentration of substrate (Table 1). The alcoholic individuals with later onset of alcohol-related problems displayed platelet MAO values quite similar to those of control subjects. A recent report by Pandey et al. (1988) also substantiates a dichotomy of MAO values in platelets of alcoholic

Table 1
MAO Activity in Platelets of Alcoholics

Age of onset of alcohol-related problems (yr)	pMole product/mg protein	
	1.2 μM PEA	12.0 μM PEA
21 and younger (19)	150 ± 17	436 ± 43
30 and older (12)	204 ± 32	528 ± 78

Values represent mean ±S.E.M. of the number of subjects in parentheses. (PEA) β-phenylethylamine.

subjects. Therefore, low platelet MAO activity may be a distinguishing feature of type II alcoholic subjects.

The specificity of platelet MAO activity as a marker for alcoholism is, however, quite low, and platelet MAO may best be described as a biological marker for vulnerability to alcoholism and other psychiatric illnesses (Buchsbaum and Rieder 1979). One may also think of *high* MAO activity as a marker of protection from alcoholism. The conceptualization of MAO activity as a measure of vulnerability is in accord with general population studies that demonstrate low platelet MAO activity to be a predominant phenotype in the population (Rice et al. 1982, 1984). Additional factors within the group distinguished by low MAO activity must be acting to promote the development of alcoholism and/or other psychopathologies. For instance, von Knorring et al. (1984) found that when they divided their low MAO subjects on the basis of intellectual capacities, those with the highest intellectual levels were also found to have higher levels of psychological functioning (greater ability to endure stress and fewer neurotic symptoms) and lower levels of alcohol-related problems. Subjects with low intellectual capacities, on the other hand, had significantly lower psychological functioning and higher levels of use and abuse of alcohol and other drugs.

Figure 2

Inhibition of MAO activity by ethanol in platelets of control and alcoholic subjects. MAO activity was measured as described (Tabakoff et al. 1988), in the presence and absence of 400 mM ethanol in vitro. The concentration of substrate (β-phenylethylamine) was 12.0 μM, and mean inhibition was significantly higher in platelet preparations of alcoholics ($p < 0.001$, Student's t-test) (Tabakoff et al. 1988).

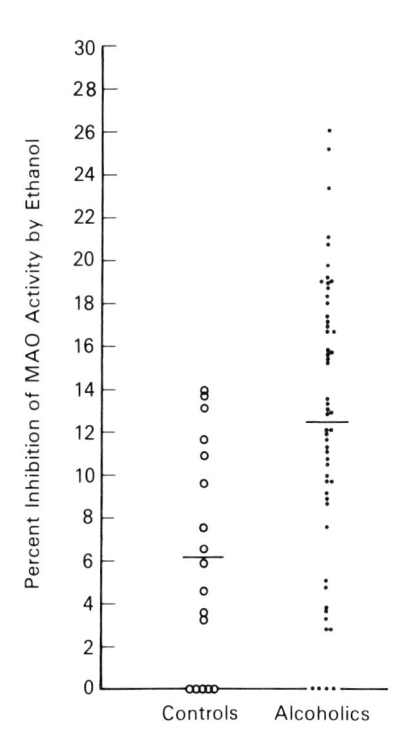

In contemplating MAO activity as a marker of psychiatric illness, one also needs to consider that the general population studies on the genetics of platelet MAO (Rice et al. 1982, 1984) do not provide evidence that the heritable activity is determined solely or primarily by the X-linked MAO-B locus (Hsu et al. 1989). In addition to factors such as posttranslational modification, e.g., flavin addition and glycosylation, the lipid microenvironment of MAO (Fowler et al. 1982) and the genes controlling lipid metabolism may play an important role in determining MAO activity. As a first approach to assessing the role of lipids in platelet MAO activity in alcoholics, we measured the effects of lipid-perturbing agents on platelet MAO activity. Ethanol was used as the lipid perturbant, and it and other alcohols were shown to inhibit platelet MAO activity in relation to their lipid/water partition coefficients (Tabakoff et al. 1985). When we examined the extent of ethanol-induced inhibition of platelet MAO at high concentrations of substrate (β-phenylethylamine), we found that inhibition was greater in the alcoholic subjects (Fig. 2) (Tabakoff et al. 1988). These observations provide another approach to considering the mechanisms that may be responsible for differences in MAO activity among individuals.

CONCLUSION

Studies of the platelet enzymes MAO and AC have provided initial evidence of utility as biochemical markers for alcoholism. MAO activity may serve best as a marker of vulnerability and as a means of distinguishing subtypes of alcoholic subjects (e.g., type II alcoholics). The data on platelet AC need to be augmented further to understand the heritability of this measure, but the lack of relationship between characteristics of type II alcoholics (age of onset of problems, aggression, and violence) and AC activity measures indicates that platelet AC activity is focusing on a dimension different from that being measured by platelet MAO. The analysis of platelet MAO and fluoride-stimulated AC activity in our studies (Tabakoff et al. 1988) indicated no significant correlation between these variables. It is possible that no single biochemical marker will distinguish satisfactorily all alcoholics from nonalcoholics; however, it is hoped that biochemical markers can be of use in the classification of alcoholic subjects and will provide insights into the genetic determinants of subtypes of alcoholism.

ACKNOWLEDGMENT

This work was supported in part by the Banbury Foundation.

REFERENCES

Belmaker, R.H., H.S. Bracha, and R.P. Ebstein. 1980. Platelet monoamine oxidase in affective illness and alcoholism. *Schizophr. Bull.* **6:** 320.

Buchsbaum, M.S. and R.O. Rieder. 1979. Biologic heterogeneity and psychiatric research. Platelet MAO as a case study. *Arch. Gen. Psychiatry* **36:** 1163.

Cloninger, C.R. 1987. Neurogenetic adaptive mechanisms in alcoholism. *Science* **236:** 410.

Faraj, B.A., J.D. Lenton, M. Kutner, V.M. Camp, T.W. Stammers, S.R. Lee, P.A. Lolies, and D. Chandora. 1987. Prevalence of low monoamine oxidase function in alcoholism. *Alcoholism* **11:** 464.

Fowler, C.J., K.F. Tipton, A.V.P. MacKay, and M.B.H. Youdim. 1982. Human platelet monoamine oxidase—A useful enzyme in the study of psychiatric disorders? *J. Neurosci.* **7:** 1577.

Giller, E., Jr. and H. Hall. 1983. Platelet MAO activity in recovered alcoholics after long-term abstinence. *Am. J. Psychiatry* **140:** 114.

Hoffman, P.L., J.M. Lee, T. Saito, B. Willard, F. De Leon-Jones, P. Valverius, S. Borg, and B. Tabakoff. 1989. Platelet enzyme activities in alcoholics. In *Genetic aspects of alcoholism* (ed. K. Kiianmaa et al.), p. 95. The Finnish Foundation for Alcohol Studies, Helsinki.

Hsu, Y.-P.P., J.F. Powell, K.B. Sims, and X.O. Breakefield. 1989. Molecular genetics of the monoamine oxidases. *J. Neurochem.* **53:** 12.

Pandey, G.N., J. Fawcett, R. Gibbons, D.C. Clark, and J.M. Davis. 1988. Platelet monoamine oxidase in alcoholism. *Biol. Psychiatry* **24:** 15.

Rice, J., P. McGuffin, and E.G. Shaskan. 1982. A commingling analysis of platelet monoamine oxidase activity. *Psychiatry Res.* **7:** 325.

Rice, J., P. McGuffin, L.R. Goldin, E.G. Shaskan, and E.S. Gershon. 1984. Platelet monoamine oxidase (MAO) activity: Evidence for a single major locus. *Am. J. Hum. Genet.* **36:** 36.

Rose, R.M., S. Castellani, J.A. Boeringa, P. Malek-Ahmadi, D.A. Lankford, J.D. Bessman, R.R. Fritz, C.B. Denney, R.M. Denney, and C.W. Abell. 1986. Platelet MAO concentration and molecular activity: II. Comparison of normal and schizophrenic populations. *Psychiatry Res.* **17:** 141.

Schuckit, M.A. 1987. Biological vulnerability to alcoholism. *J. Consult. Clin. Psychol.* **55:** 301.

Spiegel, A., A. Carter, M. Brann, R. Collins, P. Goldsmith, W. Simonds, R. Vinitsky, B. Eide, K. Rossiter, L. Weinstein, and C. Woodard. 1987. Signal transduction by guanine nucleotide-binding proteins. *Recent Prog. Horm. Res.* **44:** 337.

Szabó, G., P.L. Hoffman, and B. Tabakoff. 1988. Forskolin promotes the development of ethanol tolerance in 6-hydroxydopamine-treated mice. *Life Sci.* **42:** 615.

Tabakoff, B. and P.L. Hoffman. 1988. Hypothesis—Tolerance and the etiology of alcoholism: Hypothesis and mechanisms. *Alcohol. Clin. Exp. Res.* **12:** 184.

Tabakoff, B., J.M. Lee, F. De Leon-Jones, and P.L. Hoffman. 1985. Ethanol inhibits the activity of the B form of monoamine oxidase in human platelet and brain. *Psychopharmacology* **87:** 152.

Tabakoff, B., P.L. Hoffman, J.M. Lee, T. Saito, B. Willard, and F. De Leon-Jones. 1988. Differences in platelet enzyme activity between alcoholics and nonalcoholics. *N. Engl. J. Med.* **318:** 134.

Valverius, P., S. Borg, M.R. Valverius, P.L. Hoffman, and B. Tabakoff. 1989. β-Adrenergic receptor binding in brain of alcoholics. *Exp. Neurol.* **105:** 280.

von Knorring, L., L. Oreland, and B. Winblad. 1984. Personality traits related to monoamine oxidase activity in platelets. *Psychiatry Res.* **12:** 11.

von Knorring, A.-L., M. Bohman, L. von Knorring, and L. Oreland. 1985. Platelet MAO activity as a biological marker in subgroups of alcoholism. *Acta Psychiatr. Scand.* **72:** 52.

Wiberg, A., C.-G. Gottfries, and L. Oreland. 1977. Low platelet monoamine oxidase activity in human alcoholics. *Med. Biol.* **55:** 181.

COMMENTS

Cloninger: It may be useful to know that von Knorring and I have found that John Rice failed to use a general enough admixture analysis in his original study. Actually the distribution of scores on platelet MAO B fits a five-factor model, not a three-factor model.

Tabakoff: Yes. I was going to mention that.

Cloninger: In that case, then, you really don't have the dilemma that John Rice thought he had. That is, there are enough small components at either tail that you can have some variance. The five-factor model is certainly not compatible with the two-allele, single-locus model. There must be either multiple loci or multiple alleles. That really brings life back to the idea.

Tabakoff: Again, there is a problem even with that model, because if you're looking at subgroups, such as von Knorring does, and the frequency of the low MAO population, you still have some problems in ascertaining whether that particular low population could explain or could be an identifier of your subgroup of alcoholics. That study was also followed up by von Knorring in terms of trying to figure out whether socioeconomic status added to the propensity to become an alcoholic, and he did find that was the case.

Reich: Boris, it would be important and convenient if we could make some of the measurements in lymphoblastoid cells.

Tabakoff: We tried to measure MAO activity, and there is no MAO activity in the cells.

Reich: There is G protein in the cells, isn't there?

Tabakoff: There are G proteins and there is adenylate cyclase.

Reich: That's what I'm saying: those measurements.

Tabakoff: MAO is not measurable.

Reich: What about the adenylate cyclase?

Tabakoff: It is measurable, but we have never done the measurements.

Reich: It would be very useful, because those are renewable sources of cells that could be distributed. In contrast, of course, once you've got the platelets, you're done.

Tabakoff: Another important factor is that if it's a trait marker and you establish such a cell line and that difference persists, you would be much more assured that it is a trait marker.

Propping: The problem with the enzyme from platelets in alcoholics is that alcoholics in the intoxicated state taken to the hospitals have reduced platelet count. Did you control for that? It might be that, after several weeks, the platelet population is different in alcoholics compared to normals.

Tabakoff: Yes, we controlled for that in our studies. We did both platelet counts and expressed it per platelet and per milligram protein. The results are really quite similar.

Propping: Yes, but in the population not only the count, but the type of the platelets, the age of the platelets, may be different.

Tabakoff: Exactly. Again, there is a transient change within two or three weeks after the individual gets off alcohol, but that transient change then returns to a baseline value in the individual that is quite stable over time. This is one of the reasons to measure long-term abstinent individuals.

Chakravarti: Bob referred to the fact that the analysis shows five factors. I was just wondering if you could elaborate on that, what five factors mean.

Cloninger: We found in an admixture or commingling analysis that a mixture of five normal distributions was needed to fit the observed distribution of platelet MAO B activity.

Chakravarti: In the general population or in a population of alcoholics?

Tabakoff: General population.

Chakravarti: So it's not in a population of alcoholics?

Tabakoff: No, in the data that I showed you, the initial data, where they thought they had a major locus, it was also on the general population.

Chakravarti: Now, you were talking, of course, on the distribution of the activities.

Tabakoff: Correct.

Chakravarti: I presume that part of it must be due to the gene itself. Has anyone attempted to map the gene?

Conneally: It's on the X chromosome. It's right in the middle of the short arm.

Tabakoff: I showed where it is for both MAO A and MAO B. There may be polymorphisms in MAO A, but there are no polymorphisms in MAO B so far.

Chakravarti: If that is known, has there been any attempt to find out whether that locus itself is the determinant of the primary activity of what you see up there for MAO?

Risch: The activity in this region is not X-linked. There's no evidence for X linkage.

Tabakoff: That has been tested. This is why I brought up the fact that there may be other factors, such as lipid environment, that are important. When one tests alcoholics with lipid-perturbing agents, they seem to be different.

Cloninger: That is under investigation.

Tabakoff: Yes. It is interesting that women do have higher activity than men. That is known. It is consistent with those studies. So, there must be some sex effect, whether it's hormonal or otherwise.

Propping: The two X chromosomes.

Tabakoff: Yes, but only one is active.

Open Discussion

Searles: Marc, I know you just published a paper in the *British Journal of Addiction* about not being able to differentiate the problems between type 1 and type 2 as being differences in drinking history. I wonder if you could comment on that.

Schuckit: We have three papers that are now coming out, each related to specific types of populations. In the first paper, which was published in the *British Journal of Addiction*, we described a population of sons of alcoholics. We gave the fathers of the sons of alcoholics (there were 31 individuals) a very indirect score based on the father's age of onset of severe alcohol problems, evidence of multiple arrest, evidence of treatment, and presence or absence of first-degree female relatives. We then looked within the sons of alcoholics, to see whether there was any relationship between how type-2-like the father might have been and whether or not the son had characteristics that would relate to age of first drink, more minor problems related to alcohol, drug use, et cetera; the kinds of things we might guess would be more likely if the father was more type 2 and his type-2-ness had a chance of being passed on. We didn't find any relationship between the father's type score and the son's characteristics on drinking, drug use, and other like problems.

Cloninger: Is this a sample in which you selected people in your usual way, where they basically are well up to age 20?

Schuckit: Indeed, they are.

Cloninger: Then I'm not sure I understand the logic of your study. Since you eliminate people who have type 2 characteristics by requiring them to be nonabusers before age 20, you should not be surprised when you cannot find type 2 individuals in your study sample.

Schuckit: Your point is that if you are going to talk about people with early onset severe problems, perhaps prior to the age of 20, which is very uncommon except in people who have antisocial personality disorder, they're not going to be in our sample.

Searles: What essentially you're saying is that those people that are exhibiting this type 2 have antisocial personality disorders (ASPD).

Schuckit: We disagree somewhat, in that I think they have a totally separate disorder. The second study is coming out in *Archives of General Psychiatry*. It is now in press. Irwin is the chief author. Here it was very different. We took 171 alcoholics, mostly blue-collar, severe problems, coming into an alcohol treatment program. We interviewed the alcoholic; we interviewed at least one (and frequently two) resource person about the alcoholic; and then, we gave the alcoholic a similar kind of type 1 to type 2 type score based on that alcoholic's age of onset, that alcoholic's problems. Then, we made a number of predictions about what would be likely about drug use and other types of alcohol problems. We found almost no ability to predict anything except for one item, an item that has come in the British literature in the 1950s, and that is the age of first problem. Among these alcoholics with severe problems, but who did not prior to the age of 16 fulfill criteria for ASPD, before the onset of major life problems from alcohol, the only item that predicted major difficulties that would be associated with type 2 was a single item: age of first major life problem from alcohol.

The third study is also quite different. It consisted of 66 men. The 66 men included 33 FHPs, (these are sons of alcoholics, 8 of whom were reported on in the earlier study I mentioned, 25 of whom were not) and 33 FHNs. We gave them the TPQ. We gave these 66 men, average age about 20 or 21; matched pairs, FHPs and FHNs; the TPQ. In the TPQ, we generated 18 scores: Basically the three major scores and several subscores.

We first looked for any differences between FHPs and FHNs on the TPQ; there were none. Then we took this population and divided it into the heavier drinkers versus lighter drinkers and did a median split to see if there was any difference; there was none. Then we looked at the two extremes based on the upper drinking 20% and the lower drinking 20%, regardless of family history; there were no significant TPQ differences. Then we looked at a two-by-two. We looked at FHP versus FHN, heavy drinking median split versus lesser drinking median split; we still found no significant differences on the TPQ. Next we did something similar to what we had done before, but now on another population: We gave all of the fathers a 0–5 point scale for the FHP 33 men. Previously I reported that when we did that the sons didn't show characteristics in their course, but here we gave the fathers a score of 0–5 and looked at the TPQ on the sons. There was nothing significant; there was just nothing there on the TPQ.

Searles: I guess this shouldn't surprise you because the early onset severe type of alcoholic has been excluded by your selection procedure?

Cloninger: I think Marc has shown pretty clearly that in his sample he finds ways to restrict the sample largely to type 1 alcoholics, whether it's by age of onset or by exclusion of patients with antisocial personality disorder, or other factors. He has shown much more homogeneity within his sample than other people have. He has excluded most type 2 alcoholics by his experimental design.

Schuckit: Well, if you think type 2 alcoholism is only ASPD, then I could, if you wanted to take the time, explain why I think it makes no sense to take what looks like a separate disorder (even though a substantial proportion do have symptoms that cross over with alcoholism) and say that because the symptoms cross over it must be alcoholism, and they should all be mixed together. That makes no more sense to me than taking people who develop severe depressions while on antihypertensive medications and saying because they had a depression that looks like the other depression so let's put them all together. It also makes no more sense to me than including people who have clear bipolar illness with people with unipolar illness. Although there is some discussion there (they both have terrible depression), the course before the onset is different, the course of the disorder is different, and the course after treatment is different. Philosophically, I take the ASPDs and I put them in a separate group. They don't have this genetic disease I'm talking about, alcoholism. They have something different.

Cloninger: Well, I will make two very brief points on that. I do not feel that type 2 alcoholics have ASPD necessarily. I do think they have antisocial personality traits. There's a difference between havings traits and having the full disorder. The second point is that in the family members of people with antisocial personality (with or without alcoholism), you find that those individuals have an excess not only of antisocial personality, but also of primary alcoholism even using the diagnostic criteria used by Schuckit. However, if you evaluate these "primary" alcoholics, they have an excess of antisocial personality traits, namely high novelty seeking and low harm avoidance. Furthermore, there is no evidence whatsoever that antisocial personality disorder is inherited as a discrete entity that is separate from alcoholism.

Schuckit: You see, I don't know disorders from traits. There are, for example, traits that are said to be true of schizophrenics, that are supposed to be a schizophrenic spectrum, schizoid or schizotypal. The problem is that the human repertoire of behaviors is so limited that any disorder that we pick out, if you forget disorder and you take some of the key elements, everything we talk about is on a continuum. But, just as people with pneumococcal pneumonia may have symptoms on a continuum with me today, they probably have a separate disorder, just as schizophrenics may have some traits that go on a continuum. It's a relevant argument. I'm not saying I'm sure that Cloninger is wrong. But, just because some people are more impulsive than others doesn't imply they are variants of anisocial personality disorder.

Cloninger: What we see here is a difference in conceptual paradigms, with Marc assuming a strict Kraepelinean model of psychiatric disorders being discrete disease entities and my advocating a multidimensional model of adaptive personality traits. I have shown that we can now say conclusively that the pattern of comorbidity between multiple psychiatric disorders (such as anxiety symptoms, criminal behavior, alcohol abuse) requires us to reject a strict Kraepelinean model. If you don't accept that, then there's a lot that we need to discuss, but I don't think we can do it in five minutes here.

Lander: I'm sure you both appreciate it, but it's not a matter of choice or authority how you want to break it down. There is a genetic truth. In the comorbidity, what clusters with what is the only arbiter in the long run.

Schuckit: Oh, but he's wrong on what he said about the—

Lander: He may be wrong on the specifics. But you used the word "philosophically." I just want to underscore, philosophically is irrelevant. You have to ask what clusters with what in families, as Cloninger has said.

On that note, I want to come back to the question I asked you before about girls. The closer you are to the genetic basis of something, the more highly penetrant the trait is going to be. On Southern blots, the trait should be 100% penetrant; the phenotype as assayed on Southern blots is 100% penetrant. As you get further and further away, it begins to wander off. It seems, because of sex differences, it is highly impenetrant in females. So I have a bias that says the closer I crawl to the gene, the more I am going to expect to see it in females. There's going to be some point where it diverges for biological reasons, social reasons, whatever. So, I am particularly struck by the lack of work on evoked potentials and some of these other things in females, because the best argument to me would be to find this trait penetrating in the females, the daughters of these alcoholics, who then would pass it on. Why is this not the place to look? This is, of course, most important when I get to mapping, because if I were to ever hope to map such a thing, I would like a highly penetrant trait so I could see it through many meioses. To throw away all the female data is terrible. Also, since the females aren't abusing alcohol as much, I have less problems with confounding with the environment. I'd prefer to have them. Why isn't there more work on biological probes within the females?

Cloninger: There is work in the females that bears on this argument very directly. What we find in the females, the sisters essentially of the type 2 alcoholics, is that they have prominent somatization disorder. They have the same underlying personality traits: high in novelty seeking and low in harm avoidance. Whereas, in the type 1 alcoholics, we find that they have an excess of generalized anxiety disorders.

Lander: I was aware of that. I was actually back crawling more to the biological markers, like evoked potentials or enzyme assays, because I know you have proposed a connection between those, and I am hoping to find a common point above.

Tabakoff: With the monoamine oxidase, you do find lower levels in females as well. The few studies that have been done have looked at alcoholism; they have not tried to break down that alcoholism in any kind of subclassification. In general, there is a lower level, but no more than that has been done.

Chakravarti: Part of the original argument is in some sense not an argument. I presume you two gentlemen were talking about clinical heterogeneity. That may or may not have anything to do with genetic heterogeneity, I think, implying that there is genetic heterogeneity, but in some sense we wouldn't know it unless the genes are identified.

Cloninger: The clinical heterogeneity is associated with differences in segregation pattern, differences in inheritance in adoptees, so it is genetic as well as clinical heterogeneity.

Chakravarti: But it does not necessarily imply that they're heterogeneous at the genetic level.

Cloninger: It wouldn't necessarily, but all the data suggest that it is, based on both adoption and family studies.

Chakravarti: That brings up what Eric said, which is that as you get closer to the gene, the inheritance would increase, and that's surely true, but I don't think it will become 100%, as you imply. The problem is because of all these other behavioral traits and other things that interact with whatever genes exist to give you the phenotype.

Reich: We didn't review the literature here, although some of the models that were presented in the data yesterday, of course, included women. The main reason people stick to males in this kind of work is that there are tremendous monthly swings in the metabolism in terms of alcohol in women.

Li: No.

Reich: Sure there is.

Li: No.

Risch: Another reason to focus on males, especially in these high-risk groups, is that a larger percentage of them are going to become alcoholic. The critical aspect of all of these studies, where you come up with premorbid predictors, is to be able to say that these premorbid predictors predict alcoholism.

Schuckit: Exactly why I picked males.

Risch: You want to pick the group that is going to end up with the highest rates of alcoholism. If it's a penetrance problem, you don't want to pick the group that has the lower penetrance because you will get fewer positive outcomes.

Lander: That's if you're trying to predict. If you're trying to find the best biological markers, you may not do the same thing as if you're trying to make the best predictions for people. I think those may diverge there.

Risch: The criterion for a biological marker is that it can predict who is going to become affected.

Lander: No. If I can find a biological marker that is present in the daughters of alcoholics, or not present, or present at tremendously lower rates in the daughters of nonalcoholics, that points me to something much more useful.

Cloninger: I think you have very different clinical pictures, but with the same common denominator. We need to find the common denominator in both sexes which is closest to the gene products.

Lander: Yes. I would want to see its inheritance pattern. Even if I couldn't predict anything about these girls, it might tell me what to follow in families.

Risch: I think it has to be specific, that those who have the marker in the families who have inherited it have to be the ones that ultimately turn out to become alcoholic also.

Heath: I want to address the problem of nonrandom mating and the possibility that spouses of alcoholics may differ in multiple ways from the general population, and that in 20 years' time we may find out that we have beautiful markers, but they're not markers for alcoholism, they're markers for something quite different. So that is an important consideration. We want to be sure we've got the marker for the right thing.

Goldman: I think it can be pointed out that Marc and Bob are actually in substantial agreement. They are both saying that, whatever entity they are talking about, it is discretely found in the same family. If that's true, then the type 2/type 1 distinction is preserved genetically within families; or, if you want to call it ASPD/alcoholism distinction in certain families, then that is going to be a great aid in doing this analysis. It will be interesting to see if that distinction holds up.

Cloninger: Yes, especially if ASPD is not inherited as a discrete entity, but is the result of a combination of three or more separately inherited factors.

Begleiter: There are a couple of reasons why we chose males. One is that as Neil Risch mentioned, we wanted to start with a group where we would, at least initially, get a greater separation. We think, at least with males, we have the best chance of getting the greatest separation between high risk and low risk; that is to say, significant differences between high risk and low risk.

Lander: Significant differences in evoked potentials?

Begleiter: That's correct. So we started with that. The second is strictly a methodological problem, not a genetic one: If you do careful endocrinological follow-up of women (that is, hospitalized and in a ward) and you look at brain activity, there are endocrinological influences. You certainly cannot ask reliably about the cycling in women. I think there are difficulties with those kinds of studies, so that often you are best off having to hospitalize women volunteers, which is both time-consuming and, of course, inconvenient.

Lander: Have people tried to measure this in women and found that this quantity really cycles?

Begleiter: Yes. I think the people at U-Conn have data. Victor Hesselbrock may be able to tell us about that. They have done very careful studies, not just through interviews, but by looking at endocrines. They do find variations, there are cyclical variations, which certainly have an effect on brain function.

Lander: On this phenotypic assay?

Begleiter: Yes. And last, I think, we are also following up on children who have been with us for close to 6 or 7 years now. We also have what can be considered, at best, preliminary evidence. However, the preliminary evidence is most encouraging: There appears to be a very good predictability from the electrophysiology to drug abuse, including alcohol. So far, there is a very good relationship, but it is a small sample. It is too early.

Lander: What are the evoked potential characteristics in premenstrual girls?

Begleiter: We have not looked at that. We have not looked at women at all.

Reich: In reflecting on what we have done today, there are maybe 4 or 6 different kinds of genetic effects we have been talking about. They are all different. In understanding the genetics of alcoholism, it is not going to be a single gene; it's going to be a very complex and very rich story. That is why there are so many different aspects and why there will be so many different approaches. One of the complexities is going to be to control one aspect while you're studying the other. For example, if one wanted to study alcohol as a function of aldehyde dehydrogenases, one might want to control for other kinds of variables that might be under genetic control in order to cast in relief that kind of variation. It may make the studies more interesting and multidimensional and multidomain, and I hope, in the long run, more informative and interesting in results and how things fit together.

Comments: The NIAAA Consortium on the Genetics of Alcoholism

ENOCH GORDIS
National Institute on Alcohol Abuse and Alcoholism
Rockville, Maryland 20857

As Director of NIAAA, I want to tell you a little bit about our collaborative study on the genetics of alcoholism, which is just being unleashed. This is the first cooperative study we have done at NIAAA. We have a second study going on now on treatment matching and alcoholism. In 1987, we had our first practical review on the advisability of launching genetic studies. Many people, both in and out of the field, agreed that the time was right to do that. It took about a year before the ideas began to come together both in my mind and in the hands and minds of those investigators who hoped to participate in the project.

The announcement was put out in the winter of 1988, and it was based on a model of a collaborative agreement that had been successfully implemented at NIH in several other spheres. Essentially it was this: There would be two separate applications, one to be the coordinating center, because somebody has to watch the store and make sure that everybody is doing everything that they have promised to do and keep records of it, keep the computers happy; the other part of it was a separate application for the project itself, the hope being to marshal large pedigrees, apply some of these technologies across many families across the country which are now being done locally by the investigators who are competent in that, and finally, to move from there with the techniques of molecular biology to identify the putative gene or genes for alcoholism.

Many fine applications came in, including some that we were unable to fund because sometimes, as we all know, there are excellent ideas even in those whose scores are a shade too low to be funded. We always regret that, whether it's a collaborative agreement or not.

We do have six project cities that are going to be collaborating. The first funding actually came in before the end of the fiscal year 1989, which in government circles is September 30th. So, it is going to happen.

Each of the individual applications is not exactly how the project will be done, but represents a storehouse of wisdom and thinking from which the final method for the execution of the project will be drawn. It will also include the intramural program at NIAAA, although they did not participate (for the sake of propriety) in the design of the applications or in any part of it. They will join after the awards have been made.

Banbury Report 33: Genetics and Biology of Alcoholism
© Cold Spring Harbor Laboratory Press. 0-87969-233-2/90. $1.00 + .00

The principal investigators or their surrogates will form a steering committee. There will be input from NIAAA. We have a project officer, as well as a very excellent staff person, Dr. Kate Berg, who is a genetic epidemiologist trained at Johns Hopkins. The steering committee will, with the hospitality offered by NIAAA and the help of its staff, choose among the options provided within the individually approved applications to decide how the project will be continued.

Among the topics that will have to be resolved are the issues of ascertainment, which are perhaps even more difficult in some ways than some of the molecular biological techniques; there are different opinions on this.

Some of the official parts of this discussion in this excellent conference, as well as some of the unofficial discussions in the evening, will be a source of wisdom for some of the participants who actually have been able to be here. I am very grateful to have been invited.

We are optimistic about this project. Whether it will be easy or difficult, I think there is still some dispute. Undoubtedly, we are going to learn many things from the execution of this project.

We all know that the implications of success even in part of this project will go far beyond alcoholism, that we are going to learn about neurophysiology, about genetics, about this incredible intersection between affect and appetite, which is one way of looking at it. We welcome this.

We hope also that, as a result of the thinking, there will be a method for storing DNA and lymphocytes, and that ultimately the initial investigators in the collaborative agreement will not be the only ones who will contribute to this, but that the mechanism will permit others to enter later and to collaborate. Eventually, at a time to be discussed and decided upon by the steering committee and NIAAA, some of these samples will be available to others.

We are looking forward very much to this project.

Animal Models and Candidate Genes for Alcoholism

Genetic Animal Models for the Study of Alcoholism

TING-KAI LI
Indiana University School of Medicine
and Indianapolis VA Medical Center
Indianapolis, Indiana 46202

INTRODUCTION

Knowledge about the neurobiological basis of alcoholism can be gained by studying animals that exhibit abnormally intense alcohol-seeking behavior. Through the years, a number of investigators have attempted to develop suitable animal models of alcoholism for experimental study. Most species of laboratory animals, however, do not show a drinking preference for unflavored aqueous solutions containing moderate to high concentrations of ethanol. Among the kinds of experimental approaches to increasing ethanol consumption, the most successful has been genetic (Pohorecky 1981; Deitrich and Melchior 1985), and rat lines that differ in alcohol preference have been developed through selective breeding.

Currently, there are three pairs (high and low) of established rat lines that differ in alcohol preference, developed through selective breeding from different foundation stocks (Li et al. 1979; Eriksson and Rusi 1981; Mardones and Segozia-Riquelene 1983). One set of these, the high alcohol preference (P) and the low alcohol preference (NP) line, has been studied quite extensively in our laboratory (Li et al. 1987). Comparison of the P and NP lines has identified associated traits, opening avenues for exploration of the neurobiological basis of alcohol-seeking behavior.

More recently, we initiated a new selective breeding experiment for high and low alcohol-drinking preference, using as a heterogeneous foundation stock the N/Nih rat (Hansen and Spuhler 1984), which was developed from the cross of eight inbred strains. The new duplicate lines are the HAD-1 and HAD-2 (high alcohol-drinking) and the LAD-1 and LAD-2 (low alcohol-drinking) lines. The purpose of this new selection study is to address the issue of generality of the phenotypic associations of high alcohol-seeking behavior discovered in the P and NP lines and to establish the HAD line as another useful animal model for alcoholism research. Studies to date indicate that HAD rats are similar to P rats in many ways, behaviorally (in response to ethanol) and neurochemically.

Banbury Report 33: Genetics and Biology of Alcoholism
© Cold Spring Harbor Laboratory Press. 0-87969-233-2/90. $1.00 + .00

P/NP and HAD/LAD Rat Lines as Animal Models for the Study of Alcohol-seeking Behavior and Alcoholism

Over the last 12 years, studies have shown that P rats satisfy all of the major criteria for an animal model of alcoholism (Lester and Freed 1973; Cicero 1979):

1. P rats voluntarily drink ethanol solutions (10–30% in water [v/v] in quantities that elevate blood alcohol concentrations (BACs) into pharmacologically meaningful ranges (Li et al. 1979; Lumeng and Li 1986; Murphy et al. 1986).
2. P rats develop tolerance and physical dependence with chronic drinking (Waller et al. 1982; Gatto et al. 1987a).
3. P rats work by operant responding to obtain ethanol in concentrations as high as 30%, but not because of the caloric value, taste, or smell of the ethanol solutions (Penn et al. 1978; Waller et al. 1984; Murphy et al. 1989).

Importantly, comparison of P rats with the selectively bred, alcohol-nonpreferring NP line of rats has revealed differences that suggest new avenues for exploration of the neurobiological basis of alcohol-seeking behavior.

1. Ethanol-naive P rats exhibit lower levels of serotonin (5-HT) and dopamine (DA) in certain brain regions (Murphy et al. 1982), most notably the nucleus accumbens (Murphy et al. 1987). Higher densities of 5-HT receptors in some of these regions (cerebral cortex and hippocampus) have been found in P rats as compared with NP rats (Wong et al. 1988). Preliminary immunocytochemical studies suggest that P rats may have fewer 5-HT fibers in the affected regions as compared with NP rats (F. Zhou, L. Lumeng, and T.K. Li, unpubl.). The administration of 5-HT uptake inhibitors attenuates the alcohol-seeking behavior of P rats (Murphy et al. 1985; McBride et al. 1988).
2. P rats are behaviorally stimulated by low doses of ethanol and are less affected by sedative-hypnotic doses of ethanol (Waller et al. 1986).
3. P rats develop tolerance more quickly within a single session of exposure to a sedative-hypnotic dose of ethanol (acute tolerance), and this tolerance persists (as tested by a second dose of ethanol) for a much longer period of time (Waller et al. 1983; Gatto et al. 1987b).

The difference between lines in response to ethanol suggested the general hypothesis that an enhanced responsiveness to the low-dose reinforcing effects of ethanol, together with the rapid development and persistence of tolerance to the high-dose aversive effects of ethanol, promotes high alcohol-seeking behavior. Recent comparison studies in HAD and LAD rats have shown that, as with the P rats, selection for ethanol-drinking preference (10% v/v vs. H_2O) produced lines (HAD) that exhibit operant responding for ethanol as reward in concentrations as high as 30%. As with NP rats, LAD rats did not respond well for ethanol when alcohol concentration exceeded 5% (Levy et al. 1988). Furthermore, as was found in P and NP rats, HAD animals exhibited longer persistence of tolerance after a single, sedative-hypnotic dose of ethanol than LAD animals did (Froehlich et al. 1987). Therefore, the salient features of the hypothesis formulated from the studies of P and NP rats appear generalizable.

More recently, the contents of DA, 5-HT, and their primary acid metabolites were assayed in ten brain regions of the HAD and LAD lines of rats (Gongwer et al. 1990). Compared with the LAD line, the contents of 5-HT and/or 5-hydroxyindoleacetic acid were lower in several brain regions (cerebral cortex, striatum, nucleus accumbens, septal nuclei, hippocampus, and hypothalamus) of the HAD line. The levels of DA, 3,4-dihydroxyphenylacetic acid, and homovanillic acid were also lower in the nucleus accumbens and anterior striatum of HAD rats. These data agree generally with the findings in P and NP rats and implicate the involvement of 5-HT and DA pathways in mediating alcohol-drinking behavior. Another neurotransmitter system that may have an important role in ethanol preference is γ-aminobutyric acid (GABA). Immunocytochemical and morphometric studies have revealed more GABA-ergic terminals in the nucleus accumbens of P rats than in that of NP rats (Hwang et al. 1988). How the GABA-ergic system interfaces with the 5-HT and DA systems in the brain reward pathways is not well understood.

Molecular and Genetic Studies in Animal Models: Present and Future

Our ultimate goal in studying the selectively bred alcohol-preferring and nonpreferring rats is to identify the genes responsible for the neurobiological abnormalities that lead to excessive alcohol-seeking behavior. Alcohol-drinking is a quantitative trait and is most likely influenced by multiple genes; however, there are indications that only a few genes exert a major influence on alcohol preference. In the development of both the P and NP lines and the HAD and LAD lines, differences in the average drinking scores of the high and low lines began to emerge in the early generations, suggesting that several genes may be controlling a major portion of the variation in alcohol-drinking of these lines. From a triple-test cross analysis of ethanol preference, Drewek and Broadhurst (1981, 1983) concluded that an additive-dominance model proved adequate in the rat, and a strong directional dominance for low alcohol preference was found. Studies in B × D recombinant inbred (RI)

(C57BL/6J × DBA/2J) mice have revealed a potential single gene effect for ethanol acceptance or preference (Crabbe et al. 1983). A panel of RI strains exhibited a bimodal distribution for ethanol acceptance, implying that a single gene exerts a major control on this trait. A genetic correlation between high ethanol acceptance and the basic (electrophoretic) form of the brain protein LTW-4 was found in studies of inbred mouse strains and in B × D RI strains. The finding suggests that a locus determining ethanol intake is near the gene for the LTW-4 protein on chromosome 1 of the mouse (Goldman et al. 1987).

Recently, we tested P and NP rats for 17 different biochemical markers and found that the NP line was homozygous at all 17 loci. P rats were identical to NP rats at 14 loci and exhibited heterozygosity at 3 loci. Thus, the P line still retains some genetic heterogeneity, whereas the NP line now appears to be highly inbred. Interestingly, whereas NP rats exhibited the *ll* phenotype at the RT1-A locus of the major histocompatibility complex (MHC), P rats were predominantly *uu*, with ~20% having the *ul* heterozygous phenotype. The mean drinking score of the *uu* animals was significantly higher than that of the *ul* animals, suggesting a genetic association of ethanol preference with the RT1-A locus of the rat. We have also recently discovered a polymorphism involving the mitochondrial aldehyde dehydrogenase isozyme that appears to have an association with alcohol preference. These findings indicate that it is now timely to initiate more extensive biochemical/genetic marker studies to examine not only gene product markers, but also DNA markers.

Unfortunately, compared with man and mouse, there is relatively little information about the gene map of the rat. Fewer than 100 rat genes have been mapped (Cramer 1988). A restriction fragment length polymorphism (RFLP) linkage map for the rat genome is nonexistent. The rat MHC locus on chromosome 14 (linkage group IX) is actually the best characterized region of the rat genome, and marker enzymes and cDNA probes surrounding the RT1-A locus can be used to further characterize a potential genetic relationship to alcohol preference.

When a complete linkage map of RFLPs is established, it should be possible to resolve quantitative traits into Mendelian factors and discern the number of quantitative trait loci (QTLs) and assign them to the appropriate chromosomal locations (Paterson et al. 1988). Rat genetics is currently far from this stage, but a reasonable beginning might be the exploration of relationships of ethanol preference to a number of candidate genes for which cDNA probes are available. Because P and NP rats differ in 5-HT, DA, and GABA neuronal systems, it appears reasonable to examine the genes and mRNAs of the receptors and the enzymes of synthesis and metabolism associated with these neurotransmitter systems. This can be done on a qualitative level, i.e., RFLP analysis of genomic DNA, and on a quantitative level, through in situ and solution hybridization methodology, of the relevant mRNAs.

Other approaches to identifying potential genetic markers of ethanol preference are to screen for differences between P and NP lines in brain proteins, as has been done in inbred and B × D RI mouse strains (Goldman et al. 1987). Another "anonymous" probing technique is the use of subtractive hybridization to identify unique (to P or NP) mRNAs in brain cDNA libraries (Milner et al. 1987; Travis and Sutcliffe 1988). The use of polymorphisms involving VNTR (variable number of tandem repeat) sequences is another technique to consider for the future (White and Lalouel 1988). These loci are highly polymorphic in man. A development that shows promise for screening VNTR polymorphisms is the two-dimensional gel chromatography method reported recently by Uitterlinden et al. (1989).

ACKNOWLEDGMENT

This work was supported by U.S. Public Health grant AA-03243.

REFERENCES

Cicero, T.J. 1979. A critique of animal analogues of alcoholism. In *Biochemistry and pharmacology of ethanol* (ed. E. Majchrowicz and E.P. Noble), vol. 2, p. 533. Plenum Press, New York.

Crabbe, J.C., A. Kosobud, E.R. Young, and J.S. Janowsky. 1983. Polygenic and single-gene determination of responses to ethanol in BXD/Ty recombinant inbred mouse strains. *Neurobehav. Toxicol. Teratol.* **5:** 181.

Cramer, D.V. 1988. Biochemical loci of the rat (*Rattus norvegicus*). *Rat News Lett.* **20:** 15.

Deitrich, R.A. and C.L. Melchior. 1985. A critical assessment of animal models for testing new drugs for altering ethanol intake. In *Research advances in new psychopharmacological treatments for alcoholism* (ed. C.A. Naranjo and E.M. Sellers), p. 23. Excerpta Medica, Amsterdam.

Drewek, K.J. and P.L. Broadhurst. 1981. A simplified triple-test cross analysis of alcohol preference in the rat. *Behav. Genet.* **11:** 517.

———. 1983. The genetics of alcohol preference in the female rat confirmed by a full triple-test cross. *Behav. Genet.* **13:** 107.

Eriksson, K. and M. Rusi. 1981. Finnish selection studies on alcohol-related behaviors: General outline. In *Development of animal models as pharmacogenetic tools*, (ed. G.E. McClearn et al.), NIAAA Res. Monogr. 6, p.87. U.S. Government Printing Office, Washington, D.C.

Froehlich, J.C., J. Hostetter, L. Lumeng, and T.-K. Li. 1987. Association between alcohol preference and acute tolerance. *Alcohol. Clin. Exp. Res.* **11:** 199 (Abstr.).

Gatto, G.J., J.M. Murphy, M.B. Waller, W.J. McBride, L. Lumeng, and T.-K. Li. 1987a. Chronic ethanol tolerance through free-choice drinking in the P line of alcohol-preferring rats. *Pharmacol. Biochem. Behav.* **28:** 111.
———. 1987b. Persistence of tolerance to a single dose of ethanol in the selectively bred alcohol-preferring P rats. *Pharmacol. Biochem. Behav.* **28:** 105.
Goldman, D., R.G. Lister, and J.C. Crabbe. 1987. Mapping of a putative genetic locus determining ethanol intake in the mouse. *Brain Res.* **420:** 220.
Gongwer, M.A., L. Lumeng, J.M. Murphy, W.J. McBride, and T.-K. Li. 1989. Regional brain contents of serotonin, dopamine and their metabolites in the selectively bred high- and low-alcohol-drinking lines of rats. *Alcohol* **6:** 317.
Hansen, C. and K. Spuhler. 1984. Development of the National Institutes of Health genetically heterogeneous rat stock. *Alcohol. Clin. Exp. Res.* **8:** 477.
Hwang, B.H., L. Lumeng, J.-Y. Wu, and T.-K. Li. 1988. GABAergic neurons in nucleus accumbens: A possible role in alcohol preference. *Alcohol. Clin. Exp. Res.* **12:** 306 (Abstr.).
Lester, D. and E.X. Freed. 1973. Criteria for an animal model of alcoholism. *Pharmacol. Biochem. Behav.* **1:** 103.
Levy, A.D., W.J. McBride, J. Murphy, L. Lumeng, and T.-K. Li. 1988. Genetically selected lines of high- and low-alcohol-drinking rats: Operant studies. *Soc. Neurosci. Abstr.* **14:** 41.
Li, T.-K., L. Lumeng, W.J. McBride, and J.M. Murphy. 1987. Rodent lines selected for factors affecting alcohol consumption. *Alcohol Alcohol.* **Suppl. 1:** 91.
Li, T.-K., L. Lumeng, W.J. McBride, M.B. Waller, and D.T. Hawkins. 1979. Progress toward a voluntary oral-consumption model of alcoholism. *Drug Alcohol Depend.* **4:** 45.
Lumeng, L. and T.-K. Li. 1986. The development of metabolic tolerance in the alcohol-preferring P rats: Comparison of forced and free-choice drinking of ethanol. *Pharmacol. Biochem. Behav.* **25:** 1013.
Mardones, J. and N. Segozia-Riquelene. 1983. Thirty-two years of selection of rats by ethanol preference: UChA and UChB strains. *Neurobehav. Toxicol. Teratol.* **5:** 171.
McBride, W.J., J.M. Murphy, L. Lumeng, and T.-K. Li. 1988. Effects of Ro 15-4513, fluoxetine and desipramine on the intake of ethanol, water and food by the alcohol-preferring P and nonpreferring NP lines of rats. *Pharmacol. Biochem. Behav.* **30:** 1045.
Milner, R.J., F.E. Bloom, and J.G. Sutcliffe. 1987. Brain-specific genes: Strategies and issues. *Curr. Top. Dev. Biol.* **12:** 117.
Murphy, J.M., W.J. McBride, L. Lumeng, and T.-K. Li. 1982. Regional brain levels of monoamines in alcohol-preferring and -nonpreferring lines of rats. *Pharmacol. Biochem. Behav.* **16:** 145.
———. 1987. Contents of monoamines in forebrain regions of alcohol-preferring (P) and nonpreferring (NP) lines of rats. *Pharmacol. Biochem. Behav.* **26:** 389.
Murphy, J.M., G.J. Gatto, W.J. McBride, L. Lumeng, and T.-K. Li. 1989. Operant responding for oral ethanol in the alcohol-preferring P and alcohol-nonpreferring NP lines of rats. *Alcohol* **6:** 127.

Murphy, J.M., G.J. Gatto, M.B. Waller, W.J. McBride, L. Lumeng, and T.-K. Li. 1986. Effects of scheduled access on ethanol intake by the alcohol-preferring P line of rats. *Alcohol* **3:** 331.

Murphy, J.M., M.B. Waller, G.J. Gatto, W.J. McBride, L. Lumeng, and T.-K. Li. 1985. Monoamine uptake inhibitors attenuate alcohol intake in alcohol-preferring rats. *Alcohol* **2:** 349.

Paterson, A.H., E.S. Lander, J.D. Hewitt, S. Peterson, S.E. Lincoln, and S.D. Tanksley. 1988. Resolution of quantitative traits into Mendelian factors by using a complete linkage map of restriction fragment length polymorphism. *Nature* **335:** 721.

Penn, P.E., W.J. McBride, L. Lumeng, T.M. Gaff, and T.-K. Li. 1978. Neurochemical and operant behavioral studies of a strain of alcohol-preferring rats. *Pharmacol. Biochem. Behav.* **8:** 475.

Pohorecky, L.A. 1981. Animal analog of alcohol dependence. *Fed. Proc.* **40:** 2056.

Travis, G.H. and J.G. Sutcliffe. 1988. Phenol emulsion-enhanced DNA-driven subtractive cDNA cloning: Isolation of low-abundance monkey cortex-specific mRNAs. *Proc. Natl. Acad. Sci.* **85:** 1696.

Uitterlinden, A.G., P.E. Slagboom, D.L. Knook, and J. Vijg. 1989. Two dimensional DNA fingerprinting of human individuals. *Proc. Natl. Acad. Sci.* **86:** 2742.

Waller, M.B., W.J. McBride, L. Lumeng, and T.-K. Li. 1982. Induction of dependence on ethanol by free-choice drinking in alcohol-preferring rats. *Pharmacol. Biochem. Behav.* **16:** 501.

―――. 1983. Initial sensitivity and acute tolerance to ethanol in the P and NP lines of rats. *Pharmacol. Biochem. Behav.* **19:** 683.

Waller, M.B., W.J. McBride, G.J. Gatto, L. Lumeng, and T.-K. Li. 1984. Intragastric self-infusion of ethanol by the P and NP (alcohol-preferring and -nonpreferring) lines of rats. *Science* **225:** 78.

Waller, M.B., J.M. Murphy, W.J. McBride, L. Lumeng, and T.-K. Li. 1986. Effect of low dose ethanol on spontaneous motor activity in alcohol-preferring and -nonpreferring lines of rats. *Pharmacol. Biochem. Behav.* **24:** 617.

White, R. and J.-M. Lalouel. 1988. Sets of linked genetic markers for human chromosomes. *Annu. Rev. Genet.* **22:** 259.

Wong, D.T., L. Lumeng, P.G. Threlkeld, L.R. Reid, and T.-K. Li. 1988. Serotonergic and adrenergic receptors of alcohol-preferring and -nonpreferring rats. *J. Neural Trans.* **71:** 207.

COMMENTS

Cadoret: Do these changes you talk about from the way the enzymes are handled occur in animals that are already on alcohol, or are these found with animals before that?

Li: These are ethanol naive. In the ones that we have tested, of course, we test them first. The ones we study are usually either ethanol naive or else they have been off alcohol for a month.

Cadoret: Are there differences between the ethanol naive and the ones that have been off for a month?

Li: Not that we can see. You mean the enzyme?

Cadoret: Yes.

Li: No.

Reich: T.K., given your really wonderful results, do you think we could benefit much from a couple of high and low lines repeated to see how much variability there is?

Li: The HADs and the LADs are repeated lines.

Reich: For each line there are how many varieties?

Li: There is a P, an NP, and there are duplicate HADs, duplicate LADs. There are six lines.

Reich: And so, you could look at the variance within highs and lows and eliminate the hitchhikers and the other complexities?

Li: We hope so. We have done some selection in the Ps. They go down, so the Ps are not homozygous yet. In order to do these genetic studies, we will have to do some inbreeding before we start.

Tarter: Do you have any information about where alcohol preference lies with respect to preference for other drugs having abuse liability?

Li: That is part of a component in a program project that we submitted as a continuation of our work. This is a question asked often. We just haven't done it. Our major objective is to show that this is a good model for alcoholism studies. We are beginning to look at behavioral characteristics. That's the other question that is often asked: Are these animals aggressive, are they antisocial? Our animals appear to be aggressive toward their handlers but not toward each other, but we need to do formal testing of that.

Tarter: A few years ago, Ann Taylor published some work showing that if she handled the animals as pups (essentially stress inoculated them), she was able to reduce alcohol consumption when these animals reached adulthood. It was decreased by the investigators handling and stroking the pups.

Li: We are beginning to look at environmental influences. Hank Samson is one of the people working on this. He has been able to show that the nonpreferring animals can be induced to drink, but they never drink the same as a Wistar. They drink less than a Wistar, and a Wistar drinks less than a P. The genetic influence is still seen there, even though you can modify drinking behavior with environment. The one thing that has been replicated, and shown to increase drinking behavior, is unpredictable stress. That is raising the drinking from 2 grams to 4 grams. When we look at our preferring animals, there is nothing we can see.

Goldman: Since the Ps and NPs are marginally inbred, I wonder if you have done a backcross or F_2 experiment to estimate the number of genes.

Li: We will be doing that.

Peters: The changes in the hepatic ALDH are fascinating. Do you think that the CNS changes could be secondary, say, to higher blood acetaldehydes?

Li: Personally I don't think so. We have in the past looked at acetaldehyde content in the liver and compared the Ps and the NPs and saw no difference. However, we only did two or three experiments. We have not looked at it in greater detail. We probably should. Once we show that the polymorphic forms are different in properties, I think we would want to do that again. However, I think the serotonin difference is developmental, because there are fewer fibers.

Cadoret: It sounds to me like there could be very many different models of animal alcoholism depending on how you select. It's disturbing if that happens with humans too.

Cadoret: That's very bothersome.

Li: We have selected and only repeated this once and we are seeing the same thing. This is selecting it by a certain method. Now, if you select by some other method, you may end up with another model.

Cadoret: You may come out with a different strain.

Li: Yes, but that's the whole purpose of doing animal models.

Cadoret: If you think that, for instance, tolerance is important, you select for tolerance and see if you get a preference to go along with tolerance, and see if the biology as well goes along with that model. Then you really have some leverage.

Tarter: This may be inappropriate, but do you have any data on whether or not the P animals are more susceptible to organ system damage, liver disease, or liver injury as a result of the alcohol consumption?

Li: We haven't looked at it. In a sense, it's important to look at genetic differences in susceptibility. If I were to look at that problem, I wouldn't use this model. It could be there in the Ps, but it may not be relevant. If I wanted a model of genetic differences in liver susceptibility, I would give them forced alcohol administration and give them large maximum doses.

Tabakoff: There are a number of differences that you have noted between the P and NP. How many of those differences carry over to the HADs and LADs, and are there any that really don't carry over? The 5-HT does, but what about all the others?

Li: 5-HT, dopamine.

Tabakoff: That's different?

Li: Yes, and the operant responding. We see that in HAD and LAD.

Tabakoff: No, just the neurochemistry, I mean.

Li: That's all so far. In HAD, the serotonin abnormality is not as widespread as it is in the P. In both the P and the HAD, the dopamine is consistent.

Tabakoff: So those two are consistent.

Reich: In terms of the selection paradigm, is it possible that the mitochondria could have been selected (from the mothers' diets, for example), or is that precluded by how you selected?

Li: Aldehyde dehydrogenase is synthesized from cytosol and transported in.

Candidate Genes and Favored Loci for Alcoholism

CHRISTOPHER CHARLES HOLLAND COOK AND HUGH MALCOLM DOUGLAS GURLING

Molecular Psychiatry Laboratory
Academic Department of Psychiatry
University College and Middlesex School of Medicine
London WIN 8AA, England

OVERVIEW

To test the hypothesis that there are single major gene effects in the etiology of alcoholism, a linkage study of families multiply affected by alcoholism was carried out. Attention was paid to loci previously implicated in alcoholism, either as a result of linkage studies or because of the presence of candidate genes. Preliminary results suggestive of nonlinkage between a molecular genetic marker close to aldehyde dehydrogenase 2 (ALDH2) on chromosome 12q and alcoholism were obtained. In contrast, when the MNS blood groups on chromosome 4q were used as linkage markers to alcoholism, this region could not be excluded. It is proposed that molecular genetic techniques offer a powerful tool for the study of genetic effects in alcoholism. However, the problems of heterogeneity and difficulty in recruiting the cooperation of families suitable for linkage studies may require large-scale studies in the future.

INTRODUCTION

Family, twin, and adoption studies have indicated a genetic effect in the development of alcoholism but have not provided information on inherited traits that may account for this predisposition. Association studies employing traditional (protein) markers at a population level have yielded little useful information. This may be for two reasons: First, such markers span only a tiny fraction of the total human genome; second, alcoholism is likely to be a heterogeneous condition. In a bid to overcome these difficulties, it is necessary to employ a family linkage strategy using DNA markers.

Results from two previous linkage studies of alcoholism, using protein markers, have been published. Hill et al. (1988) showed weak linkage between alcoholism and the MNS blood group (LOD = 2.02). Tanna et al. (1988) found no linkage with MNS but did elicit weaker evidence in favor of linkage with esterase D (LOD = 1.644). These studies therefore indicate two favored loci suitable for further molecular genetic research.

On a theoretical basis, there may be many candidates for the putative alcoholism susceptibility gene (ASG). In particular, the enzymes and isoenzymes of alcohol metabolism (alcohol dehydrogenase [ADH] and aldehyde dehydrogenase [ALDH]) can be investigated by linkage. ALDH2 has already been implicated as an ASG in oriental populations, where a single base pair mutation produces an alternative form of the enzyme that is associated with an aversive "flushing" response to alcohol ingestion. Alcoholism is far less common among those individuals who possess the mutant gene. Thus, there is evidence, at least in some racial groups, that a single gene effect may exert significant influence on the susceptibility of individuals to develop alcoholism.

The present study, which is still in progress, employs restriction fragment length polymorphisms (RFLPs) as genetic markers to look for possible linkage between the favored loci or candidate genes described above and alcoholism. Eleven Caucasian families multiply affected by alcoholism have been recruited to the study. Participants have been interviewed to establish their lifetime drinking status according to various criteria, notably the Research Diagnostic Criteria (Spitzer et al. 1978) and the Alcohol Dependence Syndrome (Edwards and Gross 1976). A full psychiatric evaluation has also been made (blind to genotype), using the Schedule for Affective Disorders and Schizophrenia-Lifetime Version (SADS-L; Spitzer and Endicott 1979). Blood has been collected for DNA extraction and blood group analysis. RFLP analysis has been conducted using the techniques of gel electrophoresis, Southern blotting, and probe hybridization, as described elsewhere (see, e.g., Gurling 1985). RFLP genotype data were read from autoradiographs blind to diagnostic data by two independent raters.

RESULTS

Nuclear pedigrees (including some individuals who did not participate in the study and who therefore did not contribute to the linkage analysis) are shown in Figure 1. The broader the definition of alcoholism that is employed, the more difficult it is to find truly unilateral families suitable for linkage analysis. A detailed scrutiny of almost any extended pedigree will reveal several alcoholics or heavy drinkers if sufficient information is available and the search is extended far enough. The pedigrees shown here are unilateral in the sense that at least one parent was definitely unaffected, and significant evidence of familial alcoholism was not apparent in the ancestry of that parent.

LOD scores for preliminary linkage analyses of MNS blood group data are shown in Table 1. Three-point linkage analysis, assuming a penetrance of 99% and using either a recessive or a dominant model of transmission, produces negative LOD scores but does not exclude linkage (i.e., LOD less than -2.0) at 0.05% recombination. Assuming penetrance of 50% with the

Candidate Genes for Alcoholism / 229

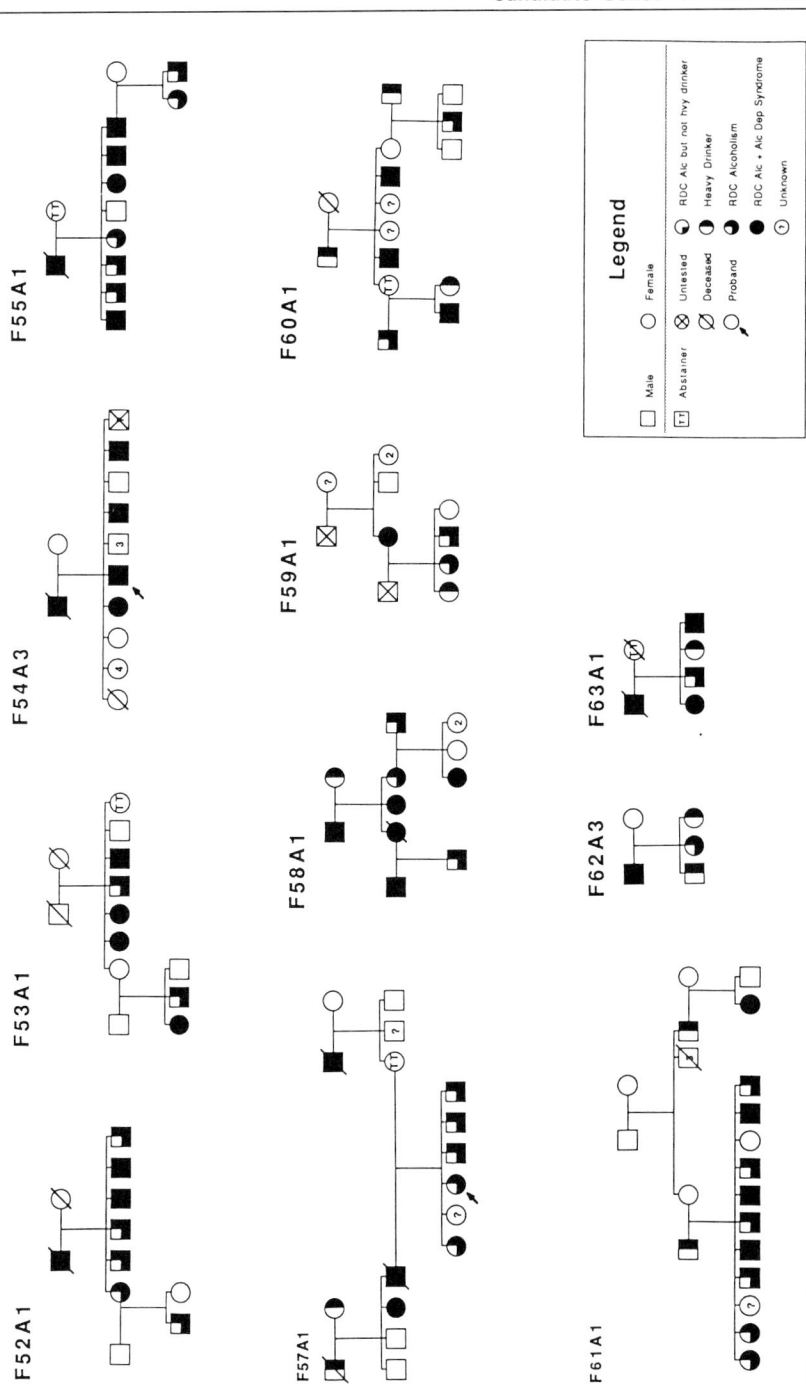

Figure 1
Linkage study of alcoholism: pedigrees.

Table 1
LOD Scores for Linkage between MNS Blood Group and Alcoholism Employing Different Models of Inheritance and Two Definitions of Caseness

Analysis	Diagnostic criteria[a]	Recombination fraction (θ)						
		0.000	0.001	0.010	0.050	0.100	0.200	0.300	0.400

Analysis	Diagnostic criteria[a]	0.000	0.001	0.010	0.050	0.100	0.200	0.300	0.400
Dominant model									
2 point, 99% penetrance	HD	−2.474	−2.426	−2.082	−1.152	−0.548	−0.047	0.063	0.018
3 point, 99% penetrance	ADS	−4.226	−4.091	−3.315	−1.954	−1.232	−0.520	−0.170	−0.031
	HD	−3.842	−3.757	−3.165	−1.733	−0.839	−0.085	−0.090	0.033
3 point, 50% penetrance	ADS	0.531	0.532	0.533	0.522	0.478	0.332	0.178	0.062
	HD	0.253	0.251	0.237	0.173	0.101	−0.001	−0.045	−0.041
Recessive model									
3 point, 99% penetrance	ADS	−7.401	−6.066	−3.679	−1.431	−0.550	0.021	0.106	0.061

[a] (HD) Heavy drinking; (ADS) Alcohol Dependence Syndrome.

dominant model yields a maximum LOD score of 0.53 at 0.01% recombination.

Table 2 shows preliminary LOD scores for data obtained from RFLP analysis, using the localized minisatellite probe pMS43 (Royle et al.1988). This probe has been localized to 12q24.3-qter, adjacent to ALDH2 at 12q24. Data from the two systems of alleles detected by this probe appear to exclude linkage with alcoholism.

DISCUSSION

Preliminary data appear to exclude ALDH2 as an ASG in the families under study. In contrast, it is not possible to exclude the MNS locus on chromosome 4q as being near a region of interest in the search for an ASG in these families; however, it must be emphasized that these results are preliminary. We intend to employ additional probes to study both the MNS and ALDH2 regions, as well as the other candidate genes or favored loci. More families are also being recruited, and we hope to extend the study of existing families.

Potentially, there are large numbers of families suitable for studies such as this one; however, two factors proved to be problematic in this respect. First, there is a paucity of multiply affected families that are truly unilateral for alcoholism. This may be a feature of recessive inheritance but may also be due to assortative mating. Second, the level of subject cooperation has been poor. In our experience, affected individuals are the least likely to give consent. In an effort to overcome these difficulties, new methods of analysis, such as the extended sib pair method (Sandkuyl 1989), can be employed.

The opportunities for studying genetic effects in alcoholism have been increased enormously by the advent of molecular genetic technology. Molecular genetic markers (RFLPs) now span the entire genome (Donis-Keller et al. 1987), and they are far more polymorphic (and, thus, more informative) than traditional protein markers. Many of the candidate genes, which are of interest as putative ASGs, have been cloned, including several of the ADH subunits, ALDH1 and ALDH2 (for review, see Smith 1986).

Studies such as this one open the way for more effective research on environmental factors, which operate interactively with genetic factors, in the development of alcoholism. Greater statistical power may be achieved in the study of environmental influences once an objective classification of genetic effects is achieved. Positive findings from such studies will also have important implications in the development of preventive measures to combat alcoholism. Such measures, aimed at reduction of alcohol-related harm in the population, may then be focused on a (genetic) group at high risk. Early signs of alcoholism will be detected sooner in those known to be vulnerable, and counseling of such individuals may include guidelines for lower "safe" drinking limits than those suggested for the general population. Finally, this

Table 2
LOD Scores for Two-point Linkage Analysis between pMS43 and RDC Alcoholism Employing Different Models of Inheritance

Analysis	Recombination fraction (θ)						
	0.000	0.001	0.010	0.050	0.100	0.200	0.300	0.400
Dominant model								
B alleles, high penetrance	−2.455	−2.308	−1.723	−0.990	−0.626	−0.267	−0.095	−0.019
A alleles, high penetrance	−3.008	−2.964	−2.653	−1.862	−1.257	−0.527	−0.193	−0.070
Recessive model								
A alleles, high penetrance	−3.735	−3.695	−3.361	−2.249	−1.343	−0.376	−0.027	0.017

(RDC) Research Diagnostic Criteria.

research may pave the way for advances in the treatment of alcoholism, either by pharmacological innovation or by identification of subgroups requiring different psychological and social approaches.

ACKNOWLEDGMENTS

We are indebted to all those individuals and organizations who assisted in contacting the families who participated in this study, including Professor G. Edwards, Drs. Gunaratna, M. Mullan, and G.K. Shaw, Broadreach House, and especially to the families themselves. Blood grouping was performed by Lewisham Hospital Blood Group Laboratory. P. Brett, Dr. D. Holmes, G. Kalsi, Dr. B. Mankoo, and R. Sherrington were very patient in teaching C.C.H.C. the necessary laboratory techniques to conduct this study. The probe, pMS43, was supplied by ICI Diagnostics. The research was funded by the University of London, the Brewer's Society, and the Wellcome Trust.

REFERENCES

Donis-Keller, H., P. Green, C. Helms, S. Cartinhour, B. Weiffenbach, K. Stephens, K.T. Keith, D.W. Bowden, D.R. Smith, E.S. Lander, D. Botstein, G. Akots, K.S. Rediker, T. Gravius, V.A. Brown, M.B. Rising, C. Parker, J.A. Powers, D.E. Watt, E.R. Kauffman, A. Bricker, P. Phipps, H. Muller-Kahle, T.R. Fulton, S. Ng, J.W. Schumm, J.C. Braman, R.G. Knowlton, D.F. Barker, S.M. Crooks, S.E. Lincoln, M.J. Daly, and J. Abrahamson. 1987. A genetic linkage map of the human genome. *Cell* **51:** 319.

Edwards, G. and M. Gross. 1976. Alcohol dependence: Provisional description of a clinical syndrome. *Br. Med. J.* **1:** 1058.

Gurling, H. 1985. Application of molecular biology to mental illness. Analysis of genomic DNA and brain mRNA. *Psychiatr. Devel.* **3:** 257.

Hill, S.Y., C. Aston, and B. Rabin. 1988. Suggestive evidence of genetic linkage between alcoholism and the MNS blood group. *Alcohol. Clin. Exp. Res.* **12(6):** 811.

Royle, N.J., R.E. Clarkson, Z. Wong, and A.J. Jeffreys. 1988. Clustering of hypervariable minisatellites in the proterminal regions of human autosomes. *Genomics* **3:** 352.

Sandkuyl, L.A. 1989. Analysis of affected sib pairs using information from extended families. In *Multipoint mapping and linkage based upon affected pedigree members: Genetic analysis workshop 6* (ed. R.C. Elston et al.). Alan R. Liss, New York.

Smith, M. 1986. Genetics of human alcohol and aldehyde dehydrogenases. *Adv. Hum. Genet.* **15:** 249.

Spitzer, R.L., J. Endicott, and E. Robins. 1978. Research diagnostic criteria. *Arch. Gen. Psychiatry* **35:** 773.

Spitzer, R.L. and J. Endicott. 1979. *The schedule for affective disorders and schizophrenia, lifetime version*, 3rd edition. New York State Institute, New York.

Tanna, V.L., A.F. Wilson, G. Winokur, and R.C. Elston. 1988. Possible linkage between alcoholism and esterase D. *J. Stud. Alcohol* **49(5):** 472.

COMMENTS

Billings: How did you decide on 11 families?

Cook: In a sense, we're stopping there for purely political reasons, once we can get some results. I would love to have a sample five times the size. There are families that are waiting to be worked on. At the moment, though, I want to get some preliminary results from these pilot studies and see where we should go, what we should concentrate on next.

Cloninger: I just wonder if any of the experts on linkage analysis would care to comment on whether they think that you can get inappropriate exclusion of an interval by assuming the wrong mode of inheritance?

Wijsman: You can.

Conneally: Sure, without a doubt.

Cook: Everything is likely to work against this.

Cloninger: So, your statement that you don't think it would be valid to use parameters derived from an actual formal segregation analysis may mean that you will inappropriately exclude a locus even if it's really there. And so, your cavalierly saying that it wouldn't be valid to use it is actually damning you to a very serious error.

Chakravarti: Actually, you shouldn't use that. I thought you meant to say that you couldn't estimate them from your families.

Cook: Sorry. That we couldn't estimate what?

Chakravarti: Parameters of the penetrance and frequency in other families.

Cook: That's right.

Chakravarti: But you should use parameters that have appeared in the literature.

Cook: We will attempt to apply particularly the parameters from formal segregation analysis for MNS.

Cloninger: I can tell you that in our own data in doing linkage analysis of this kind, where we have got parameters derived from formal segregation analysis and we have computed LOD scores under that model, and also under recessive and linkage dominant models, we can often get LOD scores far below -2 with inappropriate specification of the mode of inheritance when, in fact, with things derived from the segregation analysis, they are positive. I think it's very dangerous to not have some idea about the mode of inheritance.

Cook: I will feel happier when we have done some homogeneity tests. There might be some evidence that this is, at least, not a heterogeneous group of families. All this will be done in due course.

Risch: In response to what you are asking, Bob, there are certain parameters that are much more critical in doing a linkage analysis than others. The one that is most critical is the dominance parameter. Misspecification of penetrance—as long as you're using 50%, which he was saying, and a moderate gene frequency, the LOD score is not going to be that sensitive to that; you may misestimate the recombination fraction, but the absolute LOD score is not going to vary much. However, if you say it's dominant when it's recessive, or vice versa, then you could really kill an LOD score.

Cloninger: You can make it false negative.

Risch: If it's really dominant and you model it as recessive, you could make a very positive LOD score negative, and vice versa. But, if you say 50% penetrance when in fact it's 90%, or you say the gene frequency is 10% when in fact it's 20% or 30%, that's not going to do it.

Cloninger: So, do you think if you assume additive transmission, then you're always fairly certain?

Risch: I'm not sure. Or just do like he did, a dominant and a recessive.

Cook: Yes, that is what we should be doing. I mean, one of the advantages of the sib-pair approach would be, of course, that we don't have to place so much weight on an assumed mode of transmission.

Risch: It's also somewhat misleading to think that segregation analysis is going to answer the problem, because if there's more than one gene, the major gene, you might get a mixed model or something like that with a dominant gene, but the gene you happen to be looking at on a particular chromosome might not be that gene, it might be some other gene. So it would be totally misleading anyway to do segregation analysis and then assume that every gene you're looking for has that mode of inheritance.

Cloninger: Unless you selected the families that appear to be the ones that were segregating that major gene.

Chakravarti: You see, I think that's the whole point.

Risch: You might be segregating both of them. You don't know.

Cloninger: That's right.

Reich: The problem essentially is that we really need a simultaneous interactive analysis. There are a number of different kinds of complex segregation analyses that could be done. You can also do sib-pairs and sib relatives. The trick is going to be to find the linkage marker and the phenotype or sub-phenotype that fit the data. There is no way of talking about it as long as you have priority. You're not going to be able to look at the data or just intuit what kind of model is right and then go directly to it. It's going to be some more complex process. The statisticians of linkage analysis haven't approached situations of this complexity with their usual wisdom. A lot of work needs to be done theoretically to help out.

Chakravarti: Just to emphasize that point, choosing families that have at least the phenotype segregating in one-half or one side of the family is per se not a problem, but it is a problem if you simply assume it's dominant when in fact the weight of the evidence suggests that it probably is not the case.

Reich: There are many more models than dominant and recessive.

Risch: I disagree with one of the things you said. You don't have to put a complicated epistatic multilocus model in your linkage analysis to detect linkage. You can assume a single-locus model, be totally wrong, as long as you're not too wrong by saying it's dominant when it's recessive or vice versa, and you will detect linkage. This has been demonstrated time and again both theoretically and in practice.

Reich: To quote your own work, only if the leading character is more than 40%, as I remember.

Risch: No. I'll give you a very good example. In multiple sclerosis, there is an HLA-associated gene that has a relatively weak effect. People still aren't sure about the mode of inheritance of that gene, but you can model it. As long as you model something reasonable in a linkage analysis, you will detect linkage. You may get a recombination fraction of 15%, which is clearly wrong, but you will still get evidence for linkage and the fact that there was a gene there that influences susceptibility. It is not the major gene for that disease, it is not a gene that has a very huge impact on that disease, but it's still something that you can detect.

Genetic Variation in Serotonin and ALDH Underlying Alcoholism

DAVID GOLDMAN AND ROBERTA HABER
Laboratory of Clinical Studies
National Institute on Alcohol Abuse and Alcoholism
Bethesda, Maryland 20892

OVERVIEW

Neurochemical and ethanol metabolic genes cause heritable functional variation that not only underlies some of the differential risk for alcoholism, but also determines other normal and pathologic variation. In this paper, we discuss the role of serotonergic differences in determining inborn variations in personality and psychopathological problems associated with impulse control. Substantial heritability of serotonin function appears to exist, and several of the relevant genetic loci have been cloned. This opens the way to genetic behavioral studies focusing on this system and the underlying causes of genetic variation predisposing to alcoholism and psychophysiological differences. In this regard, a recent hypothesis ties together the genetic functional variation in aldehyde dehydrogenases (ALDHs) with selective forces of present and historical significance in the relevant populations. As summarized here, the inactive ALDH2 (mitochondrial) allele, which is associated with flushing and reduced alcohol intake, is one of three functional polymorphisms in the ethanol metabolic pathway, including two mutations that are conserved across populations. This suggests a role for selection in their maintenance. Of infectious agents capable of exerting selection pressure to maintain these polymorphisms, amebas and other anaerobic and microaerophilic organisms of the gut are the most logical candidates because they are sensitive to the nitroimidazole drugs, which, themselves, inhibit ALDH and therefore cause flushing after ethanol intake.

INTRODUCTION

At the level of the clinical phenotype, there is considerable evidence for heterogeneity in the genetic biologic factors that predispose individuals to alcoholism. Because alcoholism affects $>10\%$ of males and there is assortative mating for alcoholism, a practical consequence is that efforts to map an alcoholism vulnerability gene will typically encounter the obstacle that more than one risk-enhancing gene will segregate in extended families. Genes for "minor" subtypes would probably escape detection. The alternative to focusing on genetically or phenotypically defined subpopulations where

Banbury Report 33: Genetics and Biology of Alcoholism
© Cold Spring Harbor Laboratory Press. 0-87969-233-2/90. $1.00 + .00

heterogeneity is reduced carries with it three significant and interesting implications.

First, candidate loci for relevant biochemical and neurochemical systems can be matched to some phenotypes. Cloninger (1987) has suggested that particular combinations of three fundamental personality dimensions (novelty seeking, harm avoidance, and reward dependence) may underlie increased risk of alcoholism. Cloninger has also hypothesized that the function of a particular central neurotransmitter system determines each dimension, but the correlation between central serotonin function and impulsivity is the only relationship of this type that has been secured on the basis of cerebrospinal fluid (CSF) monoamine metabolite levels (R.N. Limson et al., unpubl.). In this paper, serotonin candidate loci will be discussed.

Second, genetic differences in neurotransmitter function not only lead to alcoholism, but also to related psychopathologies and to "normal" differences. This will be illustrated by a discussion of consequences of variation in central serotoninergic function.

Third, the occurrence of genetic variants in ALDH reducing the risk of alcoholism in Orientals raises the issue of alcoholism vulnerability genes. That is, it is possible to find a meaning for differential genetic risk for alcoholism in terms of the selective forces that have maintained the relevant genetic variants in human populations. It is probably premature to speculate on the role of genetic variation at brain neurochemical loci in determining the fitness of individuals and populations, except to make the general comment that frequency-dependent selection, the existence of multiple niches within human communities, and shifting selection pressures could maintain a high level of genetic diversity at loci contributing to differences in personality and behavior. Goldman and Enoch (1990) have recently examined the relationships of the ALDH variants to alcoholism, to alcohol-related toxicity, and to selective forces that may maintain them in particular populations. This hypothesis is summarized.

Alcoholism, Personality, and Serotonin

Some evidence has directly connected serotonin function to alcohol preference. Ethanol preference in the preferring and nonpreferring rat strains (McBride et al. 1989) and in mouse strains (Yoshimoto and Komura 1987) correlates with differences in serotonin turnover and content (McBride et al. 1989). Preferring rats had 20–30% lower levels of serotonin and 5-hydroxyindoleacetic acid (5-HIAA) in nucleus accumbens, frontal cortex, and anterior striatum. Serotonin uptake inhibitors increase the concentration of serotonin to which postsynaptic receptors are exposed and are reported to decrease ethanol intake in rats (Rockman et al. 1979; Daoust et al. 1984;

Murphy et al. 1985; Lawrin et al. 1986; McBride et al. 1989) and in humans (Naranjo et al. 1984).

However, genetic differences in neurotransmitter function are more likely to lead to multiple related phenotypes and psychiatric illnesses than to single diagnostic entities such as alcoholism. Alcoholism may be more prevalent in individuals and relatives of individuals with a variety of disorders, including affective disorder, anxiety, hysteria, sociopathy, drug abuse, and anorexia nervosa (Cotton 1979). One interpretation of data from the Stockholm adoption study (Bohman 1978; Cloninger et al. 1981, 1985) is that the "male-limited" familial alcoholism with high penetrance and early onset is associated with impulsivity and antisocial behaviors.

Serotonin inhibits a variety of behaviors (for review, see Soubrie 1986), including ingestive behavior and aggression. Serotonin also lowers body temperature and stimulates slow wave sleep. Content of the serotonin metabolite 5-HIAA in brain is reflective of the rate of serotonin release (Aghajanian et al. 1967). CSF 5-HIAA is lower in violent suicides (van Praag and Korf 1971; Asberg et al. 1976; Brown et al. 1982, 1985) and in impulsive/aggressive individuals. The correlation of CSF 5-HIAA and aggression was -0.78 to aggressive acts, -0.77 to psychopathic deviance (Minnesota Multiphasic Personality Inventory [MMPI]), and -0.63 to history of aggressive behaviors in childhood. In impulsive/violent Finns, many with exceptionally low levels of CSF 5-HIAA, 27/27 met criteria for alcoholism and 17/27 had a history of suicide attempts (Linnoila et al. 1983). Most of the impulsive young males studied by Brown et al. (1979) were alcoholic. As shown in Table 1, the negative correlation and the slope of the relationship between impulsivity and CSF 5-HIAA may be highest in more impulsive groups than in groups with less phenotypically extreme individuals, including alcoholics. As indicated in Table 1, although CSF homovanillic acid (HVA) is highly correlated with CSF 5-HIAA (Agren et al. 1986), it is not an equivalent measure, being less predictive of impulsivity in the more impulsive population of Navy alcoholics.

Pharmacologic evidence also connects serotonin function to aggression and impulsivity. In humans, lithium, which is thought to enhance serotoninergic

Table 1
Life History of Aggressive/Impulsive Behavior and CSF 5-HIAA and HVA

	Slope of relationship (correlation coefficient)		
	controls	alcoholics	Navy alcoholics
5-HIAA	−0.06 (0.18)	−0.18 (0.40)	−1.67 (0.78)
HVA	−2.67 (0.47)	−1.88 (0.33)	— (0.08)

Data from Brown et al. 1979; R.N. Limson et al. (unpubl.).

neurotransmission, has been used in clinical trials with some reduction of impulsive/aggressive behavior (Sheard 1971, 1975; Tupin et al. 1973; Myers and Melchior 1977). In rodents, serotonin turnover is lower when aggression is induced by isolation, diet, or drugs, and these aggressive states are partially reversed by the reuptake inhibitor fluoxetine and by agonists of the 5-HT$_{1A}$ receptor subtype (Valzelli and Garratini 1968; Katz 1980; Kantak et al. 1981; Berzenyi et al. 1983).

Various dimensions of personality exhibit heritabilities ranging from 0.4 to 0.6 (Loehlin 1982). These heritabilities are remarkable, considering that the true error variances associated with measurement of personality dimensions are not known but must be substantial. If genetic variation at neurotransmitter loci directly underlies normal variation in personality, it would be necessary, but not sufficient, that heritability for functional variation in neurotransmitter systems be fairly high. With respect to serotonin, its concentration in the extracellular space is a function of the rates of release, diffusion, and reuptake, with extracellular metabolism playing a minor role. Therefore, it is of interest that a study of platelet serotonin (5-hydroxytryptamine [5-HT]) uptake in pairs of monozygotic and dizygotic twins demonstrated that genetic factors significantly contribute to rate of 5-HT uptake (Meltzer and Arora 1988). Moreover, Oxenstierna et al. (1986) and Berretini et al. (1988) directly examined the heritability of CSF 5-HIAA, as well as other monoamine metabolites and neuropeptide Y (Table 2). Because the numbers of pairs studied was small, the heritability estimates are crude, and those for 5-HIAA and the dopamine metabolite HVA are nonsignificant. Oxenstierna et al. (1986) concluded that CSF 3-methoxy-4-hydroxyphenyl glycol (MMPG) and dopamine beta hydroxylase (DBH) levels are heritable, whereas 5-HIAA and HVA levels are not. However, a recent study (J.D. Higley et

Table 2
Heritability of 5-HIAA and Other CSF Neurochemical Measures

| | Intraclass correlations (n = 46 pairs) | | | |
Metabolite	MZ[a]	DZ[b]	brothers	Heritability
HVA	0.58	0.52	0.40	0.24
MHPG	0.76	0.44	0.17	0.74
5-HIAA	0.53	0.32	0.40	0.35
MAO-B	0.77	0.31	0.32	0.76
DBH	0.83	0.32	0.47	0.83
NPY[c]	0.59	0.26	0.18	0.66

Data from Oxenstierna et al. (1986); Berretini et al. (1988).
[a](MZ) Monozygotic.
[b](DZ) Dizygotic.
[c](NPY) Neuropeptide Y.

al., unpubl.) showed that the heritability of CSF 5-HIAA in rhesus macaques is >0.5.

The genetic loci determining differences in serotonin function are expressed in the raphe nuclei of the brain stem, where $\sim 40\%$ of the cells are serotoninergic (Moore 1981), but are also expressed in nonserotoninergic postsynaptic neurons, glia, and non-neuronal tissues. In the raphe neuron, the conversion of tryptophan to 5-hydroxytryptophan is catalyzed by tryptophan hydroxylase in the rate-limiting step of serotonin biosynthesis (Kaufman and Fisher 1974). Concentrations of substrate are thought to be nonsaturating and, under ordinary conditions, 5-hydroxytryptophan is rapidly decarboxylated to 5-HT.

In the pineal gland, serotonin is a precursor to melatonin; in the gut, serotonin is found in neurons of the myenteric plexus and enterochromaffin cells. Serotonin is also found in mast cells (for review, see Stoll et al. 1990). Tryptophan hydroxylases have been cloned from mouse mastocytoma and from rat, rabbit/human, and human pineal glands. On the basis of sequence identity, this enzyme is a member of the family of aromatic amino acid hydroxylases that includes phenylalanine and tyrosine hydroxylases. Although a tryptophan hydroxylase cDNA cloned from a mouse mastocytoma is hybridized to tryptophan hydroxylase mRNA derived from brain stem, there are indications, on the basis of enzymatic differences between the brain and peripheral enzymes (Kuhn et al. 1980) and levels of detected mRNA, that a different tryptophan hydroxylase is expressed in the raphe nuclei than the ones that have been cloned to date.

L-Tryptophan, an essential dietary amino acid, is specifically transported across the blood-brain barrier and then across the neuronal membrane. Dietary intake and the concentration ratio of tryptophan to other neutral amino acids determine the rate at which tryptophan is transported across the blood-brain barrier, its ultimate availability and, at least to an extent, serotonin turnover (Wurtman 1988). In the liver, tryptophan oxidase and formamidase convert L-tryptophan to kynurenine, reducing tryptophan availability.

The oxidation of serotonin to its major metabolite, 5-HIAA, is catalyzed by monoamine oxidase (MAO). The mitochondrially associated MAO-B is found in the platelet and in serotoninergic cells. MAO-A is absent in the platelet, but is the significant MAO in most regions of the brain. MAO-A has been cloned, and its deduced amino acid sequence has been compared with the sequence available for MAO-B, revealing 68% identity for the regions compared (Powell et al. 1989). From the standpoint of the patterns of transmission of behavioral traits and diseases, it is of considerable interest that both MAO-A and MAO-B are X-linked (Kochersperger et al. 1986), and MAO-A is located at Xp21-p11 (Ozelius et al. 1988).

Serotonin Receptors

Most serotonin receptors are membrane-spanning polypeptides that regulate intracellular second-messenger levels in response to extracellular ligand binding via interactions with guanine nucleotide-binding regulatory proteins (G proteins). Presynaptic receptors, sometimes called autoreceptors, are located on the membrane of the 5-HT-secreting cell and are believed to be part of a feedback mechanism that regulates serotonin synthesis and release. Postsynaptic receptors are located across the synaptic junction from sites of 5-HT release. Six serotonin receptor subtypes, 5-HT$_{1A}$, 5-HT$_{1B}$, 5-HT$_{1C}$, 5-HT$_{1D}$, 5-HT2, and 5-HT3, have been characterized pharmacologically and, to a lesser extent, behaviorally (Bradley et al. 1986).

The 5-HT$_{1A}$ receptor, found both pre- and postsynaptically (Hall et al. 1985; Dourish et al. 1987), appears to play an important role in impulsive/aggressive behaviors. The administration of the 5-HT$_{1A}$ agonist 8-OH-DPAT (8-hydroxy-2[di-n-propyl-amino]tetralin) to rats causes forepaw padding, head weaving, hind limb abduction, locomotor activity, tremor, and hypothermia. The effects of 8-OH-DPAT are reduced by electroconvulsive shock and increased by lithium (for review, see Green 1989). When 5-HT$_{1A}$ agonists are administered to wild rats, the result is a reduction of aggressive and defensive behavior and increased passivity in the face of situations that are presumably anxiety producing (Blanchard et al. 1988).

5-HT$_{1A}$ was cloned on the basis of its high sequence identity to adrenergic receptors (Fargin et al. 1988). Like adrenergic receptors, it has seven hydrophobic regions, which are probably membrane-spanning domains, and a G-protein regulatory domain. It also resembles the adrenergic receptors in that it is one of a small number of eukaryotic genes without introns. Other intronless genes include heat-shock proteins, whose transcription must be rapidly induced following cellular stress, and the phylogenetically ancient histones.

Homology (51% sequence identity) exists between two other serotonin receptors, 5-HT$_{1C}$ and 5-HT2, which were cloned and functionally expressed in mammalian cells and *Xenopus* oocytes (Lubbert et al. 1987; Julius et al. 1988; Pritchett et al. 1988). Both contain the seven putative transmembrane regions but otherwise show little homology to 5-HT$_{1A}$. 5-HT$_{1C}$ and 5-HT2 receptors regulate the function of phospholipase C (Conn and Sanders-Bush 1986; Conn et al. 1986), but 5-HT$_{1A}$ receptors regulate adenylate cyclase (Shenker et al. 1985; Markstein et al. 1986), as does 5-HT$_{1B}$ (Bouhelel et al. 1988). 5-HT$_{1C}$ and 5-HT2 are of considerable interest to behavioral geneticists. 5-HT$_{1C}$ was identified in the choroid plexus but is now known to be present in cerebral cortex (Pazos et al. 1984; Hoyer et al. 1986). The 5-HT2 antagonist ritanserin increases slow wave sleep and reduces panic, depression, and anxiety (for review, see Meert et al. 1989).

Finally, there are several 5-HT receptors that have not been cloned. Of particular interest is the pharmacologically distinct 5-HT3 subtype, an ion channel (Derkach et al. 1989). In animal studies, the 5-HT3 antagonist GR38032F reduced anxiety, aggressive behavior, agitation, and restlessness (for review, see Butler et al. 1988).

The 5-HT Transporter

Serotonin released from storage vesicles into the synapse is inactivated by reuptake mediated by a high-affinity, specific transporter located in the axon terminal, in adjacent glial cells, and in blood platelets. Both the central and peripheral serotonin transporters are pharmacologically distinct from other monoamine transporters, including transporters of dopamine and norepinephrine. Comparison of platelet and brain 5-HT transporter activities indicates that both transporters are sodium dependent and have the same drug inhibition profile. However, brain transporter activity is sensitive to ouabain, which inhibits Na^+-K^+ ATPase, whereas platelet transporter activity is relatively insensitive. This finding, which indicates that energy requirements of the platelet and brain transporters differ, suggests that the two transporters are not identical (Slotkin et al. 1986).

5-HT reuptake by platelets has been measured in a number of patient groups. A decreased level of 5-HT uptake or imipramine binding has been reported for patients suffering from depression, schizophrenia, anorexia nervosa, panic attacks, alcoholic cirrhosis, Alzheimer's disease, and Parkinson's disease (for review, see Wirz-Justice 1988). Curiously, blood serotonin levels are elevated in 30–50% of autistic children (Schain and Freedman 1961; for review, see Anderson 1987). Studies of these children indicate that they have normal levels of plasma tryptophan and 5-HIAA in CSF and urine. This suggests that the 5-HT metabolic pathway is functional. Platelets of autistic children appear to be normal in their ability to take up serotonin (Boullin et al. 1982) and to bind imipramine, an inhibitor of 5-HT uptake (Anderson et al. 1984).

A Role for Selection in ALDH Genetic Variation

Goldman and Enoch (1990) have hypothesized that ALDH variants are abundant in certain human populations (see, e.g., Teng 1981) because they confer host resistance to an infectious agent inhabiting the gut, possibly *Entamoeba histolytica*. This organism is responsible, historically and presently, for major morbidity and mortality in regions where it is endemic. Along with certain other anaerobic and microaerophilic organisms, *E. histolytica* is a candidate selective force because of its sensitivity to metronidazole and other nitroimidazoles. These drugs have an unknown mode of action but cause flushing after ethanol intake, presumably because they inhibit ALDH.

ALDH

ALDHs convert the toxic metabolite acetaldehyde to acetate, but are oxidoreductases, capable of carrying out the reverse reaction under appropriate conditions. Pharmacologic or genetic blockade of ALDH causes accumulation of acetaldehyde and alcohol sensitivity (Inoue et al. 1984). Three members of the human ALDH family have been cloned and mapped to different chromosomes, and two exhibit abundant functional polymorphism in certain populations. The mitochondrial ALDH2, encoded in the nucleus, is responsible for the majority of acetaldehyde oxidation in vivo. ALDH2 is inactive in ~50% of Orientals but rarely inactive in Caucasians. A dominantly acting (Shibuya and Yoshida 1988a) point mutation (Yoshida et al. 1984) produces the inactive ALDH2. Many Orientals also possess an inactive ALDH1, the cytosolic enzyme; ~0.5–3.3% of Japanese have both inactive variants (Yoshida et al. 1985).

ALDH and Alcoholism

The generally lower prevalences of alcoholism in Oriental countries may be due, in part, to ALDH deficiency. In a study of 175 Japanese alcoholics, 2% were ALDH2 deficient (Harada et al. 1983). In addition, only 3/31 Japanese chronic alcoholics with liver injury were deficient in ALDH2 (Yoshihara et al. 1983). In individuals with ALDH deficiency, significant elevations of acetaldehyde levels (Zeiner et al. 1979) after only one to two drinks of ethanol produce a syndrome resembling that produced in a person who has received the ALDH inhibitor disulfiram and who has imbibed alcohol. Flushing, dizziness, headache, and tachycardia are experienced.

Metabolic Genetic Variation and Ethanol Toxicity

Alcohol-associated tissue damage may be, in part, heritable: Twin studies demonstrated a two- to threefold higher concordance for alcoholic cirrhosis and psychosis in monozygotic, as compared with dizygotic, twins (Hrubec and Omenn 1981), and certain HLA antigens are associated with the development of cirrhosis (Shigeta et al. 1980; Jenkins and Thomas 1981; Saunders et al. 1982) in linkage disequilibrium studies. A specific genetic hypothesis has been advanced for the origin of Wernicke-Korsakoff syndrome, which is due to thiamine deficiency and most often results from alcoholism. The characteristic neuropathologic findings are detected in 1–3% of cases in random autopsy surveys. In two studies, one of abstinent alcoholics, a deficient transketolase with lower affinity for thiamine pyrophosphate was found (Martin et al. 1986).

Because acetaldehyde is responsible for multiple toxic effects at the subcellular level, reacting with proteins to form adducts that function abnormally

(Jennett et al. 1985) and act as immunogens (Lin et al. 1988), higher levels of damage to a variety of tissues and of alcoholic liver disease (ALD) might be hypothesized to occur in ALDH2-deficient alcoholics (Shibuya and Yoshida 1988b). Among 20 countries, the highest rate of cirrhosis per liter of ethanol consumed was in Japan, the only country in which the nonfunctional ALDH1 and ALDH2 variants are abundant. However, studies performed to date do not compare the incidence of cirrhosis in ALDH2$^-$ and ALDH2$^+$ groups in which ethanol intake is equivalent. In 23 Japanese with ALD, the ALDH2$^-$ variant occurred less often than in controls, and ALDH2-deficient alcoholics showed no characteristic differences in liver function tests or pathological findings as compared with nondeficient alcoholics (Sato et al. 1988).

Evidence for Selection at ALDH Loci and a Possible Selective Force

The occurrence of functional polymorphisms in three enzymes, ALDH1, ALDH2, and alcohol dehydrogenase 2 (ADH2) (Stomatoyannopoulos et al. 1975), involved in consecutive steps of the alcohol metabolic pathway suggests that the genetic variation is somehow maintained. It is also suggestive that the ALDH2 polymorphism is found in populations in South America, which have long been separated from Oriental populations. Genetic drift and founder effects could play significant roles in certain populations. It was hypothesized that the most likely selective force is an infectious agent inhabiting the gut; it is historically responsible for major morbidity and mortality. Human clinical infections due to a number of anaerobes and microaerophiles, including various anaerobic bacteria, *Trichomonas*, *Giardia*, *Balantidia*, and *Entamoeba,* respond to nitroimidazole drugs (metronidazole, tinidazole, nitrefazole, and ornidazole). Although the mechanism of action of the nitroimidazoles is unknown, these drugs cause flushing when subjects under treatment ingest ethanol (Suokkas et al. 1985). Because of this disulfiram-like effect, metronidazole and nitrefazole were tested, and nitrefazole was approved for treatment of alcoholism in Europe. It was proposed that nitroimidazoles act by inhibiting ALDH in host and/or parasite and that ALDH polymorphism may be most metabolically significant to organisms inhabiting the gut, where fermentation occurs, and in liver (Goldman and Enoch 1990).

E. histolytica is carried by ~10% of the world's population. Where endemic, virtually all individuals become infected and many are reinfected (Walsh 1988). Amebiasis causes significant morbidity due to ulcerative dysentery and extraintestinal infection in ~15% of those infected but causes 10,000–30,000 deaths per year in Mexico alone (Bray and Harris 1977). The cause of large differences in individual host resistance to invasive disease is unknown (National Academy of Sciences 1962). Although survey data for both amebiasis and the ALDH polymorphisms are incomplete, their distributions appear to be consistent: Rates of amebic infection have been historically high throughout East Asia, where, as well as in South America, the inactive ALDH2 is most abundant.

REFERENCES

Aghajanian, G.K., J.A. Rosecrans, and M.H. Sheard 1967. Serotonin release in the forebrain by stimulation of midbrain raphe. *Science* **15**: 402.

Agren, H., I.N. Mefford, M.V. Rudorfer, M. Linnoila, and W.Z. Potter. 1986. Interacting neurotransmitter systems. A nonexperimental approach to the 5-HIAA-HVA correlation in human CSF. *J. Psychiatr. Res.* **20**: 175.

Anderson, G.M. 1987. Monoamines in autism: An update of neurochemical research on a pervasive developmental disorder. *Med. Biol.* **65**: 67.

Anderson, G.M., R.B. Minderaa, P.G. van Benthem, F. Volkmar, and D.J. Cohen. 1984. Platelet imipramine binding in autistic subjects. *Psychiatry Res.* **11**: 133.

Asberg, M., L. Traskman, and P. Thoren. 1976. 5-HIAA in the cerebrospinal fluid— A biochemical suicide predictor? *Arch. Gen. Psychiatr.* **33**: 1193.

Berretini, W.H., G. Oxenstierna, G. Sedvall, J.I. Nurnberger, Jr., P.W. Gold, D.R. Rubinow, and L.R. Goldin. 1988. Characteristics of cerebrospinal fluid neuropeptides relevant to clinical research. *Psychiatry Res.* **25**: 349.

Berzenyi, P., E. Galateo, and L. Valzelli. 1983. Fluoxetine activity on muricidal aggression induced in rats by *p*-chlorophenylalanine. *Aggressive Behav.* **9**: 333.

Blanchard, C.D., R.J. Rodgers, C.A. Hendrie, and K. Hori. 1988. "Taming" of wild rats (*Rattus rattus*) by 5HT$_{1A}$ agonists buspirone and gepirone. *Pharmacol. Biochem. Behav.* **31**: 269.

Bohman, M. 1978. Some genetic aspects of alcoholism and criminality: A population of adoptees. *Arch. Gen. Psychiatry* **35**: 269.

Bouhelel, R., L. Smounya, and J. Bockaert. 1988. 5HT$_{1B}$ receptors are negatively coupled with adenylate cyclase in rat substantia nigra. *Eur. J. Pharmacol.* **151**: 189.

Boullin, D., B.J. Freeman, E. Geller, E. Ritvo, M. Rutter, and A. Yuwiler. 1982. Towards the resolution of conflicting findings. *J. Autism Dev. Dis.* **12**: 97.

Bray, R.S. and W.G. Harris. 1977. The epidemiology of infection with *Entamoeba histolytica* in the Gambia, West Africa. *Trans. R. Soc. Trop. Med. Hyg.* **71**: 401.

Brown, G.L., F.K. Goodwin, J.C. Ballenger, P.F. Goyer, and L.F. Major. 1979. Aggression in humans correlates with cerebrospinal fluid metabolites. *Psychiatry Res.* **1**: 131.

Brown, G.L., W.J. Kline, P.F. Goyer, M.D. Minichiello, M.J.P. Krusei, and F.K. Goodwin. 1985. Relationship of childhood characteristics to cerebrospinal fluid 5-hydroxyindoleacetic acid in aggressive adults. In *Biological psychiatry* (ed. C. Chagass), p. 177. Elsevier, New York.

Brown, G.L., M.H. Ebert, P.F. Goyer, D.C. Jimerson, W.J. Klein, W.E. Bunney, and F.K. Goodwin. 1982. Aggression, suicide and serotonin: Relationships to CSF amine metabolites. *Am. J. Psychiatry* **139**: 741.

Butler, A., J.M. Hill, S.J. Ireland, C.C. Jordan, and M.B. Tyers. 1988. Pharmacol-

ogical properties of GR38032F, a novel antagonist at 5-HT3 receptors. *Br. J. Pharmacol.* **94:** 397.
Cloninger, C.R. 1987. Neurogenetic adaptive mechanisms in alcoholism. *Science* **236:** 410.
Cloninger, C.R., M. Bohman, and S. Sigvardsson. 1981. Inheritance of alcohol abuse. Cross-fostering analysis of adopted men. *Arch. Gen. Psychiatry* **38:** 861.
Cloninger, C.R., M. Bohman, S. Sigvardsson, and A.-L. Von Knorring. 1985. Psychopathology in adopted-out children of alcoholics. *Recent Dev. Alcohol.* **3:** 37.
Conn, P.J. and E. Sanders-Bush. 1986. Regulation of serotonin-stimulated phosphoinositide hydrolysis: Relation to 5-HT-2 binding site. *J. Neurosci.* **6:** 3369.
Conn, P.J., E. Sanders-Bush, B.J. Hoffman, and P.R. Hartig. 1986. A unique serotonin receptor in choroid plexus is linked to phosphatidylinositol turnover. *Proc. Natl. Acad. Sci.* **83:** 4086.
Cotton, N.S. 1979. The familial incidence of alcoholism: A review. *J. Stud. Alcohol* **40:** 89.
Daoust, M., C. Saligaut, and M. Chadelaud. 1984. Attenuation by antidepressant drugs of alcohol intake in rats. *Alcohol* **1:** 379.
Derkach, V., A. Surprenant, and R.A. North. 1989. 5-HT$_3$ receptors are membrane ion channels. *Nature* **339:** 706.
Dourish, C.Y., S. Ahlenius, and P.H. Hutson, eds. 1987. *Brain 5-HT$_{1A}$ receptors.* Ellis Horwood, Chichester, England.
Fargin, A., J.R. Raymond, M.J. Lohse, B.K. Kobilka, M.G. Caron, and R.J. Lefkowitz. 1988. The genomic clone G-21 which resembles a B adrenergic receptor sequence encodes the 5-HT$_{1A}$ receptor. *Nature* **335:** 358.
Goldman, D. and M. Enoch. 1990. Genetic epidemiology of the ethanol metabolic enzymes: A role for selection. In *Genetic variation and nutrition* (ed. A. Simopoulos and B. Childs), Karger, New York. (In press.)
Green, A.R. 1989. Behavioural pharmacology of 5-HT: An introduction. In *Behavioural pharmacology of 5-HT* (ed. P. Bevan et al.), p. 3. Lawrence Erlbaum, Hillsdale, New Jersey.
Hall, M.D., S. El Mestikawy, M.B. Emerit, L. Pichat, M. Hamon, and H. Gozlan. 1985. [^{3}H]8-hydroxy-2-(Di-*n*-propylamino)tetralin binding to pre- and post-synaptic 5-hydroxytryptamine sites in various regions of the rat brain. *J. Neurochem.* **44:** 1685.
Harada, S., D.P. Agarwal, H.W. Goedde, and B. Ishikawa. 1983. Aldehyde dehydrogenase isozyme variation and alcoholism in Japan. *Pharmacol. Biochem. Behav.* (suppl. 1.) **18:** 151.
Hoyer, D., A. Pazos, A. Probst, and J.M. Palacios. 1986. Serotonin receptors in the human brain. II. Characterization and autoradiographic localization of 5-HT$_{1C}$ and 5-HT$_2$ recognition sites. *Brain Res.* **376:** 97.
Hrubec, Z. and G.S. Omenn. 1981. Evidence of genetic predisposition to alcoholic cirrhosis and psychosis: Twin concordance for alcoholism and its biological end points by zygosity among male veterans. *Alcoholism* **5:** 207.
Inoue, K., M. Fukunaga, T. Kiriyama, and S. Komura. 1984. Accumulation of acetaldehyde in alcohol-sensitive Japanese: Relation to ethanol and acetaldehyde oxidizing capacity. *Alcoholism* **8:** 319.

Jenkins, W.J. and H.C. Thomas. 1981. Genetic factors in determining susceptibility to alcohol dependence and development of alcohol-induced liver disease. *Clin. Gastroenterol.* **10**: 307.

Jennett, R.B., E.L. Johnson, M.F. Sorrell, and D.J. Tuma. 1985. Covalent binding of acetaldehyde to tubulin is associated with impaired polymerization. *Hepatology* **5**: 1055.

Julius, D., A.B. MacDermott, R. Axel, and T.M. Jessell. 1988. Molecular cloning of a functional cDNA encoding the serotonin 1c receptor. *Science* **241**: 558.

Kantak, K.M., L.R. Hegstrand, and B. Eichelman. 1981. Facilitation of shock-induced fighting following intraventricular 5,7 dihydroxytryptamine and 6-hydroxy DOPA. *Psychopharmacology* **74**: 157.

Katz, R.J. 1980. Role of serotonergic mechanisms in animal models of predation. *Prog. Neuro-Psychopharmacol.* **4**: 219.

Kaufman, S. and D.B. Fisher. 1974. Pterin-requiring aromatic amino acid hydroxylases. In *Molecular mechanisms of oxygen activation* (ed. O. Hayaishi), p. 285. Academic Press, New York.

Kochersperger, L.M., E.L. Parker, M. Siciliano, M. Park, D.J. Darlington, and R.M. Denney. 1986. Assignment of genes for human monoamine oxidases A and B to the X chromosome. *J. Neurosci. Res.* **16**: 601.

Kuhn, D.M., M.A. Meyer, and W. Lovenberg. 1980. Comparisons of tryptophan hydroxylase from a malignant murine mast tumor and rat mesencephalic tegmentum. *Arch. Biochem. Biophys.* **199**: 355.

Lawrin, M.O., C.A. Naranjo, and E.M. Sellers. 1986. Identification and testing of new drugs for modulating alcohol consumption. *Psychopharmacol. Bull.* **22**: 1020.

Lin, R.C., R.S. Smith, and L. Lumeng. 1988. Detection of a protein-acetaldehyde adduct in the liver of rats fed alcohol chronically. *J. Clin. Invest.* **81**: 615.

Linnoila, M., M. Virkkunen, M. Scheinin, A. Nuutila, R. Rimon, and F.K. Goodwin. 1983. Low cerebrospinal fluid 5-hydroxyindoleacetic acid concentration differentiates impulsive from nonimpulsive violent behavior. *Life Sci.* **33**: 2609.

Loehlin, J.C. 1982. Are personality traits differentially heritable? *Behav. Genet.* **12**: 417.

Lubbert, H., B.J. Hoffman, T. Snutch, T. Van Dyke, A.J. Levine, P.R. Hartig, H.A. Lester, and N. Davidson. 1987. cDNA cloning of a serotonin 5-HT-1c receptor by electrophysiological assays of mRNA-injected *Xenopus* oocytes. *Proc. Natl. Acad. Sci.* **84**: 4332.

Markstein, R., D. Hoyer, and G. Engel. 1986. 5-HT$_{1A}$-receptors mediate stimulation of adenylate cyclase in rat hippocampus. *Naunyn-Schmiedeberg's Arch. Pharmacol.* **129**: 333.

Martin, P.R., B. Adinoff, H. Weingartner, A.B. Mukherjee, and M.J. Eckardt. 1986. Alcoholic organic brain disease: Nosology and pathophysiologic mechanisms. *Prog. Neuro-Psychopharmacol. Biol. Psychiatr.* **10**: 147.

McBride, W.J., J.M. Murphy, L. Lumeng, and T.-K. Li. 1989. Serotonin and ethanol preference. In *Recent developments in alcoholism* (ed. M. Galanter), vol. 7, p. 187. Plenum Press, New York.

Meert, T.F., C.J.E. Niemegeers, Y.G. Gelders, and P.A.J. Janssen. 1989. Ritanserin (R 55 667), an original thymosthenic. In *Behavioural pharmacology of 5HT* (ed. P. Bevan et al.), p. 235. Lawrence Erlbaum, Hillsdale, New Jersey.

Meltzer, H.M. and R.C. Arora. 1988. Genetic control of serotonin uptake in blood platelets: A twin study. *Psychiatry Res.* **24:** 263.

Moore, R.Y. 1981. The anatomy of central serotonin neuron systems in the rat brain. In *Serotonin neurotransmission and behavior* (ed. B.L. Jacobs and A. Gelperin), p. 35. MIT Press, Cambridge, Massachusetts.

Murphy, J.M., M.B. Waller, E.J. Gatto, W.J. McBride, L. Lumenz, and T.-K. Li. 1985. Monoamine uptake inhibitors attenuate ethanol intake in alcohol-preferring (P) rats. *Alcohol* **2:** 349.

Myers, R.D. and C.L. Melchior. 1977. Alcohol and alcoholism: Role of serotonin. In *Serotonin in health and disease* (ed. W.B. Essman), vol. 2, p. 373. Spectrum, New York.

Naranjo, C.A., E.M. Sellers, C.A. Roach, D.V. Woodley, M. Sanchez-Craig, and K. Sykora. 1984. Zimelidine-induced variations in alcohol intake by nondepressed heavy drinkers. *Clin. Pharmacol. Ther.* **35:** 374.

National Academy of Sciences. 1962. *National Research Council Tropical Health: A Report on a Study of Needs and Resources.* Publication 996, p. 373. Washington, D.C.

Oxenstierna, G., G. Edman, L. Iselius, L. Oreland, S.B. Ross, and G. Sedvall. 1986. Concentrations of monoamine metabolites in the cerebrospinal fluid of twins and unrelated individuals—A genetic study. *J. Psychiatr. Res.* **20:** 19.

Ozelius, L., Y.-P. Hsu, G. Bruns, J.F. Powell, S. Chen, W. Weyler, M. Utterback, D. Zucker, J. Haines, J.A. Trofatter, P.M. Conneally, J.F. Gusella, and X.O. Breakefield. 1988. Human monoamine oxidase gene (MAOA): Chromosome position (Xp21-p11) and DNA polymorphism. *Genomics* **3:** 53.

Pazos, A., D. Hoyer, and J.M. Palacios. 1984. The binding of serotonergic ligands to the porcine choroid plexus: Characterization of a new type of serotonin recognition site. *Eur. J. Pharmacol.* **106:** 539.

Powell, J.F., Y.P. Shu, W. Weyler, S.A. Chen, J. Salach, K. Andrikopoulos, J. Mallet, and X.O. Breakefield. 1989. The primary structure of bovine monoamine oxidase type A. Comparison with peptide sequences of bovine monoamine oxidase type B and other flavoenzymes. *Biochem. J.* **259:** 407.

Pritchett, D.B., A.W. Bach, M. Wozny, O. Taleb, R. Dal Toso, J.C. Shih, and P.H. Seeburg. 1988. Structure and functional expression of cloned serotonin 5HT-2 receptor. *EMBO J.* **7:** 4135.

Rockman, G.R., Z. Amit, G. Carr, Z.W. Brown, and S.O. Ogren. 1979. Attenuation of ethanol intake by 5-hydroxytryptamine uptake blockade in laboratory rats. I. Involvement of brain 5-hydroxytryptamine in the mediation of the positive reinforcing properties of ethanol. *Arch. Int. Pharmacodyn. Ther.* **241:** 245.

Sato, S., T. Takagi, S. Higuchi, A. Yokoyama, T. Muramatsu, M. Saito, S. Takekawa, K. Shigemori, J. Sato, H. Tsukamoto, K. Maruyama, S. Harada, H. Ishii, K. Watanabe, and M. Tsuchiya. 1988. Alcoholic liver injuries in ALDH1 deficient subjects—Pathohistological and immunohistochemical study. In *Biomedical and social aspects of alcohol and alcoholism* (ed. K. Kuriyama et al.), p. 737. Elsevier, Amsterdam.

Saunders, J.B., A.D. Wodak, A. Haines, P.R. Powell-Jackson, B. Portmann, M. Davis, and R. Williams. 1982. Accelerated development of alcoholic cirrhosis in patients with HLA-B8. *Lancet* **I:** 1381.

Schain, R.J. and D.X. Freedman. 1961. Studies on 5-hydroxyindole metabolism in autistic and other mentally retarded children. *J. Pediatr.* **58:** 315.

Sheard, M. 1971. Effect of lithium on human aggression. *Nature* **230:** 113.

———. 1975. Lithium in the treatment of aggression. *J. Nerv. Ment. Dis.* **100:** 108.

Shenker, A., S. Maayani, H. Weinstein, and J.P. Green. 1985. Two 5-HT receptors linked to adenylate cyclase in guinea pig hippocampus are discriminated by 5-carboxamidotryptamine and spiperone. *Eur. J. Pharmacol.* **109:** 427.

Shibuya, A. and A. Yoshida. 1988a. Genotypes of alcohol-metabolizing enzymes in Japanese with alcohol liver disease: A strong association of the usual Caucasian-type aldehyde dehydrogenase gene ($ALDH_2^1$) with the disease. *Am. J. Hum. Genet.* **43:** 744.

———. 1988b. Frequency of the atypical aldehyde dehydrogenase 2 gene ($ALDH_2^2$) in Japanese and Caucasians. *Am. J. Hum. Genet.* **43:** 741.

Shigeta, Y., H. Ishii, S. Takagi, Y. Yoshitake, T. Hirano, H. Kohno, and M. Tsuchiya. 1980. HLA antigens as immunogenetic markers of alcoholism and alcoholic liver disease. *Pharmacol. Biochem. Behav.* (suppl. 1) **13:** 89.

Slotkin, T.A., W.L. Whitmore, K.L. Dew, and C.D. Kilts. 1986. Uptake of serotonin into rat platelets and synaptosomes: Comparative structure-activity relationships, energetics, and evaluation of the effects of acute and chronic nortriptyline administration. *Brain Res. Bull.* **17:** 67.

Soubrie, P. 1986. Reconciling the role of central serotonin neurons in human and animal behavior. *Behav. Brain Sci.* **9:** 319.

Stamatoyannopoulos, G., S.H. Chen, and F. Fukui. 1975. Liver alcohol dehydrogenase in Japanese: High population frequency of atypical form and its possible role in alcohol sensitivity. *Am. J. Hum. Genet.* **27:** 789.

Stoll, J., C. Kozak, and D. Goldman. 1990. Cloning and comparative mapping of a mouse mastocytoma tryptophan hydroxylase. *Genomics* (in press).

Suokkas, A., M. Kupari, J. Pettersson, and K. Lindros. 1985. The nitrefazole-ethanol interaction in man: Cardiovascular responses and the accumulation of acetaldehyde and catecholamines. *Alcohol. Clin. Exp. Res.* **9:** 221.

Teng, Y.S. 1981. Human liver aldehyde dehydrogenase in Chinese and Asiatic Indians. Gene detection and the possible implications in ethanol metabolism. *Biochem. Genet.* **19:** 107.

Tupin, J.P., D.B. Smith, T.L. Classon, L.I. Kim, A. Nugent, and A. Groupe. 1973. The long-term use of lithium in aggressive prisoners. *Compr. Psychiatry* **14:** 311.

Valzelli, L. and S. Garratini. 1968. Behavioral changes and 5-hydroxytryptamine turnover in animals. *Adv. Pharmacol.* **6B:** 249.

van Praag, H.M. and J. Korf. 1971. Endogenous depressions with and without disturbances in 5-hydroxytryptamine metabolism: A biochemical classification. *Psychopharmacology* **19:** 148.

Walsh, J.A. 1988. Prevalence of *Entamoeba histolytica* infection. In *Amoebiasis* (ed. J.I. Ravdin), p. 93. J. Wiley, New York.

Wirz-Justice, A. 1988. Platelet research in psychiatry. *Experientia* **44:** 145.

Wurtman, R.J. 1988. Effects of dietary amino acids, carbohydrates, and choline on neurotransmitter synthesis. *Mount Sinai J. Med.* **55:** 75.

Yoshida, A., I.-Y. Huang, and M. Ikawa. 1984. Molecular abnormality of an inactive aldehyde dehydrogenase variant commonly found in Orientals. *Proc. Natl. Acad. Sci.* **81**: 258.

Yoshida, A., M. Ikawa, L.C. Hsu, and K. Tani. 1985. Molecular abnormality and cDNA cloning of human aldehyde dehydrogenases. *Alcohol* **2**: 103.

Yoshihara, Y., S. Nobuhiro, T. Kamada, and H. Abe. 1983. Low Km ALDH isozyme and alcoholic liver injury. *Pharmacol. Biochem. Behav.* (suppl.) **18**: 425.

Yoshimoto, K. and S. Komura. 1987. Reexamination of the relationship between ethanol preference and brain monoamines in inbred mice including senescence-accelerated mice. *Pharmacol. Biochem. Behav.* **1**: 145.

Zeiner, A.R., A. Paredes, and D.H. Christensen. 1979. The role of acetaldehyde in mediating reactivity to an acute dose of ethanol among different racial groups. *Alcoholism* **3**: 11.

COMMENTS

Chakravarti: Is there any animal model, such as in the mouse, that can be looked at for any kind of related behavioral extensions of that?

Goldman: There are. One of the behaviors that we're most interested in, in fact, is the periodic torpor that occurs in certain mice, e.g., the deer mouse, which is not anything like a laboratory mouse. It is also possible to induce torpor in a laboratory mouse. When one does this, the temperature of the animal drops about 10 degrees and the animal stops eating. It is a state that is probably related to hibernation, but it can be induced much more readily. Another behavior it may be possible to examine is aggression in the rodents. There is a controversy as to how one measures aggression in rodents. I think the best conclusion that can be drawn from the behavioral literature in that area is that we don't know how to measure aggression in the mouse.

Reich: What are you going to do when there are multiple kinds of tryptophan hydroxylase in people and they're expressed in different parts of the brain? Is that an effect that is going to change?

Goldman: Now we have a probe that may be picking up the brain stem tryptophan hydroxylase message, which then gives us the avenue to clone that gene. Thus, one would use either one or both of those probes.

Reich: There probably is a family of tryptophan hydroxylases.

Goldman: There may be. There is one tyrosine hydroxylase, there is one phenylalanine hydroxylase. Maybe there are two or more.

Reich: Are they expressed differently in different parts of the brain?

Goldman: In fact, tryptophan hydroxylase is probably not expressed in those parts of the brain. Its expression point will probably be found to be restricted to the couple of those 100,000 or so cells of the raphe and the pineal.

Peters: You see quite a good correlation with HVA, but you put your money on tryptophan hydroxylase. What about dopamine and DBH? Is that a possibility?

Goldman: That's right. In fact, it has not only been cloned, but people have already sought to correlate genetic differences for DBH activity. The problem is that serum DBH levels reflect the genetics of how rapidly the DBH that is coreleased with norepinephrine is cleared rather than the genetics of a DBH enzyme variant. Here I have focused on one particular system. One can think of modeling other genes that would be equally useful. For example, one can study benzodiazepine receptor probes with regard to an anxiety phenotype; or one can think of specific reasons why certain genes in the acetylcholine family might be important, for example, with regard to depression.

Human Aldehyde Dehydrogenases: Genetic Implications in Alcohol Sensitivity, Alcohol-drinking Habits, and Alcoholism

DHARAM P. AGARWAL AND H. WERNER GOEDDE
Institute of Human Genetics
University of Hamburg
2000 Hamburg 54, Butenfeld 32, Federal Republic of Germany

OVERVIEW

There is a general recognition that certain biological factors may primarily regulate alcohol-drinking habits of individuals and the quantity of alcohol consumed in certain racial and ethnic groups, thus representing important genetic-metabolic determinants of alcoholism (Goedde and Agarwal 1987a, 1989a). Recent studies have consistently revealed that differences in sensitivity to alcohol (facial flushing and other vasomotor symptoms) between Caucasians and Mongoloids indicate an important physiological, rather than cultural, basis for the observed epidemiological diversity in alcohol use, abuse, and rate of alcoholism and alcohol-related disorders. Genetic variation in alcohol and aldehyde-metabolizing enzymes, particularly the deficiency of mitochondrial aldehyde dehydrogenase (ALDH) isozyme, has been found to have a direct bearing on blood acetaldehyde levels in some individuals after consumption of alcohol. Not only does elevated acetaldehyde level lead to adverse reactions after alcohol drinking in some racial/ethnic groups, but it may also enhance the general risk for alcohol-related tissue and organ damage. Acetaldehyde readily forms adducts with many cellular proteins, affecting their structural and functional properties.

INTRODUCTION

A genetic basis for alcoholism and alcohol-related disorders has been shown in family and adoption studies (Goedde and Agarwal 1989a). Changes in ethanol and acetaldehyde metabolism via genetically determined variations in the enzymes involved may be responsible, in part, for the observed individual and racial differences in alcohol-drinking habits and acute and chronic reactions to alcohol, as well as vulnerability to organ damage after chronic alcohol abuse. Whether genetic factors alone primarily influence alcohol-drinking behavior in humans or other metabolic and environmental factors determine drinking behavior has been the subject of intensive research in recent years.

In particular, ALDH (aldehyde:NAD$^+$ oxidoreductase, EC 1.2.1.3), the enzyme mainly responsible for the oxidation of acetaldehyde, has been suggested to play an important role in the toxic consequences of a deranged acetaldehyde metabolism in alcohol-related disorders. Many isozymes of ALDH, coded by different gene loci, exist in human organs and tissues and differ in their electrophoretic mobility and kinetic properties, as well as in their subcellular, cellular, and tissue distribution (Goedde et al. 1983a; Agarwal and Goedde 1987a; Goedde and Agarwal 1987b). The various isozymes also differ in their molecular size, subunit structure, and chromosomal localization. The mammalian ALDHs may be divided into three distinct classes, on the basis of their structural and kinetic properties (Weiner 1989). Members of class 1 are cytoplasmic ALDHs (e.g., ALDH1), members of class 2 are mitochondrial ALDHs (e.g., ALDH2), and members of class 3 are tumor-specific/inducible cytoplasmic ALDHs, as well as the major constitutive or inducible microsomal ALDHs (e.g., ALDH3).

Whereas ALDH1 and ALDH2 both show Michaelis constants in the micromolar range with acetaldehyde and propionaldehyde, such values for ALDH3 and ALDH4 are in the millimolar range for these substrates (Pietruszko et al. 1987; Goedde and Agarwal 1989b). The major human liver ALDH1 and ALDH2 isozymes are homotetramers, consisting of subunits of ~ 54,000 m.w. each. There are extensive subunit differences between the two isozymes, with only 68% positional identity in the primary structures. Of the residue exchanges, 27% are highly conservative (Jörnvall et al. 1987). These dissimilar regions may explain why the subunits from different isozymes do not form hybrid tetrameric molecules. The ALDH2 gene is 44 kbp in length and contains at least 13 exons, which encode 517 residues (Hsu et al. 1988). The first 17 amino acids constitute a signal peptide that is absent in the mature enzyme (Braun et al. 1987). The gene coding for the mitochondrial isozyme (ALDH2) has been assigned to chromosome 12, and the gene coding for the cytosolic isozyme (ALDH1) is located on the long arm of chromosome 9; the less-characterized stomach-specific ALDH3 isozyme has been mapped at chromosome 17.

Many direct toxic effects of alcohol and alcohol-related physical alterations have been attributed to acetaldehyde rather than to ethanol itself. Acetaldehyde might damage mitochondria, thereby reducing the level of ALDH activity and further impairing the metabolism of acetaldehyde. Reoxidation of NADH produced from NAD$^+$ during the oxidation of ethanol occurs principally in the mitochondria; therefore, any change in intracellular redox potential will produce profound metabolic consequences (Lieber 1988). Thus, the development of alcoholism involves an interplay between positively predisposing factors and factors that produce an aversion against alcohol. The widely observed genetically determined interindividual and racial variability in alcohol and acetaldehyde metabolism may explain the biomedical basis of differences in alcohol sensitivity, alcohol-drinking habits, and alcoholism (Eriksson 1987; Goedde and Agarwal 1989a).

RESULTS

Genetic Variants of ALDH2

For the first time, Goedde et al. (1979) reported that $\sim 50\%$ of Japanese and Chinese autopsy livers lack ALDH2 isozyme activity. Screening studies using hair root lysates (Goedde et al. 1980) have shown that Oriental populations of Mongoloid origin have a varying degree of this isozyme deficiency (~ 30–50%), whereas this abnormality has not been detected in Caucasian or Negroid populations (Goedde et al. 1983b; Goedde and Agarwal 1987b, 1989b). Although $\sim 40\%$ of South American Indian tribes (Mapuche, Atacameños, Shuara) show this isozyme deficiency, only a very small percentage of North American Indians (Sioux, Navajo) and Mexican Indians (Mestizo) have been found to be deficient in ALDH2 activity (Goedde et al. 1986; Bosron et al. 1988).

A structural mutation leads to the synthesis of an enzymatically inactive protein: Glutamic acid at position 14 from the carboxyl terminus (position 487 from the amino terminus) is substituted in the deficient isozyme by lysine (Hempel et al. 1984). This mutational exchange has been confirmed by the nucleotide sequence of a partial cDNA probe for human ALDH2 as well as by genomic DNA analysis (Hsu et al. 1985, 1988). The ALDH2 deficiency genotypes determined in the blood by DNA amplification and allele-specific oligonucleotide hybridization technique show a gene frequency for ALDH2^2, ranging from 0.15 to 0.35 in unrelated Japanese, Chinese, and Korean subjects (Goedde et al. 1989; Singh et al. 1989). Preliminary data from Japanese and Korean families reveal a dominance of the mutant allele over the normal allele (Singh et al. 1989).

ALDH2 Deficiency and Alcohol Intolerance in Orientals

In some individuals, ingestion of moderate amounts of alcohol exerts the so-called alcohol-sensitivity symptoms (facial flushing, increase in heart rate, enhancement of left ventricular function, hot feeling in stomach, palpitation, tachycardia, muscle weakness, etc.). Compared to Caucasians, a greater percentage of Orientals (Mongoloid ancestry) and American Indians respond to a mild dose of ethanol with marked adverse cardiovascular reactions. An abnormal alcohol metabolism by way of ALDH2 deficiency is considered to be primarily responsible for the accumulation of acetaldehyde after ethanol drinking, leading to the well-known alcohol-sensitivity reactions (Goedde et al. 1979; Goedde and Agarwal 1987b, 1989b). A positive correlation between alcohol sensitivity and elevated blood acetaldehyde level, in conjunction with ALDH2 isozyme deficiency, was noted in Japanese subjects given an acute dose of alcohol (Goedde et al. 1983a; Harada et al. 1985). ALDH2 isozyme-deficient subjects showed a significantly higher blood acetaldehyde level than nonflushers with a normal ALDH2 isozyme profile, whereas both groups of subjects showed similar blood ethanol concentrations.

ALDH2 Isozyme Deficiency and Alcohol-drinking Habits

A larger proportion of Orientals than Caucasians report no use of alcohol, whereas Caucasians generally report heavier alcohol use. A significant percentage (40–80%) of Orientals experience facial flushing and associated sensitivity symptoms after drinking alcohol (Agarwal and Goedde 1987b).

In a recent study of 101 Japanese subjects, the ALDH2-deficient phenotype was found in 42%, and the ALDH2-normal phenotype was found in 58% of the subjects (Ohmori et al. 1986). Subjects were divided into "drinking habits −" (subjects who drank only occasionally or not at all) and "drinking habits +" (subjects who drank every day or almost every day). The subjects lived in the same city and had the same occupations. When grouped according to their alcohol-drinking habits, only 19% of the ALDH2-deficient types and 49% of the ALDH2-normal types were in the + category. When nuclear families of Koreans, Taiwanese, Japanese, and Caucasians living in Hawaii were questioned about their use of alcoholic beverages and physical consequences experienced after drinking moderate amounts of alcohol, a genetic correlation between flushing and alcohol consumption was found (Nagoshi et al. 1988).

ALDH2 Isozyme Deficiency and Alcoholism

A significantly lower incidence of ALDH2 isozyme deficiency is encountered in alcoholics, as compared with psychiatric patients, drug-dependent subjects, and healthy controls in Japan (Goedde et al. 1983a; Harada et al. 1985). Similar findings have been also observed in other psychiatric clinics in Japan and Taiwan (Ohmori et al. 1986). Of 113 Japanese alcoholics, only 5 (4%) were found to be deficient in ALDH2 isozyme activity, as compared to 42% deficient among healthy controls. A similar distribution was observed in Taiwanese subjects: Of 29 alcoholics, only 3 (10%) showed ALDH2 deficiency.

Association of ALDH2 Isozyme Deficiency with Alcoholic Liver Disease

A significantly lower incidence of the ALDH2 deficiency phenotype was observed in patients with alcoholic liver disease in Japan (Yoshihara et al. 1983). The incidence of alcoholic liver disease was found significantly higher in nonflushers than in flushers. In another study, of 55 patients with alcoholic liver disease, the ALDH2 isozyme was present in 54 subjects; whereas of 96 patients without alcoholic liver disease, the ALDH2 isozyme was detected in only 48 subjects (Takase et al. 1988).

At the genotype level, a remarkable difference between unrelated healthy controls and alcoholic liver disease patients has been observed as well (Shibuya and Yoshida 1988). Of 49 control subjects, 21 were of homozygous normal (ALDH2^1/ALDH2^1), 22 were of heterozygous deficient (ALDH2^1/ALDH2^2), and 6 were of homozygous deficient (ALDH2^2/ALDH2^2) genotype. In contrast, of 23 alcoholic liver disease patients, 20 were of homozygous normal, 3 were of heterozygous deficient, and none of the patients was of homozygous deficient genotype. These studies further indicate that subjects with the ALDH2 mutant allele are at a significantly lower risk of developing alcoholism and alcohol-related organ damage, apparently due to their alcohol-induced sensitivity response.

ALDH Activity and Alcohol-Related Organ and Tissue Damage

Liver ALDH Activity

A significantly reduced in vitro total ALDH activity in surgical biopsy samples from alcoholics, as compared with nonalcoholic controls, has been reported by many investigators. The total and specific ALDH activities were found to be significantly reduced in cirrhotic liver extracts in comparison to liver extracts of nonalcoholics (Jenkins and Peters 1980; Meier-Tackmann et al. 1988). A persistently decreased liver cytosolic ALDH activity (ALDH1) in alcoholics may even indicate a primary abnormality due to a possible genetic vulnerability to alcoholism (Thomas et al. 1983). However, such a genetic propensity to alcoholism has not been confirmed in other studies (Jenkins et al. 1984; Agarwal et al. 1987); the hepatic, as well as the erythrocyte cytosolic ALDH activity, was found to rise again when alcohol intake was reduced.

Erythrocyte ALDH Activity

Reduced erythrocyte ALDH activity (ALDH1) has been noted in the blood of chronic alcoholics, as compared to healthy controls and nonalcoholic psychiatric and gastrointestinal patients (Agarwal et al. 1983). The reduced red cell ALDH activity returned to normal values after ~12 weeks of abstinence. The red cell ALDH activity decreased progressively with increasing cell age: In alcoholics, even the younger cells showed a significantly lower enzyme activity (Agarwal et al. 1985; Mezey and Rhodes 1988). Although some reports indicate that changes in erythrocyte ALDH activity in alcoholics are unrelated to alcoholic liver damage, a correlation between altered red cell enzyme activity and damage to various organs in alcohol abuse and alcoholism has yet to be established (Matthewson and Record 1986; Agarwal et al. 1987).

DISCUSSION

In the past, considerable attention has been devoted to the possible role of acetaldehyde as mediator of the psychopharmacological effects of alcohol drinking, including flushing, reinforcement, tolerance, and physical dependence. These studies and results presented here demonstrate clearly that predisposing factors determining alcohol and acetaldehyde metabolism in an individual may cause a pronounced effect on the etiology and pathophysiology of alcohol abuse and alcoholism. The ALDH2 variant with a loss in catalytic activity appears to play a major role in alcohol sensitivity and in determining the prevalence of alcoholism in Oriental populations of Mongoloid origin. Individuals with ALDH2 enzyme abnormality drink less, have the tendency not to become habitual drinkers, suffer less from alcoholic liver disease, and are rarely alcoholics. The higher the prevalence of ALDH2 isozyme deficiency is in certain racial or ethnic groups, the lower the prevalence of alcohol-related problems. However, the concept that impaired acetaldehyde metabolism might be the modulating factor for observed differences in drinking behavior, as well as for the incidence of alcoholism in certain racial and ethnic groups needs further clinical support in future studies. Moreover, the basis for the relatively high prevalence of alcoholism among native Americans, despite their inherent intolerance to alcohol, has yet to be understood.

In future research, to better assess the influence of genetically determined protective and predisposing factors in harmful alcohol-drinking behavior and alcoholism, extensive epidemiological surveys need to be carried out. Such studies may include alcohol dehydrogenase (ADH) and ALDH genotype distribution, alcohol-drinking habits, per capita alcohol consumption, and the rate of alcoholism in healthy subjects, as well as in alcoholics of different racial and ethnic backgrounds. Specifically, the metabolic and genetic basis of behavioral aspects of alcohol-drinking correlates and alcoholism among Caucasians needs special attention.

ACKNOWLEDGMENTS

This work was supported in part by the Deutsche Forschungsgemeinschaft and the Bundesministerium für Forschung und Technologie, Bonn.

REFERENCES

Agarwal, D.P. and H.W. Goedde. 1987a. Human aldehyde dehydrogenase isozymes and alcohol sensitivity. In *Isozymes: Current topics in biological and medical research* (ed. M.C. Rattazzi et al.), vol. 16, p. 21. Alan R. Liss, New York.

———. 1987b. Genetic variation in alcohol metabolizing enzymes: Implications in alcohol use and abuse. In *Genetics and alcoholism* (ed. H.W. Goedde and D.P. Agarwal), p. 121. Alan R. Liss, New York.

Agarwal, D.P., L. Tobar-Rojas, S. Harada, and H.W. Goedde. 1983. Comparative study of erythrocyte aldehyde dehydrogenase in alcoholics and control subjects. *Pharmacol. Biochem. Behav.* (**suppl. 1**) **18:** 89.

Agarwal, D.P., T. Volkens, G. Hafer, and H.W. Goedde. 1987. Erythrocyte aldehyde dehydrogenase: Studies of properties and changes in acute and chronic alcohol intoxication. In *Enzymology and molecular biology of carbonyl metabolism: Aldehyde dehydrogenase, aldo-keto reductase and alcohol dehydrogenase* (ed. H. Weiner and T.G. Flynn), p. 85. Alan R. Liss, New York.

Agarwal, D.P., C. Müller, C. Korencke, U. Mika, S. Harada, and H.W. Goedde. 1985. Changes in erythrocyte and liver aldehyde dehydrogenase isozymes in alcoholics. In *Enzymology of carbonyl metabolism: Aldehyde dehydrogenase, aldo/keto reductase, and alcohol dehydrogenase* (ed. T.G. Flynn and H. Weiner), p. 113. Alan R. Liss, New York.

Bosron, W.F., D.K. Rex, C.A. Harden, and T.K. Li. 1988. Alcohol and aldehyde dehydrogenase isoenzymes in Sioux North American Indians. *Alcohol. Clin. Exp. Res.* **12:** 454.

Braun, T., E. Bober, S. Singh, D.P. Agarwal, and H.W. Goedde. 1987. Evidence for a signal peptide at the amino-terminal end of human mitochondrial aldehyde dehydrogenase. *FEBS Lett.* **215:** 233.

Eriksson, C.J.P. 1987. Genetic aspects of the relation between alcohol metabolism and consumption in humans. *Mutat. Res.* **186:** 241.

Goedde, H.W. and D.P. Agarwal. 1987a. Genetics and alcoholism: Problems and perspectives. In *Genetics and alcoholism* (ed. H.W. Goedde and D.P. Agarwal), p. 3. Alan R. Liss, New York.

———. 1987b. Polymorphism of aldehyde dehydrogenase and alcohol sensitivity. *Enzyme* **37:** 29.

———. 1989a. Biomedical and genetic aspects of alcoholism: Current issues and future directions. In *Alcoholism: Biomedical and genetic aspects* (ed. H.W. Goedde and D.P. Agarwal), p. 348. Pergamon Press, New York.

———. 1989b. Acetaldehyde metabolism: Genetic variation and physiological impli-

cations. In *Alcoholism: Biomedical and genetic aspects* (ed. H.W. Goedde and D.P. Agarwal), p. 21. Pergamon Press, New York.
Goedde, H.W., D.P. Agarwal, and S. Harada. 1980. Genetic studies on alcohol metabolizing enzymes: Detection of isozymes in human hair roots. *Enzyme* **25**: 281.
———. 1983a. The role of alcohol dehydrogenase and aldehyde dehydrogenase isozymes in alcohol metabolism, alcohol sensitivity and alcoholism. In *Isozymes: Current topics in biological and medical research* (ed. Rattazzi et al.), vol. 8, p. 175. Alan R. Liss, New York.
Goedde, H.W., S. Harada, and D.P. Agarwal. 1979. Racial differences in alcohol sensitivity: A new hypothesis. *Hum. Genet.* **51**: 331.
Goedde, H.W., D.P. Agarwal, S. Harada, J.O. Whittaker, F. Rothhammer, and R. Lisker. 1986. Aldehyde dehydrogenase polymorphism in North American, South American and Mexican Indians. *Am. J. Hum. Genet.* **38**: 395.
Goedde, H.W., S. Singh, D.P. Agarwal, G. Fritze, K. Stapel, and Y.K. Paik. 1989. Genotyping of mitochondrial aldehyde dehydrogenase in blood samples using allele-specific oligonucleotides: Comparison with phenotyping in hair roots. *Hum. Genet.* **81**: 305.
Goedde, H.W,. D.P. Agarwal, S. Harada, D. Meier-Tackmann, D. Ruofu, U. Bienzle, A. Kroeger, and L. Hussain. 1983b. Population genetic studies on aldehyde dehydrogenase isozyme deficiency and alcohol sensitivity. *Am. J. Hum. Genet.* **35**: 769.
Harada, S., D.P. Agarwal, and H.W. Goedde. 1985. Aldehyde dehydrogenase polymorphism and alcohol metabolism in alcoholics. *Alcohol* **2**: 391.
Hempel, J., R. Kaiser, and H. Jörnvall. 1984. Human liver mitochondrial aldehyde dehydrogenase: A C-terminal segment positions and defines the structure corresponding to the one reported to differ in the Oriental enzyme variant. *FEBS Lett.* **173**: 367.
Hsu, L.C., R.E. Bendel, and A. Yoshida. 1988. Genomic structure of the human mitochondrial aldehyde dehydrogenase gene. *Genomics* **2**: 57.
Hsu, L.C., K. Tani, T. Fujiyoshi, K. Kurachi, and A. Yoshida. 1985. Cloning of cDNAs for human aldehyde dehydrogenases 1 and 2. *Proc. Natl. Acad. Sci.* **82**: 3771.
Jenkins, W.J. and T.J. Peters. 1980. Selectively reduced hepatic acetaldehyde dehydrogenase in alcoholics. *Lancet* **I**: 628.
Jenkins, W.J., K. Cakebread, and K.R. Palmer. 1984. Effect of alcohol consumption on hepatic aldehyde dehydrogenase activity in alcoholic patients. *Lancet* **I**: 1048.
Jörnvall, H., J. Hempel, and B. Vallee. 1987. Structures of human alcohol and aldehyde dehydrogenases. *Enzyme* **37**: 5.
Lieber, C.S. 1988. Metabolic effects of acetaldehyde. *Biochem. Soc. Trans.* **16**: 241.
Matthewson, K. and C.O. Record. 1986. Erythrocyte aldehyde dehydrogenase activity in alcoholic subjects and its value as a marker for hepatic aldehyde dehydrogenase in subjects with and without liver disease. *Clin. Sci.* **70**: 295.
Meier-Tackmann, D., G.C. Korenke, D.P. Agarwal, and H.W. Goedde. 1988. Aldehyde dehydrogenase isozymes: Subcellular distribution in livers from alcoholics and healthy subjects. *Alcohol* **5**: 73.

Mezey, E. and D.L. Rhodes. 1988. Changes in erythrocyte enzyme activities during erythrocyte aging in alcoholism. *Alcohol. Clin. Exp. Res.* **12**: 422.

Nagoshi, C.T., L.K. Dixon, R.C. Johnson, and S.H.L. Yuen. 1988. Familial transmission of alcohol consumption and the flushing response to alcohol in three Oriental groups. *J. Stud. Alcohol* **49**: 261.

Ohmori, T., T. Koyama, C. Chen, E. Yeh, B.V. Reyes, Jr., and I. Yamashita. 1986. The role of aldehyde dehydrogenase isozyme variance in alcohol sensitivity, drinking habits formation and the development of alcoholism in Japan, Taiwan and the Philippines. *Prog. Neuro-Psychopharmacol. Biol. Psychiatry* **10**: 229.

Pietruszko, R., M.T. Ryzlak, and C.M. Forte-McRobbie. 1987. Multiplicity and identity of human aldehyde dehydrogenases. *Alcohol Alcohol.* (**suppl. 1**): 175.

Shibuya, A. and A. Yoshida. 1988. Genotypes of alcohol-metabolizing enzymes in Japanese with alcohol liver diseases: A strong association of the usual Caucasian-type aldehyde dehydrogenase gene ($ALDH_2^1$) with the disease. *Am. J. Hum. Genet.* **43**: 744.

Singh, S., G. Fritze, B. Fang, S. Harada, Y.K. Paik, R. Eckey, D.P. Agarwal, and H.W. Goedde. 1989. Inheritance of mitochondrial aldehyde dehydrogenase: Genotyping in Chinese, Japanese and South Korean families reveals a dominance of the mutant allele. *Hum. Genet.* **83**: 119.

Takase, S., A. Takada, M. Yasuhara, and M. Tsutsumi. 1988. Hepatic aldehyde dehydrogenase activity in alcoholic liver disease. In *Biomedical and social aspects of alcohol and alcoholism* (ed. K. Kuriyama et al.), p. 721. Elsevier, Amsterdam.

Thomas, M., S. Halsall, and T.J. Peters. 1983. Role of hepatic aldehyde dehydrogenase in alcoholism: Demonstration of persistent reduction of cytosolic activity in abstaining patients. *Lancet* **II**: 1057.

Weiner, H. 1989. Letter to the editor. *Alcohol. Clin. Exp. Res.* **13**: 599.

Yoshihara, H., N. Sato, T. Kamada, and H. Abe. 1983. Low Km ALDH isozyme and alcoholic liver injury. *Pharmacol. Biochem. Behav.* (**suppl. 1**) **18**: 425.

COMMENTS

Li: I want to enlarge a bit upon what Dr. Agarwal has presented, to strengthen the perception that Chinese and Japanese are similar. With regard to the flush response, we have been studying flushing in Orientals versus flushing in Caucasians. I will discuss what happens using laser-doppler to measure the facial capillary blood flow in Orientals. Chinese flushers increase on the average of 17-fold in blood flow. It varies from 10 to about 30 in different people. Most of these people are heterozygous for the deficient allele, so the deficient allele is dominant. In the nonflushers, at most it's a threefold increase. We have also looked at Caucasians who say they flush, and they don't flush enough to be detected by facial skin blood flow. When you separate out flushers and nonflushers, you begin to see a difference in the alcohol elimination rate, even with very few subjects. Here the nonflushers are exhibiting higher rates than flushers.

Reich: That's clearance of alcohol?

Li: This is clearance of alcohol from the blood. Also, we have studied Chinese nonalcoholics versus Chinese alcoholics from Taiwan. There is a difference in frequency of the ALDH2-2, which is the allele for the deficient gene. The ALDH2 deficiency is 14% versus 50%. It's not as pronounced as what they saw in Japan, but the difference is clear. Among the Chinese nonalcoholics in Taiwan, we also see a difference in the ALDH2. This is alcohol dehydrogenase. There is a difference in allele frequency, for the $\beta 2$, as an example. This is all I wanted to show. The enzymes ALDH2 and ADH2 clearly are different in prevalence in alcoholic and nonalcoholic populations.

Gordis: T.K., could you say something about dominance, because it wasn't mentioned in your presentations?

Reich: The Chinese in Indianapolis aren't all alcoholics, are they?

Li: We haven't interviewed them in depth. The Chinese in Indianapolis are graduate students who haven't had any problems with school yet. Looking at the genotyping, what we had were livers from Japan that we genotyped and phenotyped. From that, we saw that most of the livers that were deficient in the mitochondria for the aldehyde dehydrogenase were actually heterozygotes.

Martin: Which are the Europeans for the ADH2?

Li: Europeans are about 95% $\beta 1$.

Tabakoff: When you look at alcohol elimination rates in your aldehyde-dehydrogenase-deficient individuals, do you also look at $\beta 1$ and $\beta 2$? Is there any relationship, because that could be an equilibrium difference in the aldehyde?

Li: We're looking at that. We have very small numbers. It appears that the $\beta 2$-$\beta 2$ is eliminated faster than $\beta 1$-$\beta 1$.

Tabakoff: In the presence of aldehyde dehydrogenase?

Li: With or without.

Tabakoff: That's interesting.

Li: When you separate them out, stratify them this way, you begin to see differences.

Chakravarti: The general idea is that the frequency differences in these individuals is the reason they avoid alcohol?

Li: We think so.

Chakravarti: Since you do interview some of these individuals, do you know that?

Li: I think that's what Dr. Agarwal was trying to point out. Except in the studies from Japan, they didn't have the genotyping. We do have the genotyping. People who are homozygous ALDH2-2 can't even touch alcohol. If they touch it, they break out in hives, they vomit, they get exceedingly sick.

Reich: Is this on chromosome 4?

Li: Yes.

Cadoret: Do you find your self-selected lines of animals have differences like this?

Li: They don't tell us.

Cadoret: But do you type them?

Li: Yes. What I showed yesterday was the difference in mitochondrial ALDH2. It is an isoelectric difference. We haven't looked at that any further. They are both active forms. They're just isoelectric.

Acquired and Genetic Deficiencies of Cytosolic Acetaldehyde Dehydrogenase

TIMOTHY J. PETERS,* ANDREW J.S. MACPHERSON,* ROBERTA J. WARD,*
AND AKIRA YOSHIDA[†]
*Department of Clinical Biochemistry
King's College School of Medicine and Dentistry
University of London
London SE5 8RX, United Kingdom
[†]Department of Biochemical Genetics
City of Hope Research Institute
Duarte, California 91010

OVERVIEW

Decreased enzyme activity of cytosolic acetaldehyde dehydrogenase (ALDH1) reflects either a primary (genetic) or a secondary (disease or drug-related) abnormality. Paralleling the well-defined Oriental alcohol flushing reaction, 20 female Caucasian subjects who reported alcohol-related flushing reactions were screened for reduced erythrocyte ALDH activities. Three such subjects were identified (ALDH1 Harrow, ALDH1 Colombo, ALDH1 Oxford), and the properties of the enzyme were investigated. The family of one subject (ALDH1 Harrow) was studied in detail, and the defect was shown to be inherited as an autosomal dominant trait with variable penetrance.

Two subjects (ALDH1 Colombo, ALDH1 Harrow) were challenged with a small dose (0.4 g/kg body weight) of oral ethanol. Despite the clear flush reaction, no significant increase in plasma acetaldehyde was found. This was in marked contrast to a subject with ALDH2 deficiency, who showed the expected striking increase in blood acetaldehyde.

Inherited defects in ALDH1 are thus not uncommon in Caucasian subjects exhibiting the alcohol-related flush reaction. The effect appears not to be mediated by increased systemic acetaldehyde levels but is aversive to continued alcohol abuse.

INTRODUCTION

The ALDHs play a key role in the oxidation of acetaldehyde and other aldehydes, including several pharmacologically and toxicologically active compounds, and thus in the aversive, dependency, and toxic responses to alcohol abuse. Subcellular fractionation studies have demonstrated at least two distinct enzymes, localized to the cytosolic (ALDH1) and mitochondrial (ALDH2) fractions of human liver (Koivula 1975; Jenkins and Peters 1983; Henehan et al. 1985; Smith 1986; Meier-Tackmann et al. 1988). These enzymes show ~70% homology (Hsu et al. 1985), but are coded on different chromosomes (Hsu et al. 1985, 1986) and have distinct kinetic properties (Li 1977; Bosron and Li 1986). However, their relative role in hepatic and extrahepatic acetaldehyde oxidation remains controversial. Only the cytosolic form of the enzyme is found in human erythrocytes (Inoue et al. 1978, 1979; Rawles et al. 1987), as these cells lack mitochondria.

A flushing response to alcohol is well recognized and affects ~50% of Oriental subjects but only 5–10% of Caucasian and other ethnic groups (Wolff 1972; Ewing et al. 1974; Wilson et al. 1978; Agarwal et al. 1981). The molecular basis of flushing in Oriental subjects and its effects on acetaldehyde metabolism and the prevalence of alcohol abuse and liver disease in these subjects have recently been clearly defined (Yoshida et al. 1981, 1984; Ikawa et al. 1983). Oriental subjects who show intense, unpleasant facial flushing, associated with widespread autonomic sequelae, have strikingly elevated plasma acetaldehyde levels, compared with normal subjects, following a test dose of ethanol (Mizoli et al. 1979). DNA sequencing reveals an adenine-to-guanine substitution in exon 12 in affected individuals, leading to a glutamic acid-to-lysine mutation at residue 487. This variant is enzymatically inactive, although immunoassay shows increased amounts of the null protein (Yoshida et al. 1984).

The prevalence of alcohol abuse in affected Japanese subjects is ~2%, compared to normal subjects, schizophrenics, and drug addicts (~50%) (Goedde and Agarwal 1987). A recent study of the genotype of null and normal variant ALDH2 in Japanese subjects has shown clearly that the null variant is very infrequent in patients with alcoholic liver disease. In contrast, no significant differences in the prevalence of the two variant forms of alcohol dehydrogenase (ADH_2^1 and ADH_2^2) were noted (Shibuya and Yoshida 1988a). Thus, alcohol-related flushing in Orientals is associated with a well-defined genetic defect and is highly aversive to the development of alcohol abuse and alcoholic liver disease.

In contrast to the detailed studies in this ethnic group, little is known of the flushing reaction in Caucasian subjects. Hitherto, molecular studies have not been reported, except that the possibility of the Oriental defect has been clearly excluded (Shibuya and Yoshida 1988b). The main interest to date in ALDH in Caucasians concerns the relationship between reduced enzyme activity and alcohol abuse and the secondary reduction in activity associated with the ingestion of various drugs. In this paper, we report the results of investigations of the basis of flushing in Caucasian subjects in response to small oral doses of alcohol.

RESULTS

ALDH1 Variants

A series of 20 female Caucasian subjects, who claimed to exhibit facial flushing after consuming small quantities (1–2 units [10–20 g]) of alcoholic beverages, were studied. None of the subjects were alcohol abusers or were taking any medications or drugs specifically those known to inhibit ALDH. No subject showed any hematological abnormality. Erythrocytes were isolated, washed in 0.15 M NaCl, and stored frozen until biochemical analysis. Detailed methods are reported elsewhere (Yoshida et al. 1989). Leukocyte DNA was isolated (Maniatis et al. 1982) and subjected to restriction enzyme digestion using appropriate conditions provided by suppliers. Electrophoresis and Southern blotting were by standard methods (Maniatis et al. 1982).

Table 1 summarizes the ALDH activities and properties for controls and the three subjects studied. One subject showed an enzyme activity $< 20\%$ that of control subjects, whereas the other subjects showed levels ~50% that of controls. The activity was reduced whether expressed per gram of hemoglobin or, in a partially purified enzyme fraction, per unit of glucose-6-phosphate dehydrogenase activity or per milligram of protein. Studies with NAD analogs showed clear abnormalities for ALDH1 Colombo, and both variants showed electrophoretic abnormalities.

Table 1

Activities and Properties of Erythrocyte ALDH in Normal Subjects and Index Cases from Families with Alcohol-related Flush Reactions

Activity[a]	Normal subjects	Variants[b] Harrow	Colombo	Oxford
Hemoglobin (10^{-2} U/g)	10–15	<2	6.6	10.5
G-6-PD (10^{-3} units)	1.7–2.8	<0.3	0.9	0.8
DeNAD (%) (10^{-3} U/mg)	2–4	0.2	1.9	n.a.
Protein NAD	85–105	90	25	57
NEAD (%) NAD	95–120	120	60	58
Immunoreactivity	1.0	0.5	1.0	n.a.
Electrophoretic mobility	+	+ +	−	n.a.

[a](U) Units of enzyme activity; (G-6-PD) glucose-6-phosphate dehydrogenase; (NEAD) ethanomide NAD; (DeNAD) deamino NAD.
[b](n.a.) Not available.

These results demonstrate clearly that the flushing subjects show abnormal enzyme activities presumed to reflect structural defects. In current studies, we are investigating the genetic defect at the DNA levels. This is illustrated in Figure 1, which shows a specific loss of a *Xba*I restriction enzyme cleavage site in the leukocyte DNA from the index case of ALDH1 Harrow. Similar studies with *Eco*RI, *Pst*I, *Bam*HI, and *Taq*I show no such differences.

Figure 2 shows the family tree of ALDH1 Harrow. The reduced enzyme activity is clearly familial, with both male and female members affected. Several members have not yet been studied, but the inheritance is suggestive of an autosomal dominant pattern with variable penetrance. Note also that both maternal and paternal grandfathers were alcoholics. There is no other apparent alcohol abuse in the family, although several members are too young to exclude the possibility of their subsequent development of alcoholism.

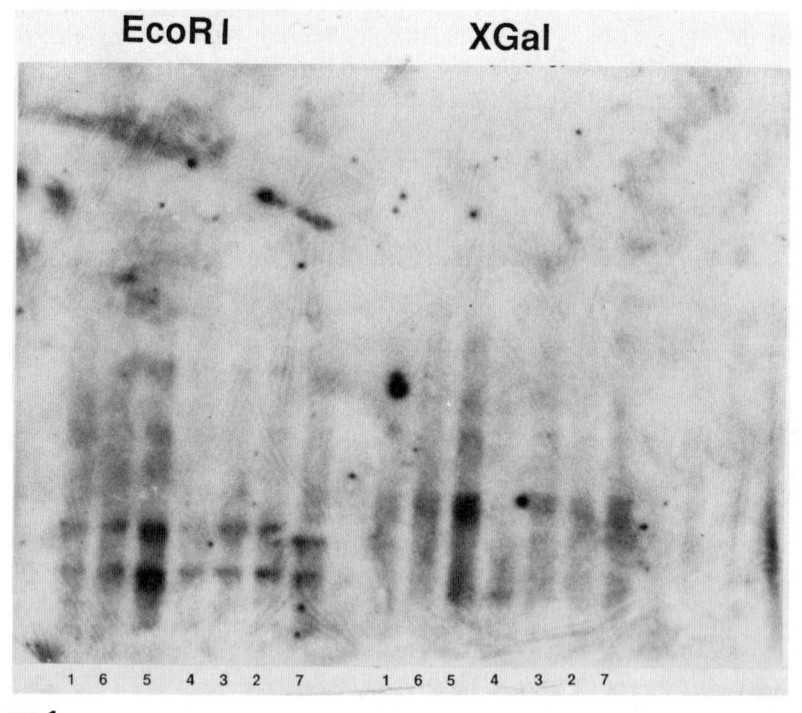

Figure 1
Southern blot analysis of restriction enzyme digests of leukocyte DNA. Leukocyte DNA from control subjects and from ALDH1 Harrow (lane *4*) digested with *Eco*RI or *Xba*I, subjected to electrophoresis, and blotted with a 1.6-kb ALDH1 probe (Yoshida and Chen 1989).

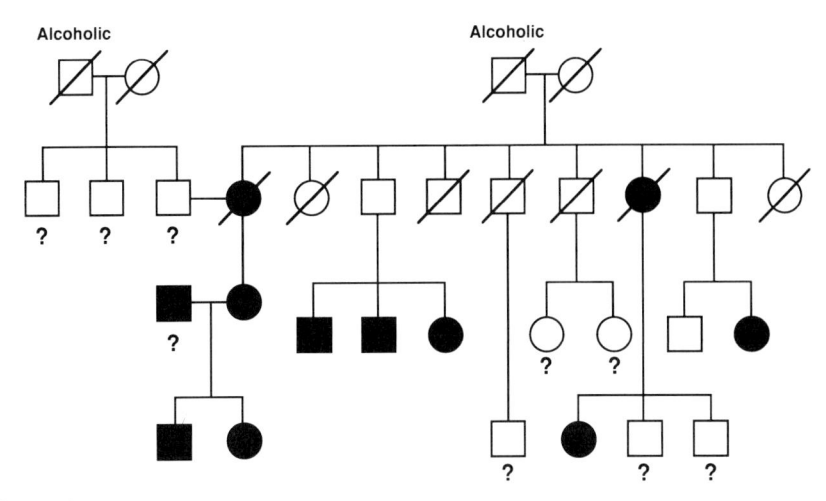

Figure 2
Family tree of ALDH1 Harrow. (Open symbols) Erythrocyte ALDH activity 2×10^3 to 4×10^3 U/mg protein, similar to control subjects. (?) Subjects not yet investigated. (Solid symbols) Erythrocyte ALDH activity $< 1.0 \times 10^{-3}$ U/mg protein.

Plasma Acetaldehyde Levels

Table 2 shows the peak acetaldehyde levels (Rideout et al. 1986) in subjects following a test dose of alcohol. The ethanol elimination rates were similar in controls and in two subjects (ALDH1 Harrow and ALDH1 Colombo). Note that the peak acetaldehyde levels were also similar at ~ 1 μmole/liter, strikingly lower than the subject with ALDH2 deficiency. These normal levels were recorded in spite of a flush reaction produced in both subjects after ingestion of ethanol. However, the nature of the flush differed. In the

Table 2
Plasma Acetaldehyde Levels and Ethanol Elimination Rates in Control and ALDH-deficient Subjects

Subjects	Ethanol elimination rates (μmole/kg/hr)	Peak plasma acetaldehyde (μmole/liter)
Controls (11)	1.00 ± 0.20	0.9 ± 0.30
ALDH2-deficient (1)	0.9	12.5
ALDH1-deficient (2)	0.90 ± 0.30	1.1 ± 0.1

Subjects consumed 0.4 grams of ethanol per kilogram of body weight over a 15-min period. Blood was sampled every 15–30 min for 3 hr and assayed for ethanol and acetaldehyde. For further detail, see Ward et al. (1989).

Oriental subject, the reaction was severe and intensely unpleasant. In the Caucasian subjects, the flush was more rapid—patchy with swelling of fingers and ankles—and occurred without the aversive autonomic effects. In these subjects, the effect was not unpleasant, and the disinhibiting and disorienting CNS effects were striking. There was no significant change in either pulse rate or blood pressure in ALDH1 Harrow during the 3 hours after alcohol ingestion. No significant changes were detectable in urinary catecholamines or their metabolites in ALDH1 Harrow or ALDH1 Colombo following a test dose of ethanol.

DISCUSSION

Variation in ALDH Activities

Table 3 lists the principal causes of impaired ALDH activity in man. These are variably associated with both quantitative and qualitative differences in the flushing reaction. The two forms of primary deficiency, Oriental and Caucasian alcohol-related flushers, appear to be associated, respectively, with genetically impaired mitochondrial and cytosolic ALDH activities. The alcohol-related flush reaction appears to be more striking and prolonged and, in particular, more unpleasant in the Oriental flushers, who show striking elevations in circulating plasma acetaldehyde levels. The study by Wolff (1972) showed increased pulse rate and blood pressure associated with the flush reaction in Oriental subjects. This implicates a direct vascular effect. In contrast, the Caucasian subjects show values similar to those of control subjects. This would imply that the mitochondrial enzyme is principally responsible for regulating the circulating acetaldehyde level, presumably by

Table 3
Inhibitors and Deficiencies of ALDH Activities

Primary

Oriental alcohol-related flushers
Caucasian alcohol-related flushers

Secondary

Alcohol abuse
Specific inhibitors: disulfiram, calcium carbimide
Antibiotics: B lactams, cephalosporins
Nitrate esters: trinitrin, isosorbide dinitrate
Nitroimidazolines: metronidazole, tinidazole
Sulfonylureas: chlorpropamide, tolazamide
Monoamine oxidase inhibitors: pargyline

catalyzing the oxidation of the high hepatic levels of acetaldehyde formed from ethanol and thus limiting its release to the peripheral circulation.

Clear differences in the DNA restriction patterns were identified after digestion with the restriction enzyme *Xba*I in ALDH1 Harrow when compared to ten control DNA samples. Although this may indicate a mutation in the ALDH1 gene, it could represent a rare polymorphism. Only the restriction enzyme *Msp*I has been shown previously to give restriction length polymorphism of both Caucasian and Oriental DNA samples when probed with cDNA ALDH1 and cDNA ALDH2 (Yoshida and Chen 1989). The biochemical data demonstrate that there are clear differences between the erythrocyte ALDH of ALDH1 Harrow and control subjects. Sequencing of the ALDH1 Harrow gene is in progress, which will show irrefutably whether a mutation in genomic ALDH1 Harrow exists. In addition, further studies of the other alcohol-metabolizing enzymes, ADH and ALDH2, at the genomic level are clearly warranted in our ALDH1-deficient subjects.

The apparently normal acetaldehyde levels in the Caucasian flushers were surprising. A possible explanation is that ALDH1 does not play a major role in hepatic acetaldehyde metabolism, at least at the relatively low ethanol loads used in the present study. This view has been proposed by Tipton and colleagues (Tipton et al. 1983; Harrington et al. 1988). The explanation of the flush would then be an abnormal peripheral and, perhaps, CNS metabolism of acetaldehyde and/or biogenic amines. It has been suggested by several workers that the natural substrates for ALDH1 are various biologically active aldehydes and semialdehydes. Alternatively, the normal acetaldehyde levels may reflect the partial enzyme deficiency in these subjects compared with the complete lack of enzyme activity in the Oriental variants. It may also reflect a difference in the plasma/erythrocyte ratio of acetaldehyde in these two groups of subjects. It is thus of interest that Lieber and colleagues (Baraona et al. 1987) have recently proposed the erythrocyte as a major carrier of peripheral blood acetaldehyde. In ALDH1-deficient subjects, red cells might be expected to have higher acetaldehyde levels.

Secondary decreases in ALDH activities are due to several different causes: (1) alcohol abuse, itself; (2) specifically designed drugs (e.g., disulfiram) used in aversive therapy for alcohol abuse; and (3) an incidental side effect of a wide range of drugs (Table 3). Reduced levels of ALDH1 activity of both erythrocytes (Lin et al. 1984; Takase et al. 1985; Matthewson and Record 1986) and hepatocytes (Jenkins and Peters 1980; Jenkins et al. 1984; Matthewson et al. 1986) are well-recognized findings in alcohol abusers. It has even been suggested that reduced hepatic ALDH1 is a primary defect in alcoholics (Thomas et al. 1982).

Reduced levels of ALDH activity, induced by the specific inhibitors disulfiram and calcium carbimide, are claimed mainly to affect ALDH1, but in light of the present studies, this may need to be reconsidered. Patients receiving these drugs, who concurrently consume alcohol, have significantly increased blood acetaldehyde levels, and exhibit an Oriental, rather than a Caucasian, flush reaction: Drug metabolites might have a potent inhibitory effect on the hepatic mitochondrial, rather than on the cytosolic, forms of the enzyme (Sanny and Weiner 1987). The other drug-induced inhibitors appear to be dose-related. Claims that diabetics—who had a sulfonylurea-induced alcohol-related flush reaction—were a genetically determined subgroup of patients with a particular predisposition to vascular lesions can probably be discounted (Hoskins et al. 1987).

Biological Implications

It appears from these limited studies that whereas Oriental flushing is due to a single mutation in ALDH2, Caucasian flushing is due to several distinct mutations leading to enzymes with reduced and/or altered activity. These are likely to influence aldehyde metabolism to differing degrees. Subtle changes in the expression and activity of alcohol and ALDH might lead to modest elevations of acetaldehyde believed to be proaddictive and reinforcing for further alcohol consumption. In contrast, marked reductions in enzyme activity, particularly of ALDH2, lead to very high and aversive levels of acetaldehyde. Whether such subtle changes contribute to the genetic basis of familial alcoholism remains to be determined.

REFERENCES

Agarwal, D.P., S. Harada, and H.W. Goedde. 1981. Racial differences in biological sensitivity to alcohol: The role of alcohol dehydrogenase and aldehyde dehydrogenase isozymes. *Alcohol* **5**: 12.

Baraona, E.D., C. Di Padova, J. Tabasco, and C.S. Lieber. 1987. Red blood cells: A new major modality for acetaldehyde transport from liver to other tissues. *Life Sci.* **40**: 253.

Bosron, W.F. and T.K. Li. 1986. Genetic polymorphism of human liver alcohol and aldehyde dehydrogenases and their relationship to alcohol metabolism and alcoholism. *Hepatology* **6**: 502.

Ewing, J.A., B.A. Rose, and E.D. Pellizzari. 1974. Alcohol sensitivity and ethnic background. *Am. J. Psychiatry* **131**: 206.

Goedde, H.W. and D.P. Agarwal. 1987. Polymorphism of aldehyde dehydrogenase and alcohol sensitivity. *Enzyme* **37**: 29.

Harrington, M.C., G.T.M. Henehan, and K.E. Tipton. 1988. The inter-relationships of alcohol dehydrogenase and the aldehyde dehydrogenases in the metabolism of ethanol in liver. *Biochem. Soc. Trans.* **16**: 239.

Henehan, G.T.M., K. Ward, N.P. Kennedy, D.G. Weir, and K.F. Tipton. 1985.

Subcellular distribution of aldehyde dehydrogenase activities in human liver. *Alcohol* **2**: 107.
Hoskins, P.J., P.G. Wiles, H.P. Volkmann, and D.A. Pyke. 1987. Chlorpropamide alcohol flushing: A normal response? *Clin. Sci.* **73**: 77.
Hsu, L.C., A. Yoshida, and T. Mohandas. 1986. Chromosomal assignment of the genes for human aldehyde dehydrogenase 1 and aldehyde dehydrogenase 2. *Am. J. Hum. Genet.* **38**: 641.
Hsu, L.C., K. Tani, T. Fujiyoshi, K. Kurachi, and A. Yoshida. 1985. Cloning of cDNAs for human aldehyde dehydrogenase 1 and 2. *Proc. Natl. Acad. Sci.* **82**: 3771.
Ikawa, M., C.C. Impraim, G. Wang, and A. Yoshida. 1983. Isolation and characterization of aldehyde dehydrogenase isozymes from usual and atypical human livers. *J. Biol. Chem.* **258**: 6282.
Inoue, K., H. Nishimukai, and K. Yamasawa. 1979. Purification and partial characterisation of aldehyde dehydrogenase from human erythrocytes. *Biochim. Biophys. Acta* **569**: 117.
Inoue, K., Y. Ohbora, and K. Yamasawa. 1978. Metabolism of acetaldehyde by human erythrocytes. *Life Sci.* **23**: 179.
Jenkins, W.J. and T.J. Peters. 1980. Selectively reduced hepatic acetaldehyde dehydrogenase in alcoholics. *Lancet* **I**: 628.
―――. 1983. Subcellular localization of acetaldehyde dehydrogenase in human liver. *Cell Biochem. Funct.* **1**: 37.
Jenkins, W.J., K. Cakebread, and K.R. Palmer. 1984. Effect of alcohol consumption on hepatic aldehyde dehydrogenase activity in alcoholic patients. *Lancet* **I**: 1048.
Koivula, T. 1975. Subcellular distribution and characterization of human liver aldehyde dehydrogenase fractions. *Life Sci.* **16**: 1563.
Li, T.-K. 1977. Enzymology of human alcohol metabolism. *Adv. Enzymol. Relat. Areas Mol. Biol.* **45**: 427.
Lin, G.-C., J.J. Potter, and E. Mezey. 1984. Erythrocyte aldehyde dehydrogenase activity in alcoholism. *Alcohol. Clin. Exp. Res.* **8**: 539.
Maniatis, T., E.F. Fritsch, and J. Sambrook. 1982. *Molecular cloning: A laboratory manual.* Cold Spring Harbor Laboratory, Cold Spring Harbor, New York.
Matthewson, K. and C.O. Record. 1986. Erythrocyte aldehyde dehydrogenase activity in alcoholic subjects and its value as a marker for hepatic aldehyde dehydrogenase in subjects with and without liver disease. *Clin. Sci.* **70**: 295.
Matthewson, K., H.A. Mardini, K. Bartlett, and C.O. Record. 1986. Impaired acetaldehyde metabolism in patients with non-alcoholic liver disorders. *Gut* **27**: 756.
Meier-Tackmann, D., G.C. Korenke, D.P. Agarwal, and H.W. Goedde. 1988. Human liver aldehyde dehydrogenase: Subcellular distribution in alcoholics and non-alcoholics. *Alcohol* **5**: 73.
Mizoli, Y., I. Ijiri, Y. Tatsuno, T. Kijima, S. Fujiwara, and J. Adachi. 1979. Relationship between facial flushing and blood acetaldehyde after alcohol intake. *Pharmacol. Biochem. Behav.* **10**: 303.
Rawles, J.W., D.L. Rhodes, J.T. Potter, and E. Mezey. 1987. Characterization of human erythrocyte aldehyde dehydrogenase. *Biochem. Pharmacol.* **36**: 3715.
Rideout, J.M., C.K. Lim, and T.J. Peters. 1986. Assay of blood acetaldehyde by

HPLC with fluorescence detection of its 2-diphenyacetyl 1,3 indanedione-1-azine derivative. *Clin. Chim. Acta* **161**: 29.

Sanny, C.G. and H. Weiner. 1987. Inactivation of horse liver mitochondria aldehyde dehydrogenase by disulfiram. Evidence that disulfiram is not an active-site directed reagent. *Biochem. J.* **242**: 499.

Shibuya, A. and A. Yoshida. 1988a. Frequency of the atypical aldehyde dehydrogenase-2 gene ($ALDH_2^2$) in Japanese and Caucasians. *Am. J. Hum. Genet.* **43**: 741.

———. 1988b. Genotypes of alcohol-metabolizing enzymes in Japanese with alcohol liver diseases: A strong association of the usual Caucasian-type aldehyde dehydrogenase gene ($ALDH_2^1$) with the disease. *Am. J. Hum. Genet.* **43**: 744.

Smith, M. 1986. Genetics of human alcohol and aldehyde dehydrogenase. *Adv. Hum. Genet.* **15**: 249.

Takase, S., A. Takada, M. Tsutsnmi, and Y. Matsuda. 1985. Biochemical markers for chronic alcoholism. *Alcohol* **2**: 405.

Thomas, M., S. Halsall, and T.J. Peters. 1982. Role of hepatic acetaldehyde dehydrogenase in alcoholism: Demonstration of persistent reduction of cytosolic activity in abstaining patients. *Lancet* **II**: 1057.

Tipton, K.F., J.M. McCrodden, D.G. Weir, and K. Ward. 1983. Isoenzymes of human liver alcohol dehydrogenase and aldehyde dehydrogenase in alcoholic and non-alcoholic subjects. *Alcohol Alcohol.* **18**: 219.

Ward, R.J., A.J.S. Macpherson, M. Warren-Perry, A. Yoshida, and T.J. Peters. 1989. Acetaldehyde dehydrogenase deficiency Caucasian flushers. *Alcohol Alcohol.* **24**: 390.

Wilson, J., R. McClearn, and R.C. Johnson. 1978. Ethnic variation in the use and effects of alcohol. *Alcohol Depend.* **3**: 147.

Wolff, P.C. 1972. Ethnic differences in alcohol sensitivity. *Science* **175**: 449.

Yoshida, A. and S. Chen. 1989. Restriction fragment length polymorphism of human aldehyde dehydrogenase 1 and aldehyde dehydrogenase 2 loci. *Hum. Genet.* **83**: 204.

Yoshida, A., I.-Y. Huang, and M. Ikawa. 1984. Molecular abnormality of an inactive aldehyde dehydrogenase variant commonly found in Orientals. *Proc. Natl. Acad. Sci.* **81**: 258.

Yoshida, A., C.C. Impraim, and I.-Y. Huang. 1981. Enzymatic and structural differences between usual and atypical human liver alcohol dehydrogenases. *J. Biol. Chem.* **256**: 12430.

Yoshida, A., V. Dare, R.J. Ward, and T.J. Peters. 1989. Cytosolic aldehyde dehydrogenase (ALDH1) variants found in alcohol flushers. *Ann. Hum. Genet.* **53**: 1.

COMMENTS

Tabakoff: Your acetaldehyde levels in at least one Oriental patient were about 12 and 2, and in your alcoholics they were in the 20s.

Peters: It's now probably 4 or 5.

Tabakoff: The alcoholics were 4 or 5?

Peters: Yes. The ethanols were in the 20s. The general hypothesis is that small increases of acetaldehyde are reinforcing; the high levels are aversive.

Goldman: What fraction of Caucasians are you labeling flushers or do you think are flushers?

Peters: At this stage, we have just decided to do the molecular structure and the bases of the enzyme activity. So, we just put out the message that Peters was interested in young ladies who flush when they drink alcohol. We were particularly interested in the family histories. We took blood samples and measured the enzyme activity. We have had about 20 so far, and I think 4 of them (we've got 1 in the sidelines that looks low) have low levels of enzyme activity, just measuring total activity.

Tabakoff: What would you postulate the mechanism is?

Peters: I think perhaps it's telling us about peripheral effects, or perhaps the CNS effect. The effects of giving ethanol to the Oriental flushers is quite different from that of giving it to Caucasians. We've heard that the effect on skin flow is quite different. I think there is a psychological CNS effect that is different, too.

Reich: Since the ALDH2 is able to protect Oriental populations, shouldn't we think of the variant in the Caucasian populations as the deficiency?

Gordis: A philosophical statement.

Reich: It's very important. When you think about risk and protective factors, and think about formulating systems to understand the interaction between risk and protective factors and exposure variables, it gets interesting.

Peters: I think we should look at some of the North American Indians. These people that are flushing almost consistently don't apparently have an ALDH2 abnormality. Do they have an ALDH1 abnormality?

Li: We have done the liver phenotyping. We see no difference in ALDH phenotyping 1 or 2 in the different tribes that we have looked at. Dr. Goedde has found some deficiency in certain of the tribes in looking at hair roots, I think, but in looking at liver specimens, we have not seen any.

Peters: You haven't looked at red cells?

Li: We haven't looked at red cells, but, you know, the liver does have the cytosolic form. I must say that we have not looked at Northwest American Indians. These are mostly Plains and Southwest Indians.

Gordis: Hasn't there been some interest in bradykinin also in explaining the original antibuse reaction? Is it possible that some other work is going on independent of acetaldehyde?

Peters: We know the Oriental flush reactions can be blocked by giving a combination of HI and H2 antagonists.

Open Discussion

Sparkes: I have been asked to make a few introductory remarks. One thing I want to focus on has to do with markers for epilepsy and other gene markers in our work with juvenile myoclonic epilepsy, a form of epilepsy that is familiar, but doesn't seem to follow, in terms of its clinical manifestations, a straightforward inheritance pattern. On the other hand, if you combine the clinical phenotype with an EEG pattern, a much clearer picture begins to emerge. Indeed, we have been able to demonstrate linkage to markers on the short arm of chromosome 6 using this approach. The main message here for alcoholism is that there may be more than one phenotype to consider in a given family to determine who is affected and who is not affected, depending on the circumstances.

My next point has to do with a consideration of altered penetrance or altered expression. Two purportedly new areas have become fashionable and have relevance in relation to unusual inheritance patterns in families. If we are carrying out linkage studies, it is important to understand what kinds of variations can contribute to the inheritance patterns even of single-gene disorders. The first area of interest is so-called uniparental disomy. The idea is that human genes and human chromosomes occur in the disomic state, but in this instance, both members of a given pair come from the same parent. Of course, if that is the case, it could be rather confusing when looking at single gene inheritance patterns. This type of thing apparently has been known in mice for some time, but has only come to human interest over the last couple of years. Interestingly, both cases in which this has been clearly demonstrated so far relate to cystic fibrosis. These were instances in which individuals were being studied because they had cystic fibrosis and, for counseling purposes, the parents were also studied. In both instances, on the cystic fibrosis chromosome, that is, the chromosome carrying the cystic fibrosis gene, both members had come from the same parent. Thus, it appears that this may not be a rare phenomenon and, indeed, may be much more common than we expected. One has to keep in the back of his mind that some of these unusual situations may occur when one looks at families to try to determine whether there is a straightforward single-gene Mendelian heritance pattern.

Lander: What's a guess as to the rate of that? When you look at the CEPH families, there is no such incidence there. So, I would say the rates can't be above 1 in 1000 probably.

Risch: Oh, no, it's much lower than that.

Sparkes: I think there are only guesses at this point. On the basis of the animal studies, it appears that it is not going to affect all chromosomes or all parts of the chromosome. But again, it's another kind of broadening of our thinking in relation to some of these problems. Whether it has any relevance in relation to alcoholism, I have no idea.

The second area that has received considerable attention recently is genome imprinting. This appears to be related to the process of meiosis. Depending on through which parent a given gene or chromosome is being transmitted, it may be expressed in the offspring or not expressed. The relationship here appears to be to methylation of the DNA. Methylation has been known for some time. If a gene is methylated in the appropriate way, it will not be expressed. This becomes particularly important if one is carrying out phenotypic studies and again looking for the usual heritance patterns. Also, in the study of some single-gene disorders, for example, the manifestation of the trait may occur earlier or later depending on which parent the gene has been inherited from. An example of this is Huntington's disease, where the early onset cases all appear to come from the father.

We bring these two issues up because you might have to consider them when you see an unusual heritance pattern, even for single-gene disorders.

Now we consider marker selection. There are different ways of looking at markers, but one important aspect concerns the disease marker and how to define the "phenotype" that is to be reflective of the mutant gene or genes. In alcoholism we're not sure if one or more than one gene is involved, or, indeed, what its manifestation could be. Related to this is genetic heterogeneity. Particularly if more than one gene is involved, genetic heterogeneity is going to be a real problem. There are different ways of handling this, and I would like to get into these during the discussion.

In carrying out linkage analysis, one can use so-called candidate genes. If one is lucky, the candidate gene will be the disease marker gene. It becomes very important to think about what are potential candidate genes for conditions such as alcoholism. Some of this involves the use of linkage information as to where the gene or genes are located for a given disorder and where the candidate gene maps; if it maps in the same area, that suggests that this could be the gene involved with the disease. On the other hand, one could look at this with an eye to biochemistry or biology, of how the gene or gene product could be related to the abnormal phenotype. You then use all that information in looking for candidate genes.

In the standard linkage analysis, one can talk about the usual phenotypic markers that have been used for many years. They are now being supplanted by DNA markers. It looks increasingly as if the standard, almost classical, RFLP-type studies are going to be replaced by other approaches to studying DNA, which will be much more informative than are the RFLPs that have been around for a number of years.

In relation to linkage analysis, one has to have some type of model of inheritance in order to test the linkage. Is it a single gene? Is it multiple genes? In addition, what approach can one use to carry out linkage analysis? There is the old standard way, if you look at parametric analysis, which Dr. Ott has been particularly instrumental in developing. There are the so-called nonparametric or related relatives methods. Also, there are methods, which Eric Lander has been quite interested in, carrying out linkage analysis for quantitative traits that can be due to multiple genes.

With this introduction, the floor is open for general discussion.

Chakravarti: Generally, there has been a frequent assumption in quantitative genetics that whenever a phenotype is normally distributed, it is probably influenced by the action of many genes. However, now there are some good examples of a single gene that determines a normally distributed phenotype. So, it's not necessarily true that just because you have a normal distribution, there are many genes. From an evolutionary viewpoint, this is quite important. Humans are not the most variable mammalian species that we know. There could be hundreds of genes that in some sense determine a phenotype. But, since genetic analysis really will relate to those genes that vary in the population, the number of genes that vary (and so are amenable to genetic analysis) would be a very small minority. As a result, we don't necessarily have to think of a large number of genes that are additive in some sense. Small numbers of genes may account for much of the variable risk for disorders like alcoholism.

Sparkes: Even with a single locus, if you have multiple alleles in a population, you could still have essentially a single Gaussian-type distribution.

Chakravarti: That's right.

Conneally: You are all probably familiar with Huntington's disease. It is a late onset disorder. The mean onset is age 38, but approximately 10% of individuals have onset before 20; we call it juvenile onset. The sex ratio is equal. There is no difference between the sexes in Huntington's with any clinical manifestations of the disease. However, if you ask from what parent did the juvenile inherit the disease, it's approximately 5–6 to 1 that it came from the father. There is obviously no simple explanation for this.

Sparkes: It also seems to be on chromosome 4, doesn't it?

Conneally: Yes. Also, there is no locus for the disease. May I define heterogeneity? I think of heterogeneity in two ways, both locus heterogeneity and allelic heterogeneity. Locus heterogeneity is different loci; and allelic heterogeneity is different alleles at the same locus. There is almost certainly no locus heterogeneity in Huntington's. We have looked at over 120 large families and all of them are linked, so if there is locus heterogeneity, it is very rare and can be essentially ignored. Allelic heterogeneity can pretty well be ruled out, because, although it is a very variable disease, you find every aspect of the disease within the one family. We have a large family consisting of over 10,000 individuals in Venezuela, and you find everything within that family. It all can be traced back, of course, to one mutant gene in that case. The interesting thing in the early onset is that it appears that the best explanation, at present, is indeed that there is differential methylation (or imprinting, as Bob calls it) going through the female line; this seems to make the gene when it goes through the female express itself much later in life. I bring all of this up because, even though Huntington's is a simple autosomal, one-locus disease, there is an awful lot of heterogeneity there, so we don't have to give up hope. Aravinda pointed out earlier today that there may not be very much genetic heterogeneity in alcoholism, even though it's clinically heterogeneous.

Sparkes: Are there any other examples in which age of expression of a disorder differs depending on in which parent a mutation occurs?

Billings: A number of multifactorial genetic conditions show that kind of thing. For instance, neural tube defects and pyloric stenosis are both conditions in which there is a sex predilection and the transmission seems to be affected by which parent has it.

Conneally: I would disagree with you to a large extent. What you have is a differential sex ratio in these cases which, as you earlier brought up, one would expect. There is a whole gamut of very common disorders, like cleft lip and palate, or pyloric stenosis, where you have a differential sex ratio, usually something like 2–3 to 1 more affected. You would expect that the least affected sex in that case would have more affected or more severely affected offspring. That isn't always quite true. In fact, that's one of the reasons the multifactorial hypothesis and the multifactorial threshold hypothesis have not been favored in more recent years among geneticists. There is a tendency in some of the diseases for this to hold, but certainly not in all of them.

Goldman: I believe that myotonic dystrophy shows the same phenomenon.

Conneally: It's the opposite, of course, in myotonic, but the mother there is carrying the disease.

Propping: In epilepsy there is an effect that is comparable to the case of Huntington's chorea or myotonic dystrophy. In epilepsy, there is a sex effect. As far as I remember, it's more frequent that the mothers are affected than the fathers are affected. This cannot be explained by the counterphenomenon you just described.

Sparkes: Certainly, that's true, I think, for the photogenic epilepsy. There are a large number of different epilepsies and there could be others.

Lander: You have to use the word "imprinting" carefully when you're saying it's the mother, because there is a tried and true thing called maternal effect that one has to deal with as well, and that could be an equally good explanation.

Sparkes: I mentioned there are at least these two types of linkage analysis, the parametric and nonparametric. Does anybody want to comment as to the value of one or the other in a situation such as alcoholism?

Lander: The dichotomy is useful, but only to a point, because many of the nonparametric methods can be seen as sort of an extension of the parametric methods in the following sense: When you do a completely parametric linkage analysis, you are saying, "I know everything. I know the chance that somebody will show the phenotype, given the genotype exactly," and you are therefore going to say in a disease of complete penetrance that if you have the genotype you do express the disease, and if you don't have the genotype you don't express the disease. Then you realize that if you are looking at a disease of incomplete penetrance, if you have the disease genotype you might get the disease or you might not get the disease. And so, in fact, conditional on the phenotype of not getting the disease, you could either have the disease genotype or you might not have the disease genotype. In other words, unaffected is not very informative; unaffected is relatively meaningless if the disease has low penetrance. You could say, "Well, does my linkage analysis depend a whole lot on the penetrance that I assume?" Roughly speaking, in a disease of low penetrance, it doesn't depend an awful lot on what low penetrance you put in. And so, you could say, "I could take a whole range of those things," or you could say, "I could pick any one of them and know it doesn't much matter." Any of those come down to the basic rule that unaffecteds don't contribute very much to any linkage analysis where the disease has low penetrance. In a limited way, you can turn that into a nonparametric sort of linkage analysis.

The key point to note in that discussion is where your information is coming from. Your information is coming primarily from the person for whom phenotype implies genotype. So, impenetrance means the *unaffecteds* aren't so useful. Phenocopy, though, means that the *affecteds* aren't so useful. If you had a high phenocopy rate and a high impenetrance rate, you couldn't trust anybody.

In some sense, the battle of linkage analysis in the face of potential phenocopy and incomplete penetrance is a battle somehow to select families that because of their segregation patterns lead you to believe that you don't have phenocopies running around, and biological markers that somehow push closer to the disease to battle back the question of penetrance. Therefore, both affected and unaffected relatives are as informative as possible.

That really underscores the whole discussion of looking for biological markers. Even if they're not the whole story, it may be far better to dissect alcoholism by finding subtypes, each one of which is tied to clear biological markers. It may be very important to take the sort of segregation analysis people are talking about and use it to say, "This is a family worth working on because the odds are very low that most of these are phenocopies that by chance happen to occur in the same family, because that's one thing you have to worry about when you select families out of a population. Everybody knows that there is the problem when you select families because they have many affected members. You've got to worry, "Was that just chance aggregation of phenocopy?" And so, two people being alcoholic in the same family does not a particularly good case make, but one can be quantitative about that. I think the full richness of how to play those off hasn't been fully developed—how to use segregation analysis to help you choose the families. However, in general terms, maybe that's a helpful start to thinking about that range of models—not really opposed to each other, but considering where your information is coming from.

Sparkes: In a way, it does determine perhaps what families you are going to sample.

Lander: Oh, yes, absolutely. If you could take the evoked potentials, for example, and demonstrate that evoked potentials segregated cleanly in families, it would determine how you would go about collecting families. It would change your strategy substantially.

Reich: The methods that are available for dealing with compound phenotypes (which is really what we're talking about) are really rather hard to utilize. They're not well enough developed yet.

Lander: What's that compound phenotype?

Reich: In the case of alcoholism, what we would end up with might be the presence or absence of certain kinds of addictive behaviors, and also the presence of certain quantitative encephalographic abnormalities. To the extent that one might be informed both by the quantitative measure and by the qualitative diagnosis, which are not fully congruent, probably it would be best in terms of signal detection to use both kinds of measures as designators of phenotype. So now, you would have a compound phenotype. The ways of handling those things can be tricky. To carry the analogy forward, it's clear that we're operating in multiple domains concerning the phenotype. A simple way to enhance the phenotype, for example, is repeated measures. It's very simple, as we know in psychology, to improve the operating characteristics of a measurement by simply making them a little more often. Then you have to integrate the information into some kind of composite measurement. In general, then, one can see that putting those phenotypes into a linkage analysis together could be quite tough.

Chakravarti: I can express another point of view. One of the promises of all this recombinant genetic technology (when it becomes easier to do more markers) may be to understand the genetics of the trait by first trying to find out what the genes are and then figuring out how many genes there are or what the effects of the genes are. We could argue a long time about how many genes are involved and how many alleles there are, or what the effects are, what the frequencies are in the populations, what the relevant environments are, and how they interact with these genes. I am sure that some very bright individual could calculate how many families you would need to find these answers; it would probably be a very impractical figure. However, it may be that even with very limited knowledge we can choose certain kinds of families and map at least a certain number of genes, and probably that will be a lot more fruitful, without ever defining genetic models in the classical sense.

Reich: Nothing I said has anything to do with the underlying genetic model. I'm speaking about deciding what constitutes a signal in the sense that Eric just indicated. Until you really understand the genetics and can measure it directly, it may be that we will have to deal with complex measurements.

Chakravarti: I thought you implied that by having either repeated measures or some other kind of method, you could distinguish between the "genetic" case and a phenocopy.

Reich: That is possible, but all people have talked about today are correlates and covariates. Nobody has said anything about cause. We would be foolish to think if there were a correlated phenomenon, that implies necessarily that that's a cause. Of course not. It could be an epiphenomenon. Biological markers are often difficult to interpret because most often they are epiphenomena that we detect. Nonetheless, they can still be helpful by triangulating a cause, by offering us different kinds of measurements that are correlated. We may have reduction in error or an increase in signal.

Lander: Yes, but the question is how do you know? What's the operational test? If you make a compound measure, how do you know it's useful for this purpose?

Reich: Well, the test of utility will be if we can use it to detect deviation at the genotypic level.

Lander: How do you know that in advance of the linkage?

Cloninger: There are straightforward empirical tests to distinguish between incomplete penetrance and phenocopies. At least in schizophrenia, they have been done fairly clearly by looking at the proportion of affected first-degree relatives of concordant and discordant pairs of monozygotic twins, at least one of whom is a schizophrenic. If you think there are a lot of phenocopies, then the discordant pair should have fewer first-degree relatives affected than the case where you have incomplete penetrance as a major explanation. You can also look at discordant pairs to see whether each member of the pair is able to transmit illness in equal proportions regardless of whether the people with the same genotype are affected or unaffected. In the case of schizophrenia, it has been shown that there really are very few sporadic cases, but there is frequent incomplete penetrance.

Those tests have not been carried out in the case of alcoholism. It's curious, because we have certainly done the twin studies and we have done the adoption studies, but the direct tests to distinguish incomplete penetrance and phenocopies haven't been carried out.

Lander: That's what I was hoping to get at with the compound measures. The compound measure is a better measure if, on tests like this, it provides fewer phenocopies of more complete penetrance.

Reich: There are other criteria also. A compound phenotype would be useful if it provided a greater deviation between the gene, the means of the genotypes we'll say, so it's a better measure for linkage analysis.

Lander: That's right.

Cloninger: What has been done, though, to test for phenocopies in alcoholism is to examine the secular trends for an increasing incidence of alcoholism over time. The presumption would be, if the rate of consumption is simply adding increasing numbers of phenocopies to the population, that the disorder would become less familial as the base rate goes up (because more of the cases would be sporadic cases). In fact, Reich and I carried out a test for that to see whether the distinction between familial and nonfamilial alcoholism was really a good distinction or not. If there really was a meaningful distinction between familial and nonfamilial cases, then, as the base rate goes up, you simply add phenocopies and the disorder becomes less familial. In fact, what has happened is that, as the base rate has gone up, the correlation between individuals in liability to alcoholism has remained constant, and the proportion of affected relatives of affected cases has gone up. Thus, it appears that there is an interaction between exposure and susceptibility, but not an increase in sporadic cases.

Lander: Is the latter test possibly subject to the following artifact: If I am actually a phenocopy, but a member of a family with alcoholics already, say due to genetic reason, I've got alcoholism there, then those individuals are now culturally more susceptible to becoming phenocopies?

Cloninger: Then you would have to presume that your cultural transmission is mimicking the genetic transmission.

Wijsman: I don't think it follows at all that raising the availability of a substance like alcohol necessarily means that an increased incidence of alcoholism is because of phenocopies.

Cloninger: I agree.

Wijsman: Clearly, in a family where you don't have alcohol, even if there is genetic predisposition, the penetrance in that family is zero. So, maybe what you are doing in the secular trends is, in essence, raising the penetrance. Now, in some sense that shouldn't be all that difficult to correct for in the linkage studies.

Cloninger: There are different liability classes by age.

Reich: It's more complicated, I think.

Chakravarti: But you're still presuming the mechanism.

Wijsman: Yes.

Reich: The general rule is that 7% or 10% of the people consume half the alcohol. That curve is very skewed to the right. If you increase the general consumption, the bulk, what happens to the right side, can be described as quite radical. There is a very big effect if you move national consumption a little bit. There is a disaster in the tail of heavy consumers.

Cloninger: The basic point is still that there isn't evidence for the presence of a substantial phenocopy rate now for alcoholism, which is surprising.

Wijsman: The other thing I found interesting in this discussion of biological markers was that there are possibly certain genotypes which are specifically aversion genotypes.

Reich: Protection.

Wijsman: Protection—whatever you want to call them. It may be worth pursuing those a bit more, because if those really exist and you can identify them in some fashion, you might be able to extract those genotypes in your analysis and build in different penetrance for those who carry the protective genotype versus the nonprotective genotypes. It would clean up your phenotype for whatever it is you are trying to follow in your analysis. Anyway, it just struck me as something that we normally don't have to look at in most other diseases.

Chakravarti: That's because we usually suffer from bias whenever we talk of a disease in terms of susceptibility. It may not work through susceptibility, but it may work through another mechanism. If it does, it occurred to me that it is a bizarre fact that there may be a number of these genes, like the ALDH and others, that may be protective in a sense. Once you take these individuals out from families because it's the presence of a very common environmental agent, the rest of the people could be affected.

Reich: Possibly. Let me just remind you that if you look at industrial exposure and a number of other major diseases, exposure variables usually have not really been taken into account in genetic modeling. There are many disorders where exposure could be measured and hasn't been.

Chakravarti: That's not quite true. We routinely take age and sex and other things into consideration.

Reich: There are very coarse measures of exposure to asbestos, for example, and the amount of dust in the air, and a number of other things that you can measure.

Chakravarti: That's true, but surely these things are taken into account by the people who study the phenotypes of cholesterol and other things.

Cloninger: Let me pose a question to you. In the adoption studies, it appears that most of the risk for adults becoming alcoholic can be explained through the childhood personality. If it's true that most of the variability in risk is attributable to personality traits that appear to be polygenic, how do we go about linkage trials in alcoholism to be sure that we get something out of them? If it doesn't turn out that we really have many single-locus effects that are large, how are we going to proceed to get useful information? It may turn out that there are a substantial number of genes, but each has relatively small effects. Are we ready for that in linkage trials?

Lander: Could you, for the sake of argument, toss out several models that might be operating, because it may be relevant: Polygenic means many things to different people.

Cloninger: Well, here I'm talking about traits where if you do selection in rodents, either mice or rats, you get divergence over at least 40 generations. This indicates that there are fairly large numbers of genes, each contributing small amounts to the variability. However, we also have evidence from segregation analysis for a major gene effect in the type 2 group of alcoholics. I'm not sure whether that's an artifact or not. I hope it isn't. I hope we will be able to identify the gene and map it someplace quickly; but I think we have to go into this with open eyes and be sure that we at least planned our description of cases and our approach to analysis so as to be prepared for substantial polygenic inheritance.

Reich: In that same vein, let us consider tolerance, which seems to be under selective control in rats, and since the human and the rat evidence seems to converge on that as a major factor in the susceptibility or susceptible offspring. What would be the best way to study the genetics of the development of tolerance in human populations, where tolerance may be an important characteristic that is related to the onset of addictive behaviors?

Wijsman: It seems to me that in tolerance there actually may be a real way of proceeding. It's wonderful when you have an animal model. You can do all sorts of things with that. You can certainly try to map that and try to understand that because you can manipulate the organism and see if you can learn something from that. I would certainly encourage that.

Cloninger: I think that's probably the overall significance of what T.K. said yesterday. T.K. Li is able to identify a number of brain transmitters and receptors that may be involved in modulation of motivated behavior in his animal model. We can then begin to use those as candidate genes in our human linkage studies.

Lander: Let me dissect a bit further the possible models you mean when you say polygenic. The word polygenic is often used in our community to mean just what you said: "additive" effects of multiple loci. The hallmark is the selection studies where this will go up over the course of generations. You make an F_1, it's in the middle; then the F_2s, it's spread around. That's one sort of multigene genetics we could be talking about. Another type is pure locus heterogeneity. Here there are multiple genes, any one of which would be sufficient to cause a trait. In this case, if they were all, say, dominant, and you did segregation analysis in a population, it would behave perfectly dominantly. You wouldn't know that it was ten different loci unless you by chance did a cross between those families.

Cloninger: You wouldn't get that kind of response to selection.

Lander: That's right, exactly. Finally, I am going to say synthetic traits. This is the word that is used among lower-organism geneticists. I don't know what word gets used among higher-organism geneticists. Here I mean multiple loci, all of which are necessary. So, in the extreme case, no phenotype unless you have the mutant at both or all three or all four loci. Do other people have other names for this?

Martin: Epistasis.

Lander: Well, epistasis is a whole lot of things.

Martin: Here it's extreme epistasis. Homogenesis is another term.

Lander: That's a horrible term. This predates mutagenesis by at least 40 years. Fine. Synthetic traits will do.

In animal studies, you can set up a single cross between two rats with the same genotype from inbred lines and get progeny who are all genetically identical. You know the phase, and you know it's homogeneous. You stand a chance of mapping even five or six loci in there because of the fact that any locus that contributes to this additive phenotype will have a distorted segregation pattern among the highs and the lows.

What's the trouble with doing that in human families? One, very small number of offspring. Now, small family size wouldn't be a problem provided you could get a whole lot of small families who were identical in the parents. So, if I didn't have heterogeneity, if I could ensure homogeneity, and here I mean both locus homogeneity and phase homogeneity, because, as you know, you take one meiosis or so and you use it to set phase, and if I've got a lot of loci running around I may actually use up a couple of my meioses setting phase and I would have no kids left. So, the problem is the inability to get a large number of small families with the same phase relationships and the same loci segregating. In fact, if one believes in a purely polygenic model, and one simply does a little bit of arithmetic or simulation, assuming there is heterogeneity for ten loci, any five of which would add up enough to push you over some liability threshold, the numbers are completely impossible. I know a couple of people who have done such simulations and such arithmetic. I don't actually know that any of this has gotten published. It may be worth writing this stuff up because past some point the heterogeneity, the inability to set up a large cross, kills you.

Now let me make a remark about that. If you do it in animals, you may well be able to transfer it to humans. I think this is an extremely nice direction, and one that has gotten far too little attention, because people have been pessimistic about being able to handle the data, worried to death about "Is this really a good model for the human?" Who cares? These loci will be involved and they will teach us things. They may or may not. They're better candidates than anything else. Here I am going to say something I would have thought heretical maybe a little while ago. It may be important not just to try these as candidate genes for linkage, but for association studies. In a linkage study, one is looking for the fact that the locus segregates with the trait. One needs to know the phase it is in, or at least one meiosis in which to set that phase, and then see another meiosis in which it is phased with the trait. Admittedly, if it's a candidate gene, you are expecting zero centimorgans. That's fine. But I think an interesting question to ask is: If you can go further, and say not just whatever was on this chromosome and went into this person, did it also go into the other affected, if I can assign a particular genotype and say that genotype in this gene is associated in a population sense, I may be able to see true cases that are polygenic, even though I can't see those cases by linkage analysis. A good example of that may be the ADH studies, where it is not going to be easy to see linkage, but I can see an association stand out.

I am very pessimistic on just looking at random associations all over the genome. If you have a very meaningful locus, there are cases where association is more powerful than linkage; for example, when there is much polygenic variation you can still notice that a particular genotype stands out. I think both need to be tried.

Wijsman: If you could map something in mouse or rat, since we now have a fairly good idea of the relationship between where things are on the mouse chromosomes versus the human chromosomes, you could then look in the appropriate place on the human chromosome, which means that you could potentially skip that laborious cloning process.

Lander: The rodent genome and the human genome have blocks of about 10 cM of recombination that basically correspond. It should be noted, though, that if you transfer without knowing the gene, you could only do linkage, you couldn't do association. Anyway, that is going to be fruitful. It may be the only hope for truly polygenic inheritance, if that's what you're talking about, in human families.

The other possible hope is through a subphenotype. Saying that some aspect of alcoholism is evoked potential—not all, but some—and let's map evoked potential. Another aspect is something else, and another aspect is something else, and the constellation together produces, etc. and, in essence, I'm not mapping a polygenic trait. I'm saying this polygenic trait tends to happen when there is a constellation of more Mendelian traits, so I will cheat. But I think that is a very reasonable approach to this as well, and it greatly emphasizes the importance of those subphenotypes. It says that it doesn't matter whether those subphenotypes are found more broadly in the population than in alcoholics; if they're found very often in alcoholics, we want to understand what that's about. Sometimes people will say, "Well, it's not a good predictor of alcoholism in the general population." That's not necessarily relevant at all. If there are subphenotypes, you may still want to find them.

If it's just simple Mendelian locus heterogeneity, you are in a much happier case because within a family, it's a Mendelian trait that will map somewhere. The only problem is that in Family 1 it's mapping to chromosome 3, in Family 2 it's mapping to chromosome 5, the next one to chromosome 3. You may be able to deal with that by various analytical methods and just assume it maps to one of three locations. We make a joint hypothesis: Yes, we have to look at more families, but that's okay. You may be able to do it, though, by getting rid of the locus heterogeneity by looking at isolated populations, well-defined populations. One oughtn't necessarily to be working in New York City when we might do better to do this in Lapland or something, where one just hopes that due to population genetics that there are fewer of those loci in the locus heterogeneity running around.

So, I will ask, out of naivete, how much work is done in big city hospitals and how much work is done in well-defined isolated groups where there is locus heterogeneity and one has minimized it as much as possible? Should more work be done on better isolated genetic populations?

Cloninger: In isolates how do you generalize, because you don't get replication?

Lander: You don't need to replicate the isolates. It is the right thing to do because that will reduce the heterogeneity, but it's a problem because usually only one investigator ends up having access to those families. That's a sociological problem you have to deal with.

Risch: What about your assumption of within-family homogeneity in the presence of assortative mating? I think that model is fine when you are dealing with a disease with a frequency of 1 in 1000 or 1 in 10,000, and when there's no assortative mating, and when you have a clear Mendelian pattern of inheritance. I think we should make it clear to everybody here that that's not what we are dealing with when we are talking about this particular disease.

Lander: That's right. I completely agree. There is a tendency to want to get huge families doing this. One of the problems with diseases like this is stretching out to get huger and huger families; you run the risk for a disease of reasonably high prevalence in the population that you will quickly find yourself including things that have another cause, or you will find the cause coming in from another direction.

Risch: It's even worse than that because affected individuals are likely to carry more of the genes themselves because of assortative mating. Assortative mating causes allelic association.

Lander: It depends on the rates in the population. You could certainly make up models where that's completely hopeless. It will again be better in isolated populations. You never know in advance what it's going to be.

Finally, synthetic traits are a happy situation because in fact a synthetic trait maps the loci; it's very simple. The problem is if you think about something with high prevalence, if you actually need multiple factors, all of them have to be very frequent, and you can get in trouble with that. Nevertheless, it's a framework for thinking about your question.

Cloninger: When there is epistasis, do you think multipoint mapping is robust for detection of the individual loci?

Lander: Sure. Why wouldn't you think it's robust?

Cloninger: The leap from two points to multipoint mapping is not a problem?

Lander: The leap from two-point to multipoint mapping is not a problem with multiple loci provided one is robust in penetrance, which arise because of not knowing what should happen within the locus. In fact, we have just mapped this one, and we don't know what the penetrance factor is, and you're just asking yourself, "How much trouble do I get into because of this other penetrance?" In fact, you can do multipoint, so, you're really asking, "How much trouble do I get into with multipoint mapping with impenetrance?"

Conneally: Regardless of the model we use and how attached we are to it, we must be very careful not to exclude linkage for any given region of a chromosome based on our model, because we got, say, a LOD score less than -2 or some other magic number, and that we get into a rut in that case.

Risch: Would you be willing to exclude it if it was -7 or -8?

Conneally: That's a good question.

Chakravarti: No.

Lander: If it's 20% from the population and the other 80% is due to another locus, it will be easy to get minus whatever you want to.

Conneally: Especially if you go at 0.5.

Chakravarti: One thing you should mention is the models are not really three different models as you present them, because there will be variation at every given trait, so over families, for example, a synthetic trait does not always segregate at the same loci. You always have to do linkage analysis on the heterogeneity.

Lander: Right.

Chakravarti: The second point is proposing association in some sense is really quite difficult. I think, at one time, association studies were done more out of frustration than anything else; but now, if you can do linkage, then it's imperative that more people start thinking about how to implement these. I really don't think association studies will be so important, especially because you have missed one critical aspect and you call the one model polygenic. It probably should be called multifactorial, because there will definitely be environmental components for some of these.

Lander: Absolutely. I'm as scared as you are about association studies. If something had been proven in the rat to be important, I would think it worth undertaking an association study.

Chakravarti: From my perspective, the reason for being scared is that people go out and collect the data. Then, eventually, it filters down to analysts like me, and I've got to produce.

Lander: As you know, there is an HLA-A association in San Francisco for the ability to use chopsticks.

Risch: Not if the controls are done properly.

Lander: That's the problem.

Risch: No, I know how to pick the controls.

Goldman: A question I have for some of the mathematical geneticists concerns the significance of LOD scores, given that a wide variety of models might be applied to a particular data set. At what point do you decide there is evidence of linkage?

Ott: I have recently done a computer simulation analysis to address exactly that problem. It's clear that when you try linkage analyses across various genetic markers, you inflate the LOD score. If you do it the way people do psychiatric studies, that means you do the linkage analysis and then report the maximum LOD score you observe. But, I think, one way of handling this is doing computer simulation under the assumption of absence of linkage and basically repeating the whole process of maximizing the LOD score across genetic markers, so that then you have something to compare the actually observed maximum LOD score with the run that you will get, and a computer simulation in which also you maximize over genetic markers, and then compare those two. That gives you a good value comparison.

Risch: I want to reiterate some of the points that were made here. I take a somewhat different view from Aravinda. First, among the three models that were put on the board, I think we probably already have some information about which of these are more plausible for alcoholism, although I don't see as much difference between 1 and 3 maybe as you do. I think they are actually very similar, because they're both models of epistasis. Model 1 is really a model of epistasis also, if you're talking about a discrete trait.

Lander: If you're talking about a discrete trait, yes.

Risch: Right. So, the problem here is that we are dealing with a trait that is not awfully familial. In fact, I think one of the problems is that, from my reading of the literature, the genetic data are not totally consistent. At best, you could say from the adoption studies maybe there is a threefold increased risk to a first-degree relative of an alcoholic.

Cloninger: That risk is ninefold.

Risch: Well, fine. If you can define a subform which is specific so that the risk of type 2 among relatives of type 2 probands is ninefold, and it's a specific entity in and of itself, I would say fine, go for it. Then, maybe you have much more power to detect genes by a random genome search. I would be entirely in agreement with that, if that finding is robust and holds up. But, in the absence of that, if you have a relatively low relative risk like that—in fact, from my reading of the half-sib studies, they show rates that are very comparable to siblings, which is problematic, because it should be really much lower.

I think the genetic data right now for alcoholism are very confounded and not very clear. Certainly, what they are *not* saying is that we have a major gene segregating here with a large effect that can be easily found. I would like to see a replicated finding that was robust to demonstrate that.

Reich: Didn't you listen this morning to T.K.'s talk?

Risch: You mean the protective gene? You're talking about a different phenotype. You're talking about unaffected. Now, when you have genes that don't have very large effects, they can be very difficult to find through a linkage search paradigm. However, if you have candidate loci that again don't have very large effects, like the enzyme he is talking about, you are much better off doing an association study. You have a much better chance of finding it and demonstrating something significant. The only trick is you have to be careful in how you pick your controls (and there are very clearly defined ways to do that) so you don't run into the problem of population stratification to give a spurious association. When the gene effects are weak, it may be impossible or next to impossible to find them through linkage analysis.

Reich: A couple of points should be mentioned that come out of our meeting. One thing we have discussed here is that the appropriate approach from the epidemiological and clinical point of view is to try to measure common environmental effects and to control for them, or at least to statistically control for them, so that we can cast the genetic effects in greater relief. That is an extremely important feature.

Some of the problems we have talked about are easy to assess—namely, women who, because of their religious beliefs, are teetotalers and have never been exposed to alcohol—and are unknowns as far as phenotype is concerned. Doing even that simple thing on a number of those people—in certain parts of the country, it's up to 40% of women, for example—would clarify and improve the meaning of our phenogram, for example, or the pedigree, if you knew who those people were. One thing that people have to do in these complex diseases (and not only alcoholism, but other gene/environment disorders) is to learn effectively how to measure nongenic effects and control for them in order to cast or make more obvious our genetic factors.

Chakravarti: I think Neil disagreed with me, but he qualified his statement when he said "by choosing an appropriate control." Ted brings up that there are individuals who could be genetically susceptible, but they are teetotalers. I find it difficult to rationalize any way to really choose an appropriate control. In that sense, a linkage study is a lot better.

Risch: There is the "mystery" control, known as the two alleles not inherited by that individual that the parents possess.

Chakravarti: Which means you are essentially doing a sib-pair analysis?

Risch: No, not a sib-pair. You take the two alleles. You type both parents. The alcoholic child inherited one allele from each parent. You take the two other alleles that weren't inherited and that's your control.

Lander: That's really the only perfect control.

Chakravarti: That's fine.

Reich: The other question I would like to bring up that we haven't talked about, but should, is the distribution of points for markers given the various approaches to the strategy. One thing workers in this field will have to do, and which we plan to do, is to try to work out optimal strategies for minimizing the amount of effort and maximizing the amount of genetic analysis bang we could get using various methods and various models, rather than picking one and going with it, to try to work out a strategy that is most convenient, recognizing that we will have various different kinds or subforms of alcoholism, and, perhaps, various different kinds of analyses that we plan to do.

Lander: Let me disagree with that. In principle I agree, it's always good to be efficient. But they're not such different strategies. You are never going to be able to do much with markers more than 20 cM apart. There's nothing on the board where it pays to have markers closer than 5 cM. It's a factor of 4. In fact, the biggest problem right now is that we do not have somebody distributing to everybody a set of markers across the whole human genome in DNA form that you could easily label. It's actually more of an organizational problem. The markers are out there. Somewhere between 1000 and 2000 markers have been used on the CEPH families already. If those were available to everybody, mapped and in good DNA form, so you didn't have to get them in your lab, grow up the plasmid, make the insert, and do it, if you could buy them as a preprocessed kit, the factor of 4 would not be as important. I think that NIAAA and some of the other people ought to try to instigate a more organized world for linkage analysis. It's no longer the markers that are the problem, it's the distribution.

Sparkes: Sequence-tagged sites (STS) may do away with the need to have the actual genes, as long as you have the information about them in terms of their sequence.

Lander: Sadly, the STS that are going to be made for the human genome in the near future are not being selected because the STS themselves detect polymorphism. I would like to see a substantial portion of those STS put aside to insist that they be polymorphic, but there are little tricks—like the best polymorphisms we have right now are at the NTR loci that are actually hard to PCR across because of slippage and mispriming and being too long. And so, people have these little C-A repeats, but not enough of them are known; they're not trivial to PCR. Much important work will have to go into making these STS also points of polymorphism. Unfortunately, the physical mappers out there have no real appreciation for how important it is to make them polymorphic. We should put pressure on for them to be polymorphic.

Chakravarti: One point to add is that, again, in principle, what Ted said is correct, the kinds of markers you need are probably different depending on what trait you want to map. However, there has been a continuing trend to try to find more and more polymorphic markers simply because the amount of effort eventually you've got to put in would be much less if you had highly polymorphic markers.

Reich: With common diseases and using affected relative methods, of cousins for example, if your polymorphism information content (PIC) value is less than 0.6, it could be that there's no information at all in cousins.

Lander: That's right.

Risch: You would just have to type more relatives. When you have low PIC values, you just have to type all the intervening relatives. If you had a very high PIC value, like 0.9 or 0.95, you could just do the cousins and not anybody else.

Chakravarti: That's right, but that's a lot more work in typing all of the intervening relatives.

Risch: But you may have more power in more distant relatives also.

Conneally: I don't think markers are a problem, because by the time we have done all the VNTRs and all Jim Webber's C-As (and he's putting them out now at a rapid rate too) there will be a lot more available for us. That's the least of our problems.

Risch: I agree with that.

Sparkes: In terms of the markers, which is something we haven't spent too much time on, is it really worth while to think about "candidate" genes, or is it worth while just to think about the broad distribution, and in a sense go through and kind of saturate, if you will, the markers we talked about?

Billings: I was curious about this candidate gene. The metabolism of alcohol has yielded alcohol dehydrogenase and aldehyde dehydrogenase, which are apparently going to be relatively useful in a subset of individuals. Are there other likely genetic candidates that are related to this epidemiological factor in alcoholism, i.e., alcohol, which anybody has in mind?

Cloninger: We have heard from T.K. and Boris today that some genes that influence neuroreceptor function appear promising.

Billings: Right, predictors for the animal model.

Sparkes: I think it's worth while thinking about the candidate genes because if you really have a candidate gene, it is very likely you are going to know the function of that gene very quickly. Even though they have the CF gene, as far as I know, at least, they haven't published or come up publicly with the real function of that gene. That's not a trivial step.

Cloninger: But the candidate gene strategy hasn't worked ever for non-Mendelian disorders, has it?

Sparkes: Oh, yes.

Lander: Sure. Didn't work for CF.

Martin: What are the examples? Cholesterol?

Wijsman: In collagen disorders it worked.

Cloninger: That may be true for Mendelian disorders, but maybe for something as complex as cardiovascular disease or alcoholism, we will have to identify specific physiological components.

Wijsman: Yes. I would tend to agree that, by and large, it hasn't been a very useful strategy, but it doesn't hurt either.

Sparkes: It hasn't been widely used.

Cloninger: When you're trying to reconstruct the physiology and the genetics of the components of a complex system, that's true.

Conneally: If you take a candidate gene, and if it's polymorphic, even though it really isn't a candidate, it is as likely to be next door to the locus as any other anonymous piece of DNA.

Wijsman: There's no harm.

Lander: If you generate 20 candidate genes, it's a trivial investment.

Cloninger: T.K., could you comment on how you think we could better use the results of the animal studies?

Li: Yes. First of all, there has only been one model. That is part of the weakness. So, how much we can generalize we really don't know. There are three animal models that show alcohol preference. In one of them David has shown there is a major gene effect on alcohol preference. From our repeated selection, we get segregation very early, so it is likely that there are major gene effects in drinking behavior. Now, that depends on how you want to define human alcoholism. One area that we have some handle on is tolerance. Boris is right now selecting for tolerance, but this is chronic tolerance, tolerance with chronic exposure. That is different from what we see in our animals experimentally, although it may be the same thing. He just told me today that his high-tolerance animals have increased vasopressin in mRNA in brain. Our animals do, as well. So, some things are beginning to look promising. I think, for example, that may be one aspect to look at as a candidate gene. There are abnormalities in the serotonin system that are existent in the C57s as well as in our animals, but they are different. Ours seems to be a decrease in fiber density in certain brain regions and theirs is a metabolic effect of deficiency in tryptophan. I think, from that theory, we will look at many things—tryptophan hydroxylase, et cetera, and serotonin receptors. We know geneticists have cloned the 5HT-1A receptor. That's the one that is up-regulated in our animal model. Then, 1A, 1C, 2, 3—I think they are all cloned right now. Is that right?

Goldman: I'm not sure about 3.

Li: Somebody is working on 3, I think. There are others we should take note of, for example, benzodiazepine, which seems to show an effect of alcohol. There is the NMDA receptor, which alcohol has very high specificity on. All of these are things that we can look at.

The study that has been proposed that we are all focusing on happens to be an all-Caucasian study, so the polymorphisms that I described and Dr. Agarwal described in Orientals won't pertain. They are just not relevant in that population. The only polymorphisms that are common enough in the Caucasians in alcohol dehydrogenase is the ADH3 gene where there is gamma 1 and gamma 2; and then, there is the cytosolic aldehyde dehydrogenase polymorphism that Tim Peters described. I guess this would be some kind of a beginning for candidate probes.

As far as other enzyme systems, there is the cytochrome P-450 for alcohol, which is an inducible enzyme; there are polymorphic forms of that, I think, and that may be another possibility. Humans show differences in catalase, but we don't know how well that functions in alcohol metabolism anyway.

Goldman: If you look to the example of non-insulin-dependent diabetes mellitus, where they looked for a linkage with insulin receptor, it turned out that the effect was principally not there in NIDDM. However, they did find that defect in leprechanism. Similarly, we would expect that for every one of the key enzymes involved in neurotransmitter synthesis and reception, there would be some population of people who carry the defect that would be phenotypically significant. It might be a small population, but nevertheless, you have the advantage then of finding something that connects at the level of the phenotype to the fundamental molecular level. That should teach us something. I think it's worth while looking for that reason alone. It's a somewhat different situation than with some other diseases, because there is a whole host of good candidates here. Granted, for many of them there is no RFLP at the locus available to date, but for some there is a nearby highly polymorphic locus. Looking down the road to a few years from now, it might be very important to make sure that we have a highly polymorphic locus near any particularly good candidates.

Li: The major direction or strategy that we plan to adopt is to use the candidate genes to tell us where we are and then look for the highly polymorphic sites nearby.

Reich: I would like to go back to the electroencephalographic phenotypes and ask Henri about the history. He once recounted to me how the original features were extracted from EEGs. My understanding was they kind of smoothed everything and averaged everything in order to get the humps and lumps. One of the plans that I have heard discussed was the idea of going back to the raw data, being informed about segregation and other kinds of variation that might occur, and trying to pull out the features from the raw information that might be more congenial to or have the properties of major loci. I wonder if Henri would comment on how these things were done and whether he thinks that might be feasible.

Begleiter: I think it's feasible now. There are a number of features that can be extracted at the various levels. What has been done up to now is to look at brain function in a very static manner. People have recorded a number of trials and have averaged over those trials. Moreover, while confronted with about 500–1000 data points, they have actually focused on three or four and thrown out the rest, which, of course, is not good sampling. Now, you can examine features at many different levels. You can look at dynamic features that change from trial to trial and are extremely varied. That is, the interindividual variability is great. You can look at the features that are in the average response and allow you to look at the dynamic properties across sites on the skull. There again, there is a tremendous interindividual variation. You can look at the features that have a specific topographical distribution in time. This, again, represents a set of really new techniques. Probably most exciting, you can actually begin to model the dipoles, which provide you with interesting information in terms of location or intensity or orientation. That is extremely individually based, so that there is a tremendous amount of interindividual variability. Even though some similar effects may be produced, they are reproduced by different generators that are different in terms of intensity or orientation or even location, for that matter.

Reich: If we define a major locus as one that produces a 2-s.d. difference between the means of the homozygotes, could one ever hope for deviations in that magnitude from those kinds of materials?

Begleiter: I think within a year it's absolutely possible, yes.

Peters: I have a point related to T.K. Li's comments. There is considerable interest now in the area of free radicals. To add to your list, I think superoxide dismutase has been cloned and there are polymorphisms for three forms.

Li: There was actually an abnormality in superoxide dismutase described in black alcoholics.

Conneally: Some years ago, but not in Caucasians. Nobody has confirmed it. It is in the literature.

Peters: The other point is whether the classical geneticists have anything to tell us. Are there any associations (either positive or negative) between chromosome abnormalities and alcohol abuse? The most severe patient I ever saw, earliest onset, was an XYY aggressive psychopath. Are there any clues like that you could use to point us in the right direction?

Sparkes: Something like what has been done with Duchenne's muscular dystrophy?

Peters: Yes.

Sparkes: I'm not aware of anything like that.

Peters: X-chromosomal defects in bowel disease have been quite helpful in giving us clues as to which way to go. I wonder if you have any suggestions, Michael?

Conneally: You could do chromosomes in some of these families, but it's very expensive.

Reich: Part of the problem is that the people who are in hospital for retardation or some abnormality, where you could get breaks and all sorts of tears and things, are supervised so they don't have access to alcohol. I think it's much better for other phenotypes like bipolar illness or schizophrenia where psychosis or pathological behavior may have an effect.

Sparkes: Yes. I think what Tim is suggesting, though, is the possibility of a congenital rearrangement that is predisposing in an unusual association, which could be very useful if you could find it.

Peters: Like the XYY.

Martin: Does that hold up?

Cloninger: I don't know about the association of XYY and alcoholism. Certainly, XYY is associated with increasing criminal behavior.

Cadoret: Could you get an idea for extra candidate genes from animal studies that have looked at behavioral traits, like exploration and defecation? You have done a lot of work, Bob, in developing your theory of personality from animal studies. I would wonder if there hasn't been a lot of work done with animals, breeding them for exploratory behavior, or risk-taking behavior, and then examining biochemical differences in those animals.

Cloninger: You are correct. The findings are in line with much of what T.K. talked about earlier.

Cadoret: Not necessarily that those animals go on to become alcoholic, but they may have some of the behavioral traits that you think are important for development of alcoholism.

Wijsman: I think, though, that if you take the tactic of trying to breed a high risk-taking line, or something of that sort, you run the risk of removing yourself too far from the particular trait you are interested in. If you are trying to select first and then map afterward, you are probably much better off sticking with the specific kind of behavior you are interested in, in this case with alcoholism, some measure of alcoholism, rather than some correlate.

Cadoret: We also know that a lot of people who are alcoholic take a lot of risks.

Wijsman: Yes, but you also, I think, then remove yourself too far from the fundamental defect.

Lander: Unless you consider taking risks the phenomenon.

Begleiter: There is a well-known strain called the Maudsley reactive strain, which manifests a great deal of exploratory behavior and, coincidentally, also likes alcohol. They don't take it in as great an amount as T.K.'s rat, but they show a preference for alcohol. This is also true of Norway wild rats.

Li: There are also two lines, low-avoidance and high-avoidance, with Bob Brush at Purdue, and they are sort of like Maudsleys. They also show a difference in alcohol preference, again, not as much as the ones we select for.

Billings: What about the candidate genes in other psychiatric disorders? We have batted around the problems with the Amish pedigree and the schizophrenia pedigrees, but, presumably, there will be candidate linked markers in some of those. Are those going to be candidate genes for alcoholism as well?

Reich: We're better off here than the other diseases. This is the best for candidate genes.

Risch: Chromosome 5 for those pedigrees had some alcoholics, as I recall, so maybe that would be a good region to try for alcoholism.

Billings: Psychiatric disorder and alcoholism are epidemiologically associated, so it's a possible candidate gene.

Sparkes: You have to keep in mind, just at the genetic level, that you can have different mutations at the same locus and have different manifestations. Evidence of that is in the hemoglobin story, where you can have the same tissue affected, but different manifestations, depending on which mutation. So, I think Paul's suggestion shouldn't be too readily discarded.

Conneally: Ted, I'm curious as to why you say we're better off here. There is no equivalent of a teetotaler in bipolar illness, for example.

Reich: But there are no candidate loci.

Conneally: Oh, I see, for that reason.

Reich: Schizophrenia is probably even more primitive. There are some other kinds of effects, but, by and large, the number of interesting candidate loci is much less. There is nothing, for example, the equivalent of protective loci.

Wijsman: To go back to the question of looking at exploratory animals: In *Drosophila* work, selection experiments on fecundity and longevity and various kinds of aging phenomena shed some light on correlated responses. Because you can manipulate the organism, you can ask whether or not changing fecundity is a by-product of changing longevity in these strains, and what not. It may not be efficient to do this in rats, but maybe if you want to ask questions like, "Is it specifically the exploratory behavior that is predisposing people to seek out alcohol?" then one might consider pursuing that line of work in rats or mice or some other organism.

Goldman: There is a nice body of work in that area with LSS mice. Many people are looking at correlated behavioral responses in that system. Furthermore, other strains are being developed that we haven't even discussed, for example, strains that have high and low withdrawals or high and low activations after alcohol. These sorts of correlated responses are being looked at. I think it is a very important approach.

Genetic Linkage Analysis in Alcoholism—Obstacles, Opportunities, and Consequences

Genetic Approaches to the Dissection of Complex Diseases

ARAVINDA CHAKRAVARTI[1] AND ERIC S. LANDER[2]
[1]Department of Human Genetics
University of Pittsburgh
Pittsburgh, Pennsylvania 15261
[2]Whitehead Institute for Biomedical Research
Cambridge, Massachusetts 02142

INTRODUCTION

The two great problems confronting the human geneticist are (1) a given genotype may not always result in the same phenotype and (2) a given phenotype does not always result from the same genotype. The first aspect is generally explained by the phenomenon of penetrance or expressivity; the second aspect may be explained by multiple allelism, multiple loci, or the occurrence of phenocopies. These are the major reasons for the complex patterns of inheritance observed for many phenotypes. This complexity is inferred for a phenotype whenever the incidence of the trait is increased among the relatives of probands and yet no simple Mendelian pattern of inheritance is evident.

Brother Gregor Mendel taught us not to attempt to study all genetic differences at one time, but rather to study the inheritance of differences that depend on a single gene. This precept, followed by the early human geneticists from the beginning of this century, allowed the rapid elucidation of the mode of inheritance for several rare and common human traits and diseases (McKusick 1988). These studies also emphasized that human traits followed the same regular rules of genetic transmission discovered in other organisms. Since human family data arise from uncontrolled matings and small families, these early investigators also proposed statistical methods for objectively analyzing these data to infer the mode of inheritance (Nicholas 1982). However, two problems still remained: First, many traits truly seemed complex, and, second, for many traits there did not seem to be any objective way to identify a sub-phenotype that could be due to single gene differences. For several traits, the inheritance was simply assumed to be "multifactorial"—this often being a definition masquerading as an explanation. There have been several developments that allow a resolution of this dilemma, and these promise to dissect a complex trait into identifiable components.

DISCUSSION

Models of Complex Genetic Systems

For a complex organism such as the human, the pattern of inheritance for most phenotypes is not simple. Of 4344 uncommon traits listed in McKusick's (1988) catalog, only 2208 (51%) have a recognizable inheritance pattern; of the latter only $\sim 20\%$ are due to single gene differences. The three major causes of this complexity are (1) reduction in penetrance; (2) segregation of multiple, independent, monogenic traits; and (3) segregation of multiple, interacting genes together with environmental influences. For this last model, we generally assume an oligogenic system with a limited number of segregating loci. In the extreme case, where a large number of loci each with only a minor, additive effect on the phenotype are considered, this could be termed a polygenic or multifactorial model.

Of the three postulated causes of genetic complexity, the third scenario is the most general, of which the other two may be considered as special cases. Thus, interaction of a single gene with a common environment or subject to stochastic factors may lead to reduced penetrance (model 1), but this reduction is random and independent of the genetic background of an individual. On the other hand, interaction between a primary gene and its genetic modifiers may also lead to reduced penetrance (model 1), but this reduction is nonrandom and depends on the genotypes at the modifier loci. Finally, when only a few (2 or 3) genes interact to produce a trait, there is a substantial probability that in certain families only one of these loci will segregate, thus giving the impression of single gene inheritance. Since, by chance, different genes will segregate in different families, one may obtain multiple, independent monogenic traits (model 2). This is a model of genetic heterogeneity.

Other scenarios exist, of course. Environmental effects can modify traits, but there is increasing recognition that environments common to a family may lead to familial aggregation and simulate genetic transmission. There is also the suspicion that the large number of isolated cases observed for many complex disorders are sporadic, probably due to phenocopies, and thus of environmental origin. However, as is the case in many cancers, a large majority of these sporadic occurrences may be due to specific genetic mutations in somatic cells and often at the same locus involved in the hereditary cases. Thus, many phenocopies may, in fact, be genocopies. Finally, epigenetic modification of a phenotype, such as due to genomic imprinting, may also be possible (Sapienza 1989). All of these factors may lead to a complex pattern of inheritance.

A final point regarding the number of genes that contribute to a trait should be discussed. Although a large number of genes may be involved, only those genes that are polymorphic and segregate within families are relevant to genetic analysis. For a fixed incidence of a rare trait, the trait causing alleles is typically not expected to be rare but rather common under an oligogenic model. As discussed by Chakravarti (1990), observed levels of genetic variation at structural genes and the frequency distribution of their alleles suggest that many complex traits are probably determined by only 2–5 segregating loci.

Under this scenario, the genetic questions of direct interest are:

1. How many genes are involved?
2. What are the allelic effects of individual genes?
3. Are these allelic effects independent, additive, or interactive?
4. Are there environmental influences and, if so, are they genotype-dependent?
5. What are the genomic locations of the relevant genes?

The Resolution of Complexity

The resolution of a complex trait into simpler components has been attempted on the basis of four different methods as outlined below.

Trait Definition

Clearly, the most crucial exercise in studying complex diseases is an objective definition of the trait. Knowing the biology of the disorder can always help in defining a phenotype that has a greater probability of being homogeneous. The current success in understanding the familial nature of human cancer has largely come not from identifying patients as being affected, nor from noting the organs affected, but from classifying cancer according to histological types. It is also helpful to identify biological correlates of a disease, since these may often be more amenable to genetic or biochemical analyses. It has been suggested that classifying families according to these biological markers may be more helpful than a direct study of the segregation of the complex phenotype (Lander 1988).

Ascertainment of Families

For reasons of efficiency and practicality, for rare or uncommon phenotypes, families must be ascertained through affected individuals. These probands lead to the ascertainment of other relatives, both affected and unaffected, and thus of families in which the probands are either parents or offspring or both. This latter characteristic is determined by many factors, the most important being the survival age of probands.

Even though families may be ascertained on an ad hoc basis, the difficulty lies in interpreting the pattern of inheritance in the sampled families. The primary object in the past has been to use the sampled families for analysis of the segregation patterns, which, in turn, depend on the expected distribution of *genotypes*, and thus of phenotypes, among ascertained families. These distributions can theoretically be predicted if families are sampled at random. Often, random sampling cannot be achieved for practical reasons; this effect is compounded when families with multiple affected members are selected in frequency greater than their proportional representation in the population. There is thus the need for an ascertainment rule determined prior to the selection of families, a rule that determines how relatives of probands and relatives of secondary affected individuals are selected.

A major unanswered question is whether only the nuclear family containing the proband or large pedigrees consisting of the proband and all first, second, etc. relatives should be ascertained. The genetic characteristics of nuclear families selected through a proband are well known (Morton 1982), whereas characteristics of large pedigrees are generally not well known. However, nuclear families are inefficient for most types of genetic analyses. Second, it is commonly argued that assembling a collection of independent nuclear families has a higher risk of introducing etiologic heterogeneity than would be obtained in large pedigrees. This need not be true, since the many individuals who marry into a large pedigree may also contribute to heterogeneity; this is especially important for common traits. A compromise appears to be the selection of a primary nuclear family through the proband and subsequent ascertainment of other nuclear families of predetermined relationship to the proband (Lalouel and Morton 1981).

Segregation Analysis

The primary reason for ascertaining families in a defined manner is to facilitate segregation analysis for inferring the mode of inheritance. For several ascertainment schemes, the analysis of single gene traits is well known; analysis of traits of multifactorial origin is also possible (see Morton 1982). Classically, segregation analysis has proceeded via tests of goodness-of-fit of observed to expected segregation patterns; the expected patterns are those derived from random aggregation, single gene models, and the multifactorial model. The intermediate oligogenic models are not usually considered. Furthermore, tests of heterogeneity cannot be performed per se unless the family material is divided according to independent, clinical, or biological criteria.

For complex phenotypes, the aim of segregation analysis is to identify a major locus, that is, a single gene with a large effect on the phenotype. Residual genetic factors, if present, are assumed to be multifactorial. Thus, segregation analysis by itself can only provide a partial answer, and even then, requires a large number of families. To increase efficiency, some investigators (MacLean et al. 1984) have proposed segregation analysis using marker loci linked to one of the putative genetic loci. In these circumstances, the residual segregation unexplained by the known marker locus is explored for additional genetic effects. This method can be extended as additional single genes known to affect the phenotype are identified, but it first requires the identification of genes by linkage analysis.

Linkage Analysis

The genetic epidemiologist's paradigm of first ascertaining families, next performing segregation analysis, and finally identifying the genes involved through linkage analysis does not seem very efficient. Several developments in molecular genetics now make it practical to establish linkage directly without knowledge of the exact genetic model. Once linkage is determined, the genetics of the phenotype can be easily dissected.

Following the discovery of restriction fragment length polymorphisms (RFLPs), Botstein et al. (1980) were the first to propose using RFLPs to develop a comprehensive genetic linkage map and subsequently to use this map for mapping disease genes of unknown biochemical function. This method has been extremely successful in mapping several disease-causing genes, notably those for Huntington's disease, Duchenne/Becker muscular dystrophy, and cystic fibrosis (for further examples, see McKusick 1988). Once the gross location of the disease gene is known, molecular methods to isolate the gene of interest on the basis of map position are possible and have been successful, as in cystic fibrosis (Rommens et al. 1989).

A human genetic linkage map at an average resolution of 10 map units is currently available (Donis-Keller et al. 1987), and efforts are under way to increase the resolution to 1–2 map units. More than a thousand RFLPs are currently known, and molecular methods now permit the identification of very highly polymorphic genetic markers (Nakamura et al. 1987; Weber and May 1989). The recent developments in statistical and computer-based methods to detect linkage for complex diseases, when multiple genes are involved and genetic heterogeneity is present, make it feasible to search for linkage even for complex genetic systems (Lander and Botstein 1986, Risch 1990). Thus, all the elements to identify the genes for a complex phenotype are now available. The genetic dissection of complex diseases will probably occur through linkage studies. This will have two major advantages. First, the reliance on ascertainment schemes is not as critical. Second, linkage studies can utilize any family structure, including pairs of relatives. The reliance on large pedigrees assumed to segregate a rare autosomal dominant gene is now neither necessary nor recommended.

REFERENCES

Botstein, D., R.L. White, M. Skolnick, and R.W. Davis. 1980. Construction of a genetic linkage map in man using restriction fragment length polymorphism. *Am. J. Hum. Genet.* **32:** 314.

Chakravarti, A. 1990. Impact of genetic, somatic and epigenetic variation on phenotype. In *Genetic variability in human diseases: Cells, individuals, families and populations* (ed. C.F. Sing and C.L. Hanis). Oxford University Press, New York.

Donis-Keller, H. et al. (32 additional authors). 1987. A genetic linkage map of the human genome. *Cell* **51:** 319.

Lalouel, J.-M. and N.E. Morton. 1981. Complex segregation analysis with pointers. *Hum. Hered.* **31:** 312.

Lander, E.S. 1988. Splitting schizophrenia. *Nature* **336:** 105.

Lander, E.S. and D. Botstein. 1986. Mapping complex genetic traits in humans: New strategies using a complete RFLP linkage map. *Cold Spring Harbor Symp. Quant. Biol.* **51:** 49.

MacLean, C.J., N.E. Morton, and S. Yee. 1984. Combined analysis of genetic segregation and linkage under an oligogenic model. *Comput. Biomed. Res.* **17:** 471.

McKusick, V.A. 1988. *Mendelian inheritance in man: Catalogs of autosomal dominant, autosomal recessive, and X-linked phenotypes.* 8th edition. Johns Hopkins University Press, Baltimore.

Morton, N.E. 1982. *An outline of genetic epidemiology.* S. Karger, Basel.

Nakamura, Y., M. Leppert, P. O'Connell, R. Wolff, T. Holm, M. Culver, C. Martin, E. Fujimoto, M. Hoff, E. Kumlin, and R. White. 1987. Variable number of tandem repeat (VNTR) markers for human gene mapping. *Science* **235:** 1616.

Nicholas, F.W. 1982. Simple segregation analysis: A review of its history and terminology. *J. Hered.* **73:** 444.

Risch, N. 1990. Linkage strategies for genetically complex traits. II. The power of affected relative pairs. *Am. J. Hum. Genet.* **46:** 229.

Rommens, J.M., M.C. Iannuzzi, B.-S. Kerem, M.L. Drumm, G. Melmer, M. Dean, R. Rozmahel, J.L. Cole, D. Kennedy, N. Hidaka, M. Zsiga, M. Buchwald, J.R. Riordan, L.-C. Tsui, and F.S. Collins. 1989. Identification of the cystic fibrosis gene: Chromosome walking and jumping. *Science* **245:** 1059.

Sapienza, C. 1989. Genome imprinting and dominance modification. *Ann. N.Y. Acad. Sci.* **564:** 24.

Weber, J.L. and P.E. May. 1989. Abundant class of human DNA polymorphisms which can be typed using the polymerase chain reaction. *Am. J. Hum. Genet.* **44:** 388.

COMMENTS

Cloninger: Aravinda, a major consideration in focusing only on the affected individuals in families when you have phenotypes like alcoholism is deciding just what is "affected." It's not a simple situation where you can either say that someone is or is not affected; often there is a spectrum of conditions that may be considered affected. For example, few of the women who have children susceptible to alcoholism are alcoholic themselves. There may be personality traits or associated psychiatric disorders, like somatization or depression, that actually may be the equivalent in women of what alcohol abuse is in men. It often is impossible to decide rationally who to consider affected and who not to consider affected. You may need to follow these individuals through time also. Thus, given the problems of instability of diagnosis, variable expression, and variation in penetrance by sex, I would submit that the strategy of considering only affected individuals is really unworkable.

Chakravarti: Not really. I think, even when we talk of using "affecteds," that word should be used in quotes. As you will realize, in any kind of genetic analysis, or linkage analysis in particular, the people who are more extreme on the quantitative scale that you measure probably have a more stable diagnosis and will surely give more information either for or against linkage. So, you don't have to use the term affected in any strict sense, as long as you define a specific set of criteria. I don't think "affected" is used in any other sense.

Cloninger: What I mean is, in practice, if you're going to decide whether you need to interview the person, draw a sample of his blood, establish a cell line, there are very few individuals whom you should feel comfortable excluding. Then, once you have collected all of that data, are you just going to put it aside and ignore it in the linkage analysis? I doubt it.

Chakravarti: No.

Cloninger: You may in some analyses.

Chakravarti: No, no. There are two parts, I guess. One is to find methods to map the genes, because I think having that information would be more useful to the general genetic analysis than not. I don't think that you have to set those individuals aside. They would still be important to find out which individuals have the gene and don't express it, or who have the gene and don't have some other gene and either express it or not.

Reich: I think what Aravinda is driving at is that we're talking about several different issues here. One is doing diagnostic assessments on everybody in a family. What do you do with those assessments once you have them; who do you include as affected; and what do you do with unaffected individuals? Now, who you sample for blood to do a linkage analysis are not necessarily the same people that you want to do diagnoses on or get detailed clinical interviews, which is the most expensive part of the study. For example, if you know there are two alcoholics in a family, and they are clear blue-ribbon alcoholics, and the other people are less clear, you might want to get blood from other relatives to clearly define whether they are sharing genes identical by descent or not, but that doesn't necessarily mean you have to have diagnostic assessments on those individuals. When you're dealing with complex diseases, the real guts of the linkage proof rests in the people who you are defining as "affected" in the analysis. On the other hand, linkage marker information may be critical on unaffected individuals or intervening people, but not their diagnoses.

Sambrook: Can you get some estimates of how stable your diagnosis is by, let's say, looking at pairs of identical twins, how stable the diagnosis is for that, and then comparing them with sibs and comparing them with half-sibs?

Cloninger: I think there are extensive data about the test-retest reliability of the diagnosis of alcoholism. It's probably among the highest of all the psychiatric disorders. Test-retest correlations over long periods of time are on the order of 0.8–0.85 for alcoholism, but that itself is a function of severity too, and the more severe cases very seldom lead to any changes in diagnosis. The mild or borderline cases can be quite variable. Some of the spectrum conditions, like somatization and depression, might be even more unreliable.

Chakravarti: More unreliable in the sense of less stable?

Cloninger: That's right.

Chakravarti: The thing is, if you're doing that, you obviously have some index of how stable a particular diagnosis is, so you can just choose any individual with any diagnosis with a stability above a certain percent.

Cadoret: George Valliant has studied alcoholics over a long term, and he finds that at one time you can call Individual A an alcoholic and a couple of years later that person has cleaned up his act and no longer meets the criteria for alcoholism; then a few years further down the line that person may again go back into being more alcoholic than he had been. There is that type of variability to be concerned about as well.

Chakravarti: I guess that is part of what Bob is saying: Alcoholism is not like other common diseases where you can just take an instantaneous phenotype.

Cloninger: There are age effects too. If you have someone age 20 who is unaffected, you may want to follow them until they're 40 to see whether they develop alcoholism. That could be a critical person. We have seen changes in diagnosis in the Amish study of Egeland. Changes in two diagnoses lead to major changes in the LOD scores so that there is now very questionable evidence for linkage between bipolar illness and 11p.

Linkage Analysis of Alcoholism: Problems and Solutions

ELLEN M. WIJSMAN
Division of Medical Genetics
Department of Medicine and Department of Biostatistics
University of Washington
Seattle, Washington 98195

OVERVIEW

Mapping genes for alcoholism by linkage analysis will be much more difficult than for clear Mendelian defects, because alcoholism is likely to be a multifactorial disease and the relationship between the phenotype and genotype is unknown and may be weak. Identification of at least one phenotype that is measured at the physiological level, can be shown to segregate with alcoholism, and gives good discrimination between individuals at risk and not at risk for the disease could improve the power of the technique to detect linkage. Identification of possible subgroups of families prior to performing linkage analysis could provide another avenue for increasing the chances of success. Finally, to prevent an increase in false-positive results, it may be necessary to make all decisions about mode of inheritance and about phenotypes in pedigrees prior to the collection and analysis of any marker data.

INTRODUCTION

Evidence supports the premise that there is a genetic component to alcoholism, as reviewed in this volume (Cadoret and Wesner; Cloninger; Reich and Cloninger, all this volume). It is therefore possible that the genetic approach to the study of disease may be of use in understanding mechanisms behind predisposition to alcoholism. This approach can be summarized as follows: If differences in phenotypes among individuals are at least partially caused by genetic differences among individuals, it is possible to use statistical techniques of linkage analysis to localize the gene(s) responsible for these phenotypic differences on a genetic map. After gene localization, molecular techniques can be used to identify and characterize the gene(s) involved. With this technique, it is possible to identify proteins and pathways that are currently unknown and to study their interactions with other proteins and metabolites. It is important to note that this approach can lead to some understanding of not only genetic aspects of the disease, but also environmental aspects.

Banbury Report 33: Genetics and Biology of Alcoholism
© Cold Spring Harbor Laboratory Press. 0-87969-233-2/90. $1.00 + .00

Linkage analysis has worked very well for placing many genetic disorders on the human genetic map. The basic idea behind this application of the technique of maximum likelihood is as follows. Assume that pedigrees containing affected individuals have been sampled and that there is a single locus responsible for the disease in question. If genotypes at some marker locus are also known for the pedigree members and if the disease allele and an allele at the marker locus are inherited together more often than expected by chance alone, there is evidence for linkage between the two loci. This is measured by a LOD score exceeding +3.0, corresponding to a significance level of ~5%. A LOD score below −2.0 demonstrates significant evidence against linkage to the recombination fraction at which the LOD score is −2.0. (For a thorough discussion of the LOD score method of linkage analysis, see, e.g., Ott 1985.)

It is not easy to isolate a gene once it has been mapped. However, the mapping of disease loci has led to the cloning of genes responsible for Duchenne muscular dystrophy (Monaco et al. 1985; Ray et al. 1985; Kunkel et al. 1986) and, most recently, cystic fibrosis (Riordan et al. 1989; Rommens et al. 1989). These successes for single-locus disorders indicate that the successful mapping and eventual isolation of genes reponsible for single-locus disorders may be primarily a function of the availability of sufficient resources.

Although the strategies used for mapping and isolating single-gene defects might provide a guide for approaches that aid in the isolation of loci involved in alcoholism, it is doubtful that the mapping of such loci will be nearly as easy as that for known single-locus defects. This is because a disease such as alcoholism differs from the disorders mentioned above in at least four ways: (1) The mode of inheritance is unknown; (2) environmental factors probably influence manifestation of the disease; (3) it seems likely that there may be multiple loci involved in the development and expression of the disease, and (4) the current phenotype of alcoholism is neither unambiguously qualitative (affected vs. unaffected) nor quantitative. These factors will complicate data collection and analysis, although they will not necessarily prevent its eventual successful execution. As a result, it seems probable that an understanding of alcoholism through dissection of genetic mechanisms will not come suddenly with the identification and cloning of a single gene, but slowly, as individual genes are identified that play some role in the predisposition to alcoholism. My goal is to outline the potential problems and pitfalls that may occur in the attempt to map the genes involved in alcoholism and to suggest possible procedures that may miminize these problems. I will do this by breaking down the approach into its component parts and indicating possible problems and solutions for each part.

Linkage Analysis of Alcoholism

Phenotype

Linkage analysis will only be appropriate for mapping genes involved in alcoholism if alleles at individual loci have detectable effects on the phenotype. Therefore, linkage analysis of alcoholism must not begin with the final computation of LOD scores, but with the initial identification of one or more phenotypes that are associated with alcoholism and that give some evidence for the segregation of a major locus in pedigrees. Throughout the remainder of this paper, the term alcoholism will refer to any of these phenotypes that may be used in lieu of alcoholism. The phenotypes may be either quantitative (measured on a univariate or multivariate continuous scale) or qualitative (categorized into two or more discrete groups, such as affected and unaffected). To apply likelihood methods to these data, it is also necessary to have estimates of the probabilities of the various phenotypes as a function of the genotypes at the locus to be mapped. That is, it is necessary to have estimates of the penetrance functions of the genotypes and the mode of inheritance of the locus.

It is best to estimate penetrance at the point when the phenotypes are being defined rather than waiting until linkage analyses have been initiated. There are three reasons for this. (1) It avoids the desire to try the linkage analyses later over a variety of definitions of the disease phenotype; (2) it allows one to assess the value of the phenotype for use in a linkage study before the study has been initiated; and (3) it engages investigators in discussion of this topic before controversy arises over linkage results. These topics will be discussed further.

Penetrance is useful not only for describing random effects of environment on the phenotype, but also for coping with problems of multifactorial inheritance. Although the technique of linkage analysis requires the assumption that the phenotype is controlled by a single genetic locus, the effects on the locus being mapped of additional necessary loci can be described with a penetrance parameter. If the model is correctly parameterized, simulations indicate that the conclusion of linkage may be correctly obtained and that little bias occurs in the estimates of parameters (Greenberg and Hodge 1989). Therefore, as long as the evidence for a major locus is not spurious, it should be possible to determine that linkage analysis is feasible on the basis of the value of the phenotype. This requires a reasonable separation of distributions in the case of a quantitative trait (Boehnke and Moll 1989) and a low misclassification probability of affected individuals for a qualitative trait (Ott 1985, p. 125).

To achieve a reasonable phenotype for a linkage study, it is likely that the end point, alcoholism, may be an undesirable phenotype with which to perform genetic analyses if there are multiple underlying causes for the disease. It may be more efficient to find a physiological phenotype, even if it is rare in the general population of alcoholics. Suggestive data on various physiological parameters need to be confirmed and extended and may shed some additional light on the problem of defining the phenotype(s) of alcoholism.

The study of the genetics of heart disease can be used as an example. The end point of heart disease, myocardial infarction, is a poor indicator of the underlying phenotype. It was the observation that a specific rare subset of families had a particularly severe form of the disease (familial hypercholesterolemia, or FH) that led to the eventual identification of the defect in these families (Brown and Goldstein 1986). This, in turn, opened up investigation on the biochemical pathways involved in cholesterol transport and led to some understanding of many of the steps involved in this process. Although FH is responsible for only a small fraction of all heart disease, identification of these pathways was instrumental in identifying other loci that also influence the risk of developing heart disease, including lipoprotein a (Utermann 1989) and apolipoprotein E (Boerwinkle and Sing 1987; Boerwinkle et al. 1987).

Collection of Families

The next stage of a linkage study consists of identifying families that contain one or more individuals with the phenotype of interest. The optimal size and configuration of pedigrees to be collected at this stage will depend, to some extent, on how common the phenotype is and on whether or not the assumption of genetic homogeneity is valid. (Genetic homogeneity implies that all individuals with the phenotype have a defect at the same locus.)

If apparently identical phenotypes can be caused by defects in different genes (genetic heterogeneity) and if these phenotypes are common, as is the basic phenotype of alcoholism, then a large pedigree with affected individuals in two or more branches of the pedigree may be segregating at more than one disease locus. If this occurs, it will be very difficult to obtain significant evidence for linkage. Therefore, for common disorders, it may be advantageous to collect smaller pedigrees under the expectation that genetic heterogeneity, if it exists, might be detectable between (Morton 1956; Ott 1977; Risch and Baron 1982; Risch 1988), but not within, pedigrees.

If the phenotype in question is rare, large pedigrees that show the disorder in multiple branches are unlikely to be segregating for two different genetic forms of the phenotype. In such cases, large pedigrees are advantageous because they may be big enough, individually, to definitively demonstrate or exclude linkage. Hence, heterogeneity is considerably easier to detect in large pedigrees than in a mixed group of smaller pedigrees.

If the phenotype is rare and extreme compared to the "average" alcoholic family, genetic heterogeneity for the phenotype is less likely than if the phenotype is similar to more common phenotypes. This, again, was the case for FH and was an important facet in unraveling the defect. The study of alcoholism could benefit from the same sort of very rare phenotype, if one exists, even if that phenotype cannot be considered, by any means, to be "typical" of the more common version of the disease.

It is also important at this stage to make any decisions about the subtyping of pedigrees, as differences in severity of phenotype, age of onset, or other symptoms may be indicative of genetic heterogeneity. The presence of subtypes may indicate genetic heterogeneity of the disorder. Even mildly different phenotypes in different sets of families may be indicative of genetic heterogeneity; a recent report of heterogeneity of linkage of Charcot-Marie-Tooth disease to chromosomes 1 and 17 has indicated that the families with linkage to chromosome 1 show a more severe form of the disease than families with linkage to chromosome 17 (Chance et al. 1989).

Linkage analysis can be performed on predefined subgroups of pedigrees, but only if the assignment of each pedigree to one or more subgroup has been made irreversibly before the results of any linkage analysis for the pedigree in question are known. If pedigrees are added to or removed from a subgroup after LOD scores for those pedigrees have been computed, there is danger of allowing unconscious experimenter bias into the analysis with the possibility of achieving apparently significant, yet unconfirmable (spurious), evidence for linkage. This may explain why, after both positive (St. George-Hyslop et al. 1987; Goate et al. 1989) and negative (Pericak-Vance et al. 1988; Schellenberg et al. 1988) reports of linkage of Alzheimer's disease (AD) to chromosome 21, there is still great disagreement as to whether there is a subset of pedigrees with linkage of AD to chromosome 21 (Roses 1989; St. George-Hyslop et al. 1989).

The effect of unconscious bias can be understood as follows. Linkage analysis is carried out in a sequential manner until a significant positive or negative total LOD score is achieved on a group of pedigrees. Overall LOD scores are summed over the scores obtained for individual pedigrees. If there is an unconscious bias that causes the experimenter, for example, to include a previously excluded pedigree in a subgroup because of the sign of the LOD score obtained for that pedigree, the LOD scores obtained will be biased toward positive or negative numbers, depending on the bias. Because the sum of numbers that tend to be greater than zero will eventually reach +3.0, this could produce a situation where false evidence in favor of linkage would be produced.

This same caution holds for the assignments of phenotypes to individuals within pedigrees when the phenotype has a judgmental component to it. Once marker information has been collected on some or all individuals in the pedigree, it is very important to avoid unconscious bias in the person(s) making the diagnosis or collecting the clinical information. In practical terms, this usually means that it is useful to discourage a great deal of communication between individuals responsible for the diagnosis and for the analysis. The person collecting clinical data should not also perform the linkage analysis unless no new cases are admitted to a given pedigree once the collection of marker data has begun. Similarly, the possible effects on the LOD score of changing phenotypes of individuals should not be made available to the investigator responsible for collecting the clinical data.

Choice of Markers

Three approaches can be used to identify markers to be tested for linkage to alcoholism: (1) the random marker approach; (2) the use of several candidate loci, on the basis of current understanding of the physiology of alcoholism; and (3) the use of markers that are linked to a disease locus in animal studies. The first approach assumes no prior knowledge of the location of the locus; the latter two are different candidate gene approaches, with the third approach based on the assumption that a gene linked to a disease locus in an animal might show the same linkage in man. The candidate gene approaches have the advantage that the strength of the evidence needed to accept linkage is less than that for the random marker approach because of the high prior expectation that the candidate loci may be involved. That is, a LOD score may be statistically significant even if it is $< +3.0$. The candidate gene approaches have the following disadvantages: (1) Loci that produce operational definitions of alcoholism in animals may be irrelevant to the disease state in humans; (2) we know very little about physiological details that might provide solid candidate loci; and (3) it is less likely that we would learn something about physiology relevant to alcoholism that we do not already know. Therefore, it is likely that at least some mapping attempts will be done with the random marker approach.

For random mapping, evidence in favor of linkage must be very strong before it can be accepted. It is a waste of resources to embark on a study unless the statistical power of the study is high enough to provide some reasonable chance of success. Recently, Ploughman and Boehnke (1989) suggested that it is possible to perform a power analysis by simulation on a set of pedigrees that have already been collected. They have written a computer program, SIMLINK, to perform these computations. Although such a power analysis is rather time-consuming, it does not seem unreasonable to expect such an analysis to be performed prior to embarking on data collection and analysis that may take years. The power computations can indicate not only which pedigrees may be most or least useful for detecting linkage, but also what degree of polymorphism is needed for the marker loci to detect linkage at a specified distance.

Linkage Analyses

The final step in linkage analysis of alcoholism is the computation of LOD scores, followed by their interpretation. Computation is straightforward and will not be addressed here. If the mode of inheritance, phenotypes of individuals in the pedigrees, and subgroups of pedigrees have been established prior to any analysis, then, at most, several different analyses need to be performed, possibly under different gene frequencies and rates of sporadic affected phenotypes, if the phenotype is discrete.

Interpretation of the results is likely to be more difficult, particularly because of the high probability of both genetic heterogeneity and multifactorial inheritance involved in the disease. The results of a linkage analysis between alcoholism and a marker locus will have one of three possible outcomes for the total set of pedigrees or for some subset of pedigrees: (1) a LOD score of $> +3.0$ for some recombination fraction, indicative of linkage; (2) a nonsignificant LOD score in the range -2.0 to $+3.0$; or (3) a LOD score < -2.0 for recombination fractions below some value, usually interpreted as evidence against linkage when the locus is known or strongly suspected to be a single locus.

For single gene defects, evidence against linkage for a series of independent marker loci can be accumulated as an overall exclusion map (Edwards 1987). This can be useful for choosing markers for further typing, as markers in regions with the highest probability of showing linkage can be preferentially chosen. However, if genetic heterogeneity indicates that some, but not all, families are linked to a particular marker and if the marker is sufficiently polymorphic, the unlinked families tend to show sufficiently strong evidence against linkage; therefore, the conclusion of no linkage for the whole set may be obtained. For this reason, subtyping of families may be useful: Exclusion maps for the individual subtypes, as well as the whole data set, can be generated. If subtypes are more likely to be genetically homogeneous, conclusions about absence of linkage are more likely to provide a reliable exclusion map for the subtypes than for the total data set.

If linkage results are positive, either for the total data set or for some subset, confirmation of the results needs to be obtained from a completely independent set of pedigrees that have the same phenotype. If the phenotype is a qualitative affected/unaffected phenotype with reduced penetrance, it is also useful to reanalyze the data under the assumption of close to 0% penetrance because this will expose any weakness in the assumption about the mode of inheritance.

Finally, if independent confirmation is not possible, it will probably be necessary to establish a collaborative effort to evaluate all of the data used both to establish and to reject evidence for linkage. This may involve exchange of DNA as well as an independent (and blind) reevaluation of some or all pedigree members to determine whether such failure to replicate the results is due to some subtle difference in phenotype definition or to either genetic heterogeneity or chance.

CONCLUSIONS

It may be possible to eventually map the gene(s) involved in susceptibility to alcoholism and determine the functions of the gene(s) involved. However, this will probably involve the definition of better phenotypes, careful attention to possible phenotypic heterogeneity, and avoidance of all sources of human bias. Alcoholism is likely to be a heterogeneous disease and is likely to require considerably more care than simpler genetic diseases in terms of experimental design, establishing diagnostic criteria ahead of time, and interpretation of the final results.

ACKNOWLEDGMENTS

This work was supported in part by National Institute of Health grants AG-05136 and HHLBI HL-3-0086.

REFERENCES

Boehnke, N. and P.P. Moll. 1989. Identifying pedigrees segregating at a major locus for a quantitative trait: An efficient strategy for linkage analysis. *Am. J. Hum. Genet.* **44:** 216.

Boerwinkle, E. and C.F. Sing. 1987. The use of measured genotype information in the analysis of quantitative phenotypes in man. III. Simultaneous estimation of the frequencies and effects of the apolipoprotein E polymorphism and residual polygenetic effects on cholesterol, betalipoprotein and triglyceride levels. *Ann. Hum. Genet.* **51:** 211.

Boerwinkle, E., S. Visvikis, D. Welsh, J. Steinmetz, S.N. Hanash, and C.F. Sing. 1987. The use of measured genotype information in the analysis of quantitative phenotypes in man. II. The role of the apolipoprotein E polymorphism in determining levels, variablity, and covariability of cholesterol, betalipoprotein, and triglycerides in a sample of unrelated individuals. *Am. J. Med. Genet.* **27:** 567.

Brown, M.S. and J.L. Goldstein. 1986. A receptor-mediated pathway for cholesterol homeostasis. *Science* **232:** 34.

Chance, P.F., T.D. Bird, D. Atkinson, P. O'Connell, M. Leppert, H. Lipe, R. Ketting, J.-M. Lalouel, and R.W. White. 1989. Linkage evidence for genetic heterogeneity in type I Charcot-Marie-Tooth neuropathy. *Am. J. Hum. Genet.* **45:** A135.

Edwards, J. 1987. Exclusion mapping. *J. Med. Genet.* **24:** 539.

Goate, A.M., A.R. Haynes, M.J. Owen, M. Farrall, L.A. James, L.Y. Lai, J.J. Mullan, P. Roques, M.N. Rosser, and R. Williamson. 1989. Predisposing locus for AD on chromosome 21. *Lancet* **I:** 352.

Greenberg, D. and S. Hodge. 1989. Linkage analysis under "random" and "genetic" reduced penetrance. *Genet. Epidemiol.* **6:** 259.

Kunkel, L.M., et al. (including 73 contributors from 25 different centers). 1986. Analysis of deletions in DNA from patients with Becker and Duchenne muscular dystrophy. *Nature* **322:** 73.

Monaco, A.P., C.J. Bertelson, W. Middlesworth, C.-A. Colletti, J. Aldridge, K.H. Fischbeck, R. Bartlett, M.A. Pericak-Vance, A.D. Roses, and L.M. Kunkel. 1985. Detection of deletions spanning the Duchenne muscular dystrophy locus using a tightly linked DNA segment. *Nature* **316:** 842.

Morton, N.E. 1956. The detection and estimation of linkage between the genes for elliptocytosis and the Rh blood type. *Am. J. Hum. Genet.* **8:** 80.

Ott, J. 1977. Counting methods (EM algorithm) in human pedigree analysis: Linkage and segregation analysis. *Ann. Hum. Genet.* **40:** 443.

―――. 1985. *Analysis of human genetic linkage.* The Johns Hopkins University Press, Baltimore.

Pericak-Vance, J.A., L.H. Yamaoka, C.S. Haynes, M.C. Speer, J.L. Haines, P.C. Gaskell, W.-Y. Hung, C.M. Clark, A.L. Heyman, J.A. Trofatter, J.P. Eisenmenger, J.R. Gilbert, J.E. Lee, M.J. Alberts, D.V. Dawson, R.J. Bartlett, N.L. Earl, T. Siddique, J.M. Vance, P.M. Conneally, and A.D. Roses. 1988. Genetic linkage studies in Alzheimer's disease. *Ann. Neurol.* **19:** 415.

Ploughman, L. and M. Boehnke. 1989. Estimating the power of a proposed linkage study of a complex genetic trait. *Am. J. Hum. Genet.* **44:** 543.

Ray, P.N., B. Belfall, C. Duff, C. Logan, V. Kean, M.W. Thompson, J.E. Sylvester, J.L. Gorski, R.D. Schmickel, and R.G. Worton. 1985. Cloning of the breakpoint of an X:21 translocation associated with Duchenne muscular dystrophy. *Nature* **318:** 672.

Riordan, J.R., J.M. Rommens, B.-S. Kerem, N. Alon, R. Rozmahel, Z. Grzelczak, J. Zielenski, S. Lok, N. Plavsic, J.-L. Chou, M.L. Drumm, M.C. Iannuzzi, F.S. Collins, and L.-C. Tsui. 1989. Identification of the cystic fibrosis gene: Cloning and characterization of complementary DNA. *Science* **245:** 1066.

Risch, N. 1988. A new statistical test for linkage heterogeneity. *Am. J. Hum. Genet.* **42:** 353.

Risch, N. and M. Baron. 1982. X-linkage and genetic heterogeneity in bipolar related major affective illness: Reanalysis of linkage data. *Ann. Hum. Genet.* **46:** 153.

Rommens, J.M., M.C. Iannuzzi, B.-S. Kerem, M.L. Drumm, G. Melmer, M. Dean,

R. Rozmahel, J.L. Cole, D. Kennedy, N. Hidaka, M. Zsiga, M. Buchwald, J.E. Riordan, L.-C. Twui, and F.S. Collins. 1989. Identification of the cystic fibrosis gene: Chromosome walking and jumping. *Science* **245:** 1059.

Roses, A.D. 1989. A conservative viewpoint on linkage in Alzheimer's disease. *Neurobiol. Aging* **10:** 427.

Schellenberg, G.D., T.D. Bird, E.M. Wijsman, D.K. Moore, M. Boehnke, E.M. Bryant, T.H. Lampe, D. Nochlin, S.M. Sumi, S.S. Deeb, K. Beyreuther, and G.M. Martin. 1988. Absence of linkage of chromosome 21q21 markers to familial Alzheimer's disease. *Science* **241:** 1507.

St. George-Hyslop, P.H., R.H. Meyers, J.L. Haines, L.A. Farrer, R.E. Tanzi, K. Abe, M.F. James, P.M. Conneally, R. Polinsky, and J.F. Gusella. 1989. Familial Alzheimer's disease: Progress and problems. *Neurobiol. Aging* **10:** 417.

St. George-Hyslop, P., R. Tanzi, R. Polinsky, J.L. Haines, L. Nee, P.C. Watkins, R.H. Meyers, R.G. Feldman, D. Pollen, D. Drachman, J. Growdonn, A. Bruni, J.F. Foncin, G. Salmon, P. Fromheld, L. Amaducci, S. Sorgi, S. Placentini, D. Stewart, W. Hobbs, P.M. Conneally, and J.F. Gusella. 1987. The genetic defect causing Alzheimer disease maps on chromosome 21. *Science* **234:** 885.

Utermann, G., F. Hoppichler, H. Dieplinger, M. Seed, G. Thompson, and E. Boerwinkle. 1989. Defects in the low density lipoprotein receptor gene affect lipoprotein (a) levels: Multiplicative interaction of two gene loci associated with premature atherosclerosis. *Proc. Natl. Acad. Sci.* **86:** 4171.

Genetic Linkage Analysis under Uncertain Disease Definition

JURG OTT
Columbia University
New York, New York 10032

Carrying out genetic analyses of alcoholism poses problems similar to those encountered in many diseases, e.g., in schizophrenia and other mental disorders. One of the problems is that the mode of inheritance of these diseases is unknown, although involvement of some genetic factors appears quite convincing. Another problem relates to the definition of disease phenotypes, affected and unaffected: It is often unclear which disease classification is genetically most relevant. Possible ways of dealing with this second problem of classification are proposed in this paper, where it is assumed, for argument's sake, that the disease in question is, at least partially, under the influence of a single gene.

Affection status is usually based on certain well-defined rules (medical classification systems). Classification of cases near the boundary between affected and unaffected often appears somewhat equivocal. Therefore, linkage analyses sometimes are carried out for several different classification schemes, because one does not want to run the risk of restricting the analysis to a diagnostic scheme in which the phenotype categories poorly reflect underlying genotypes. On the other hand, one has to be aware that carrying out linkage analyses for several diagnostic schemes and reporting the overall maximum LOD score will lead to an inflation of that score and, thus, the evidence for linkage (J. Ott et al., in prep.). Instead of using several different schemes of defining affected and unaffected cases, one might disregard information from questionable cases, i.e., distinguish known affected and unaffected cases and define every other case as having phenotype *unknown*. Such a coding scheme was used, for example, in an analysis of familial osteoarthrosis (Palotie et al. 1989). This approach largely avoids possible misclassifications.

An extension of the three-class system, affected, unknown, and unaffected, to a larger number of phenotype classes is possible when a hierarchical classification scheme is employed so that phenotypes range more gradually from one extreme (known affected) to the other (known unaffected). This is discussed below (see Equivocal Affection Status).

Biological Variables

In addition to those variables used to directly define affection status, other variables may be correlated with the disease and may be used as indicators of disease status. Such concomitant variables are also called biological variables or endophenotypes. The hope is that they may reflect underlying genotypes more closely and show higher penetrance than the affection status categories. That is, they should be *trait*-related and not simply *state*-related. A variable that is state-related is not very useful for genetic analyses because it is a consequence of being affected rather than being an expression of the underlying disease genotype. To judge the usefulness of a biological variable and avoid problems of state relatedness, one might examine its distribution among unaffected relatives of affected individuals. A biological variable that is indicative of the genotype should then occur in two clusters, corresponding to gene carriers and noncarriers. For example, if some enzyme level is such a biological variable, it should ideally have a bimodal distribution among unaffected close relatives of known affected individuals. A well-known example is the distribution of the creatine kinase (CK) levels in female members of families segregating for the X-linked gene for Duchenne muscular dystrophy: Generally, if a cutoff point between a normal and elevated level is chosen so that only 5% of noncarriers show an elevated CK level, approximately two-thirds of carriers have elevated CK levels.

One possible endophenotype is the subjective impression of a physician. Although this is not a very objective criterion, subjective judgments may be very useful, as they may indicate some as yet unmeasurable quantity. As long as subjective judgments are given independently of variables already taken into account, they may be used the same way as one would classify equivocal disease cases as probably affected or highly probably affected, etc. For example, consider an older, phenotypically questionable individual at risk for a dominant disease with age-dependent penetrance. On the basis of the appearance of the individual, one may have the impression that he or she is likely to be unaffected, but this impression should not be based on the individual's advanced age, as age-dependent penetrances are already taken into account in the linkage analysis. The following simple scheme for implementing levels of belief and a larger number of hierarchical affection status classes is proposed.

Equivocal Affection Status

Consider the penetrances displayed in Table 1. They represent conditional probabilities of a phenotype, given an individual's genotype at an assumed dominantly inherited disease. The two extreme, unequivocal phenotypes are affected and unaffected (for penetrances other than 0 and 1, see below). Equivocal phenotype classes and their associated penetrances may now be defined by attaching weights (w) to the two extreme classes and forming a weighted average penetrance, i.e., by multiplying the penetrances for affect-

Table 1
Example Penetrances for Phenotypes of Known and Uncertain Affection Status

	Phenotype			
Genotype	affected	unaffected	unknown	affected (80% certain)
D/D	1	0	0.5	0.8
D/d	1	0	0.5	0.8
d/d	0	1	0.5	0.2

ed by w and those for unaffected by $1 - w$ and summing the two results. A trivial compound phenotype, unknown, is obtained with $w=0.5$ (any phenotype with penetrances all equal represents unknown). If the consensus is that a certain equivocal individual should be scored as affected, with 80% confidence, the appropriate weight is $w=0.8$, resulting in the right-most phenotype category of Table 1.

In many diseases, including alcoholism, penetrance is reduced and age-dependent. Then, e.g., the affected phenotype may be characterized by penetrances of $t, t, 0$ instead of 1, 1, 0 and, correspondingly, penetrances for unaffected are $1 - t, 1 - t, 1$. Starting from these two phenotypes as the extreme classes, one may proceed exactly as before by attaching weights w and $1 - w$ to the affected and unaffected penetrances and forming a weighted average. For example, an individual likely to be affected (80% level of belief) then has a penetrance of $0.8t + 0.2(1 - t)$, given the genotypes D/D or D/d. Although this approach is intuitively appealing, its statistical basis has not yet been formulated.

Inclusion of additional independently acting variables does not represent a problem. For example, if an enzyme level such as the CK values in Duchenne muscular dystrophy discriminates probabilistically between carriers and non-carriers of the putative disease gene, a given observed level may be associated with penetrances f_1, f_1, f_2. These penetrances may then simply be multiplied into the penetrances for an equivocal phenotype so that, e.g., one obtains $f_1(0.8t + 0.2[1-t])$ for the D/D or D/d genotypes. If the resulting penetrances become very small, it may be convenient to rescale them by a constant factor so that, e.g., they sum to 1 for each phenotype. Although such rescaling will affect the likelihood, $L(\theta)$, where θ = recombination fraction, it will have no effect on the likelihood ratio, $L(\theta)/L(1/2)$, or the location or LOD scores in linkage analysis. Only the ratios of the penetrances for the various genotypes, not the actual penetrance values, are relevant for linkage analysis.

The analysis techniques discussed above centered around the concept of a qualitative phenotype with two classes, affected and unaffected, which was extended to allow for the effect of biological variables. Alternatively, one may want to work directly with those variables that are used to define affection status in the first place, e.g., amount of alcohol consumed per day and number of days absent from workplace. These variables would then either be combined by forming a weighted sum, which would serve as a qualitative phenotype, discriminating well between carriers and noncarriers of the putative single gene, or the variables could be used directly as a multivariate phenotype with different mean vectors for the different genotypes. Means and covariances would have to be estimated before the analysis. On statistical grounds, the latter approach appears most promising, but it may require more data and parameter estimates that may not be readily available.

Risk Factors

Environmental risk or stress factors are conditions that predispose individuals to disease. For example, a worker in a distillery may be more prone to alcoholism than other people. If that worker is genetically susceptible to alcoholism, he may succumb to the disease more readily than other genetically susceptible individuals who are not exposed to the particular predisposing environment. On the other hand, if someone does not develop alcoholism despite being exposed to a high-risk environment, it is more likely that he or she is not genetically at risk.

Risk factors influence expression of a genotype, and endophenotypes are expressions of the genotype; there may also be interactions between risk factors and endophenotypes. Despite the differences between these two classes of variables, the effects of risk factors may be taken into account by techniques similar to those outlined above, i.e., by suitably modifying penetrances. One current technique is to increase the current age of an individual, for analysis purposes. The situation of an individual subjected to a more stressful environment is then considered to be analogous to that of an individual at higher age but free of the stress factors. Equivalently, the current age of someone living in a particularly low-risk environment may be decreased for analytical purposes.

A more general approach might be to define different penetrance functions (age-of-onset curves) for different environments. The particular form of the age-dependent penetrance function will depend on the influences of the various environments under consideration. For example, if someone lives under a very protective environment in which access to alcoholic beverages is practically impossible, the corresponding penetrance function would be almost flat for gene carriers and essentially zero for noncarriers of all ages. In such a situation, unaffected individuals of any age are practically uninformative for linkage, and all information will come from affected individuals. Due to the low penetrance, there may only be a small number of affected individuals so that a very protective environment may furnish little information for linkage analysis.

ACKNOWLEDGMENTS

This work has been supported by grant MH-44292 from the National Institute of Mental Health and by the W.M. Keck Foundation. Fruitful discussions with Dr. Daniel Weeks are gratefully acknowledged.

REFERENCES

Palotie, A., P. Väisänen, J. Ott, L. Ryhänen, K. Elima, M. Vikkula, K. Cheah, E. Vuorio, and L. Peltonen. 1989. Predisposition to familial osteoarthrosis linked to type II collagen gene. *Lancet* **I**: 924.

Brewing Genes and Behavior: The Potential Consequences of Genetic Screening for Alcoholism

PAUL R. BILLINGS
Department of Medicine
Harvard Medical School
Boston, Massachusetts 02115

OVERVIEW

Major genes associated with human alcohol addiction and its medical complications may be discovered. Screening programs to identify alcoholics or those susceptible to this disorder using genetic tests could then be proposed. The predictive value of genetic tests for alcoholism will likely be low, given known environmental modifiers. Individuals with genetic conditions currently experience prejudices arising from misconceptions about the importance of genes in disease causation. Practically, this results in discriminatory practices in insurance procurement, employment, adoption eligibility, and the availability of other social entitlements. Prior to establishing genetically based screening programs for alcoholism, it will be necessary to investigate the effectiveness and social outcomes of testing for behavioral traits and to improve "genetic public education."

INTRODUCTION

There is burgeoning interest in the role of genes in the development of human disease. Research efforts to identify major genes for rare and common disorders have been fueled by (1) rapid advances in the methods used to study specific genes and DNA biochemistry; (2) increased sophistication in genetic epidemiology and linkage analysis; (3) success in identifying the genes for certain disorders (e.g., phenylketonuria, muscular dystrophy, cystic fibrosis, and retinoblastoma); and (4) a significant increase in funding of genetic investigations by the federal government, private foundations, and biotechnology companies.

Not only are relatively rare Mendelian disorders being investigated, but major genes producing common human conditions such as behavioral disorders, heart disease, cancer, and hypertension are also being sought. It is notable that (1) this research makes genetic explanations of disease of interest to larger fractions of the population; (2) management of genetically based common diseases is a potential source of immense profits for physicians and industry; and (3) for each of these common ailments, causative associations with disease-producing environmental factors are already established.

Although the importance of environmental and nongenetically determined factors in disease causation has been shown, the media and the public remain enthralled by the inherited aspects of illness. This persistent public fascination with genetics may arise from a deep-seated desire to attribute seemingly inexplicable human characteristics and behaviors (such as alcohol addiction) to one's inevitable and uncontrollable ancestral inheritance—the genes. It may seem possible to escape personal responsibility for disappointing aspects of life or personal failures, or to avoid facing the inevitability of illness and death by studying, investing in, and, at times, blaming genes (Billings 1989). Geneticists' routine exaggeration of the importance and promise of their work is accepted by this receptive public.

Research in alcoholism has many similarities to work on other common disorders. Alcoholism's impact in terms of morbidity and mortality on individuals, and its socioeconomic effect on our country as a whole, are significant. Many alcoholics wish to be cured of their addiction; they also wish to prevent the stigmatization of their family that results from their alcoholism. In addition, insurers, employers, governments, physicians, educators, and others may benefit from the study of this disorder and the development of a predictive test for individuals likely to become alcohol abusers. Unfortunately, past conflicts in scientific, social, economic, political, cultural, and personal viewpoints have obfuscated definitions of and investigations into alcoholism and alcohol abuse.

Alcoholism has been difficult to define precisely; criteria vary among studies. Despite this uncertainty, alcoholism is widely assumed to have a determined, genetic etiology. This position has arisen in part from the "blaming the genes" trend (see above) but is also supported by adoption and twin studies (Goodwin et al. 1974; Cloninger et al. 1981; Schuckit 1981; Gurling 1984). The problems with this work have been reviewed (Murray et al. 1983; Lester 1988; Searles 1988). These studies do not support the hypothesis that there is a simple genetic cause of alcoholism.

Because of the high prevalence of alcoholism, if a genetic test for this disorder were universally applied, the program would likely identify 10–30% of the population as being ill or disease susceptible. The social, political, and economic consequences of genetic screening for alcoholism would therefore be significant. Given this situation, three questions arise in considering the genetic analysis of alcoholism:

1. Is development of a genetic test for alcoholism likely?
2. Does the history of behavioral genetics in general, and of alcohol research in particular, suggest concerns in applying genetic analyses to human behaviors?

3. What are the current problems experienced by nonclinically disabled individuals diagnosed with genetic conditions (a group I have called the "asymptomatic ill") (P. Billings et al., unpubl.), a situation common in preclinical or sober alcoholics?

In discussing these questions, I use case material from my medical genetics practice whenever possible.

RESULTS AND DISCUSSION

Is a Genetic Test for Alcoholism Likely?

The recent experiments of Yoshida and collaborators (Shibuya and Yoshida 1988a) on the genes encoding the aldehyde dehydrogenase enzyme confirm earlier work of Goedde et al. (1979) and support the hypothesis that the genes regulating the metabolism of alcohol could play a role in alcoholism. Mutant alleles affecting the enzymes, cofactors, and receptors involved in alcohol processing by the human body may influence alcohol ingestion or its effects.

However, the environmental context in which genetic variation is measured is usually important, as indicated by the aldehyde dehydrogenase findings. The predisposing genotype in Japanese subjects is not associated with alcoholism in the United States. A different isoenzyme pattern (and presumably genotype) is more common in British alcoholics than in nonalcoholic controls, and the "flushing response" cannot explain the aversion to alcohol in Caucasians. These results already suggest that genetic heterogeneity, modifier genes, and important epigenetic and environmental factors influence the expression of clinical alcoholism. The predictive accuracy of a genetically-based test, given these numerous modifying factors (biological, cultural, economic, etc.), will likely be low.

Table 1 suggests other approaches that may yield genes and genetically-based tests relevant to clinical alcoholism. Of particular importance are the rodent models, which already suggest that genetic factors influence preference and acceptance of diets containing alcohol. Extensive gene mapping has been completed in rodents and humans, and syntenic genetic relationships have been demonstrated. Testable genetic influences in rodent models may therefore quickly lead to identification of human genes that can be assessed in clinical alcoholism. As in human studies using identical twins, genetic variation in inbred animals at modifying genetic loci may be restricted, producing unusual "genetic background" effects. This background homogeneity may distort genetic findings, exaggerating the influence of genes in animal models. Variation *within* inbred animal strains with respect to alcohol consumption is

Table 1
Hypothetical Major Genes Influencing Alcoholism

Source	Examples
1. Metabolic pathway(s) of alcohol	alcohol dehydrogenase aldehyde dehydrogenase
2. Animal models	C57BL/6 insensitivity to 10% alcohol diet
3. Major psychiatric disorders	manic depressive illness schizophrenia obsessive compulsive disorder
4. Variability in alcohol-induced disorders	cirrhosis (liver) Korsakoff's syndrome/Wernicke's encephalopathy (brain) cardiomyopathy (heart) fetal alcohol effects (fetus)
5. Variability in alcohol treatment responses	alcohol tolerance suggests action of endogenous opioid/antianxiety agents and their receptors pharmacologic measures fail to control alcohol withdrawal in some individuals
6. Chromosomal disorders	dysmorphic psychiatric/alcoholic patients familial alcoholism

important and may be attributable to many somatic, developmental, and environmental factors (Dole et al. 1988).

Each of the sources noted in Table 1 may yield one or more genetically based test(s) that could prove relevant to the care of certain alcoholic subjects or those predisposed to alcoholism. There is no current evidence that any of these potential lines of experimentation (or others) will yield a major gene that might be predictive of most or all of alcoholism in this country. In fact, the major contribution of genetic analyses of most common disorders, particularly of behavior, may be to help create subgroups of individuals who share a particular genotype, and on whom further clinical studies, including variation in disease expression and outcome, can be done. Clinically important subgroups are already suggested by the findings that alcoholics who flush may have a different likelihood for developing liver disease than those who do not (Orientals) (Shibuya and Yoshida 1988b) and that alcoholics with other major psychiatric disorders have poor clinical outcomes when compared to those not afflicted with other conditions (Powell et al. 1982; Mirin 1984; Richard et al. 1985; Safer 1987; Rounsaville et al. 1987).

If common sense dictates that the study of alcohol metabolism and animal models of alcoholism will likely yield genetically based tests with possible relevance to human alcoholism, then what should be the goals in applying these tests?

1. *An increase in basic understanding of the etiology of alcoholism.* Knowledge of the precise genetic mutation producing a disease susceptibility does not always yield information about disease causation. The precise genetic lesion in the condition sickle cell anemia has been known for more than 20 years. This knowledge has not been accompanied by great progress in understanding how the mutant hemoglobin produces disease or in the clinical care of this condition. In fact, developments in infectious disease treatments and transfusion medicine have been more crucial to the care of individuals with sickle cell anemia than knowledge of the genetic lesion. Similarly, the role of the dystrophin gene in muscular dystrophy will not likely explain why about one third of affected boys with Duchenne muscular dystrophy are mentally retarded. All individuals with this disorder (to date) have abnormalities in dystrophin expression (Kunkel 1986; Bonilla et al. 1988). Genetic insights do not always lead quickly or directly to useful information about a disease.
2. *To develop new prevention or treatment approaches.* This is a *prerequisite* for any universal genetic screening program. Without effective preventive or therapeutic schemes, there is little chance that genetic screening will be successful or satisfactory to the general public. If a genetic test were developed for alcoholism, not only would its validity need to be demonstrated on large and diverse populations, but also those individuals identified by the test would need to have a proven plan to lessen or avert the possibility that their genetic predisposition would lead to clinical disease. At present, failures in preventing and treating alcoholism are common and do not offer enough hope to justify the identification of all individuals who are susceptible to the disease.

The American experience with alcohol prohibition laws suggests that environmental approaches to controlling alcoholism need renewed study. In other disorders influenced by genes, the importance of environmentally based treatment approaches is clear. In phenylketonuria (PKU), an illness that can severely affect mentation and behavior, compliance with and the availability of a phenylalanine-restricted diet are essential to treatment of affected individuals (Scriver et al. 1989). Those receiving adequate early care have no genetic reason for continued illness. Similarly, the societal response to hereditary deafness in Martha's Vineyard suggests the range

and effectiveness of cultural approaches that may ameliorate devastating hereditary conditions (Groce 1985).
3. *To establish clinical and genotypic correlations.* A definition of alcoholism based on genotypes and clinical manifestations may arise. Such a definition may produce less measurement bias and observer variability than previous descriptions of alcoholism.

That these important goals need to be cautiously pursued is illustrated by a recent CBS radio report of a "new genetic test for alcoholism." This story suggested that a validated test predicting alcoholism was ready for clinical use. Press reports often ignore scientists' comments emphasizing the limitations and/or preliminary nature of published data offered. Such stories can create expectations that tests for a disorder will soon be available and helpful. Yet review of the article from which the news report was drawn indicates that the distortion did not arise in the popular press. The research authors state, "The new data are also anticipated to be of value in identifying subjects at risk, in guiding genetic counseling, and in developing effective therapies for alcohol-dependent subjects" (Mueller et al. 1988). Surely, it is unrealistic to expect reporters to verify this statement. Comments like these in research reports may also foster unrealistic expectations in the public, and reflect pressure on investigators to overstate the findings of experiments and their importance. There is no indication that genetic counselors should advise alcoholic clients or their families to undergo testing. As genetic approaches are applied to alcoholism, investigators must take a leading role in educating the public on the limitations of their work and the slow course of scientific and medical investigation.

Does the History of Genetics Suggest Problems in Studying Human Behavior and Alcoholism?

Comprehensive reviews of this subject exist (Lewontin et al. 1984; Vogel and Motulsky 1986). Certain points deserve reemphasis:

1. Misuse of behavioral genetic research results has occurred. Immigration laws and decisions allowing sterilization of the mentally retarded in the United States and sterilization of alcoholics in Germany, and current socioeconomic incentives for selective mating (based, in part, on behavioral traits) in Singapore and Malaysia demonstrate past and current problems. The societal forces that foster and promote eugenic thinking are poorly understood and require further investigation. Before genetic screening is universally applied, greater understanding of eugenic uses of data and mechanisms to lessen its pernicious impact need to be identified.
2. The study of behavioral genetics can be historically divided into the

genetic evaluation of normal development and intelligence, and the study of behavioral disorders. Within each of these fields, problems have arisen in the normal process of scientific investigation, verification, and clinical application. The premature and overzealous interpretation of hereditary influences on the performance of individuals on "intelligence tests" in order to influence educational programs and the purported genetic predisposition to criminality of males with the karyotype 47 XYY are examples of such problems.
3. There have been several widely quoted studies within the field of behavioral genetics that have proven to be incorrect or false. Sir Cyril Burt's data on intelligence in twins, the linkage of ABO blood group antigens to social class demographics, the linkage of manic depressive illness to chromosome 6 and 11, and the chromosome 5 linkage of schizophrenia are examples of published data being incorrect, prematurely considered verified, or too broadly interpreted to the public. It is possible that these problems are peculiar in their type, frequency, or in extent of public knowledge to the field of behavioral genetics.

Other illustrations of current problems in this field include:

1. While discussing the genetics of behavior and the usefulness of twin methods on the national television show *Nightline*, Dr. Thomas Bouchard, Jr., the "leader of the largest study of human behavior using identical twins ever" stated that his project had produced "more than thirty publications" to support his widely reprinted claim of genetic influences on behaviors such as aggressivity, creativity, traditionality, and toilet training. Dr. Bouchard repeatedly noted that most of the behaviors their group studied were "about fifty percent genetic," suggesting that tests of the genes involved in behavioral traits are possible and made more imminent by the Minnesota group's work.

    Review of Dr. Bouchard's project publication list as of October, 1989 (for the period, 1981–1989) reveals that only 6 of the total of 29 articles in print (in English) concern behavior and appear in peer-reviewed journals. Furthermore, none allows an appraisal of the twin method used; this type of study has frequently been invalidated by significant biases (Kamin 1974; Feldman and Lewontin 1975; Hrubec and Robinette 1984). Nonetheless, this project and its striking conclusions have been the subject of articles in most of the widely circulated popular national periodicals (Dusek 1987). A tradition of premature publicity and overinterpretation of data may continue to bedevil behavioral genetics and create conditions producing misuses of preliminary information.
2. A recent headline in a widely circulated governmentally produced mental health newspaper announced, "Gene for Schizophrenia Found." When a

justification for this incorrect interpretation of a recent publication (Sherrington et al. 1988) was solicited, the publisher of the paper noted that the journal was read by legislators who might be influenced to fund biological behavioral research rather than studies on "schizophrenogenic mothers." A gene would reduce the guilt, stigma, and prejudice faced by families affected by schizophrenia.

Unfortunately, hereditary explanations are associated with stigmas (see below) and, in the case of this scientific report on schizophrenia, its usefulness, validity, and general applicability have been questioned (Byerley 1989). Despite good intentions, the use of unestablished or unconfirmed reports and data to influence funding and reduce the prejudice experienced by the behaviorally disordered and their relatives only replaces one "belief" system with another; it does not lead to better care or understanding of this condition or individuals affected by it. The intent of this practice seems more in the tradition of misuses of data than the normal dissemination of scientific findings.

Table 2 lists some of the parties who may be anxious to promote genetic screening programs along with potential outcomes of their development. Other investigators have come to similar conclusions (Holtzman 1989; Nelkin and Tancredi 1989). The outcomes noted are hypothetical and do not empha-

Table 2
Potential Consequences of Genetic Screening

Groups interested in expanded genetic testing	Possible outcomes
1. Affected individuals and their families	increased presymptomatic identification and abortion
2. Employers	increased preemployment screening, transfers, and terminations
3. Insurers	increased stratification and more uninsured asymptomatic individuals
4. Governments (federal/state/local)	increasing public knowledge of individual genetic makeup and eugenic social planning
5. Educational institutions	tracking based on intelligence and behavior-related genetic tests

size possible benefits to individuals from screening. It is striking that most of the groups likely to advocate genetic screening (Table 2) are usually not privy to personal medical information. Some are forbidden by law to use medical information in operating processes. Individual rights, including the confidentiality of personal medical information, may suffer when powerful interest groups (with notably poor information security) attempt to gain information about health predispositions (Marx and Sherizen 1986).

The history of human genetics is, in part, a story of a eugenic tradition. There have been persistent attempts to the present day to use the limited findings of genetic research to shape social policy and to enact social, economic, and political programs. The field of behavioral genetics contains examples of discredited scientific findings being used for nonscientific purposes. Premature publicity and distortions currently tend to foster the myths of controllability and determinism on which eugenic thinking depends. The interest of large employers, insurers, governments, and others in promoting genetic screening represents a threat to the privacy of personal health information. When personal health matters become the concern of such groups, the potential for coercion and discrimination, characteristics of eugenically influenced misuse of science, increase. Thus, the astonishing advances in molecular genetics and human genetic information are arising in a society where prejudice, discrimination, and eugenic practices can occur. Protections must be developed, studied, and in place before large populations (e.g., auto workers) undergo testing to identify a susceptibility to alcoholism.

What are the Current Consequences of Genetic Labeling?

One approach to assess the risk of widespread genetic screening is to evaluate the outcomes of current diagnostic labeling. Although the ability to make clinical decisions with DNA-based data is a relatively new phenomenon, reliable disease indicators have been available for many conditions in the presymptomatic or early clinical stages of disease. Many healthy consultees have been told that they have a gene associated with an illness after a brief clinical evaluation, primarily because the disease has been found in other family members.

In a preliminary survey conducted by mailing a solicitation to genetic counselors, a journal, and several newsletters, evidence that individuals with genetic conditions currently experience stigmatization, including genetic discrimination, was uncovered (P. Billings et al., unpubl.). Twenty-nine cases were evaluated. Nonclinically disabled individuals labeled with predispositions to illness (often based in part on family history information) report difficulties in adopting children, finding or changing the site or type of employment, and garnering the full range of social entitlements, including insurance. Even when effective preventive or therapeutic measures are used to lessen or abrogate the expression of a gene (e.g., the use of phlebotomies in hemochromatosis or dietary treatment in PKU), those asymptomatic individuals labeled as genetically ill are often unable to procure entitlements. The intercession of medical professionals is generally ineffective in reversing the process of stripping these individuals of social protections. Close family relatives of those identified with genetic predispositions also may experience prejudice as if they are disabled or ill. Despite laws prohibiting discrimination, law enforcement is difficult and ineffective. Individuals who experience discrimination are afraid or financially unable to make legal appeals. Genetic discrimination may occur when illness and handicap are believed to arise from a gene(s) and to be transmitted intrafamilially (including to nongenetically related relatives, i.e., spouses).

Another troubling aspect of current responses to the hereditary nature of certain illnesses and genetic diagnostic labeling is illustrated by the following case:

> Mr. X, a recent arrival to our state, is a 25-year-old accountant who visits the office for a general physical exam. He reports a family history of alcoholism and several arrests, brawls with trauma, a divorce, and job termination because of alcoholism in another state. He currently has been sober for one and a half years. He takes Antabuse, a medication causing alcohol aversion, daily. Mr. X requested during his visit that I not note his alcoholism as a diagnosis on any document that would leave my office. He mentioned that his previous employer had learned of his condition through an insurance company document. I represcribed his medication, which is routinely used only in treating alcohol addiction. Mr. X called my office the next day to inform me that if he had filled his prescription at the pharmacy where his insurer covered part of the cost of medication, the exact type of medication he was ordering would be recorded in a computer file available to the insurer. This might violate the confidentiality he had requested. He paid for the medication at a pharmacy unaffiliated with his insurer.

Private medical information, including diagnostic information about genetic conditions, is already stored outside of the office medical record (Dezell 1984; Norton 1989). Insurers, employers through collaborating insurance representatives, and others may gain access to this information for a fee. Many individuals with such records are not aware that they exist, have not consented to their storage, and do not know that they may be used when applications for insurance are initiated. Although safeguards have been established to ensure that current and correct information is present in these files, if their existence is generally not known, their content cannot be effectively challenged by the subject of the file. Furthermore, the company maintaining these files does not guarantee the correctness of the diagnoses within its records.

An individual with a hereditary biochemical illness was listed as having a "blood disorder, non-specified type" in an M.I.B., Inc. record and was denied all coverages.

It would not be difficult to store information on large numbers of individuals with alcoholism, irrespective of their current behaviors and sobriety, without mentioning the disease directly. For instance, alcoholics could be listed under "toxic disorder" of a particular organ affected by alcohol (brain, heart, liver, pancreas, etc.). In addition, the current system for reimbursing physicians promotes violations of the confidentiality of medical information. Physicians are not paid unless they attach a diagnosis to third-party billing information. The more serious or chronic the disorder indicated, the better likelihood of adequate payment. This information is subject to review by nonmedical personnel and storage by insurance company computers. The entire process often occurs without patient knowledge or consent. The potential for significant violations of privacy rights and abuse resulting in discrimination are obvious.

It is apparent that current understanding of genetics and our system of medical practice can generate cases of prejudicial treatment and frank discrimination directed at those with genetic conditions seeking jobs, insurance, and other social entitlements. The explosion of genetic information and the social/economic/political forces promoting its use will not reduce the incidence of these serious problems in the future. Current laws are ineffective in preventing problems, because the laws are not enforced and victims are afraid to seek legal redress. If genetic testing for alcoholism were to be developed, many healthy individuals would likely suffer serious and destructive social consequences directed against those with hereditary disorders.

CONCLUSIONS

Exciting advances in genetic methods are being applied to the study of alcoholism. New etiological hypotheses, clinical approaches, and tests relevant to the disorder will likely arise. Whether a genetically based test will be found that can predict susceptibility to alcoholism in the general population is uncertain.

Both historical trends and current practices suggest caution in applying new genetic tests to behavioral disorders. Unacceptable outcomes of genetic screening programs—including prejudice, stigmatization, and discrimination—occur when new tests are not properly validated, when preventive and/or therapeutic options are inadequate, and when the decision to undergo testing is significantly influenced by nonmedical considerations (e.g., the desire to get or retain a job or to secure personal rights). These conditions are currently extant and require further study and modification before screening programs are attempted.

Research in alcoholism should include studies delineating the potential misuses of hereditary information in this disorder. Several other changes in the environment in which genetic research is currently conducted might lessen the risks posed by future genetic screening programs. First, investigators should rededicate themselves to careful science. They should take personal responsibility for educating the public about the diversity of influences producing alcohol addiction and the limited insights genetic research yields. The grandiose exaggerations that are common in grant writing and publicity surrounding new findings should be avoided. Unfortunate myths and anxieties about alcoholism and genetic information are prevalent and may be ameliorated if researchers studying alcoholism attack these problems.

Public education about genetic diversity in humans and about disease variation needs systematic and comprehensive improvement and should be the subject of active research. Ideas leading to new strategies for disease prevention and therapy, and which consider the complexity of human behavioral disorders and the important environmental determinants of these conditions, need to be fostered. Finally, statutes protecting individuals against adverse uses of genetic information in medical settings, the workplace, insurance offices, and other sites must be enacted and enforced. Only when these efforts have yielded results—when notions and conditions that lead to genetic screening failures, the misuse of genetic information, eugenics, and genetic discrimination are altered—will universal testing for inherited factors in the predisposition to alcoholism be satisfying to the consuming public.

ACKNOWLEDGMENTS

The author acknowledges Jon Beckwith and members of the Boston-based public interest cooperative, the Genetic Screening Study Group, for stimulating discussions. Julie Schneider provided excellent editorial assistance. Christine McNulty expertly prepared the manuscript.

REFERENCES

Billings, P. 1989. Responsible genetics? *Cell* **59**: 12.
Bonilla, E., C.E. Samitt, A.F. Miranda, A.P. Hays, G. Salviati, S. DiMauro, L.M. Kunkel, E.P. Hoffman, and L.P. Rowland. 1988. Duchenne muscular dystrophy: Deficiency of dystrophin at the muscle cell surface. *Cell* **54**: 447.

Byerly, W.F. 1989. Genetic linkage revisited. *Nature* **340:** 340.
Cloninger, C.R., M. Bohman, and S. Sivardsson. 1981. Inheritance of alcohol abuse: Cross-fostering analysis of adopted men. *Arch. Gen. Psychiatry* **38:** 861.
Dezell, M. 1984. It's 1984: Do you know where your medical records end up? *Boston Bus. J.* **4:** 1.
Dole, V.P., A. Ho, R.T. Gentry, and A. Chin. 1988. Toward an analogue of alcoholism in mice: Analysis of nongenetic variance in consumption of alcohol. *Proc. Natl. Acad. Sci.* **85:** 827.
Dusek, V. 1987. Bewitching science. *Sci. for the People* **19:** 19.
Feldman, M.W. and R.C. Lewtonin. 1975. The heritability hand-up. *Science* **190:** 163.
Goedde, H.W., S. Harada, and D.P. Agarwal. 1979. Racial differences in alcohol sensitivity: A new hypothesis. *Hum. Genet.* **51:** 331.
Goodwin, D.W., F. Schulsinger, N. Moller, L. Hermansen, G. Winokur, and S.B. Guze. 1974. Drinking problems in adopted and nonadopted sons of alcoholics. *Arch. Gen. Psychiatry* **31:** 164.
Groce, N.E. 1985. *Everyone here spoke sign language: Hereditary deafness on Martha's Vineyard.* Harvard University Press, Cambridge.
Gurling, H.M. 1984. Genetic epidemiology in medicine—Recent twin research. *Br. Med. J.* **288:** 3.
Holtzman, N. 1989. *Proceed with caution: The use of recombinant DNA technology for genetic testing.* Johns Hopkins University Press, Baltimore.
Hrubec, Z. and C.D. Robinette. 1984. The study of human twins in medical research. *N. Engl. J. Med.* **310:** 435.
Kamin, L. 1974. *The science and politics of I.Q.* Earlbaum Associates, Potomac.
Kunkel, L.M. 1986. Analysis of deletions in DNA from patients with Becker and Duchenne muscular dystrophy. *Nature* **322:** 73.
Lester, D. 1988. Genetic Theory: An assessment of the heritability of alcoholism. In *Theories on alcoholism* (ed. C.D. Chaudron and D.A. Walkinson), p. 1. Addiction Research Foundation, Toronto.
Lewontin, R.C., S. Rose, and L.J. Kamin. 1984. *Not in our genes: Biology, ideology and human nature.* Pantheon Books, New York.
Marx, G. and S. Sherizen. 1986. Monitoring on the job: How to protect privacy as well as property. *Tech. Rev.* **8:** 63.
Mirin, S.M., ed. 1984. *Substance abuse and psychopathology.* American Psychiatric Press, Washington, D.C.
Mueller, G.C., M.F. Fleming, M.A. LeMahieu, G.S. Lybrand, and K.J. Barry. 1988. Synthesis of phosphatidylethanol—A potential marker for adult males at risk for alcoholism. *Proc. Natl. Acad. Sci.* **85:** 9778.
Murray, R.M., C.A. Clifford, and H.M. Gurling. 1983. Twin and adoption studies: How good is the evidence for a genetic role? In *Recent developments in alcoholism* (ed. M. Galanter), vol. 1, p. 25. Plenum Press, New York.
Nelkin, D. and L. Tancredi. 1989. *Dangerous diagnostics: The social power of biological information.* Basic Books, New York.
Norton, C. 1989. Absolutely not confidential. *Hippocrates* **2:** 53.
Powell, B.J., E.C. Penick, E. Othmer, S.F. Bingham, and A.S. Rice. 1982. Prevalence of additional psychiatric syndromes among male alcoholics. *J. Clin. Psychiatry* **43:** 404.

Richard, M.L., B.I. Liskow, and P.J. Perry. 1985. Recent psychostimulant use in hospitalized schizophrenics. *J. Clin. Psychiatry* **46:** 79.

Rounsaville, B.J., Z.S. Dolinsky, T.F. Babor, and R.E. Meyer. 1987. Psychopathology as a predictor of treatment outcome in alcoholics. *Arch. Gen. Psychiatry* **44:** 505.

Safer, D. 1987. Substance abuse by young adult chronic patients. *Hosp. Community Psychiatry* **38:** 511.

Schuckit, M.A. 1981. Twin studies on substance abuse: An overview. In *Twin research: 3. Epidemiological and clinical studies* (ed. L. Gedda et al.), p. 61. A.R. Liss, New York.

Scriver, C.R., S. Kaufman, and S.L.C. Woo. 1989. The hyperphenylalaninemias. In *The metabolic basis of inherited diseases*, 6th edition. (ed. C.R. Scriver et al.), p. 495. McGraw-Hill, New York.

Searles, J.S. 1988. The role of genetics in the pathogenesis of alcoholism. *J. Abnorm. Psychol.* **97:** 153.

Sherrington, R., M. Potter, K. Dudleston, B. Barrablough, J. Wasmuth, M. Dobbs, and H. Gurling. 1988. Localisation of a susceptibility locus for schizophrenia on chromosome 5. *Nature* **336:** 164.

Shibuya, A. and A. Yoshida. 1988a. Frequency of the atypical aldehyde dehydrogenase-2 gene ($ALDH_2^2$) in Japanese and Caucasians. *Am. J. Hum. Genet.* **43:** 741.

———. 1988b. Genotypes of alcohol-metabolizing enzymes in Japanese with alcohol liver diseases: A strong association of the usual Caucasian-type aldehyde dehydrogenase gene ($ALDH_2^1$) with the disease. *Am. J. Hum. Genet.* **43:** 744.

Vogel, F. and A.G. Motulsky. 1986. *Human genetics: Problems and approaches.* Springer-Verlag, New York.

COMMENTS

Martin: I want to reiterate some points that were raised at the beginning of your talk about Tom Bouchard's work because I think you left an impression that is perhaps slightly unfair. It is important to realize that Tom Bouchard has only gotten these twins because he has made vigorous use of the press in every English-speaking country he could get. Of course, *The New York Times* is not particularly important in itself, but that story has been picked up by almost every other newspaper in the world. It is precisely through those contacts that he has found these twins.

Lander: Doesn't that methodology invalidate the study? If I write an article that says, as was written in *Discover*, "They both drink the same beer and they flush the toilet the same number of times and we're doing a study on folks like that," how in the world is this a random sample of anything?

Martin: The point is that the number of monozygotic twins reared apart in the world is very small.

Lander: And you're going to subselect those who found each other and have some interesting similarity and an interest in this study. You are guaranteeing it is going to be meaningless in any statistical sense.

Martin: I don't think there is really a sample out there from which one subsamples. He is probably getting just about complete ascertainment of all the ones that exist.

Reich: We don't know that.

Lander: I doubt that. You're saying a meaningless study is better than no study at all.

Reich: First, there is a very deep issue here that I think we have glossed over, and that has to do with advertisement by scientists, among scientists, and with respect to the general public. It is a very serious business because we can look at major findings among scientists. Who gets the credit? When does the credit go to whom? We could ask ourselves: Does the discoverer of a major discovery, let's say—or an idea, which is even harder to come by than a discovery—always get the credit? And, for the person who gets the credit, what are the elements of the credit that accrue to that individual?

There are some obvious examples all the way through the history of science, of course, from the very beginning, of the fact that it pays to advertise. In many ways they're very sad and they're very peculiar, but that's certainly true. So, our journals are not only advertisements on the advertising page, but there are advertisements on the reporting page and there are advertisements in the articles and there are advertisements among ourselves. There is a very big business there.

Second, in competing for scarce resources at the government level, it's perfectly clear that there are more piggies at the trough than there is food. We are talking business here. So, when the linear accelerator people come up against the human genome project people, they fight. In contrast, Tom Bouchard is a tyro. The truth to tell is that advertising remains, as it has been since the time of Newton, since this is the 300th anniversary of the fights that Newton had—he also had advertising battles, by the way—it obtains today.

Billings: It has been my experience in my training in genetics that there is something different about behavioral genetics. The concepts built into the society in which we are doing our research are different for issues of behavior than they are for the inheritance of any particular trait, like crooked fingers, which is a very common autosomal dominant trait.

Reich: But not cancer.

Chakravarti: I think the problem is not the risk, which is what most of the scientists are used to dealing with, but how that risk is perceived, either as or not as a burden. So, when you bring up the question of crooked fingers and cancer, those are two rather extreme cases, because, as you probably realize, even though there are very clear diagnostic tests for Down's syndrome in women at the age of 35, not everyone deals with that.

Reich: Many of us in the field go on to interact with organizations for the families of people with alcoholics and people with major mental illness. Part of their major thrust is destigmatization. What we have to do is to treat, and what we are asked to do by the consumers, if you like, is to treat mental disorders as other disorders in several important respects. One is they're not to be ashamed of it, although it takes some courage. Two, equal funding and equal support in the scientific community ought to be given to those disorders using commonly accepted public standards. So, it's not appropriate for schizophrenia or other major mental disorders to get less support than the muscular dystrophies, even though muscular dystrophy is a terrible illness and deserves a lot of work. In that context your comments about genetics and mental disorders should be balanced. I think these disorders need a lot more light, a lot more support, a lot more money, a lot more discussion, and a lot more destigmatization, if you like, in the scientific community and outside it.

Conneally: To change the subject, talking about confidentiality and people concerned about knowing their risk status, there is now presymptomatic diagnosis in Huntington's disease. In fact, approximately 40 to 50 people have been told that they have a very high probability of having the gene. Their number one overriding concern is confidentiality. They are scared stiff that their employer and their insurance company will find out about it.

Billings: Right. In the three published experiences about the Huntington's presymptomatic question (that is, the Harvard experience, the Johns Hopkins experience, and now the British experience), of the people who began the testing program, about half dropped out for a variety of reasons. Clearly, the fear of what might happen to them is one of the reasons—not only the fear of being labeled with a presumably degenerative and incurable illness, but also other kinds of more immediate and social concerns.

Cloninger: I want to make three points. One is that I think the evidence for the heritability of personality being around 50% is really very persuasive. The Bouchard experiment is more of a curiosity than it is anything that will help us to have heritability estimates. These estimates are based on very well-designed studies on thousands of pairs of twins as well as on adoptees. The estimates are fairly consistent.

The second point is that premature overstatements by scientists are not unique to people with hereditarian persuasions, but have been equally offensive by people with environmental biases. It is misleading to think that there isn't a need for balanced discussion. I think we all strive for that.

The third, and I think the most important, point is that many of your comments, Paul, could be taken to encourage repression of research and to discourage public discussion. Your very final conclusion and recommendation was for education of the public. I think the very fact that you had an opportunity with Eric and Bouchard to be on national TV to have public discussion is what we need. I think Tom sometimes does need to be questioned about possible overstatement, but, at least, you had the opportunity for open public discussion. We should take the position that we need to educate the public by having more of these things in *The New York Times* and having appropriate balanced critique, rather than to keep things from being done. That's the unhealthy undertone of many discussions about whether we should have behavioral research or not. I think it's very good that we're having more open discussion, not less.

Lander: For the record, I am just going to note, Bob, that taped footage from some entirely other subject was used. I don't know Tom Bouchard. I was not on that program nor invited to be on that program. The tape they took for some other purpose. Relevant to Paul's discussion, I want to try to rephrase in a sentence what I think we all can agree on. The purpose of understanding the hereditary basis and the environmental basis of any of these things is to get a mechanism. The more we understand about mechanism, the more we can destigmatize, the more we can think about helping. That's very good.

The problem with both political and environmental uses for hereditary arguments is that there are many people whose interest is not in understanding mechanism and therefore acting on it; it is in some sense for washing one's hands of responsibility. If something is called hereditary, this is to some people and to some politicians an excuse for saying, "I can't do anything about it." That, I think, is the line. I do not think most people here who do work on the heritability of various traits have that motivation at all. However, I do think there are folks out there who do have that motivation; for example, it's hard to look at the IQ debate and not see politicians saying, "It's heritable and therefore there's no point in putting money into these schools." That doesn't follow logically, but it follows very often in the political discussions. For the hereditary and the environmental work to move forward and to help the environment, people on both sides must say, "That is not a valid conclusion either way. We now have to draw lessons about mechanisms, we have to attempt to destigmatize." I think that is common ground that everybody, whatever their prior prejudices are, in the scientific community can agree on and can push for.

Chakravarti: Partly, the problem is that facing the public and having to explain applications of genetics for humans is also a rather new area for most people in genetics. This is part of an ongoing process. The amount of ignorance on the part of the public, and even some science reporters, is absolutely incredible.

Open Discussion

Lander: I mentioned briefly polygenic traits. I would like to amplify that just a bit. In the last couple of years it has become practical to dissect polygenic traits in animal studies. It is something that has been neglected up to now for very good reason: (1) It hasn't really been possible to dissect the traits and (2) people think about animal models in many fields and immediately worry whether these exactly copy the human situation. If you can find a distinction between the animal and the human situation, you say this isn't a good model. That's fine if you want to test a drug on the animal and see whether that drug can be used on the human. It's not an excuse if you want to understand the molecular basis of a phenotype, in which case you go after as many of the bits and pieces of the molecular apparatus that produce alcoholism or whatever else you want.

Ott: I think that blind assessment is extremely important for various reasons. I have seen cases where people are so convinced that they are pursuing a linkage that they just cannot escape the tendency to minimize the number of recombinants. Of course, as soon as you look at both loci, the disease locus and the marker locus, you recognize who is a recombinant and who is not. There is a tendency, then, to try to minimize the number of recombinants. It is important to do the diagnosis irrespective of marker determination, and possibly also irrespective of family relationships. I fully agree with that.

I have something of a problem seeing the usefulness of ascertaining pedigrees according to certain rules. Ted pointed out that for linkage analysis it is less important than for segregation analysis. I think it helps comparability of studies. In that sense, I certainly agree. The question is, then, how easy is it to do segregation analysis in these pedigrees. I think it will be difficult, but, at least, it is certainly easier when you have fixed rules and you know these rules.

Reich: I didn't specify the rules. It's just that there should be some, and people should take careful notes of how they got their material.

Sparkes: I would like to raise one kind of general alternative approach to linkage and segregation analysis. This is the candidate approach. With the improved technology, particularly with PCR, in terms of sequencing genes, finding mutations in them, might it get around some of these problems by taking the candidate gene that you think for various reasons could be the susceptibility gene and looking in the affected individuals for any evidence of mutation? Admittedly, that is a lot of work currently. But for many problems being raised in the discussion, certainly that would be one alternative approach. Admittedly, a lot of resources would be required to do that.

Cloninger: At least the data will be there. The material you would need to do that would be available. It would be generated in the studies that you're doing and that are planned in the program that we're doing.

Reich: I agree. I think that's a very useful approach. When you're going after a candidate gene in this field, you've got to be aware that there are many different genetic mechanisms. The genetic mechanism will suggest the kind of experiment. You do a very different job if you're looking for allelic forms of ALDH-1, as opposed to some kind of underlying biological measurement correlated with acute tolerance. You could do the different kinds of candidate gene approaches with different kinds of things. It certainly complements what we're doing.

Goldman: The great strength is that there will be the extreme individuals who because of their phenotype you might associate with a particular candidate gene. Even though the whole study won't have been done to select for those individuals, they will emerge. So, yes, it could be targeted.

Reich: We should target. If we knew that there was a variety of alcoholism or nonalcoholism, for example, related to the presence of ALDH-1, it certainly would be very useful to stratify or amend our sample in some way to be able to study that because that gives us another dimension in studying the genetics of the disorder.

Wijsman: I am pessimistic about the likelihood of success taking that approach, for several reasons. First, in general, identification of candidate genes and then subsequent attempts to use those to delete has failed in almost all cases. Collagen works, but there haven't been very many others. Candidate genes didn't work for most of the other ones, like amyloid and Alzheimer's. That's another one. A lot of people thought it might very well be.

Sparkes: From what Mike says, that is still a possibility.

Wijsman: But amyloid isn't an issue any more.

Conneally: No. They're 18 cM apart. But still, they latch onto 21, so in a way that's one. It's not the gene.

Wijsman: Insulin is another one.

Goldman: But it did work for leprechanism.

Wijsman: But that wasn't the one.

Conneally: Well, but there is some work on that.

Wijsman: All right. People always pick out candidate genes from these studies, but, by and large, they are kind of pulling them out of a hat.
Second, if you take the candidate gene approach, you don't really find a surprise. You are never going to find a gene that you don't know about. We don't know very much about the underlying genetic mechanism for most things. We know what a few genes might do, but we aren't going to find surprises that way. One of the beauties of, shall we say, a traditional genetic analysis, is if you start with the phenotype and you find the gene that's defective in the phenotype, then it leads you to the pathways and physiology that you don't have to now know about.

Sparkes: That's a kind of serendipity.

Wijsman: Right. Third, I am concerned that if one takes a series of affected people in a family and types them, does the sequencing, and compares them to, say, the unaffecteds in the families and you see some differences in the sequence, that you may be hanging yourself by interpreting what may be a normal polymorphism as perhaps something significant. If the gene you are looking at maybe even has a slight effect on manifestation of the phenotype, if the phenotype is mitigated strongly by background genetic effect, you may have an association in the family without that gene having much at all to do with the phenotype you are looking at. So, you will still have to do a linkage analysis to demonstrate that that gene is the primary cause of that phenotype rather than some sort of mild secondary cause. Considering all these things, I don't think you can get away from linkage analysis. I don't say that the candidate gene approach isn't a useful way of taking an initial step, but it doesn't get you away from linkage analysis.

Goldman: I would like to point out that, in essence, a lot of the anemias that have been genetically mapped really were mapped using candidate gene approaches; for example, all of the glycolytic pathway enzymes that caused chronic hemolytic anemias, plus the G6PDs of the world.

Conneally: That's not reverse genetics, that was forward genetics.

Goldman: It wasn't reverse genetics, but it was taking something that was known and using that as a tool. It was molecular. But I think your comments in general are very well taken, that you won't find something unknown.

Wijsman: I think the candidate gene approach depends on how secure your knowledge is of the underlying physiology. If you're very sure that this enzyme or protein that you're looking at is of major importance in whatever you might be looking at, it's more likely to succeed. That was true for collagen, but with many of the candidate gene approaches, you are just kind of pulling something out of a hat. It may be involved, but it's really not a secure kind of knowledge. I think there are not going to be many cases where that approach will succeed.

Sparkes: A third approach is the animal model. I think it is a useful approach in trying to understand or identify human genes. I don't think there is going to be any single method that is going to be *the* best way, and I think we need to consider all the possibilities.

Conneally: Another thing we need to talk about is the marker phenotype itself.

Li: I think all of these are relevant. To the extent that we know about biological mechanisms that underlie these and we can identify proteins and genes that go with these phenomena, they may be useful as candidate probes.

The only area in which we have very firm understanding of the physiology of the genetics is the difference in alcohol sensitivity in the LS and SS mice. That has been correlated with a very high degree of correlation coefficient to the sensitivity within the neurons in the cerebellum. The LS and SS model is really the loss of righting reflex in these animals, the sensitivity of the cerebellar Purkinje cells to the effects of alcohol. That has been defined. Also, at the biochemical level, there seems to be a difference in the sensitivity of the GABA benzodiazepine chloride channel complex. Those data are softer than the physiologic data, but that is what people are working on now. Boris Tabakoff is currently selecting for chronic tolerance. As he mentioned yesterday, there may be a difference in vasopressin level between the two lines. We also see a difference in vasopressin levels, at least in the mRNA in the brain regions of alcohol-naive, alcohol-preferring, and alcohol nonpreferring animals. So, I think, either vasopressin or vasopressin receptor certainly is another candidate. Of course, none of these may exhibit polymorphism, and so we need to look for that, but these are certainly candidates. I don't know how much is known about the withdrawal model that David has. Do you know, in terms of the biochemistry, the differences in withdrawal?

Goldman: I think it's known that it's not a metabolic difference, that it's some sort of difference in CNS sensitivity. Beyond that, we don't know.

Reich: Why do you say it's different in sensitivity?

Goldman: Because the rate of ethanol elimination is not appreciably different.

Reich: Why do you say it's CNS sensitivity?

Goldman: If, presumably, the brain is exposed to the same levels of ethanol that you are seeing peripherally and that are being measured peripherally, then what is seen is that one strain responds to the virtually identical rate of ethanol elimination with a dramatically different syndrome of withdrawal, with not only nervousness and stiffness of the tail preparatory to seizures, but with actual seizures.

Li: Finally, we know several things about the alcohol preference model. There are abnormalities in dopamine, so dopamine D2 receptors. In serotonin, we have identified the serotonin 1A receptor as an area of concern. There are differences also in GABA fiber content; that is new data that is not published yet. The benzodiazepine-chloride complex is again implicated there. Vasopressin I have spoken about. And maybe, opioids. These are the general areas that I think are targeted for research in the future in this model.

If one thinks that alcohol-seeking behavior is the model that is most relevant for looking for a mechanism, one needs to develop additional lines to see whether there is generalizability of mechanisms and look for new mechanisms. As I showed, it doesn't take too many generations before you start seeing separation of the lines. I think that may be, in terms of animal work, the most fruitful way to see new candidate probes and mechanisms.

Sparkes: These studies have all been done on rats up to this point, is that correct?

Li: And mice.

Sparkes: Mice are particularly useful at this stage because so much is known about the mapping of many genes. What is the possibility of setting up back-crosses to see whether you can map any of these characteristics that are related to alcohol?

Li: These are some of the things that people in Colorado are looking at right now with the LS and SS mice. They have recombinant inbred animals and that is exactly what they are doing. So, there is some effort in that direction. We are planning to begin some work in that area ourselves.

The reason I say it is important to establish other lines is that, as I mentioned, with the C-57s, which is an inbred line that happens to like alcohol, the underlying mechanism seems to be quite different. Their brains are also deficient in serotonin, but it looks like a metabolic abnormality and not a neuronal one, wherein there is induction of tryptophan purolase and a lowering of the circulating tryptophan content and subsequently lower serotonin in the brain. Their drinking can be stopped, for example, by giving them a high carbohydrate diet; that is known to increase brain serotonin content, to increase availability of tryptophan. That doesn't work in our animals. So, there are multiple underlying mechanisms. They go to the same final path, but there are different ways of doing it. We need to look at different receptors and enzymes as a result.

Sparkes: It seems to me this would be very fruitful because, as we heard, there is considerable homology in terms of linkage maps between mice and humans, and that will probably be true with rats as well, although less is known there. By setting up the appropriate matings, one could perhaps get an answer reasonably quickly once these recombinant inbred strains are available—at least to know where to look in humans, and if there are any candidate genes mapped in those areas—that would be a useful approach. Even if there aren't, at least the possibility of testing in humans using even anonymous probes becomes very useful in seeing whether there is any evidence of segregation with those anonymous probes in the familial cases.

Martin: T.K., when you refer to the Purkinje cell response and its relationship to the righting response, in what detail is that story understood?

Li: It's an electrophysiological correlation of the inhibition of firing of the Purkinje cells by alcohol in situ. That is also being done by taking out the fetal cerebella for Purkinje cells and implanting them in the anterior chamber of the eye of the opposite animal. It can show the opposite strain or opposite line, and they are able to show that the phenomenon belongs to the Purkinje cells and not to the medium.

Martin: Has anyone obtained DNA libraries from those cells?

Li: Oh, yes. That's what they're working on.

Propping: You mentioned a correlation between this peculiarity and the sensitivity to alcohol in mice. How was the sensitivity measured in mice?

Li: Righting reflex. They give the animals a dose of alcohol, put them on their backs in a trough, and measure the time it takes them to regain the righting reflex. The time it takes to regain the righting reflex and the degree of inhibition of the neurons in different animals are the correlate.

Propping: Do you think that in humans there is an equivalent to this sensitivity measure?

Li: The equivalence in humans is something that I would like to look at. For example, I have been telling Marc Schuckit the responses that his family history positive individuals exhibit (because they are drinkers, they are not ethanol-naive) could be "tolerant" because they are less sensitive. You would have to test that. That was one reason, I presume, that he gave the benzodiazepines to see whether they differ also in benzodiazepine sensitivity, because they had never been exposed to benzodiazepines. If he sees no difference, the next test is to see if they are given benzodiazepines first, do they then exhibit greater tolerance to benzodiazepines in the family history positive individuals.

Propping: There exist, rather rarely, of course, certain humans who do not possess a cerebellum, just the congenital traces, and that has more or less no consequence at all.

Li: What are you suggesting?

Propping: That the sensitivity to alcohol in humans might be related to other mechanisms.

Li: When you do experimental observations of "sensitivity," all of that is very specific to the test or the measure that you use. This goes for tolerance development, as well as withdrawal, depending on whether you hold the mice by their tails to induce convulsion or what. All of these drug effects are task-specific. So, of course, if you don't have a cerebellum, that may not be a good way to measure Purkinje cell sensitivity, but there are other tests you could look at.

Sparkes: Thanks very much, T.K. Now, let us move on to Mike's suggestion regarding the phenotype. Mike, would you like to comment at this time on this issue?

Conneally: No, we haven't talked about it yet. It's not one fixed phenotype; there is gradation.

Reich: It's not just a gradation, but differences.

Sparkes: One concern with the phenotype would be in terms of the possible different expressions in different individuals, whether one could be looking at the same gene, same mutant, in different individuals, but having a slightly different phenotype, much as I mentioned with the juvenile myotonic epilepsy. It is difficult to control for until you have some idea what the basic mechanisms are. One would hope that, at least in family studies, one is going to be dealing with the same mutation or mutations, assuming that this is hereditary. I guess we are all making the assumption for the moment that there are strong hereditary components, at least in some instances of alcoholism.

Conneally: Maybe Bob or Ted could tell us how you define phenotypes in type 1, type 2.

Cloninger: The question of how to diagnose alcoholism, what set of criteria to use, is not entirely clear-cut. In our family and linkage studies of alcoholism, we have been using Feighner diagnostic criteria, which involve four groups of symptoms, and then we looked for symptoms in at least three of those four groups, or only in two groups, and so on.

We find some people who are severe alcoholics who, in addition to those criteria, meet anyone's criteria for dependence and have been hospitalized. Others are fairly definite, with symptoms in three or more groups, but haven't been hospitalized and aren't severely dependent. Others, who only have symptoms in two groups, are considered probable alcoholics. If we include probable alcoholics, we can push the rate of alcoholism in brothers up to 60–70%. In our segregation analyses, we have usually limited it to definite alcoholics who had symptoms in three groups, just because the numbers were so high. In part, you get into some problems in segregation analysis just from high base rates. But that's not a clear-cut decision because it may be that you can show that the number of probable parents influences the recurrence risk in siblings, and so it is actually probably part of the inherited spectrum. That is already a problem, then, before we talk about subtypes.

The subtyping procedures are also not that clean, in that they require rating age of onset of the individual symptoms, at least in severe cases that get treated. What we really try to do is to see the differences in patterns of development over time. That is why I have advocated use of personality variables as an adjunct to the assessment, because I think that may be easier. There are positive correlations between the two sets of discriminating symptoms (type 1 and type 2 features) that I described in my presentation. There are many people with an admixture of those symptoms. In large families, we are not going to have the luxury of being able to limit it to only cases that are cleanly of one type or another. These are not discrete diseases in the usual way we think of discrete diseases, in the Kraepelinean sense, but probably reflect different processes.

Sparkes: Then, presumably, the subtyping proposal that you have is hypothetical at the moment.

Cloninger: No. Those symptom patterns do discriminate, the types of families are different in their segregation patterns, and it works very well in the relatives of cases who aren't selected for being treated. However, with probands, for example, you often get people who have combined forms of susceptibility.

The third class of problems is, once you get beyond the diagnosis of alcoholism and subtyping of alcoholism, what other disorders you want to take into account as part of the disease spectrum in doing a linkage study.

Ted Reich showed a very elegant analysis suggesting that depression probably is genetically independent from susceptibility to alcoholism. Most people would agree with that, I think. We haven't seen evidence of depression, for example, in the Swedish data either, so there are both family and genetic data to support making the distinction, and I tend to favor not including depression. However, I would want to include somatization disorder. That could have major implications. The question would be whether you would take pedigrees when the father is the alcoholic proband and he has a somatizing spouse. There is a lot of assortative mating, correlations of around 0.4–0.5, between women with somatization and men with alcoholism and antisocial personality.

I think those are the major issues. I haven't told you what the right answer is because no one knows yet. We only have hypotheses with varying amounts of support.

Reich: I would like to add some things. First, in psychiatric parlance, the test-retest stability and the test-retest reliability in the diagnosis of alcoholism are excellent, even if one comes back, after some hours or after some days, with a different interviewer. We usually hear comments about people with alcohol problems being liars, reprobates, cheats, but the diagnosis is actually highly reliable. If the questions are asked in the appropriate way, the operating characteristics of that decision are excellent. If one goes back in 6 years blindly and asks an individual, "Have you ever had these problems?" the operating characteristics of that are also very good—much better, for example, than with schizophrenia and manic-depressive illness. Among psychiatric disorders, then, the most stable, reliable, repeatable measure, I believe, is the diagnosis of definite alcoholism.

You then look at different sets of criteria that have grown up internationally, in part because of different cultural attitudes about alcoholism within the society. For a long time, for example, some of the Mediterranean societies denied that they ever had alcoholism at all. France denied it for a long time, even though even a casual visitor to Paris who hung around the Seine would see all the hobos with bottles in their pockets. But now, they are serious, as the French say, and they're making measurements. In doing so, they have, as in many behavioral disorders, written criteria in their own idiom. We also know there are different patterns of drinking in north and south Europe, which may well lead to different kinds of alcoholism.

With respect to the diagnosis of alcoholism using different kinds of criteria, some based more on pathological behaviors of the sort that occur in northern Europe, some based more on perhaps addictive phenomena that may occur without behavioral abnormalities in southern Europe, there still appears to be considerable overlap, and the diagnosis remains good. But it does make the international aspects of this diagnosis more difficult.

Finally, with respect to international diagnosis, it is most difficult because in some societies drinking anything, especially in Islam, is not permitted. Even if you drink a little bit consistently, it appears one has to have a pathological bent. In Saudi Arabia, where they do horrible things to regular drinkers, like cutting a hand off, you really have to be motivated to drink even a little bit regularly. Maybe in those countries we need different categories compared to our country. In doing genetic studies, one goal is not only to make a diagnosis, but to characterize the phenotype so we can subdivide it according to some very coarse type 1-type 2 characteristics. We hope to do that in the collaborative study of alcoholism.

The old way was to first subdivide and produce your phenotypes, and then do the genetics. With this disorder, doing the genetics and subdividing at the same time may be part of the same scientific exploration. That is a little bit different from the usual, and I am hopeful that will happen.

Among young people, in childhood, when alcoholism begins, there are other disorders that seem closely related. They aren't as easily diagnosed, nor are they as specifically diagnosed, as alcoholism.

Cloninger: I would make one brief addition: That is, the criteria that have been best validated in many ways in family studies are the Feighner, Robins, and Guze criteria, but they are really terrible from the point of view of helping to take leads from animal studies about alcohol-seeking behavior, susceptibility to tolerance, and so on. One advantage of the type 1-type 2 distinction is that it tries to capture differences in susceptibility to tolerance, dependence, and alcohol-seeking behavior.

Noble: Henri asked me to make a comment about the neurocognitive profile. I think we should be concerned about taking only single measures. I think when we're talking about alcohol-dependence, the central nervous system really is a very important place to look. (Of course, cirrhosis of the liver is an entirely different situation and may require looking at aldehyde dehydrogenase, etc.) If we are looking at the CNS, we should not look only at a single criterion, because that could be involved in other disorders also. The best thing here, from my point of view, is to look at a number of things that go into a composite that reflects CNS activity.

We talk about the neuropsychological factors that are important, and we should look at those in conjunction with electrophysiological factors plus personality. The more we examine the composite, the more that composite becomes reflective of the disorder we are looking at. I think we should strive more to look at what is typical, if there is such a thing, about alcoholism or alcohol dependency.

Sparkes: Look at the combination, not just single components.

Noble: Yes, because, Henri, you would say, wouldn't you, that in schizophrenia we've got some differences in the P300 also?

Begleiter: Yes.

Noble: So, be careful of personality characteristics, Bob, that might also be related to other kinds of mental disorders. Therefore, I think, we should bring this out more and more as we can, if we are going to be specific, otherwise a number of disorders would be involved.

Cadoret: I think it is evident that these criteria are quite arbitrary. A number of years ago, I wrote a textbook of psychiatry for general practitioners. I used the Feighner, Robins, and Guze criteria. I tabulated the criteria and their frequency found in various groups. I made a list—such a percentage has criterion 1, such a percentage has criterion 2, etc. From the literature you can get a tremendous list called the non-criterion symptoms. These were equally easily determinable symptoms or signs that occurred more frequently in affected people, but which never appeared in the criteria list. You can do that for any condition. For instance, in antisocial personality, there are a great many antisocials who have a large number of somatic symptoms. That doesn't appear at all in anybody's criteria list of antisocial. Yet, it is significantly increased in those individuals over and above control groups. It might be reasonable to look at your criteria, or to gather a whole bunch of criteria like that that have proven to be higher in the group of interest. Maybe you will find a more reliable set of criteria.

Reich: Henri drew my attention to one comment that I think the psychiatrists and the phenomenologists can agree to. The natural history of alcoholism is largely unknown. It's rather remarkable. I don't think the life course prospective follow-up studies have been done in an appropriate way for alcoholism.

Cloninger: There have been many follow-up studies.

Reich: Not long-term follow-ups. I don't think prospective follow-ups in modern times show exactly what happens to alcoholics over their life spans.

Begleiter: Not the kinds of things that, for instance, Strauss and Carpenter did for schizophrenia.

Cadoret: How about George Valliant's study?

Cloninger: We've got follow-up studies in St. Louis, three different studies I can think of immediately. There was a study that Guze, Clayton, and I published 2 years ago about 200 alcoholics followed 6–12 years. Liz Smith did studies of material originally collected by Ted Reich, Remi Cadoret, and George Winokur, over a 15-year period. There are follow-up studies by Valliant and others. But, I agree that we need to do careful repeated measurements of our subject to help us characterize it.

Reich: I was referring mostly to the fact that as alcoholics get older they seem to disappear. How many die, how many abstain, and how many get institutionalized, and what pathways do they take? I don't think that is well known, especially in modern times, not that cirrhosis is declining because it's better treated.

Cloninger: Remember, getting back to the diagnosis issue, the linkage analysis requires that we use explicit categorical classifications. This wavering about whether we count a probable or a questionable as affected or unaffected, if we start classifying half of our relatives as question marks, we are going to be throwing away a lot of data, and we probably can't afford to do it. We can test alternative classification schemes, but we'd better specify those ahead of time before we get into data analysis if that's what we plan to do.

Li: This is not a unique problem to alcohol research. How do people go about doing studies on hypertension, diabetes, hypercholesterolemia?

Wijsman: There is a disorder called familial combined hypercholesterolemia, where it's not an individual who is affected, but a family. I don't know how they define these things.

Li: So, this is not a unique problem. We can always make a diagnosis of the obvious, but it's the borderline, gray area where we have problems.

Cloninger: About a third of the relatives are in that borderline category.

Martin: Why don't you just assign these phenotypes to maximize your LOD score?

Ott: We do need to try out various classification schemes, but there are certainly alternative approaches. One approach might be to allow for the fact that one person is less likely to be affected than another one. There are certain impressions you people may have—this is a very clear-cut case, that is a less clear-cut case—and such impressions can perhaps be put into a number and that number can be used in the linkage analysis. I am planning on developing a scheme for incorporating such impressions into the linkage analysis.

Conneally: Well, in your central phenotype-genotype matrix, can't you include it right there?

Ott: Yes. The question is how.

Conneally: You mean the probability to attach to it? You are talking about the probability of the phenotype given the genotype.

Ott: Yes.

Cloninger: How do you estimate that probability?

Martin: But that's the probability in the population. You want the probability for the individual. That's quite different. So you just give them a different age of onset.

Reich: There are two questions on the table. One is the question raised by Bob, who said that for psychiatric phenotypes they are really semicontinuous, in the sense that in the borderline there are preclinical and fringe cases who you could show have an excess of children with the major phenotype. So, to some extent, they are genetically related, but, on the other hand, maybe less so; or there are more phenocopies in that group of individuals; or the diagnoses are less stable; or there is more noise in some way. One issue is how to handle individuals with those phenotypes. We can see who they are quite precisely. We will know that their diagnoses can be less reliable, or whatever. That's one group. The second group are individuals whose cases are definitely diagnosed, but who can be very atypical. You don't know what to do with them either. Therefore, there are two kinds of problems with diagnosis that may require, in my view, different statistical treatments, because the relationship of the uncertainty to the genotypes is different in both cases.

Cloninger: Last week, we were discussing this in relation to schizophrenia and were able to agree fairly well on things that were core cases, some other cases that were in between, and some things that were definitely excluded from the spectrum. Jurg suggested the idea of having a continuous rating that would rank things 1 to 7 or whatever. Then, ideally, it would be nice to have probabilities to assign to each level, but we didn't know how we would come up with those probability estimates. Others argued that the alternative would be to take everyone in the middle who is around 50% probability and count them as unknowns (not count them one way or the other). These two approaches may be roughly equivalent. I don't think we have the luxury of going with the latter procedure in the case of alcoholism. I think the kind of approach that you were suggesting, Jurg, is almost inevitable for us to try because of the high proportion of cases that are probably in the spectrum.

Reich: So there will be a new kind of phenotype and a new kind of linkage analysis?

Cloninger: It is a very challenging problem.

Conneally: The 50% or so are uninformative.

Cloninger: Yes, but we're going to have a lot of those.

Li: Do you know the stability of that group?

Cloninger: We have done a follow-up study over 6–12 years of the probables, and they are less reliable, less stable, than the definites. But instead of a stability κ of around 0.85 for the definite severe cases, it's on the order of 0.6, which is still as good as you get with major affective disorder, for example.

Li: How many move up to the definite category?

Cloninger: Some move in and some move out. Some move up and some deny that they ever had the symptoms.

Martin: It's not really different from the age-of-onset problem, is it?

Ott: It's more complicated. Environmental factors also may come into play here. I have seen this, for example, in the linkage analysis of osteoarthrosis. If someone lives in an environment that doesn't give much exposure to getting a disease and if he does get it, that is a much clearer case. The other way around, if you don't get it but you live in an environment that makes you prone to disease, you are a clear non-case. Such environmental conditions should also be incorporated in the linkage analysis.

Sparkes: I would like to shift the discussion to a related area, and this concerns the genetic models for alcoholism. Is there any strong feeling that there is a more likely model than another, for example, a single gene versus multigene? Are there any indications from what we have at this point as to what that model might be?

Cloninger: I didn't show all the data, but we have done segregation analysis studies of large sets of pedigrees of alcoholics. The evidence overall is for a combined model with a detectable major gene effect, a substantial multifactorial background, and modest amounts of nonfamilial environmental contributions. On the other hand, you can subtype that and, as I presented, get one group that appears to have the segregated locus and another that looks more purely multifactorial. I don't know that you can talk about there being one mode of inheritance. It will depend on how you specify the phenotype. For example, just the very clear-cut decision that Ernie Noble showed us about requiring that you get alcoholics who have been abstinent for 2 years clearly has a major impact on the kind of alcoholic you have. I would bet that the segregation pattern of those people is much more like the type 1 alcoholics with the multifactorial component and no major locus than the type 2 patterns, like Henri has been showing, with multiple generations with high heritability, where we had evidence for a dominant major gene plus a multifactorial component.

Reich: We should also note that there have been a number of different mechanisms that have been bandied around, so you can't really say that there is a single mechanism or a single model.

Sparkes: Is there general agreement that, at least in some instances, there appears to be a Number 1 model, as Bob was suggesting, a major locus plus some other effects?

Reich: I think there are major genes in there, and more than one. We have evidence for the ALDH and the ALDH-2. There are classic Mendelian genes in there that are relevant and I think can be mapped. It's a very complex mixture.

Wijsman: I want to raise one point about the segregation analysis. This is a very complex set of modeling. We don't really know how robust it is. There are a lot of assumptions that go into that modeling process. It's nice when you get a result that works, like you got from your major locus segregating, but when you have this large polygenic background and all that, all sorts of violations of your assumptions could give you this apparent result. The fact that you get a certain analysis in itself doesn't indicate that you have something homogeneous going on.

Reich: Of course. I don't think anybody would disagree with that.

Wijsman: I think that is important to keep in mind, that that is by no means proof of a single gene. It's nice that it's there.

Reich: Everybody agrees.

Wijsman: It is certainly a place to start.

Reich: The real proof is going to be in the linkage. I don't think we are used to using linkage in that way, but in this context the real proof will be in the linkage, I think, not in the segregation analysis.

Cloninger: Absolutely.

Sparkes: It seems that in many conditions where there is a laboratory test, one can make a decision and people often feel much more comfortable. We have heard a little about the EEG studies. Peter indicated that at least some EEG patterns were hereditary, and it looks like there may be some associated changes, as Henri and Ernie have pointed out. This area really needs to receive a lot of attention to see whether these patterns are hereditary or not.

Begleiter: It is still under investigation. How well it segregates in families is not something that I can answer in the form of statistical data. Certainly, my impression is that it segregates quite well in families. This is only an impression, and we need to do more work and do a formal analysis before we can provide you with some kind of answer, but it is very encouraging.

Searles: The difference you are seeing in high-risk and low-risk is not alcohol-specific, is it?

Begleiter: By "alcohol-specific" do you mean does it lead to alcoholism or does it lead to drinking alcohol?

Searles: No, I mean, is it also found in other disorders?

Begleiter: Yes. The particular deficit that I initially reported in 1984 is certainly unique to that high-risk population. It is not unique to other psychiatric disorders. For instance, in schizophrenics you have a significant deficit of P300. Because of that, we have gone on to look at other electrophysiological deficits. The combination of three very specific deficits that we have identified in high-risk are, indeed, seemingly unique to the high-risk population.

Searles: Of alcoholics?

Begleiter: Of high risk for alcoholism. So, we will have a set of electrophysiological phenomena, specifically anomalies, that are unique to alcoholism.

Searles: But the P300 itself is not?

Begleiter: That is correct, absolutely not.

Searles: I want to ask Bob and Ted about environmental measures in the studies you are doing. You tell me that you can't find any. That's disturbing. How is that going to be taken into consideration, since there obviously has to be a huge environmental component in the development of alcoholism?

Reich: We are going to have our steering committee meeting and we are going to try to prepare measures, including environmental and family ones, and then we are going to have a fight. The fight is going to be to bring the measurement or assessment procedure down to some reasonable amount of time. And then, among the investigators, all of whom have a certain interest, to try to get some kind of rational compromise on how to measure what. What comes out should be of interest to many investigators.

Searles: This is a study of families, correct?

Cloninger: Yes.

Searles: There is an instrument available that has garnered a modest amount of attention, and that is the sibling inventory differential experience model of Denise Danielson at Stanford.

Heath: There are a lot of problems with that instrument. It has come under a lot of criticism in the behavioral genetics field because of the way it was constructed.

Searles: Yes. I am just suggesting it is an instrument that's available that hasn't been terribly well used at this point.

Reich: For good reasons. There are better things. Why would you suggest we use an inferior instrument?

Cloninger: Lee Robins has also developed an instrument designed especially to pick up environmental factors.

Searles: That's the home environment interview? I'm using that myself also. I've only used it on 10 pairs. It's a cumbersome instrument. One of the appeals to me of the Stanford instrument is its brevity.

Heath: The only disadvantage is you can't analyze the data when you get it because it's not well structured.

Cadoret: One variable we are going to measure is exposure to alcohol. I think that is an important environmental variable. I would like to reiterate the possibility of using adoption studies to find environments that are conducive to either greater or lesser drinking; and also, environments that may interact in some way to magnify the effects of genes. I think we can still get more information about these environmental factors from adoption-type designs.

Propping: Henri, in reference to the electrophysiological parameters you extracted, have you any knowledge about the distribution in your proband? Is there evidence for bimodality of the distribution or is it a unimodal distribution?

Begleiter: I am not sure it's bimodal, but it's definitely not unimodal, that much we can say.

Reich: I think one of the best laboratories to look for relevant environmental effects would be discordant MZ twins and their children. That really hasn't been exploited. I would like to see more work done in that field.

Cloninger: One way to approach this is to follow the lead suggested by Andrew [Heath] and Nick [Martin]. That is, we need to model the frequency and amount of alcohol intake as a separate variable in these families. Those are partly heritable traits themselves, yet they don't overlap entirely with susceptibility to problem drinking. We may need to simultaneously analyze variables that influence frequency and amount of intake, as well as susceptibility to problems from alcohol intake. That again is a major challenge for simultaneous analyses.

Heath: Why?

Cloninger: There may be genetic factors that contribute to the exposure phase, and then other factors that contribute to the various kinds of complications to exposure.

Heath: That's okay. However, some of the genetic factors may be contributing to both. That makes it much more complicated.

Sparkes: Particularly for the mathematical geneticists, we have a question: *How serious is the problem of heterogeneity going to be?* It seems quite clear from the discussion I have heard that one can expect considerable heterogeneity. How much of a practical problem will that be in doing the genetic studies?

Wijsman: It seems obvious that it is going to make exclusion mapping almost worthless. Where you've got a simple, clear Mendelian of any sort, you can hope that your exclusion map tells a great deal about where something is, where you haven't excluded it. If you have a lot of heterogeneity in a LOD score, that doesn't give you much information at all.

Reich: And remember, it's not a unitary phenotype. For some of our phenotypes it will be useful, for others it won't.

Wijsman: Only if you're sure that that's a specific disorder. That's the problem with heterogeneity.

Reich: We will be doing aldehyde dehydrogenase alleles. That's one example, but there will be others.

Cloninger: That's an interesting point: If the exclusion mapping isn't very useful, then all we need to do is look for home runs (i.e., detection of major genes)?

Wijsman: Yes.

Conneally: Of course, that's the importance of large families. It is a clear method, in this case, because of heterogeneity.

Martin: Shouldn't the approach be to start off getting all these families and then evaluate the informativeness of the pedigree, using something like Boenke's algorithm? Basically, you don't even bother with families that aren't going to give you a LOD of at least 3 under ideal conditions. It's likely that heterogeneity is going to be the major problem here and, therefore, studies across families are going to be quite meaningless.

Reich: I think there is a body of research that would disagree with you. We can pick up genetic effects that account for 10% or 20% of the variability by using affected sib-pairs.

Martin: But that's across families.

Wijsman: That's right, it's across families, and you need a lot.

Martin: That's the whole point. That's the problem.

Reich: We'll have a lot in the planned NIAAA study called the Consortium on Genetics of Alcoholism (COGA).

Wijsman: Even if you have a lot of genetic heterogeneity, with a linkage study you can still detect linkage.

Martin: You have a lot of data from a lot of different pedigrees, but maybe they will all just cancel each other out.

Wijsman: No, they don't cancel each other. You can still get a bias of shared haplotypes because some fraction of them will be sharing it. You just need a lot of data.

Cloninger: The plan in COGA is to start out with affected sib-pairs and then their nuclear families and then extend from there. That's a minimal inclusion criterion.

Reich: The idea is to exploit the family of technologies available to linkage analyzers, reckoning that if one lists the advantages and disadvantages of all the different methods, they're useful in different circumstances. If one looks at the range of the family of phenotypes we will be studying and genotypes we will be studying, they are also quite variable. Our goal is to try to collect material so that we could use both approaches and sometimes one approach or another would be useful for different phenotypes that we will be studying, including, as David and T.K. do, measured genotype approaches and candidate gene approaches.

Martin: But that's all words, Ted.

Reich: It's not all words. We do the work.

Martin: I know, the fact is if you've got a completely heterogeneous disease here and it's a different gene in every pedigree...

Reich: God is not so unkind.

Martin: On the contrary. That's a convenient assumption for you to do this work.

Reich: If you're going to tell me that every case of the disorder is due to a different cause, then we have no business studying the disorder at all.

Martin: Precisely.

Reich: That's not science. You're looking at the worst-case scenario. I think there is some commonality between affected individuals and we are going to try to use those commonalities to figure out what's going on.

Cloninger: We have strong evidence of heritability, many biological markers, and many candidate genes. It will take at least 10 years before we can come to firm conclusions.

Martin: $26 million later.

Cloninger: The assumption is that this may be a heterogeneous disorder, but it's unlikely to be as bad as you would have us believe. On the other hand, we know that we are going to have well-characterized pedigrees, we are going to be able to study multiple phenotypes, and we will be able to do our linkage analysis on a wide range of phenotypes. There will certainly be something useful that will come out of this.

Conneally: Nick, I want to comment on your idea of using, for example, Boenke's algorithm. The problem is that the LOD score is dependent on the mode of inheritance. If you happen to give an improper mode of inheritance, you won't get a proper LOD score to begin with.

Martin: But it's all right because you know the mode of inheritance.

Conneally: We just have to be very conservative in rejecting linkage using a -2 or something for the same kind of reason.

Wijsman: Right. But it can give you some indication about your likelihood of being able to see something positive.

Cloninger: Using that, though, you would have to somehow feed in a way to search on the mode of inheritance too.

Wijsman: That's right. You'd have to specify, but you could do that in the analysis.

Cloninger: You should maximize the LOD score for whatever mode of inheritance gave you the maximum LOD score.

Martin: Yes. So what's wrong with my suggestion, that we need a new kind of program that you feed in the pedigrees and some basic raw information, and it generates the maximum regression weights to maximize the LOD score and the mode of inheritance?

Cloninger: That's a good project.

Martin: The way you do that is to test half of your pedigrees and then you test it out on the other half.

Sparkes: Along those same lines, are there any other ideas that perhaps would relate to additional mathematical approaches to the issue than what have been discussed so far?

Wijsman: I was intrigued by a couple of comments that Jurg has made about trying to build in some of the uncertainty in various subcategories of the phenotype, trying to define the phenotype in a multivariate fashion, or something like that.

Ott: This is what Bob referred to just a minute ago. We discussed this at the schizophrenia meeting. It hasn't been done.

Wijsman: Yes, I know, but intuitively or intellectually you can imagine that it could be done.

Ott: Yes. In principle, you have all these variables. Now, instead of treating them as such, one could just use them as part of the phenotype and then define a multivariate phenotype. One would then imagine a joint mean vector for the unaffecteds and a different mean vector for the affecteds and do a linkage analysis on those multivariate phenotypes. Technically it's not a problem because in the linkage programs there is provision to do that. One would have to specify the covariates between the variables, but this is probably not too much of a problem either.

Cloninger: Jurg, something that we didn't think of before was how to come up with a way of scaling the relationship between some of these intermediate phenotypes. You might use something akin to what Ted Reich had described, using multiple threshold techniques to measure the degree of dependence or independence of some putative spectrum condition with the core phenotype. Essentially, it uses what is the relative risk of disorder Y in the families of probands with disorder X.

Ott: This is a different approach. I just want to say about the multivariate phenotypes that to estimate these variates and covariates it would be useful to have pedigrees that allow you to do that so that your ascertained pedigrees would be suitable for that purpose. The other approach to that kind of hierarchical scheme of disease definition would lead to a univariate phenotype, a phenotype that has a linear relation (on one side you have the clearly unaffecteds, on the other the clearly affecteds) and then use the classes as phenotypes; class 1, 2, 3, and so on would then be the phenotype.

Reich: They're both complementary approaches.

Wijsman: You might be able to get from one to the other if you could think of projecting that multivariate spectrum onto a set of categories and use that as a crude estimate.

Reich: Every time you compound your measurement, you can make a decision about whether there is a latent genotype whose effect you are amplifying. That, I would assume, is the goal.

Martin: This all makes very bold assumptions about the causes of covariation between the different measurements which is a problem that behavioral geneticists have been tackling for about 10 or 15 years.

Reich: That's why we can use linkage to solve those problems.

Martin: You're talking about getting a compound measurement by adding up phenotypes.

Reich: Combining phenotypes.

Martin: Yes. I'm saying that if you just combine those phenotypes according to the weights from some effect analysis, you can be completely misleading yourself as to what the true underlying genotypic scores are that you ought to look at.

Heath: Those are tractable measurements.

Martin: The point is that it is tractable. That is precisely the problem we have been working on in twins.

Heath: Some of this stuff in the context of segregation analysis is being written up and published by Linda Mays in *Behavior Genetics* and is probably available for circulation on the back of napkins too.

Martin: I think it is also important to draw attention to the work of Boomsua and Peter Melmar, who have been working on maximum ways of getting genotypic and environmental scores of individuals after you fitted the correct covariate structure model to your covariates. You can assign a genetic and environmental weight for each individual. The weights are best assigned from twin studies because that is a much cleaner way than family studies. You can then use that when you go to your families.

Reich: What Nick says is very interesting. He is talking about a quantitative environmental approach, and we were talking more in this context about a linkage approach. In my view, the linkage approach is a higher order of proof.

Cloninger: We may do better in a linkage analysis if we have probabilities derived from twins.

Reich: I think that when we do the linkage approach and begin to understand the compound versions like that, it may or may not be that the assumptions of the quantitative environmental approaches will be very useful.

Heath: I think what Nick is suggesting is that one can use the focus of the environmental approach on actual observations precisely in the context of segregation analysis and a linkage analysis.

Martin: That's right.

Cloninger: They're complementary.

Martin: You are going to be making your compound phenotypes on an almost arbitrary basis. How are you going to assign the weights with which you add them up in the very basic phenotypic analysis of some multiple regression analysis of phenotypes? In getting that compound score, you are going to be adding some phenotypes that are 10% genetic and others that are 90% genetic and using that as the phenotype for linkage analysis. I think that's crazy. If you're serious about doing that, you ought to assign more weight to the variables that are more genetic and less to those that are more environmental. You also want to have some idea about the dimensionality of those variables that you are adding up. Just because you can stick them on a single multiple regression equation doesn't mean they're not on more than one dimension. These are not things to "to and fro" about. There are rigorous methods of analyzing and answering these questions that we have been working on for a long time. There are ways of sorting out the dimensions of the equation and then coming up with the optimum weights with which to combine these variables. I would strongly urge you to look at those methods before you start to work out compound phenotypes.

Cloninger: I think we have heard two useful suggestions of ways to assign the probabilities of an individual having a certain genotype. One, as Nick has just said, could use analyses based on twins and their families to try to resolve the genetic and environmental contributors to the phenotypes we are observing. The second would be segregation analysis, which would give probabilities of an individual having a particular genotype. Both of those could be fed into the linkage analysis, or you could do simultaneous segregation and linkage analysis. Other people prefer the attitude of just assuming a single gene and relying on the robustness of the linkage analysis to detect the major genotype when it's there.

Wijsman: It seems to me what you are trying to do is just to make sure that your phenotype is a little cleaner so that you get high penetrance, so you can rely on your penetrance. That is the goal.

Author Index

Agarwal, D.P., 253

Begleiter, H., 137
Billings, P.R., 333

Cadoret R.J., 31
Chakravarti, A., 307
Cloninger, C.R., 55, 105
Cook, C.C.H., 227

Goedde, H.W., 253
Goldman, D., 237
Gordis, E., 213
Gurling, H.M.D., 227

Haber, R., 237
Heath, A.C., 3
Hesselbrock, M., 75

Hesselbrock, V., 75
Hoffman, P.L., 195

Lander, E.S., 307
Li, T.-K., 217

Macpherson, A.J.S., 265
Martin, N.G., 3, 15
Meyer, J.M., 3

Noble, E.P., 159

Ott, J., 327

Peters, T.J., 265
Porjesz, B., 137

Propping, P., 175

Reich, T., 55

Schuckit, M.A., 183
Searles, J.S., 89

Tabakoff, B., 195
Tarter, R.E., 43

Ward, R.J., 265
Wesner, R.B., 31
Whelan, J.P., 195
Wijsman, E.M., 317

Yoshida, A., 265

Subject Index

Acetaldehyde, 225, 269–271, 275
Additive genetic variance and alcohol consumption in twins, 15–17, 113
Adenylate cyclase as biological marker for alcoholism, 195–204
Adoption paradigm, hereditary versus environmental factors, 32–42, 287, 364
Adrenergic receptors, 242
Adrenocorticotropin hormone, 187
Alcohol abuse, 56, 258, 270. *See also* Alcoholism
  in adoptees, 118, 287
  criteria for diagnosis
    in Iowa adoption study, 96
    in Stockholm adoption study, 94, 117–118, 120
  genetic and environmental percursors, 36, 79–80, 129–130, 294, 330, 364. *See also* Genetic effects and alcoholism
  in Japan, 266
  prediction by level of risk, 125, 285, 366
  secular trends in, 57, 71–72
  in Swedish men, 106
Alcohol and other drug-use behaviors, 69, 168
Alcohol consumption patterns, 172, 185, 285. *See also* Genetics of alcohol sensitivity
  abstinence, 3, 8, 10–11
  in adults, 8–10
  in Australian twins, 3–13
  and flushing response, 228, 231, 268, 335
  individual differences in, 15–17, 19
  per capita in U.S., 56, 65
  relationship to P300 amplitude, 147–148, 192, 361
  in twin studies, 15–29, 113–114, 138, 175–177
Alcohol dehydrogenase (ADH), 28–29, 228, 297
  ADH3 gene, 299
Alcohol elimination rate, 18
Alcoholism, 115–116, 228
  alcohol-related symptoms, 108, 121–122
  and ALDH, 244, 286, 335. *See also* Aldehyde dehydrogenase
  age-specific distribution, 62–64
  definition according to Stockholm Adoption Project, 94

familial distribution and transmission, 55, 57–60, 67, 89–90, 138, 183–194, 366
frequency in males versus females, 60–62
genetic epidemiology, 105–133, 364–365
genetic screening, 333–350
genetic test, 335–338
and hyperactivity, correlation between, 43–45
and liver disease, 257–258
methodological limitations of research on genetics of, 89–103
poor school achievement as marker, 77–78
types 1 and 2, 118–119
vulnerability to alcoholism, 43–54, 238
Alcoholism susceptibility gene, 228
Alcohol metabolism, in twin studies, 15–29, 113–114, 175
Alcohol-seeking behavior in animal models, 218–226, 302
Alcohol-specific genetic effects and psychomotor sensitivity, 15, 20
Alcohol tolerance, 195
  in animal models, 218, 287–289, 354
Aldehyde dehydrogenase (ALDH), 226, 231, 286, 297, 335
  and alcoholism, 244, 286, 335
  ALDH1 variants, 267–268
  ALDH2, 227–228, 237, 244–245, 255, 266, 270–272
  ALDH2 deficiency, 255–257
  deficiencies of ALDH1, 255-258, 261, 265–276
  erythrocyte ALDH, 257–258
  genetic implications in alcohol sensitivity, 253–263
  inhibition by nitroimidazole drugs, 237, 244–245, 270
  selection in ALDH genetic variation, 243–244
  selection at ALDH loci, 245
  variation in ALDH activities, 270–272
γ-Aminobutyric acid (GABA), 219, 354
Animal models for studying alcoholism, 217–226, 354–355
  gene mapping in, 301–302, 335
  tolerance, 287–289
Antisocial personality (ASP), 34, 36–37, 75–77, 95, 115, 127, 207
Ascending reticular activating system, 178

377

Assortative mating and alcoholism, 4, 83, 231
Attention deficit disorder, 43–44, 75–77
Australian twin register, 3, 15

Biological markers of alcoholism, 189–190, 195–204, 210
Blood alcohol concentration (BAC) and alcohol metabolism, 17–19, 91, 186
  psychomotor sensitivity, 21–23
Body sway test, 19–21, 91, 185, 187, 193
  reproducibility, 24–26
  righting reflex, 356
Brain stem auditory evoked response, in alcoholics (BAER), 137

Calcium carbimide, 270, 271
Candidate genes, 69, 127, 227–236, 278, 297, 322, 351
  in animal models, 301–302
Cognitive test results in sons of alcoholics, 46–48
Compound phenotype, 283–284
Conduct problems and antisocial personality, 77, 127
Continuous performance test, 144, 164
Cortisol level after alcohol challenge, 187, 188

Danish adoption study, 91–92
Desmethyldiazepam, 186
Desynchronizing influence on EEG, 178
Diazepam, 184, 186, 188, 193, 299
Discrimination, as consequence of genetic screening for alcoholism, 340–341
Disulfiram, 182, 244–245, 270–271
Dopamine, 218
Dopamine beta hydroxylase, 240
Drinking habits, 15–17, 256, 258
Driving competence, genetics of alcohol sensitivity, 23

Electroencephalogram (EEG), 181–182, 185, 187, 211, 299–300
  activity in alcoholics, 137–142, 161
  effect of alcohol on, 175–182
  response to acute alcohol loading, 176–178
  synchronization in alcoholics, 178–180

Electrophysiology, 368
  in alcoholic fathers and their sons, 161–166
  as phenotypic marker of alcoholism, 149–152, 187
  recovery in alcoholics, 138–139
Entamoeba histolytica, 243
Environmental effects on alcoholism, 16–20, 97–98, 294–295
  academic competence, 81
  adoption studies and, 31–42, 287
  attenuation or enhancement of genetic factors, 75–88, 93, 116, 355–356
  availability of alcohol, 86–88
  family, 79–80, 151, 167–168, 183–194, 320–322
  life events, 80–81, 100
  peer influences, 80
  risk factors, 330–331, 366
  social competence, 81
Epistasis, 288, 291
Event-related-potential (ERP) in alcoholics, 137, 161–162, 187
Exposure to alcohol and alcoholism, in teenagers, 3–13

False-positive results of linkage analysis, 317
First pass metabolism, 28
Fluoride activity in alcoholics, 196–197
Fluoxetine, 240
Flushing response to alcohol, 228, 231, 255–258, 261, 335

Gene-environment correlation to alcoholism, 90, 93, 95, 116
Genetic effects and alcoholism, 16–17, 116, 283. *See also* Linkage analysis
  adoption studies, 31–42
  ALDH deficiency in Orientals, 255–258, 261, 265
  EEG response to alcohol, 176–178
  socioeconomic status effect, 39, 78, 82–83
  versus environmental effects, 89–103
Genetic screening for alcoholism, consequences of, 333–350
Genetics of alcohol sensitivity, 16–17, 20, 355, 357
  and ALDH, 243
  ALDH deficiency and alcoholism, 255–257

Subject Index / 379

CNS functioning, 159-174
  heritability, 18, 50, 125-127, 159-160
  psychomotor sensitivity, 19-23
Genome imprinting, 278
G proteins, 196, 202-203, 242
Guanine nucleotide-binding coupling protein. *See* G proteins

Halotype sharing, molecular genetics in alcoholics, 179
Heterogeneity, locus, 227, 288, 290
5-HIAA, heritability, 240
High risk, familial alcoholism, 55, 89-90, 138, 366
  children of alcoholics, 183-194
  EEG activity, 139-142, 151
5-HT$_{1A}$ receptor, 242
5-HT$_{1C}$ receptor, 242
5-HT2 receptor, 242
5-HT3 transporter, 243
Hyperactivity in children and alcoholism, 43-45, 75-77

Imipramine, 243
Impulsiveness and attention deficit disorder, as markers for alcoholism, 76
Iowa adoption study, 95-98

Linkage analysis, 126, 229, 232, 327-331
  choice of markers, 278, 322-323
  heterogeneity, 321
  LOD scores, 228-231, 292-293, 317-318, 321, 327, 363
  phenotype penetrance, 277, 281-282, 319-320, 329
  and RFLPs, 179, 220, 227, 231, 279, 311
  ALDH deficiencies, 271
Lithium, 239, 242

Metronidazole, 243, 245, 270
MNS blood group and alcoholism, 227-228
Monoamine oxidase (MAO), 209, 241, 270
  activity inhibition by ethanol, 199
  activity in platelets of alcoholics, 198
  and alcohol tolerance, 196
Monomeric alpha waves, 179
Multidimensional scaling, 3-7

National Institute on Alcohol Abuse and Alcoholism, 213-214

Neurophysiological studies in alcoholic fathers and their sons, 160-161
Neurotransmitter function, 238
Nitrefazole, 245
Nitroimidazole drugs, inhibition of ALDH, 237, 243, 245, 270

Oligogenic models of segregation analysis, 310
Ornidazole, 245
Ouabain, 243

P300, electrophysiology of alcoholics vs. nonalcoholics, 90-91, 142-147
Penetrance and linkage analysis, 279, 319. *See also* Linkage analysis
Personality traits in alcoholic fathers and their sons, 166-167, 171-172, 185
Phenylalanine hydroxylase, 241
Phospholipase C, 242
Platelet enzymes, 196
Polymorphism information content, 296-297
Prediction of alcohol-related problems in children of alcoholics, 185-188
Prejudice, as result of genetic screening for alcoholism, 340-341
Prolactin level after alcohol challenge, 187-188
Psychiatric illnesses and occurrence of alcoholism, 34, 38-39
Psychomotor sensitivity to alcohol, 15, 19-21. *See also* Body sway test

Race and susceptibility to alcoholism, 228, 238. *See also* Flushing response to alcohol
Restriction fragment length polymorphism (RFLP), 170, 179, 220, 228, 231
Ritanserin, 242
RT1-A locus and ethanol preference in rats, 220

Segregation analysis, 110-112, 235, 282, 310-311, 351, 358, 365
Selective breeding for alcohol tolerance in animal models, 217, 287-289
Sequence target sites, 296
Serotonin, 218, 298, 356. *See also* Tryptophan hydroxylase
  heritability of serotonin function, 237-240

receptors, 242–243. *See also specific receptors*
uptake inhibitors, 238–239
Single-locus disorders in alcoholism, 318
Socioeconomic status, use of adoption paradigm, 37
Static ataxia, 91
Stockholm adoption study, 92–94, 117–118, 120
Subjective high assessment scale, 185
Superoxide dismutase, 300
Sway test. *See* Body sway test
Synchronizing influence on EEG, 178

TAU path analytic model for alcoholism, 59, 66

Teenage drinking onset, 3–7
Temperance boards, used in Stockholm adoption study, 93–94
Tinidazole, 245, 270
Transmissibility of familial alcoholism, 58–60
Tridimensional Personality Questionnaire, 187
Tryptophan hydroxylase, 241, 251–252
Tyrosine hydroxylase, 241

Uniparental disomy, 277

Weight, effect on alcohol sensitivity, 27–28

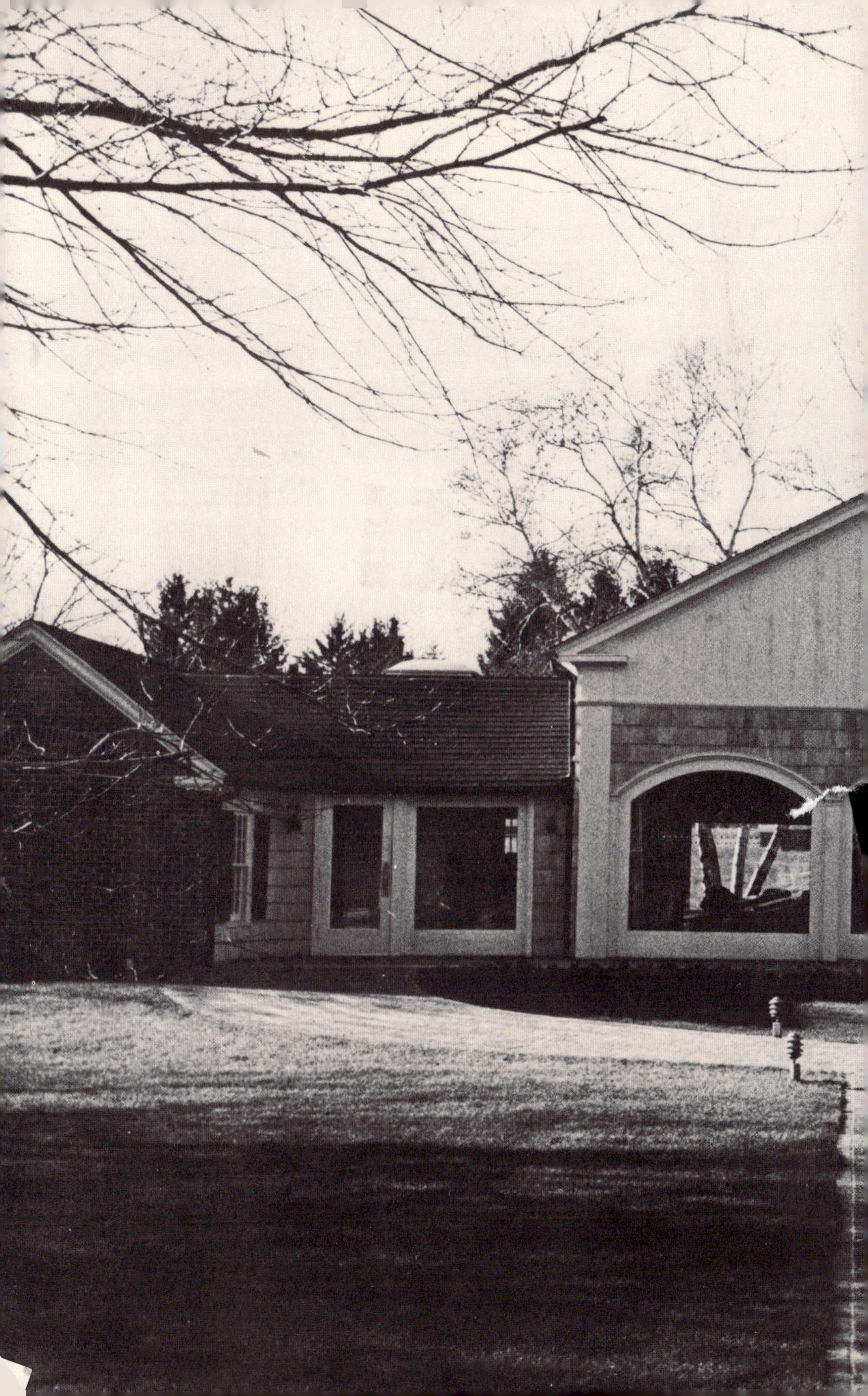

GETTYSBURG COLLEGE

3326800 02565328

WITHDRAWN

DEMCO